CULTURE AND AGENCY

The Place of Culture in Social Theory

MARGARET S. ARCHER

University of Warwick

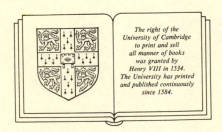

The right of the
University of Cambridge
to print and sell
all manner of books
was granted by
Henry VIII in 1534.
The University has printed
and published continuously
since 1584.

Cambridge University Press

Cambridge
New York New Rochelle Melbourne Sydney

Published by the Press Syndicate of the University of Cambridge
The Pitt Building, Trumpington Street, Cambridge, CB2 1RP
32 East 57th Street, New York, NY 10022, USA
10 Stamford Road, Oakleigh, Melbourne 3166, Australia

First published 1988

Printed in Great Britain at the University Press, Cambridge

British Library cataloguing in publication data

Archer, Margaret Scotford
   Culture and agency: the place of culture
in social theory.
   1. Culture
   I. Title
   306   HM101

Library of Congress cataloguing in publication data

Archer, Margaret Scotford.
   Culture and agency: the place of culture in social theory/
Margaret S. Archer.
     p.   cm.
   Includes index.
   ISBN 0 521 34623 1
   1. Culture   I. Title.
   HM101.A654 1988
   306–dc19   87–19722 CIP

ISBN 0 521 34623 1

Dla Profesora Jerzego Stefana Langroda

z wyrazami szacunku, wdzięcznośći
i wiernej przyjaźni.

Contents

Preface

The problem of structure and agency has rightly come to be seen as the basic issue in modern social theory. However, in acquiring this centrality it has completely overshadowed the problem of culture and agency. The main thesis of this book is that in fact the two problems do directly parallel one another: they raise identical difficulties and the method by which these can be resolved turns out to be exactly the same.

Nevertheless the structural and cultural domains are substantively very different, as well as being relatively autonomous from one another. These two considerations have crucial bearings on my main thesis. The first consideration means that the concepts used have both to respect and to capture the substantive differences between structures and culture; otherwise these would simply be clamped together in a conceptual vice, doing violence to our subject matter by eliding the material and the ideational aspects of social life. The second means that theories developed about the relationship between structures and social agents and between cultures and cultural actors have to recognize the relative autonomy of structure and culture. Otherwise we would be violating our ability to understand social life as the interplay between interests and ideas. In short, if these considerations are not acknowledged, then we would not be dealing with two parallel problems but simply collapsing the one into the other.

The problem of structure and agency is now a familiar phrase used to denote central dilemmas in social theory – especially the rival claims of Voluntarism versus Determinism, Subjectivism versus Objectivism, and the micro- versus the macroscopic in sociology.

These issues are central for the simple reason that it is impossible to do sociology at all without dealing with them and coming to some personal decisions about them. When writing, these decisions affect the statements that we advance, and when reading they affect the sentences that we can accept. These issues are problematic for any social theorist who cannot come down with conviction on one side or the other; and that means a great many of us, each of whom is then of necessity in the job of reconciliation. Imperative as this is, the urgency of the problem of structure and agency is not one which imposes itself on academics alone, but on every human being.

For it is part and parcel of daily experience to feel both free and enchained, capable of shaping our own future and yet confronted by towering, seemingly impersonal, constraints. Those whose reflection leads them to reject the grandiose delusion of being puppet-masters but also to resist the supine conclusion that they are mere marionettes then have the same task of reconciling this experiential bivalance, and must do so if their moral choice is not to become inert or their 'political' action ineffectual. Consequently in facing up to the problem of structure and agency social theorists are not just addressing crucial technical problems in the study of society, they are also confronting the most pressing social problem of the human condition.

Thus what has happened is that theorists dealing with the structuring and transformation of social organization have at least (and at last) converged on a common problem. Provision of a promising solution to this central problem is now accepted by many as a kind of litmus paper: theories which fail the acid test do effectively cede any claim to provide the framework for general social theory. (For example to find that some approach is wholly deterministic, entirely objectivistic, or exclusively microscopic is ground enough for ceasing to consider it as a serious claimant.) Theories which pass the test may still be at all sorts of loggerheads with one another but they do now share a criterion for the assessment of their competing concepts and explanations, namely how well these contribute to the solution of the central problem. Moreover the very fact of addressing the same issue increases the chances of synthesis to the extent that the proffered solutions are based on compatible premises.

In this respect, cultural analysis lags behind: indeed in general it seems to be the poor relation of structural analysis. For purposes of description there is a glaring lack of descriptive cultural 'units', and for purposes of explanation culture swings wildly from being the supremely independent variable in some theories to become the passive dependent variable in others. Perhaps because of this state of the art, it is not common to find references to the problem of culture and agency or any significant convergence on it as the focal issue. Nevertheless this phrase denotes exactly the same dilemmas as those which have become widely recognized in the structural domain.

There is the same tension to be resolved both theoretically and experientially between the fund of ideas which in a real sense we feel free to accept or reject, and the fact (sometimes known but sometimes happening behind our backs) that the pool itself has been restricted or contaminated and that our sensed freedoms can be more a matter of manipulated feelings than of genuine liberty. There is a similar task of reconciling objective knowledge (however this is defined, and none but the radical relativists leave this category empty) with human subjectivity and our capacity for generating new interpretations within our heads or for the interpersonal negotiation of new meanings. There is an equivalent dilemma about how to transcend the divide between small-scale accountancy procedures, often contextually bound, and the existence of macroscopic symbol systems, operating trans-situationally.

The same problem then is just as central as in the structural field, but it involves different entia: namely the relations pertaining between ideas and the ideational influences operating between people. However, the status of cultural analysis as a poor relation means that any attempt to deal with the problem of culture and agency is going to have to confront conceptual poverty as far as these entities are concerned and will have to forge many of its own tools *en route*.

In undertaking the problem I have deliberately tried to travel light, working in the barest and sparest terms and thus giving room to only those components which seem necessary and sufficient to an utterly basic account of the linkage between culture and agency. Because of this most readers will probably be surprised by the lack of any reference to huge chunks of the literature on culture, by the total neglect of certain issues preoccupying major cultural theorists, and also by the failure of many of these giants to figure in the text at all.

Such absences are intentional: there is only an element of arbitrariness in that sometimes other thinkers could have been substituted for those examined and that usually alternative illustrations would have done just as well as those employed. So these absences can only be justified by showing how the tool-kit used here was put together because the 'problem of culture and agency' was conceived of in a particular way, which in turn made this equipment appropriate for tackling it. Thus I have tried to clarify the task as I see it, and to justify the tools selected for it, in the following five theses.

On conflation

The way in which both problems are approached in the present work rests on one fundamental assertion, namely that what is being sought is a theoretical stance which is capable of *linking* 'structure and agency' or 'culture and agency', rather than *sinking* the difference between the 'parts' (organizational or ideational) and the 'people', who hold positions or ideas within them. Thus from the outset it must be made clear that these two problems are both being viewed in a distinctive way and, moreover, one which is far from commanding general assent – especially in the cultural field.

Thus when discussing 'structure' or 'culture' in relation to 'agency' I am talking about a relationship between two aspects of social life. However intimately they are intertwined (in, say, our experiences of marriage as both legal institution and daily practice), these are none the less analytically distinct. Few would disagree with this characterization of social reality as Janus-faced: indeed too many have concluded too quickly that the task is therefore how to look at both faces of the same medallion at once. It is precisely this methodological notion of trying to peer at the two simultaneously which is resisted here. The basic reason for avoiding this is that the 'parts' and the 'people' are *not* co-existent through time and therefore any approach which amalgamates them wrongly foregoes the possibility of examining the interplay between them over time. Thus for example, a particular marital structure pre-dates *our* contemporary constitution as married social subjects – which is an entirely different point from the perfectly compatible statements that previous actors through their prior social practices themselves constituted a given institution of marriage earlier in history (since this refers to agents long-dead), or that our present actions as married subjects are contributing to the transformation of this institution at some future time (since this refers to distant re-structuring). Any form of conceptualization which prevents examination of this interplay should therefore be resisted.

However, the dominant theoretical tendency in the structural domain and even more markedly in the cultural field, has indeed been to elide the 'parts' and the 'people'. I have called this generic error the Fallacy of Conflation and devoted Chapters 2, 3 and 4 to exploring the different versions it has taken in cultural analysis and to examining their specific drawbacks. Fundamentally what is wrong with conflationary theorizing is that it prevents the interplay between 'parts' and 'people' from being the foundation of cultural dynamics. This is because in every version of the Fallacy, the elision of the two elements withdraws any autonomy or independence from one of them, if not from both.

Conflation of the two levels of analysis always takes place in a particular direction and there are only three possible logical directions. The first pair make either the 'parts' or the 'people' an epiphenomenon of the other: they differ about which is held to be epiphenomenal but not about the legitimacy of elision *per se*. Thus either version renders the dependent element inert, be it 'parts' or 'people'. Consequently, adherents to either type of epiphenomemalism advance rather crude unilateral accounts when explaining cultural stability and change. In the one, cultural properties are simply formed and transformed by some untrammelled dominant group or placed at the mercy of capricious renegotiation by unconstrained agency. In the other, some cultural code or central value system imposes its choreography on cultural life and agents are reduced to *träger* or bearers of its properties, whether through oversocialization or mystification. If, as my initial assertion maintained, an adequate theoretical stance is one which acknowledges the interplay between culture and agency, then it must be predicated on some autonomy or independence being assigned to each.

However, the errors attaching to conflation do not depend on epiphenomenalism, or rendering one aspect of social life itself lifeless – whether in the structural or cultural domain. This is shown by the remaining possibility, namely 'central' conflation, where elision occurs in the 'middle'. Instead what happens is that autonomy is withheld from both 'parts' and 'people' and this has precisely the same effect of precluding any examination of their interplay. Here the properties of cultural systems and the properties of cultural interaction are conflated because they are presented as being so tightly constitutive of one another. Unlike everyday terms which involve mutual constitution, such as 'singing' (where song and singer have separate properties, some of which are irrelevant to the practice – such as the circumstances of composition or the marital circumstances of singers, and some of which have an interplay that is vital to it – the song's difficulty and the singer's virtuosity), in central conflation matters are very different. For the intimacy of reciprocal constitution amounts to an actual elision of the two elements, which cannot be untied, and thus their influences upon one another cannot be unravelled. Once again the net effect of conflation is that the possibility of gaining explanatory leverage on cultural dynamics from the interplay between 'parts' and 'people' is relinquished from the outset.

On analytical dualism

In contradistinction to every version of conflation in social theory is the approach endorsed here, which is based four-square on analytical dualism. This emphatically is not the same thing as philosophical dualism, for there is no suggestion that we are dealing with separate entities, only analytically separable ones and ones which it is theoretically useful to treat separately. However, to forestall the obvious counter-objections from those whom I have just been criticizing it is necessary to justify both the utility and the feasibility of analytical dualism. Its usefulness will be briefly commended by reference to the increase in explanatory power which Lockwood gained in relation to social change by distinguishing between 'social integration' and 'system integration'. Obviously I will have to demonstrate that a parallel distinction can be employed in the cultural realm. This will involve showing not only the desirability but also the practicability of its use there. In other words, I will have to produce some workable means *of* distinguishing between 'parts' and 'people' in the field of culture – some way of overcoming the methodological difficulties undoubtedly involved in rendering analytical dualism operational and thus of repelling the charge that these are matters of philosophical intractability.

Lockwood insisted on the possibility and profitability of distinguishing the orderly or conflictual relations pertaining between groups of actors (the degree of social integration) from the orderly or contradictory relations prevailing between parts of the social structure (the degree of system integration). The point of the exercise was to theorize about the *interplay* between them, for he rightly argued that neither element alone provided the sufficient conditions of structural change. Thus System integration could be low but unless its contradictions were actualized and amplified by sectional social groups, they could be contained and stasis would persist because of this high social integration. Alternatively group antagonism could be profound (low social integration) without leading to significant change in society, unless it was linked to Systemic contradictions. In short it was the conjunction between the two elements which furnished the key to structural stability or change.

The aim is obviously to see whether the same explanatory pay-off can be gained by using a parallel distinction in the cultural field. In attempting to draw it, the first major obstacle was that culture has rarely been viewed as something susceptible to malintegration, let alone been conceptualized in terms of its degree of integration (either comparatively or historically). Instead there has been a pervasive Myth of Cultural Integration, appropriated by sociology from early anthropology, which perpetuates an image of culture as a coherent pattern, a uniform ethos or a symbolically consistent universe. The net results of this enduring Mythology, the defects of which are examined in Chapter 1, is that no concept of 'cultural contradictions' was readily available to stand as the counterpart to the familiar notion of 'structural contradiction'. Ironically, in view of his reputation as a normative consensus theorist, it was Durkheim, in his lesser known work on the evolution of educational thought, who furnished the ingredients for conceptualizing cultural contradictions and their contrast category, cultural complementarities.

In other words the utilization of analytical dualism in the cultural domain meant first forging the appropriate concepts – after abandoning the traditional selective perception of nothing but cultural coherence. The distinction which was finally drawn was a deliberate attempt to parallel the way in which Lockwood had differentiated between the structural relations of 'parts' and of 'people'. On the one hand, then, there is *logical consistency*, that is the degree of consistency between the component parts of culture. This is a property of the world of ideas, of World Three, as Popper would put it; or, if preferred, of the contents of libraries. In fact we utilize this concept every day when we say that the ideas of X are consistent with those of Y, or that theory or belief A contradicts theory or belief B. These are quite different from another kind of everyday statement, namely that the ideas of X were influenced by those of Y, where we are talking about causal effects which are properties of people – such as the influences of teachers on pupils, of television on its audience, or of earlier thinkers on later ones. This latter, is *causal consensus*, that is the degree of cultural uniformity produced by the imposition of ideas by one set of people on another through the whole gamut of familiar techniques – manipulation, mystification, legitimation, naturalization, persuasion and argument. Causal consensus is thus intimately allied to the use of power and influence, whereas logical consistency is entirely independent of them since it exists whether or not it is socially exploited or concealed or, to clinch the point, regardless of its even being recognized.

To underline the parallel with Lockwood's distinction, the degree of logical consistency was labelled 'Cultural System integration' (hereafter CS) and the extent of causal cohesion was termed 'Socio-Cultural integration' (hereafter S-C). The former refers to relations between the components of culture; the latter to the relationships between cultural agents. The CS/S-C distinction therefore maps onto that between culture without a knowing subject and culture with a knowing subject. However, it is one thing to accept the advantages of drawing such distinctions in principle (because they promise increased explanatory power), or even to affirm their validity (because they confirm two different everyday encounters). It is quite another to operationalize the dividing line between 'parts' and 'people' satisfactorily, and some critics took Lockwood to task on precisely this point.

This problem takes up the whole of Chapter 5 which argues in favour of using the rules of logic as the method for delineating between the two. As an attempt to develop a methodology for utilizing analytical dualism in cultural analysis it basically works as follows: culture as a whole is taken to refer to all intelligibilia, that is to any item which has the dispositional capacity of being understood by someone. Within this I then distinguish the Cultural System, which is that sub-set of items to which the law of contradiction can be applied. These are propositions, for only statements which assert truth or falsity can be deemed to be in contradiction or to be consistent with one another. In turn this means that the Cultural System is restricted to the propositional register of society at any given time. The justification for defining the CS in this way rests partly on the fact that it meets the criterion of methodological workability, but partly, too, on the self-evident importance of those things held to be true or false in society at any given time or place.

Obviously we do not live by propositions alone (any more than we live logically); in addition, we generate myths, are moved by mysteries, become rich in symbolics and ruthless in manipulating hidden persuaders. But all of these elements are precisely the stuff of Socio-Cultural interaction. For they are all matters of inter-personal influence, whether we are talking at one extreme of hermeneutic understanding (including religious experience at the furthest extremity) or of the manipulative assault and battery of ideas used ideologically. All those other non-propositional things to which we assent or over which we dissent — such as tastes and preferences, likes and dislikes, affinities and animosities, patriotism and prejudice — lie in between. And all of this takes place outside of, *en dépit de*, the canons of logic, whether knowingly on the part of actors (proclaiming the mystery of faith), or whether imposed on unknowing others (recipients of symbolic machinations), or whether as that semi-knowledgeable mish-mash called 'public opinion'.

Clearly the Cultural System and Socio-Cultural life do not exist or operate independently of one another; they overlap, intertwine and are mutually influential. But this is precisely the point, for I am *not* asserting dualism but rather the utility of an *analytically* dualistic approach, the main recommendation for which is the very fact that it allows this interplay to be explored. It will be obvious too that making the distinction in this way depends on endorsing the universality of the law of contradiction (universal applicability being its great comparative and historical attraction). However, since this itself is not universally accepted, much of Chapter 5 is devoted to justifying its endorsement.

None of this means that there is no other way of distinguishing between 'parts' and 'people' in the cultural domain: perhaps others with greater ingenuity can produce alternatives and will do so in the future. But in this work the tools had to be forged as it proceeded, for I could discover no systematic attempt to use analytical dualism in the cultural field and therefore had little upon which to build, except the hunch that to parallel Lockwood's approach to the struc-tural domain would prove fruitful. It may indeed be that by criticiz-ing this preliminary attempt to draw a parallel distinction, a better form of delineation emerges to render this parallelism even more profitable in the explanation of cultural dynamics.

On the interface

Having made this distinction between the Cultural System and Socio-Cultural interaction, two major questions have to be addressed: how do we conceptualize their interplay; and, through this, how do we gain theoretical leverage upon cultural dynamics? Our starting point, the distinguishing of logical relations (pertaining to the CS) from causal ones (pertaining to the S-C), allows for their independent variation and in turn makes the *interface* between them the site of intensive investigation. Our procedure – the attempt to conceptualize how certain properties of the 'parts' and certain properties of the 'people' actually combine at the interface – is of course at variance with any form of conflationary theorizing. For this task, which takes Chapters 6, 7 and 8 to accomplish, is brushed aside by conflationists who sweep through the interface because of their epiphenomenalism or sweep it away due to their notion of mutual constitution. My objective is to theorize about the *conditions* for cultural stability or change, and my basic hypothesis is that these conditions are rooted in the *conjunction* between the Cultural System and Socio-Cultural interaction – just as they are grounded in the conjuncture between social and system integration in the structural domain.

Another way of putting this is that the present enterprise seeks to avoid being stung by either of Foucault's ways of tangling with these nettles. In his earlier works, where 'discourse' was presented as an abstract structure of thought (not without similarities to the present notion of the Cultural System), it was also viewed as uninfluenced by non-discursive elements like interests and power (which in the present text are held to fuel Socio-Cultural interaction). Consequently at that stage he had to emphasize the *arbitrariness of discursive changes*, which was effectively to conclude that cultural dynamics can be described but cannot be grasped theoretically. In his later work he switched his stress to the other side of the divide and overemphasized the role of power in constituting knowledge, which now became *relative to* Socio-Cultural contingencies. However, such contingencies were viewed as patternless processes where domination was confronted by a recalcitrant 'agonism', a sort of inveterate thirst for struggle, independent of particular conditions. Consequently the later work endorses the *arbitrariness of Socio-Cultural interaction* because no account is given of why, when or how people do struggle. Now, the processes of cultural change can be described but a theoretical account of the different forms and consequences of cultural struggles cannot be provided. Thus the early work is confined to one side of the interface and the later work to the other: my aim is rather to grasp the nettle firmly in the middle, dragging up its roots on either side. This is to deny an arbitrary

character both to the changes taking place and to the processes producing them.

The underlying approach can be summarized quite succinctly.
Generically it is how contradictory or complementary relations between 'parts' of the Cultural System map onto orderly or conflictual
relationships between 'people' at the Socio-Cultural level which
determines whether the outcome is cultural stability or change.
This means that we need to specify, first, which Systemic relations
impinge upon agency and how they do so; and, second, which
social relations affect how agents respond to and react back on the
Cultural System.

We begin with the Cultural System and we do so because any
Socio-Cultural action, wherever it is situated historically, takes
place in the context of innumerable interrelated theories, beliefs
and ideas which had developed prior to it, and, as will be seen, exert
a conditional influence on it. For as Cohen has convincingly
argued,

in all sociological enquiry it *is* assumed that some features of social structure and culture are strategically important and enduring and that they
provide the limits within which particular social situations can occur. On
this assumption the action approach can help to explain the nature of the
situations and how they affect conduct. It does not explain the social structure and culture as such, except by lending itself to a developmental
enquiry which must start from some previous point at which structural
and cultural elements are treated as given.[1]

The strength of this point does not depend on the infinite-regress
argument: it lies in the fact that by moving *one* stage further back in
time, in order to explain the *present* cultural context, one has to take
into account the *previous* Cultural System from which it developed.
However, the question still remains, which of these Systemic relations do impinge on action contexts at any given time? It has
already been mentioned that the law of contradiction will be used
to assess the inconsistency or complementarity of items in the
Cultural System at any point in time. However, at that time not all
of these will or can be known, and of those which are known, many
involve propositions which no one then supports. Therefore
analysis does *not* begin with a complete description of the Cultural
System: a full itemization of its contradictions and complementarities being both impossible and irrelevant. Instead we start with
the ideas which at any given time have holders, and restrict ourselves to
these items. For only if an item is held by someone can its logical
relationships with other items have any effect on agency.

In short, analysis opens by examining the effects of holding ideas with particular logical relations (of contradiction or complementarity to others) – not with the (Socio-Cultural) reasons for these being held, reasons which would necessarily have been conditioned by an anterior cultural context. It is then maintained that to uphold ideas which are embroiled in a contradiction or enmeshed in complementarities places those who do so in different action contexts where they are confronted with different situational logics.

In brief, contradictions mould problem-ridden situations for actors which they must confront *if and when* they realize, or are made to acknowledge, that the proposition(s) they endorse is enmeshed in some inconsistency. What they do next is not determined: they have the options of irrational dogmatism or of abandoning the theory or belief altogether, *but* if they want to go on holding it non-dogmatically then their only recourse is to repair the inconsistency, that is the force of the situational logic. By contrast, complementarities mould problem-free situations for agents who can explore their ideational environments without danger or difficulty and from this build up an elaborate conspectus, the elements of which are mutually consistent and reinforcing. This by contrast fosters a situational logic of reproduction aimed at retaining this felicitous cluster and discouraging alterations in it.

On the other hand, these Systemic influences are only part of the story about how cultural situations are moulded for actors. The other part is made up of the causal relations operating between groups and individuals at the Socio-Cultural level. Such relationships have their own dynamics, rooted in different material interests, producing various forms of social stratification and different ideal interests, such as ethnic, religious or linguistic divides (which are ideational but not propositional). These make their own contribution to cultural stability or change through the influences they exert upon what actors do on the spot. They form the other side of the interface and are thus co-determinants (with Systemic conditioning) of what actually takes place there. Systemic conditioning only appears (and this is nothing more than appearance) to be decisive when Socio-Cultural influences happen to be pulling in the same direction. It is, therefore, easier to pin-point their independent contribution when social orderliness or disorderliness are pulling in different directions, that is operating at variance with Systemic conditioning. Under such conditions one can readily identify the main ways in which they work at the interface.

It is universally the case that Socio-Cultural imbalances, and the power differentials deriving from them, affect the degree of awareness or 'discursive penetration' that actors have of ideational contradictions or complementarities themselves. Thus, for example, when some dominant material-interest group supports a set of propositions which are embroiled in contradiction, they will use their power to control the visibility of inconsistent items through a variety of 'containment strategies', the most blatant of which is censorship. If successful, the subordinate agents will remain unruffled by the inconsistencies attending the group's beliefs for they are in the dark about them; the Systemic fault-line represented by the contradiction will remain unexploited, even by those who have the interests to split it wide open, because power has kept it unperceived. Consequently, in this instance, social imbalance produces orderly Socio-Cultural relations, maintaining the cultural status quo whilever agents' access to information can be controlled.

Nevertheless, power relations still affect Systemic stability, even when they do pull in the same direction. This can be illustrated from a set of complementary items, like the cluster of propositions about caste and Karma that Weber discusses. The Hindu elite was the most culturally proficient and it used its power to protect this mastery from change which would threaten the benefits associated with it. Here the Brahminate beneficiaries responded by elaborative reproduction, exemplary leadership and the encouragement of imitative practice, together with the repression of internal innovation because of its disruptive potential. Socio-Cultural action thus protects, preserves and prolongs the Systemic status quo.

Finally, however, the nature of Socio-Cultural relations affects which of the responses forged under the pressure of the situational logic can actually be made to stick. Again, fundamentally and universally no corrective formula (generated to repair contradictions) and no reproductive scheme (elaborated to protect complementarities) can be made to 'take' in society when the contemporaneous distribution of interests and power do not gel with it. Instead a variety of ideational shifts will be registered depending on the nature of the disjuncture, ranging from progressive accommodation to counter-actualization and including schismatism and Specialization. (Which of these will occur under what conditions is the subject of Chapters 7 and 8.)

In short, cultural stability or Cultural Elaboration are at the mercy of the conjunction between the two levels. Cultural dynamics are governed by how the influences stemming from the

Cultural System gel with those emanating from Socio-Cultural relations, at the interface where they intersect. This is why we turn to the morphogenetic perspective to provide an overall framework for conceptualizing and theorizing about cultural elaboration.

On morphogenesis and morphostasis

What has been said so far about advancing on this shapeless, seething and shifting thing that we call culture is that the most promising way of coming to grips with it (exposing the patterning of processes and end-products within this flux) is through the use of analytical dualism. Thus in the previous three theses I have been sketching in how one might achieve this aim through conceptualizing culture in terms of parts and people and examining the interface between them.

In the structural domain the theoretical framework which is most explicitly based on analytical dualism is the morphogenetic approach. In social theory this perspective recognizes that the unique feature distinguishing social Systems from organic or mechanical ones is their capacity to undergo radical restructuring. As a process 'morphogenesis' refers to the complex interchanges that produce change in a System's given form, structure or state ('morphostasis' is the reverse), the end-product being termed 'Elaboration'. Of course action is ceaseless and essential to both the stable continuation or the further elaboration of the system. However, when morphogenesis results, then subsequent interaction will be different from earlier action precisely because it is now conditioned by the elaborated consequences of that prior action. Hence the morphogenetic perspective is not only dualistic but sequential, dealing in endless three-part cycles of Structural Conditioning ⟶ Social interaction ⟶ Structural Elaboration. The suggestion is that this framework be transferred to the cultural field, using equivalent analytical phases (i.e. Cultural Conditioning ⟶ Socio-Cultural interaction ⟶ Cultural Elaboration), in order to unravel the dialectical interplay of culture and agency over time.

To work in terms of these three-part cycles is to accord *time* a central place in social theory. Time is incorporated as a theoretical variable rather than simply as a medium in which events take place. This represents the methodological key to the experiential problem of how we can simultaneously feel bound to plod round the cultural treadmill yet also brim over with criticism and creativity – the tension between being conditioned to do things one way but being able to conceive of doing them differently. It is also the way of avoiding the transposition of this experience into a theoretical stance which embraces its eternal duality but then ends up unable to specify under what conditions we are condemned to reproduce our culture versus which conditions allow us the freedom to transform it. Those who endorse the 'duality of culture', rather than analytical dualism, then simply oscillate between the two, insisting on both but unable to tell us when one rather than the other will predominate. Thus they talk about our inescapable contribution to the recursiveness of culture, because our very practices have, per-force, to draw on language, rules and signification schemes and thus reproduce them, but simultaneously they insist that praxis itself can always introduce cultural transformations. Cultural change thus becomes an immanent but indeterminate possibility, equally likely or unlikely at any given moment and therefore unpredictable and inexplicable.

What is crucially different about the morphogenetic perspective is the core notion that culture and agency operate over different time periods. This is what enables us to decipher our experiential bivalence and to disentangle that which seems to make for theoretical indeterminacy. This core notion which is fundamental to the morphogenetic perspective is based on two simple propositions: that the Cultural System logically predates the Socio-Cultural action(s) which transform it; and that Cultural Elaboration logically post-dates such interaction.

Thus the interface that was discussed in the last thesis is always 'the present', wherever that happens to be situated historically. However, this T_1 (present-time) is peculiarly pivotal in the morphogenetic approach. As Markovic expressed it, both 'past and future are *living in the present*. Whatever human beings do in the present is decisively influenced by the past and by the future . . . the future is not something that will come later, independently of our will. There are *several possible futures* and one of them *has to be made*.'[2] Thus what was being disentangled at the interface was, first, anterior cultural conditioning, that is how the prior development of ideas (from earlier interaction) conditions the current context of action, confronting agents with both problem-free and problem-ridden clusters of beliefs, theories and ideas. But this is no bland confrontation in which actors survey the ideational array and unconstrainedly take their pick. For we are all born into and can only live embedded in an ideational context which is not of our own making. Our very knowledge about it, our vested interests in rejecting it or retaining it and our objective capacities for changing it have already been distributed to us *before* the action starts.

Second, however, there is the actual response of agency to this inherited cultural context and, in responding, actors can exploit their degrees of cultural freedom to great (elaborative) effect. For what was said above about the existence of cultural constraints should never be taken as an endorsement of cultural Determinism, partly because the structural conditioning of material interests is also operative in the same 'present' and pulling in different directions. More importantly, however, is the quintessential reflective ability of human beings to fight back against their conditioning (not nullifying it for if nothing else it dictates language and topic), giving them the capacity to respond with originality to their present context. (Specifically they do this either by taking advantage of inconsistencies within it and then generating new forms of syncretism and pluralism from it, or by exploring novel combinations of compatible elements within it and then advancing new types of systematization and specialization in the field of ideas.) If this insistence upon our reflective originality seems to be a theological aberration on my part, so be it, but it was one universal enough to commend itself to Marx when he maintained that men make history but not under the circumstances of their choosing. Hence Voluntarism has an important place in this perspective but it is ever-trammelled by past cultural conditioning and by the current politics of the possible.

Thus Cultural Elaboration is the future which is forged in the present, hammered out of past inheritance by current innovation. Because of this, the elaborated sequences through which culture is transformed are the joint products of the situational logics impinging from the Cultural System on contexts in which agents find themselves *and* their Socio-Cultural responses to them. This is the generic process by which the cultural future is made in the present. It is also what determines which form of future (not its contents) is made, and in turn makes this a patterned not a patternless process.

Thus we will be discussing different scenarios which culminate in cultural morphogenesis and in none of these are the discursive changes which result in the least way arbitrary – any more than the interplay between the Cultural System and Socio-Cultural interaction is a patternless process. Obviously considerable effort will have to be devoted in the text to the derivation of morphogenetic sequences culminating in Cultural Elaboration as well as to their

counterparts, the negative feed-back loops resulting in morphostasis or cultural reproduction – the two, of course, often
operating simultaneously in different parts of the cultural domain.
All that is being signalled here is that the morphogenetic perspective will provide a helpful framework for understanding the structuring of culture over time and one which enables specific forms of
Cultural Elaboration to be explained. This way of formulating the
theoretical enterprise leads directly to the last thesis.

On unification

This work ends by reconsidering its starting point. I opened
with the assertion that the problem of culture and agency directly
paralleled the much more familiar problem of structure and
agency. All of the intervening theses have signalled how this
parallelism is perceived and explored. In particular much of the
text is devoted to examining the hunch that Lockwood's approach
to the explanation of structural change might prove equally useful
if it could be transferred to the cultural field. Despite all the
difficulties encountered in adapting it to this purpose, the pay-off
seems well worth the effort. Indeed it exceeds expectations for it
opens out a whole new vista – the possible conceptual and theoretical
unification of structural and cultural analysis from the morphogenetic
perspective.

But why is this unification so desirable and why is its promise
considered to be such a bonus? The answer is basically that it enables us to go beyond the mere assertion that structure and culture
enjoy relative autonomy from one another. Crucial as this is, as the
ultimate reason for resisting the Fallacy of Conflation, it simply
does not go far enough. To assert that the two are relatively
autonomous is to say nothing about their relative importance for
social stability and change at any given time. Yet without this there
is the danger of unjustifiably slipping into giving one the dominant
role for all time, or of unnecessarily throwing in the sponge and
deeming this to be an empirically variable matter dependent on
episodic contingencies.

The second reason for pursuing their unification under the same
conceptual umbrella is that if structure and culture do have relative
autonomy from one another, then there is interplay between them
which it is necessary to explore theoretically. For unless this is done,
we remain stuck with the valid but vacuous assertion that ideas are
forces in social conflict and that the socially forceful are also

culturally influential. None save the complete materialist or idealist would deny this, but we would still remain mute about how these processes operate and whether their influences are reciprocal.

Analysing both structure and culture from the morphogenetic perspective allows one to get to grips with these problems. By utilizing this common framework it becomes easier to see *how* structure and culture intersect in the middle element of their respective morphogenetic cycles: through structural-interest groups endorsing some corpus of ideas in order to advance their material concerns but then becoming enmeshed in the situational logic of that part of the cultural domain; and through ideal-interest groups seeking powerful sponsors to promote their ideas but then immediately embroiling cultural discourse in power-play within the structural domain. Using the same conceptual framework thus enables one to pin-point the mechanics of the inter-penetration between structure and culture. Even so, to show how they are mutually influential is still not to answer the question as to whether these effects are of equal importance.

The final step, then, is to argue that the question 'when does structure exert more influence over culture and vice versa?' is one which now becomes amenable to solution. If structural and cultural dynamics are both conceptualized in terms of morphogenetic/morphostatic cycles, it becomes possible to theorize about their influence on one another by examining how the cycles proper to each can mesh together in various ways and with varying consequences. Thus Chapter 9 is devoted to inspecting different combinations of morphostasis and morphogenesis in structure and culture. It is then argued that particular configurations are associated with reciprocal influences between the two, while other patterns make either structure or culture more influential for the other and for social change – for the time being. There is also some promise here of being able to explain what sorts of structural and cultural changes are induced under the different configurations.

However, much of this work remains at a high level of theoretical abstraction and at certain points becomes purely speculative for want of appropriate data. Thus the latter part of Chapter 8 contains a free-ranging sketch of how this approach to culture could be pushed forward as a research programme and what material would be needed for its advancement and application. Since cultural analysis still remains the poor relation of structural analysis, this gap will have to be closed before full advantage can be derived from the theoretical unification of the two fields which Chapter 9 presents in skeletal form. When some flesh has been put on these bare theoretical bones, then it should become possible to explain two key issues – whether historically or comparatively and whether societally or sectionally. When theoretical unification is complete it will enable a specification to be provided of the conditions under which structural and cultural dynamics are interrelated in determinate but varying ways. Equally, at any given point in time, a unified theoretical approach will permit a full account to be given of how discursive struggles are socially organized and of how social struggles are culturally conditioned.

The object of this book is not merely to put the problem of culture and agency on the agenda for social theory but to position it there alongside the problem of structure and agency. For, whatever the shortcomings of this text itself, the conviction remains that what proves to be an adequate solution to the one problem will also serve for the other and that substantial benefits must accrue from their theoretical unification.

1   The Myth of Cultural Integration*

The conceptualization of culture is extraordinary in two respects. It has displayed the weakest analytical development of any key concept in sociology and it has played the most wildly vacillating role within sociological theory.

(1) At the *descriptive* level, the notion of 'culture' remains inordinately vague despite little dispute that it is indeed a core concept. In every way 'culture' is the poor relation of 'structure'. Definition of the former has not undergone an elaboration equivalent to that of the latter. Consequently there is no ready fund of analytical terms for designating the components of the cultural realm corresponding to those which delineate parts of the structural domain (roles, organizations, institutions, systems, etc.). Methodologically, such is the poverty of conceptualization that there are as yet no 'units' for describing culture: essentially cultures are still 'grasped', in contrast to structures which are now 'analysed'. Basically the notion of cultures *being* structured is uncommonly rare outside of structuralism: instead of different 'cultural structures' there are endless 'cultural differences'.

(2) At the *explanatory* level the status of culture oscillates between that of a supremely independent variable, the superordinate power in society and, with a large sweep of the pendulum, a position of supine dependence on other social institutions. Hence, in various sociological theories, culture swings from being the prime mover (credited with engulfing and orchestrating the entire social structure) to the opposite extreme where it is reduced to a mere epiphenomenon (charged only with providing an ideational representation of structure).

Together, this descriptive vagueness and these theoretical vagaries, mean that culture occupies no clear place in sociological analysis. What culture is and what culture does are issues bogged down in a conceptual morass from which no adequate sociology of culture has been able to emerge. Obviously such a state of affairs begs for explanation and I believe that the reason for it is embedded in the generic assumptions of an all-pervasive 'Myth of Cultural Integration'. This Myth embodies 'one of the most deep-seated fallacies in social science . . . the . . . assumption of a high degree of consistency in the interpretations produced by societal units'.[1] Yet it projected an image of culture which proved so powerful that it scored the retina, leaving a perpetual after-image, which distorted subsequent perception.

Originating at the descriptive level, the Myth created an archetype of culture(s) as the perfectly woven and all-enmeshing web, the intricate construction of which only added to its strength. Today, instead of analogy, one would simply say that the Myth portrayed culture as the perfectly integrated system, in which every element was interdependent with every other – the ultimate exemplar of compact and coherent organization. Held in thrall by this archetype, theorists of various persuasions concerned themselves only with *how* to accommodate it in their theories; there was no questioning of whether it should be given house-room. Their problem was to find a place *for* the Myth since the Myth itself was not problematic. In turn, the Myth derived power and durability precisely *because* it was endorsed by schools of sociological thought which were otherwise hostile to one another.

That the same theorists who were in bitter dispute over the extent of structural integration (institutional complementarity or contradiction) could simultaneously agree on the subject of *cultural* integration, only buttressed this mythology. Moreover, the fact that they produced differing versions of the Myth helped to insulate its core premise from scrutiny: the *existence* of cultural integration could never be at issue in a debate on the rival mechanisms held to be responsible for it. Thus profound differences over *how* cultural unity was achieved only served to reinforce a fundamentalist accord on the generic nature of cultural coherence.

The most proximate and powerful origins of the Myth are undoubtedly the heritage of anthropology. Despite definitional wrangling over the term 'culture', there was substantial concord among anthropologists about its main property – strong and coherent patterning. This central notion of culture as an integrated whole,[2] grounded in German historicism (*Historismus*), echoes down the decades. Malinowski's conceptualization of 'an individual culture as a coherent whole'[3] reverberates through Ruth Benedict's 'cultural patterns',[4] Meyer Shapiro's 'cultural style'[5] and Kroeber's 'ethos of total culture patterns',[6] to resurface in Mary Douglas's notion of 'one single, symbolically consistent universe'.[7] Two features of this heritage should be underlined. On the one hand its strong aesthetic rather than analytical orientation, which led to an endorsement of ' "artistic" hermeneutics as the method for grasping the inner sense of cultural wholes'.[8] On the other hand this approach, based on the intuitive understanding of cultural configurations, entailed a crucial prejudgement, namely an insistence that coherence was there to be found, that is a mental closure against the discovery of cultural inconsistencies.[9]

This *a priori* assumption, that there always was a discoverable coherence in culture and this total reliance on inspirational grasp as the method for discovering it, spilt over to soak the most diverse varieties of sociological theory. The Myth surfaced intact in Functionalist thought, transmitted by Sorokin. His insistence on the internal logic of culture, which would be apprehended by sweeping up a mountain of cultural fragments the inner coherence of which could then be intuitively deciphered, was finally enshrined in the Parsonian central-value system – that *a prioristic* guarantor of further societal integration. If Parsons had taken on board and given pride of place to a notion of an overt and readily detectable cultural system (being somewhat more analytical in his attempt to grasp it through his 'pattern variables'), linguistic structuralism did the reverse. It accepted incoherence as being the surface characteristic of overt and seemingly unconnected cultural symbols but then revealed their underlying structuration by a hidden code – again grasped intuitively, by some form of deciphering or interpolation, though always lacking any external context of justification.

Finally, the Myth received monumental reinforcement by its adoption into Western humanistic Marxism. The notion of 'hegemonic culture' and its offspring, the 'dominant-ideology' thesis, embodied the same assumption about cultural coherence: certainly it was inspired by sectional interests, generally it distorted the nature of reality and undoubtedly the consensus it generated was the product of manipulation, but nevertheless mystification and misguidedness did not deny it the basic property of coherence shared equally by the Parsonian normative system. Significantly the now-familiar reliance on aesthetic grasp dominated Marxist methodology here, as evidenced by the growing preoccupation of Euro-Marxists with literary criticism[10] with laying bare the ideological impregnation of works of art, by a kind of 'class decoding' which had distinct affinities with the enterprise of linguistic structuralism.

The conventional anthropological approach to culture in fact contained two distinct strands within the concept:

- The notion of a *cultural pattern* with an underlying unity and a fundamental coherence.
- The notion of *uniform action*, identified with the above and stemming from it to produce social homogeneity.

In other words, to view culture as 'a community of shared meanings' meant eliding the community with the meanings. In so doing a vital analytical distinction was obfuscated and this was to have far-reaching consequences when the Myth was transmitted to sociology. For the Myth contains a basic analytical confusion between two elements which are both logically and sociologically distinct. Teasing them out involves separating the two strands above which were tautly intertwined in the anthropological image.

What remain inextricably confounded in the Myth of cultural consistency are

- *Logical consistency*, that is the degree of internal compatibility between the components of culture (however these two terms are defined).
- *Causal consensus*, that is the degree of social uniformity produced by the imposition of culture (again however these two terms are defined) by one set of people on another.

The former concerns *the consistency* of our attempts to impose ideational order on experiential chaos; the latter concerns the *success* of attempts to order other people. Logical consistency is a property of the world of ideas; causal consensus is a property of people.

The main proposition advanced here is that the two are logically and empirically distinct, hence they can vary independently of one another. Thus it is perfectly conceivable that any social unit, from a community to a civilization, could be found the principal ideational elements (knowledge, belief, norms, language, mythology, etc.) of which do indeed display considerable logical consistency – that is, the components are consistent not contradictory – yet the same social unit may be low on causal consensus. For example, this may be especially true where the 'culture' in all its logical coherence is the prerogative of an elite (priesthood, caste, intelligentsia, estate or ruling class). Because of this, the non-elites may behave differently (absence of social uniformity), given that they only have access to more restricted ideas.

Restricted access may give rise to defective or divergent syntheses of the cultural stock resulting in schism through the differential accentuation of the cultural elements received. Furthermore, such action is the joint product of the notions inculcated and the response to enforced inculcation. Unlike the elite, these actors are not responding to the power of precept alone but also to preceptual power. Power relations are the causal element in cultural consensus building and, far from unproblematically guaranteeing behavioural conformity, they can provoke anything from ritualistic acceptance to outright rejection of the culture imposed.

It should be noted that these cases where high logical coherence is accompanied by low causally induced consensus do not depend upon the existence of cultural alternatives within the social unit in question. Although these are generally extremely important in amplifying the lack of social uniformity, their presence is not a necessary pre-condition for the independent variation of logical coherence and causal consensus in the cultural realm. In brief, this distinction can be sustained *even if* we uncritically accept the existence of a single, unified central-value system or cultural scheme.

Equally the opposite situation can be found in society: causal consensus may be high while logical consistency is low. Again there is nothing inconceivable about a social unit the members of which display considerable cultural accord in their basic values, interpretations and language, yet the Cultural System itself is riven with inconsistencies. Successful imposition does not require high coherence of the cultural package imposed. Partly this is because humankind does not necessarily notice inconsistency or unexceptionally find it intolerable (individually we all give house-room to incompatible mental furnishings through intellectual idleness, patches of ignorance, nostalgia or closing the emotional shutters). Again, more important in empirical terms, are the power relations implicated in imposition. Whether we are talking about parental socialization of political indoctrination, the success achieved may reflect coercion rather than conviction. As in the glaring case of German Fascism, considerable behavioural uniformity can co-exist with *both* substantial doctrinal inconsistencies and significant mental reservations in the population.

Thus my basic proposition is that it is essential to distinguish

5

logical consistency from causal cohesion in order to gain an analytical grip on the cultural components and upon Socio-Cultural dynamics. This distinction would closely parallel that between System integration and social integration,[11] made by Lockwood, in the structural domain. Indeed, much of the following argument seeks not merely to bring the analysis of culture on a par with that of structure but also to suggest that the two can be analysed in very similar generic terms. In line with this conviction, what has so far been discussed as the logical consistency of culture will henceforth be referred to as Cultural System integration. Similarly causal cohesion will now be termed Socio-Cultural integration. As in the structural field, so here the point of this distinction is to improve our explanatory purchase on cultural statics and dynamics.

Lockwood rightly argued that neither element alone provided the sufficient condition for structural change. On the one hand, System integration could be low but unless its contradictions were actualized and amplified by sectional social groups they could be contained and stasis would persist because of this high social integration. Alternatively, group antagonism could be profound (low social integration) without leading to significant change in society, unless it was linked to Systemic contradictions. Obviously the cultural parallels require a detailed specification, which will follow later, but for the moment the key point is that in both structural and cultural fields the analysis of stability and change depends on making such analytical distinctions.

The error underlying the Myth of Cultural Integration was that it elided this crucial distinction: the basic deficiency of the anthropological heritage, as appropriated in sociology, was that it resisted making any analytical distinctions at all. The net effect of this insistence on cultural compactness was that it precluded any theory of cultural development springing from internal dynamics. Logically the component parts of any complex have to be accorded some autonomy if they are to interact and to change (or actively to maintain) one another, or the state of the whole. Yet this is precisely what the image of a coherent pattern, a uniform style or an all-pervading ethos effectively denied. Consequently *internal* dynamics were surrendered to external ones – the forces for development were located anywhere other than within the Cultural System itself. At their most sociological they were pictured as diffusing inwards from the exterior; at their least, as giant mirrors of individual psychology[12] the traits of which were independent of their cultural context.

However, the interest of this Myth for sociology does not concern its genesis, maintenance and vitality in the history of thought, but instead relates to its analytical premises and consequences. Its evergreen quality is mainly of significance in protecting and protracting these. Thus I now want to link three things together over time, but the linkage to be accentuated between them concerns conceptual continuity. (Obviously this is mirrored in the history of ideas but it is not their chronology which will be traced here.)

– The genesis of the Myth of Cultural Integration in anthropology.
– Sociological support for the Myth.
– The weak analytical development of a sociology of culture.

My main argument is that the current theoretical deficiencies in the sociological analysis of culture are directly attributable to the conflation of Cultural System integration with Socio-Cultural integration – a confusion of the two which could be found within the anthropological heritage but which was intensified by the Myth of Cultural Integration in all its subsequent sociological manifestations. Consequently the premisses and implications enshrined in the Myth must be disentangled and demolished before culture can assume a proper place in sociological analysis.

The origins of the Myth

(1) The image of cultural coherence is grounded in traditional society. It is most persuasive where traditionalism prevails, largely because the enduring enruttedness of primitive society can immediately be taken as exemplifying the force of cultural consistency. (This logical leap is far too precipitous and requires close re-inspection.) Almost automatically, however, the durability of routine was attributed to its enmeshment in an all-pervasive perfectly integrated Cultural System which had imposed itself as the printed circuit of the primitive mind. Thus, in the classic statement about compact coherence among the Azande we should note that Evans-Pritchard in fact elides the cultural, structural and personality systems:

In this web of belief every strand depends upon every other strand, and a Zande cannot get out of its meshes because it is the only world he knows. The web is not an external structure in which he is enclosed. It is the texture of his thought and he cannot think that his thought is wrong.[13]

Not only was this taken as the epitome of the primitive Cultural System by many social theorists but certain anthropologists also sponsored the extension of such imagery beyond traditional society. Thus it percolated up the centuries of the 'stages' of social development; a seepage undoubtedly encouraged by a neglect of the interregnum, that vast tract representing the greater part of human history which fell between the increasingly popular dichotomies of primitive and modern, undeveloped and developed, traditional and scientific societies. Thus in 1924 we find Edward Sapir generalizing the Myth from one side of the gap to the other; both sides displayed cultural coherence and so, by extension, did the phrases and forms in between:

A genuine culture is perfectly conceivable in any type or stage of civilization . . . It is merely inherently harmonious, balanced, self-satisfactory . . . It is a culture in which nothing is spiritually meaningless, in which no important part of the general functioning brings with it a sense of frustration, of misdirected or unsympathetic effort.[14]

Hence the 'anthropological image', with its co-insistence upon a complete interdependence (every strand depending on every other) and an inherent harmony of the whole Cultural System (balanced, self-satisfactory) passed into sociology. And this despite the existence of at least one school of thought which had consistently repudiated the association of interdependence with harmony – the Marxist tradition accentuating contradictions between interdependent parts and their disruptive social potential.[15]

(2) But before moving on to the sociological inheritance it is important to enter certain severe objections to the conception of cultural integration where it originated – in relation to primitive society. First, it is a strange tribute to the influence of German Historicism and Romanticism that something like Zande culture, which Evans-Pritchard himself called 'a thing of shreds and patches'[16] should have become the supreme exemplar of coherent integration. As Gellner comments, it is

ironical that this culture of shreds and patches, incorporating at least 20 culturally alien groups and speaking at least 8 diverse languages in what is but part of its total territory, should have come to have been systematically invoked, by philosophers making facile and superficial use of anthropology, as an illustration of the quite erroneous view that cultures are islands unto themselves, *whose supposedly coherent internal norms of what is real and what is not real may not be challenged*[17]. (my emphasis)

The irony is compounded if it is recalled that the famous passage about the tightly interwoven cultural strands which completely enmesh the Zande population is immediately qualified in the text: 'Nevertheless' (a caveat perhaps so large as to swamp the initial proposition) Zande 'beliefs are not absolutely set but are variable and fluctuating to allow for different situations and to permit empirical observations and even doubts'.[18]

Evans-Pritchard himself attempts to save his argument from this obvious objection by introducing the notion of a kind of moving cultural equilibrium whereby the Azande 'adapt themselves without undue difficulty to new conditions of life',[19] adaptation preserving coherence. This theme of course echoes down the corridors of later Functionalist thought. But given that he has acceded to the presence of doubts and to the importing or implanting of external influences, why should we assume that these are unproblematically reintegrated into a new form of cultural coherence?

In fact, the assumption has not been acceded to universally. The work of certain later anthropologists has questioned this view of Cultural System integration as generic to primitive societies. There is, for example, Edmund Leach's record of Burmese tribesmen alternating between two quite incompatible visions of their society.[20] There are the frequent instances of frontier dwellers who literally and linguistically bestride two different (thus potentially inconsistent) cultures, and there is the well-documented effect of exogamy in marriage rules which enforces exposure to and incorporation of cultural differences to varying degrees. These are simply a few examples of the occurrence of cultural pluralism and the accompanying incursion of inconsistencies. Usually, however, these have been deprived of cultural significance through an easy acceptance of adaptive reintegration but, as Gellner argues, the implications of this view are unacceptably unrealistic. It presumes that 'there can be no syncretism, no doctrinal pluralism, no deep treason, no dramatic conversion or doctrinal oscillation, no holding of alternative belief systems up one's sleeve, ready for the opportune moment of betrayal'.[21] It denies the readiness of opportunistic gurus, ambitious younger sons or disgruntled minorities to capitalize on cultural ambiguities and discontinuities which would advance their ambitions. If the standard view does not give us the noble savage it leaves us with the primitive cultural dope, unable to exploit the intricacies of his own *Lebenswelt*.

(3) Yet if it is indeed the case that pluralism is common, inconsistency is pervasive and syncretism is general practice, why has the

image of high Cultural System integration possessed such staying power? Why, too, has there been the complementary and stubborn resistance to assigning cultural inconsistencies any importance in mainstream social theory? Two reasons are usually given to account for this situation by those who, like me, see perversity and prejudice in its perpetuation. Both reasons are rooted in the debate about the nature of the so-called primitive mind. Although they themselves are mutually opposed, they jointly repulse the notion of cultural inconsistencies and their social importance.

On the one hand the long-lasting school of thought which has endorsed some concept of a 'savage mind' has enshrined the notion of a mentality which is constituted entirely differently from our own. No amount of information or instruction would alter its basic difference in constitution, its (romanticized or regrettable) fusion with nature, which, in turn, repudiates clear distinctions between the mundane and the spiritual, the animate and the inanimate, the self and others or other things. What is crucial in this generic concept of a 'savage mind' is that it is one where the rules of identity and contradiction do not operate. For from this perspective these are not 'the' rules, they are 'our' rules, part of a wholly different mentality. Consequently the reactions which *we* might expect towards inconsistency and incoherence are predicated upon *our* own mental constitution. Hence cultural discontinuities are theoretically discounted from this point of view which holds them unimportant because the 'savage mind' discountenances them. It cannot act on what it does not sense. For us to accord theoretical significance to unsensed contradictions would be an unwarranted act of cultural importation, to proponents of this kind of theory.

I have no interest here in debating the demerits of this 'booming buzzing confusion' portrayal of primitive mentality except on one point. Since a substantial amount of evidence indicates that the perceptual discrimination of primitive people in everyday and experimental settings is just as acute as that of their investigators, and that their linguistic capacities for differentiation in various areas (snow, cattle, kin) may well exceed that of the anthropologist, there are no grounds on which to *presume* that the cultural inconsistencies we perceive and could/would act on, *must necessarily* remain inert to the 'savage mind' and therefore *will be of no significance* in primitive society. What I am more concerned to stress is the odd affinity in this connection shared by those holding a diametrically opposed view of primitive mentality.

Ironically, the harshest opponents of the 'pre-logical mind' notion seek to make their case by a demonstration of the total coherence of primitive thought: intense hermeneutic ingenuity is deployed to defend seemingly contradictory statements/beliefs from the charge of incoherence; extensive interpretative schemes are erected to decode superficially inconsistent elements by revealing their underlying compatibility. Once again the effect is systematically to deprive cultural inconsistency of any social or theoretical significance – not by arguing that such contradictions are unsensed but by contending that they are 'merely' sensed, that is they are apparent rather than real. But, as Gellner argues, the

trouble with such all-embracing logical charity is . . . that it is unwittingly quite *a priori*: it may delude anthropologists into thinking that they have *found* that no society upholds absurd or self-contradictory beliefs, whilst in fact the principle employed has ensured in advance of any inquiry that nothing may count as pre-logical, inconsistent or categorically absurd though it may be. And this, apart from anything else, would blind one to at least one socially significant phenomenon: the social role of absurdity.[22]

(4) However, without diminishing the significance of these two views for founding and buttressing the Myth of high Cultural System Integration – through their *a prioristic* denial of the existence or the significance of inconsistency – I believe that there is an even more pervasive reason accounting for its longevity. This reason is more general since it also characterizes the work of many who remain completely agnostic about the constitution of primitive mentality. Basically it consists in attributing the massive uniformity of behaviour, displayed over time, in 'cold' societies, to the *binding logic of the Cultural System*. In other words, the predominance of routine, repetition and reproduction in the traditional society are interpreted as properties of high Cultural System integration. Primitive peoples are seen as inexorably trapped in a coherent cultural code which generates the behavioural uniformities observed. Thus, to give a recent example, Giddens writes of 'societies confined implacably within the grip of tradition'[23] because of the 'ontological security' conferred by unquestioned codes of signification and forms of normative regulation. Now in all such cases there seems to be a fundamental confusion between the 'grip of tradition' (which I do not denigrate) and its source in the bindingness of the cultural logic. In brief, *high Cultural System integration is consistently being confused with high Socio-Cultural integration.*

The uniform and lasting patterns of behaviour accredited to properties of the Cultural System are never considered to be engendered and encouraged by contingencies of the traditional terrain.[24]

In other words, the force of tradition is seen as the force of the traditional belief system rather than of the traditional way of life. On the contrary, I would argue that it is the latter which fosters uniformity and continuity in collective patterns of behaviour, whereas it is an illusion foisted on traditional life that its regularities are *orchestrated* by an overarching Cultural System. Instead they are merely manifestations of high Socio-Cultural integration. That is to say that given a relatively stable environment, individuals could largely live inductively from past contexts to future ones *because* they were engaged in unchanging activities. But this was due to the stability of the structured context which promoted high Socio-Cultural integration since customary practices did continue to 'work', rather than to their constrained enmeshment by an integrated belief system. On the contrary it should be ventured that it was precisely this high level of day-to-day and generation-to-generation workability of practices which created an optical illusion about the coherence of Cultural Systems and simultaneously discouraged the thorough exploitation or exploration of their contradictions.

Instead the two are elided, the effects of Socio-Cultural integration have generally been seen as the consequences of Cultural System integration. Even a thinker like Bauman, who conceptualizes 'culture as praxis', gives more power to the Systemic elbow. The *univers du discours*, from which meanings are derived, is seen as 'fostering itself, with the force of an external inevitability, on each particular member of the community and on each particular communication-event'.[25] What is much rarer to find in the literature is any full-blooded assertion that the crucial element in traditionalism is the *social* integration aspect. Gellner provides this, but also recognizes the controversial nature of his following proposition: where 'relationships are fairly well-known (because the community is small, and because the types of relationship are small in number), shared culture is not a precondition of effective communication'. In support of this he cites Lévi-Strauss's example of a Red Indian band in the Brazilian jungle, made up of two smaller groups, neither of which understood the other's language. Here, given 'the smallness of the total group, and the simplicity of the problems and situations facing it, this absence of linguistic communication did not apparently prevent it forming an effective co-operating group'.[26]

In fact I suspect that Gellner is deliberately over-accentuating his case in stating that given a highly structured society then culture is not indispensable, in order to put gunpowder under the Myth of Cultural System integration and integration through Cultural Systems. What I think he is really accentuating is the independent contribution of Socio-Cultural integration to traditionalism, dissociated from any orchestration by a binding Cultural System. For the reasons why he holds that 'an effective co-operating group', or other kinds of repetitive relationship, can work are *not* without a cultural dimension: those involved 'have long ago sized each other up: each knows what the other wants, the tricks he may get up to, the defenses and counter-measures which, in the given situation, are available, and so on'.[27] But this of course is at the Socio-Cultural level.

Even if I am guilty of misconstruing Gellner's intentions, such an interpretation of his position is at least of value in highlighting the fact that much of the uniformity which has been confused with and attributed to the bindingness of cultural belief systems, merely reflects a high degree of Socio-Cultural integration. Another, more contentious, way of putting this is that *traditionalistic practices are not necessarily shared because the Cultural System is binding, but can be binding because they are shared at the Socio-Cultural level.* In fact I would argue that this is not an *a prioristic* matter, a view which strengthens but is not essential to the main argument – namely the necessity of distinguishing analytically between the two types of cultural integration, the Systemic and the social. So far this necessity has been established negatively, by reference to the errors arising from elision of the two elements; next I will seek to establish the positive advantages of this analytic distinction.

(5) We turn now to four flaws in the original Myth. So far I have tried to show *how* the Myth of Cultural integration originated in terms of its constitutive assumptions – the most basic one being the conflation of Cultural System integration with Socio-Cultural integration. Now I want to disentangle certain sins of commission and omission perpetrated within the Myth in relation to these two elements. For the crucial point here is that their combined effect serves to extinguish exactly those features the combination of which could give explanatory purchase on cultural change. In teasing them out the object is, of course, the reverse. It is to delineate those components the interplay of which would form the kernel of a theory of cultural development.

(i) Where Cultural System integration is concerned, the main sin of omission has been touched on already – the refusal to recognize or attach any importance to the existence of inconsistencies at this level. Commitment in advance to cultural coherence

blinds us to the possibility that social change may occur through the replacement of an inconsistent doctrine or ethic by a better one, or through a more consistent application of either. It equally blinds us to the possibility of, for instance, social control through the employment of absurd, ambiguous, inconsistent or unintelligible doctrines ... even if they never occurred it would be wrong to employ a method which excludes their possibility *a priori*.[28]

What Gellner is pointing to here are certain far-reaching social consequences which *may* result from Systemic cultural contradictions. Whether these do occur depends, I will argue, on conditions in the Socio-Cultural realm. So far Gellner has touched on a necessary but insufficient condition for consequential cultural change, which is suppressed by the upholders of Systemic consistency.

Simultaneously he has done something else of equivalent importance. This is to explode the assumption that the *interdependence* of cultural elements automatically equals the *integration* of the Cultural System (as exemplified in the image of each strand depending on every other and forming an escape-free web). Quite simply, what he demonstrates is that when inconsistencies pertain between interdependent elements (as in the case of the role expectations attaching to *igurramen* of the High Atlas, who must behave generously, appear unmaterialistic and yet remain prosperous), then *cultural manipulation* is inescapable (in the above case in order to balance the books). In other words, far from a coherent Cultural System being passively received, its active mediation is required if it is to be translated into a semblance of social coherence. Thus interpretative manipulation is involved, whether to sustain the Cultural System or to change it.

In brief, the theoretical incorporation of inconsistency at the Systemic level does two things: it specifies certain necessary conditions for stability or change in the Cultural System. Every contradiction represents a potential for change. Whether it does lead to this rather than to active containment depends on the activities of groups and individuals at the Socio-Cultural level. Thus the second implication of giving due attention to the flaws in Cultural System integration is the necessity of distinguishing this level analytically from Socio-Cultural integration – for the latter determines the fate of these discontinuities, that is whether they are amplified into recognisable changes or damped down to preserve the picture of social continuity.

(ii) Still at the level of Cultural System integration an equally important sin of commission is covertly committed in the process of conceptualization. The presence of a high degree of interdependence among cultural components is taken as a straightforward manifestation of high Systemic integration. Already we have seen the fallacy of assuming that because the strands are tied together they necessarily form a neat web. This erroneously presumes that interdependent elements must be compatible and empirically we have seen that this is not always the case. However, the coherence of the Cultural System may not derive from the harmonious integration of its parts as tends to be assumed (for we have seen that harmony and interdependence need not be synonymous). Instead the coherence presented, and any integrative force it exerts, may be due not to something the Cultural System possesses (harmonious integration of parts) but to something it lacks, namely autonomous elements (relatively independent of the connected components). To use the traditional imagery, these would be 'loose ends' unknit with the main web. Empirically they might be things like pockets of deviant cultic practice, novel practices penetrating from frontier regions or ancient mythological survivals. If at all extensive such autonomous elements would constitute a fund of alternatives at the Systemic level. The Myth, however, is committed to the absence of such 'loose ends'.

The crucial point here is that cultural coherence may not stem from the integration of the Cultural System but from lack of alternatives to it – and this itself is a property of the System. Too frequently it has been presumed to be a property of the Socio-Cultural level. Primitive people, because of their low individuation, are held to lack a *sense* of alternatives (rather than alternatives being Systemically unavailable). Thus Horton exemplifies this view when he writes that 'in traditional cultures there is no developed awareness of alternatives to the established body of theoretical tenets; whereas in scientifically oriented cultures, such an awareness is highly developed'.[29] But the (Systemic) existence of options cannot be elided with people's sense of them. In modern societies a variety of options are known to be available but some people can also close their minds to this plurality: in traditional societies we cannot assume that everyone has a closed mind until we know whether they have any option. Once again this point serves to bring home the need to distinguish between the two levels.

Equally this question of alternatives (like our discussion of inconsistencies) is linked to the conditions of cultural stability or change.

The existence of alternatives at the Systemic level, or the presence of *variety* as it is termed in information theory,[30] is essential for *adaptive Systems*. This mathematical theory postulates some source which continuously generates variety (new signals, symbols, messages) and some receiver who can put this variety to use. I am not concerned here with the 'adaptive' aspect or with the notion of 'successful mapping' (through which the fund of variety is sorted into those modifications which most closely match the environment and those which do not) but simply with the question of change (which may turn out to be non-adaptive, always assuming that this term can be operationalized). However, in the context of cultural change, information theory does contain two invaluable insights: first that alternatives (variety) must be available to be drawn upon the Systemic level; and, second, that there must be receivers at the Socio-Cultural level who are willing and able to make use of them. (Yet again the distinction between the levels is indispensable.)

To put some meat on the bones of this abstract discussion let us briefly refer to Roger C. Owen's example of the inter-penetration of certain independent Indian patrilocal bands of Northern Baja California.[31] Here the source of variety at the Systemic level was the operation of the exogamy rule for marriage partners. This meant the continuous importation of females from other bands which were linguistically and culturally different. The local band was thus a hybrid residence unit, in terms of language and culture, where the children differed from either parent given their bi-lingual and bi-cultural characteristics. Here, in other words, the children constituted the group which could draw on the pool of variety. To Owen, who pursued the notion of adaptation, this meant that 'contained in any given population would be a diversified set of adaptive symbols derived from the females: to any situation of rigorous selective stress, there would be available a number of possible responses, thus giving to the culturally hybrid band a high survival potential'.[32] I would prefer to say more simply that this unit had a high Systemic potential for change, requiring actualization by its bi-cultural agents.

(iii) Turning now to Socio-Cultural integration, the main sin of omission here was a conventional unwillingness to concede that there was *ever* enough differentiation in the population to make interpretative innovations, to manipulate cultural loopholes, or to exploit inconsistencies. I would not for a moment deny that the relatively low levels of social differentiation in most traditional societies do act as a severe drag upon large-scale collective action for cultural and any other sort of change. But at the same time it seems to me that our modern notions of the kind of collectivity which introduces significant modifications, and also the kinds of modification which count as significant, have blocked an appreciation of smaller scale differences *and* the qualitative changes which they can introduce.

Certainly in the Durkheimian tradition low social differentiation is closely associated with low personal individuation and, in general terms, I do not contest this. However 'individuation' is a comparative social term, never meant by Durkheim to rob tribal man of any element of individual*ism*: indeed it was precisely his egotism, self-seeking and opportunism which required normative control. Yet all such character traits tended to be banished by the makers of the original Myth. This was particularly true of the holistic anthropologists; 'the individuals they so respect and exalt, jealously guarding them against subsumption under the typical or the general, are always *collective wholes* . . . Historicists may like individuality; yet as good holists, they feel no affection towards *individualism*.'[33] Homogenous individuals as standard-bearers (in both senses) of shared cultural uniqueness were the humanoids of this type of theorizing. These were the oversocialized populaces which made for high Socio-Cultural integration. What is lacking here is the acceptance of a few individual personality differences – a bit of gumption, a sense of grudge or grievance, an eye to the main chance, a touch of adventurism and so on. For these are all that need to be postulated as the initial mechanisms through which the contradictions of the Cultural System begin to be exploited.

Unfortunately, and partly because of this dominant orientation in anthropology, what we lack is a 'high politics' of traditional society. There seems to be a glaring paucity of case-studies dealing with individual machinations to gain power, to establish independence or to generate legitimacy, which would have been very revealing about the Cultural Elaboration associated with these manoeuvres. There is another reason for this neglect which is just as powerful. Quite simply, the manifestations of early Cultural Elaboration which I have in mind were often not recognized as such. Shifts in cosmologies, in doctrinal emphasis, in symbolic combinations, or in ritualistic practices have not been accorded much significance because they did not represent an obvious shift towards cultural modernity. Very likely they do not, but this does not mean that they are merely a kind of symbolic Brownian motion inside a sealed cultural vessel. Instead, by Elaboration, Accretion, syncretism, or re-interpretation, a winding path may lead away from the original Cultural System. Though there is no reason to assume that this will either constitute or join the highway to modernity, this is *not* to deprive it of subsequent social significance.

(iv) Finally, to view Socio-Cultural integration as the product of the bindingness of the Cultural System involves an equally serious error of commission. Namely the assumption that the shared beliefs, values and symbols will continue to integrate society for as long as the Cultural System remains intact. As far as change is concerned, it is presumed to be a one-way relationship, working from the top down. I believe it is more realistically conceptualized as a two-way relationship, but once again this would depend upon utilizing analytical dualism for dealing with the interplay between the two levels. In support of the latter approach let us pursue the implications of the view that culture is *not* always shared because it is binding but may sometimes be *binding because shared*. The latter allows the Socio-Cultural level the possibility of pushing open the door to cultural change through actions which diminish integration-through-sharing and to do so independently of any co-terminous alteration in the Cultural System.

Undoubtedly integration-through-sharing is a powerful binding force in traditional societies; by its very nature it discourages innovation. Where there is a high level of co-action this does serve to promote co-thought,[34] especially when we are dealing with subsistence living. As a generalization, it does seem to be the case that there is roughly parity between the available variety and active variety of cultural elements in such societies and that they are pretty equally distributed. There is no significant vocabulary of concepts, meanings, beliefs or knowledge for some to draw upon, thus distinguishing themselves from others and fragmenting Socio-Cultural integration. Second, although this does not preclude individualistic innovation (primitive creativity should not be ruled out *a priori*), it is the individual who accumulates variety in the co-action System and who then confronts severe difficulties over its retention and transmission. In other words, cultural poverty is like physical poverty – grinding. Primitive cultural accumulation is almost as difficult as primitive capital accumulation and is, of course, related to it. So far these may look like further good reasons for not anticipating an independent contribution to cultural change from the Socio-Cultural level. They are not; they are simply reasons why this contribution will be slow and hard-won.

On the one hand the generalization about available variety and active variety being on a par is nothing more than that – it represents an 'average type' of traditional society not a universal characterization of traditional societies. For in many such social groupings small pools of variety do exist, in the form of surviving practices which can be activated and legitimated through a claim to represent the authentic 'tradition'. At any time this diversity may also be augmented by external contact, or more likely the latter sets up a tripartite, though rudimentary, Pluralism between cultural recusants, conventionalists and converts. Then we have only to return to the postulate of elementary differences in personality and interests for the erosion of sharing to be set in train. The second argument about the difficulties of accumulation is basically that the train can never gather enough speed to leave the station. Undeniably there is strength in the assertion that without the written word, cultural variations and innovations will be condemned to protracted recapitulation and oral embroidery. But this, it seems to me, is a general characteristic of any form of cultural transmission in traditional societies: it is not particular to ideas outside the mainstream, or more difficult for those holding them. This would only be the case if the individual alone accumulated them. But while he/she may be the first to originate or adopt them, we cannot universally assume that such people will be unsuccessful in transmitting them to their families, to a particular locality or to some subgroup with the same opportunism or general outlook as themselves. Only by assuming complete homogeneity at the level of structure, geography and personality *as well as* culture, can lack of success be a foregone conclusion. Without this assumption there is no reason why slow cultural fissiparousness cannot undermine previous Socio-Cultural integration, by eating into the 'sharedness' which was its mainstay.

Altogether, four major criticisms have been made of the original Myth, and are summarized below:

- A refusal to recognize or attach importance to inconsistencies within the Cultural System.
- Inattention to the presence or absence of alternatives at the Systemic level.
- Unwillingness to concede any modicum of differentiation in the population.
- A rejection of any conditions capable of damaging Socio-Cultural integration.

When considered in conjunction these points totally preclude a theory of cultural change because they eliminate precisely those elements essential to one. At each of the four points it has been seen that there is a common defect – the lack of any distinction between properties of the Cultural System and the features of Socio-Cultural integration. In brief, it is this central aspect of the Myth which militates against examination of the interplay between the two levels and thus obstructs the investigation of cultural dynamics.

Yet the origin of the Myth was grounded in primitive society which at least accounts for the playing down of inconsistency, alternatives, diversity and discontinuity, though it does not exculpate those who advanced theories which were predicated upon their total absence. Even if the

discovery of incoherences were never more than a contributory rather than a sufficient cause, it still would not be legitimate for us to employ a method which inherently prevents any possible appreciation of this fact. When anthropologists were concerned primarily with stable societies (or societies held to be such), the mistake was perhaps excusable: but nowadays it is not.[35]

Instead the Myth has gone from strength to strength. As at its origins it continues to draw its power from the elision of Cultural System integration with Socio-Cultural integration.

In the first place its appeal was redoubled since it became buttressed from two different and usually opposed schools of thought. However, it is vital to be clear that the one re-inforced it in an entirely different way from the other. In the first case (typical of normative functionalism) the Myth was restated in terms of 'downwards' conflation. Here, Cultural System integration engulfs Socio-Cultural integration through processes of orchestration, regulation and internalization. In the opposite case (represented by neo-Marxism) the Myth was re-instated in the form of 'upwards' conflation. Basically the Socio-Cultural level swallows up the Cultural System as the effect of social domination and ideological manipulation. Finally, just as both of these versions were becoming rather frayed under the wear and tear of criticism, the Myth was suddenly revitalized by a brand new exposition of it – this time taking the form of 'central' conflation (typified by the 'structuration' approach)[36] This was not merely another shot in the arm: rather it extended an eternal life-support system to the Myth by seeking to banish for good the analytical dualism, on which the present critique depends. To these theorists the Myth did indeed elide the Systemic and Socio-Cultural levels – but rightly so. Since the two were mutually constitutive and consequently inseparable, it was therefore improper to analyse them dualistically. That this full-frontal defence of the inexorable duality of culture was even less capable of providing a theory of cultural change[37] than the two preceding forms of conflation, is taken here to constitute the final condemnation of the whole conflationary procedure. However, not only do these bold assertions require justification but it also remains to demonstrate that these three new forms of the old elision were and are just as inimical to the understanding of cultural morphogenesis or morphostasis as was the original Myth.

The common denominator of the various conflationists who buttress the Myth of Cultural integration is that they elide logical relations with causal connections and then judge this *ensemble* to make a coherent whole. On the contrary, an approach based on analytical dualism challenges this judgement and the premises on which it is founded. Instead, by distinguishing logical relations (pertaining to the Cultural System) from causal relations (pertaining to the Socio-Cultural level) and allowing of their independent variation, the interface between them becomes a problematic area for intensive exploration. The results of this would identify the *conditions* for integration in the cultural realm, without that state of affairs being taken as a foregone conclusion – any more than it can be in the structural domain. Cultural integration is demythologized by rendering it contingent upon the particular patterning of interconnections *at* the two different levels and *between* the two different levels.

PART I
Rejecting Cultural Conflation

2 'Downwards Conflation': on keys, codes and cohesion

The original Myth did not pass unscrutinized from early anthropology into twentieth-century sociology: it was inspected, curiously handled and finally passed with reservations by the grand old sociologists of civilizations. The affinities between these two approaches were warm. The even older school of civilizational analysis had also placed cultural coherence on a pedestal, the main difference being that it had been pictured in cyclical terms, rather than as a stable pattern frozen by tradition. One of the key bridging thinkers here was Pitrim Sorokin, whose work made four distinct contributions to revitalizing the Myth:

(1)   It lent it civilizational sweep by 'gathering up' the centuries intervening between primitive and modern societies, which then justified the transfer of propositions about the former to the latter. In brief, it served to universalize the Myth.

(2)   It transmitted the Myth into mainstream sociology. Directly this mythology was built into the foundations of Functionalist thought, its immediate future was assured. More indirectly, by preserving and extending the 'artistic' approach to grasping cultural cohesion, civilizational analysis stocked a methodological armoury, from which later non-Functionalists could take up their main conceptual weapons, namely the notions of cultural keys and codes.

(3)   It elucidated the mechanisms responsible for 'downwards conflation', in a powerful account of how the internal logical consistency of Cultural Systems actually generated social uniformities in both mentality and behaviour, thus producing Socio-Cultural cohesion. In short, it actively justified a more precise formulation of the Myth rather than uncritically endorsing the elision of Cultural System and Socio-Cultural integration.

(4)   It made the claim, embodied in one of Sorokin's main titles, *Social and Cultural dynamics*, that this whole approach was not only compatible with the notion of cultural change but was actually a theory of it. In other words it asserted that the major premises of the Myth, far from being inimical to theorizing about change, were in fact adequate to explain it.

Because these four implications were so bold and far-reaching Sorokin's theory merits attention, not only in order to understand how this massive shot in the arm was administered to the Myth, but also to pinpoint why it appears to have been fundamentally misguided. Sorokin begins by asking two basic questions:

   – Do cultures have internal logical consistency?
   – If so, do such cultures shape uniformities in social behaviour and personality?

Quite properly, these questions are distinct, as the first refers to Cultural System integration while the second relates to Socio-Cultural integration.

Essentially he answers both questions with a qualified 'yes': 'In integrated cultures both behaviour and mentality become parts of one integrated system. The integration is not perfect, but it is tangible.'[1] In fact it seems to me that the qualifications turn out to be a good deal more interesting than the affirmations – as far as both levels are concerned.

At the Cultural System level Sorokin makes an interesting distinction between two kinds of integration among cultural components. First, there is functional integration which refers to their causal interdependence and which he resoundingly rejects, thus repudiating all

theories that take some specific variable internal to a culture (whether it be modes of production, technique and invention, religion, morals, art and science, philosophy and forms of government) and try to 'explain' all or the majority of the other characteristics of the culture in question as a 'function' or 'superstructure' or 'effect' of this variable: all such theories . . . assume the existence of a causal–functional integration between the parts. In other words, their promulgators appear to be partisans of the view of the functional unity of all cultural elements.[2]

This is deemed fallacious because not *all* the components of any culture *are* linked together causally and anyway the existence of some components is exclusively due to external influence or accidents of spatial adjacence – matters of contingency rather than functionality. Here his acceptance of both 'autonomy' and 'alternatives' amongst the components of culture (which thus becomes pregnant with contradiction and potential clashes) may seem to strike at the roots of the Myth as well as its Functionalist and Marxist outgrowths.

It might indeed have done just this if it had been Sorokin's main concern but it was not. For distinct from and towering over causal–functional integration is the 'Logico-Meaningful Integration of Culture'. This, like a superb work of art, is ' "supremely integrated" because in such instances each part, when set in its designated position, is no longer noticeable as a part, but all the parts together form, as it were, a seamless garment.'[3] It is this 'property' which is ultimately sought for among the world's Cultural Systems: correspondingly the causal import of 'autonomy' and 'alternatives' and their 'contradiction' and 'conflict' fade from theoretical significance, not just at the Systemic level but also at the level of Socio-Cultural integration.

On the one hand, what is looked for at the Cultural System level are 'the *logical* laws of identity, contradiction, consistency; and it is these laws of logic which must be employed to discover whether any synthesis is or is not *logico-meaningful*'.[4] I would of course applaud this as a starting point for examining the Systemic level. Unfortunately the quotation immediately goes on to make clear that it is *not* the 'logical laws' as such on which analysis will depend but the much vaguer notion of *meaningful coherence* – which effectively comes full-circle to return to artistic hermeneutics.

Side by side with such logical laws, *in the narrow sense*, the *broader principles of 'keeping'*, of internal consistency, must also be used to determine the existence of this higher unity, or the lack of it. These are the principles expressed in the terms 'consistent style', 'consistent and harmonious whole', in contradistinction to 'inconsistent mingling of styles', 'hodgepodge', 'clashing' patterns or forms, and they apply especially to the examination of artistic creation. Many such *superlative unities cannot be described in analytical verbal terms; they are just felt as such, but this in no way makes their unity questionable.* One cannot prove by mere words . . . the inner consistency and supreme integration of the Cathedral of Chartres . . . *But not being completely describable in terms of language, their supreme unity is felt by competent persons as certainly as if they could be analysed with mathematical or logical exactness.*[5] (my emphasis)

On the other hand it is this 'higher unity' which is held to generate integration and uniformity at the Socio-Cultural level. The argument is simple: artistic peregrinations through the welter of civilizations demonstrate that 'the dominant type of culture moulds the type of mentality of human beings who are born and live in it'.[6] This is the intervening variable which links consistency at the level of Cultural Systems to Socio-Cultural uniformities. It is not a perfect translation because of the human capacity for not practising what we preach but within 'these limits *the conduct and behaviour of the members of any such culture is conditioned by it, and stands in a consistent and clear association with it'*.[7] So, though imperfect, the relationship between the two levels is still tight. 'Overall' cultural integration thus comes about through the 'downward' influence of the Systemic upon the Socio-Cultural.

Ironically, perhaps, I have no real quarrel with Sorokin's main conclusion, would he have accepted the following formulation, with its points of emphasis, analytical distinctions and the full implications of its vice versa clause – '*where* and *when* there is a high degree of logical consistency in the Cultural System, this is a *necessary but insufficient condition* for Socio-Cultural integration: conversely extensive contradictions in the Cultural System *encourage but do not determine* Socio-Cultural conflict'. Unfortunately his conceptualization of coherence, and particularly his method of detecting it, would seem to preclude acceptance of this formulation. For the methodology serves to establish consistency, to elide the two levels, to eliminate a two-way interplay and to evade the import of Systemic incoherence and Socio-Cultural conflict for change. Even more unfortunately it was precisely this 'artistic' methodology and the attendant commitment to 'downwards' conflation which passed into subsequent sociological theory. Let us look briefly at these conceptual and methodological deficiencies, especially as they relate to the treatment of the two levels.

As far as the analysis of the Cultural System is concerned the 'essence of the logico-meaningful method of cognition is . . . in the finding of the central principle (the "reason") which permeates all the components, gives sense and significance to each of them, and in this way makes cosmos of a chaos of unintegrated fragments'.[8] But how do we avoid imposing a meaning which is simply not there, or how do we validate the meanings we claim to detect? Sorokin's answer is that we avoid false attribution by identifying the 'major premise of each system',[9] and are subsequently confirmed in the correctness of our identification by the fact that this 'major premise' will then act as 'the key', in conjunction with the canons of logic, to 'the nature of the entire unity'.[10] The presumption that there is a key to be found, which is itself predicated on the assumption that Cultural Systems are coherently ordered, though not obviously so at first glance, is Sorokin's lasting bequest to sociology.

Yet it seems to me that he has merely restated the problem, that is, how do we know that what we choose to call the 'major premise' is in fact that? What protection is there against defective perception reinforced by selective illustration, and indeed what compelling reason exists for supposing that Systemic organization must be based on a single key principle? In practice I do not believe that Sorokin solved these problems: given that 'major premisses' do not announce themselves. What he did quite bluntly was to invent them by inductive artistry. Various cultures were then designated as either 'Ideational' or 'Sensate' in their basic premises (which roughly coincide with Weber's 'other-worldly' and 'this-worldly' orientations), since to him 'all integrated cultures have in fact been composed of divers combinations of these two pure logico-meaningful forms'.[11] Leaving aside the glaring absence of any context of justification (which continues to dog modern exponents of the key or the code), there is another major difficulty with this procedure.

Ideally this method sweeps up an enormous number of cultural fragments, revealing their internal coherence.[12] But only ideally, for these two architectonic principles are admitted never to have existed in pure form.[13] The problem is that when the majority of cultures are examined they turn out to be 'mixed' in nature, that is unassimilable to either ideal type. Initially Sorokin extricates his approach from this difficulty by simply designating a 'Mixed' type — a solution which is internally inconsistent because, as a *mélange* of the two pure types, there cannot be a single 'major premise' operative within them. However, the obvious attraction of this 'solution' is that it *appears* to enable more cultures to be considered as integrated and thus amenable to being 'logically read'. Nevertheless as a supremely honest theorist Sorokin is then driven to recognize that the majority of 'Cultural Systems' were in fact *incoherent* mixes:

As to the Mixed forms which represent a highly eclectic and low-grade integration of Ideational and Sensate elements, they have probably always been very widespread . . . mixtures of this sort probably represent the most common type of mentality to be found among individuals and groups. Since the major premises of such mentalities are eclectic, sometimes even irreconcilable, the mentalities as a whole are also eclectic and sometimes self-contradictory. Thus the logic of such a cultural type is often nonlogical or illogical.[14]

29

Now, first, this deprives him of a method of 'reading' *all* Cultural Systems. At best it results in a distinction between a minority of cultures with great internal coherence (roughly, the world religions) and a majority of inconsistent ones which lack a key and are therefore not just different but defective in a way which defies sociological analysis. Immediately this distinction has implications for the theory of change. While Systemic coherence is held to be a powerful directive factor, Systemic inconsistency is deemed of no account for it simply signals defectiveness and, consequently, directionlessness and impotence. Thus the coherent System contains the seeds of its own destiny: change is the unfolding of its immanent potentialities, which can be crushed but never altered by external events.[15] In contrast the contradictions of unintegrated Systems are neither viewed as fractures along which splits are most likely to occur (that is as directional indicators of change) nor as forces positively encouraging change (through exploitation of internal tensions). Thus far from contradiction representing a crucial source of change from inside the System, here it merely leaves it prey to outside forces.[16]

This represents a proclamation of the insignifcance of internal inconsistency *for* change but it simultaneously restricts his theory *of* change to a very limited number of cases. In view of Sorokin's earlier admission that integration Cultural Systems are empirically in the minority, then we are left with a theory of change in which for *most cultures it is externally induced*, while for a few it is explained as the realization of their 'immanent life career'. As in the original Myth, the positive contribution of contradiction to change is dismissed and the theory of cultural change is correspondingly deficient.

Moving to the level of Socio-Cultural integration, Sorokin's *leitmotif* is that this is an epiphenomenon of Cultural Systems integration – without independent or reciprocal influence upon the former. There are only two refinements of the original Myth: first, that the phenomenon is explicitly one of *downwards* conflation; and second, that the mechanisms reducing the Socio-Cultural to the epiphenomenal realm are spelt out. Again, what will be accentuated here are the twin difficulties and defects of this enterprise, particularly in relation to theorizing about cultural change.

As we have already seen, the Cultural System supposedly orchestrates the Socio-Cultural domain through the creation of a particular mentality. Then 'from the fact that there is hardly any clear-cut boundary line between mentality and behaviour', it is argued that they 'imperceptibly merge into each other'.[17] The net result is held to be that 'activities assume one form in an Ideational and quite a different form in a Sensate society with respect to all the sociocultural compartments'. Moreover, these conclusions are held to be 'so self-evident that there is hardly any need to develop the argument further'.[18] Hence the integrated Cultural System shapes men and sweeps their interaction along with its logic. The very notion of any independent thought or action at this level is branded as a theoretical fallacy: 'In integrated cultures both behaviour and mentality become parts of one integrated system.'[19]

Yet difficulties immediately arise which *do* require much more argument. Because of the empirical predominance of 'mixture' at the Systemic level, Sorokin is driven to talk not about influence of *the* Cultural System but about the effect of the *dominant* culture. Thus considerable back-tracking is entailed when he states: 'the evidence is that historically there is an association between the type of dominant culture and the frequency of the type of conduct and personality'.[20] For here *pluralism* is conceded at the Systemic level, though its relations to *power* at the Socio-Cultural level are not examined. Thus what makes the dominant dominate remains an enigma, since Sorokin never grounds domination in social interaction.

Secondly, although pluralism is conceded to be universal in reality (both styles naturally occur 'in almost every socio-cultural constellation'),[21] this is seen as a fluctuation between the ideal types at the Systemic level, and never as representing a set of alternatives which people can exploit in relation to their interests. Yet his own data indicate that the *existence of pluralism* does give people the choice (or some choice) as to which mentality they develop and what form their action takes. Even certain Popes, as heads of a preponderantly 'Ideational' institution, were found to be of the 'Sensate' type of personality. Although this was always attributed exclusively to Systemic features (periods of institutional decline and corruption)[22] and never to autonomous Socio-Cultural action, it is difficult on the basis of such evidence to resist the conclusion that the Socio-Cultural realm does possess considerable autonomy in relation to the (pluralistic) Cultural System. Far from being passively shaped, it involves active choices which can in turn intensify contradiction, as was indeed the case in the papal examples.

Finally, however, the implications of power, domination, choice and conflict at the Socio-Cultural level for the theory of cultural change are never considered. These, of course, would constitute 'upward' influences and would represent a dynamic interplay between the two levels. Not only would I argue that their inclusion would make for a much better theory of cultural dynamics, but having recognized something of their existence then to exclude them from it appears to be a matter of pure theoretical *fiat*. This is explained though not justified by commitment to 'downwards conflation' – but the number of counter-factuals this assumption confronts are sufficient to consign it too to the land of myth.

The Functionalist version

Despite the deficiencies which have been underlined, Sorokin's work perceptively noted the problems and honestly confronted the difficulties of maintaining the Myth. Future theorists had the option of rebuilding from new foundations or papering over the widening cracks. Although Sorokin provided a towering defence of the Myth of Cultural Integration, he had, in the course of his studies, explicitly highlighted four problematic elements, but these were to be sedulously overlooked by later normative functionalists:

- The discovery of a fairly ubiquitous lack of cultural integration at the Systemic level (that is, the empirical predominance of low-grade Mixed systems) demanded much more theoretical attention especially if it was *not* (held) to undermine the Myth of cultural coherence. For fundamentally it raised the whole issue about the social role of Systemic *inconsistency*, which could not simply be brushed aside.
- The detection of a significant degree of independence at the Socio-Cultural level and the admission of an equally significant amount of pluralism at the Systemic level, posed the question of their relative autonomy and paved the way for a serious examination of their inter-play. Furthermore this rendered the assumed predominance of the Systemic over the Social (or logical connections over causal relations) at least questionable.
- The introduction of the notion of *dominant* Cultural Systems pointed up the necessity of addressing power and its role in establishing domination and subordination between alternative Systems. Obviously this would entail an investigation of power relations at the Socio-Cultural level – thus reinforcing the previous point. The only alternative to this would be a specification of *additional* Systemic properties which accounted for certain Systems attaining dominance. (However if holism is to be avoided here – were it argued, say, that the most internally consistent system dominates – then explanation of why this is the case still requires reference to human agency: exploration

of the Socio-Cultural level cannot be avoided if the mechanisms by which domination is established are to be elucidated.)

The methodological procedure whereby the sensitive observer unerringly detects that the key element articulating the Cultural System was revealed as defective in one crucial respect. It was predicated upon the assumption that each Cultural System possessed a major architectonic premiss – which was admitted not to be the case for the Mixed Systems with which the majority of societies somehow managed. This problem required a better conceptualization of the cultural components themselves than the simple model of a master key to all the scattered elements. Moreover if this was going to be needed in *most* cases then it should have led to heart-searching as to the adequacy of artistic hermeneutics, which at best *appeared* to work for a small minority of Systems.

In the Parsonian re-working of the Myth none of these problematic elements (with the partial exception of the last) was seriously addressed. Instead mainstream Functionalism pressed on with downwards conflation in a more sophisticated but also a more rigid form. To state the case briefly, since this is not the place for a detailed examination of Parsons's thought, normative Functionalism gave primary emphasis to 'the integration of social systems at the level of patterns of value orientations as institutionalized in role-expectations'.[23] In this brief formulation we have both the *leitmotif* of the Myth (consistent cultural patterning), the downwards inflection (systemic values shape role activities) and the net result (social integration). When dealing with the cultural realm, Parsons thus fails to make exactly the same distinction over which Lockwood took him to task in relation to the structural domain – the confusion of Systemic and social integration.[24] However, the downwards direction of the elision is of equivalent significance and was neatly criticized by Blake and Davis as 'the fallacy of normative determinism'[25] – namely the error of assuming that because norms (at the Cultural System level) are meant to control behaviour, then this is sufficient ground for assuming that they successfully do so (at the Socio-Cultural level).

In this context it is particularly instructive to pin-point the ways in which the four problems raised by Sorokin's work were evaded by Parsons, for their continued avoidance was what assured the continuation of the Myth.

First, instead of exploring the social role of inconsistency at the Systemic level Parsons does precisely the opposite. He makes the *a priori* assumption about a 'general strain to consistency in a cultural tradition'[26] as a property of functioning social systems. The various components of the Cultural System (beliefs, values, symbols) are not just held to *be* broadly compatible, they are pressed into mutual consistency by the tradition of which they form a part. 'Belief systems and systems of value-orientation are both parts of the cultural tradition and, *as such*, there is pressure for them to form a consistent system of patterns'[27] (my emphasis). We are told that their 'interdependence may be assumed',[28] but even if we presume it, why should we make the further assumption that interdependent elements cannot contain contradictions? For interrelationship does not preclude incompatibility. Moreover, Parsons readily admits that consistency will be imperfect but simultaneously asserts the insignificance of such imperfections. Again why should we write off incoherence (or any degree of it) as unimportant?

The answers to these questions are all contained in the imperatives of functioning social systems. We are back in the groove of circular Functional argument – the imputation of properties because of the necessity of those properties to adequate functioning – and back too to the well-worn criticisms that this form of argument merely states what the properties must be in order for the System to work in one particular way, namely smooth adaptive equilibration. None of this requires recapitulation here: suffice it to say that Parsons endorses the notion of a high degree of coherence at the level of Cultural Systems, elevates this to a matter of functional necessity and again deprives inconsistency of any positive theoretical role in cultural change.

Secondly, and of more importance for the present argument, is the complete elision of Cultural System integration with Socio-Cultural integration: 'Culture, in terms of the conceptual scheme of this work, consists . . . in patterned or ordered systems of symbols which are objects of the orientation of action, internalized components of the personalities of individual actors and institutionalized patterns of social systems.'[29] The conflation of the two levels is intrinsic to the whole approach which postulates that the same theory is adequate for any action system, from the dyad to the civilization. In asserting the homological nature of small and large social systems he simultaneously denies any necessity of theorizing about them in different terms. Since there 'are continuities all the way from the two-person interaction to the USA as a social system', it follows that 'we can translate back and forth between large-scale social systems and small groups'.[30] This is a classic case of the 'displacement of scope'[31] and it embodies the contentious assumption, in this connection, that all essential components of Cultural Systems are already contained in small-scale Socio-Cultural constellations.

On the one hand, the homology notion allows Parsons to introduce and justify the key element of his theory – normative consensus. In the dyad he showed how the simplest form of regular interaction between two actors required the establishment of norms, therefore he concludes that homologically there can be no social system, however large, without an equivalent form of normative regulation. Thus what had been vital but problematic to Durkheim – engineering the normative conditions of organic solidarity in modern societies – is precisely the opposite for Parsons, normative consensus is the cornerstone making regular systems of action possible.[32] Thus the conflation of Cultural Systems integration and Socio-Cultural integration is not just a feature of Parsonian theory, the whole theoretical structure rests upon it.

On the other hand, the generic assumption about homology which enables Parsons to work from the micro to the macro and vice versa does not imply mutual influence between them. The micro and the macro may share the same *kinds* of properties, but it is the Systemic level which determines what these properties in fact are. This represents the endorsement of a downwards influence which is quintessential to the whole scheme. As Parsons declares the '*keynote of the conceptualization we have chosen* is that cultural elements are elements of *patterned order* which *mediate and regulate* communication and other aspects of the mutuality of orientations in *inter-actional processes*'[33] (my emphasis). It is here in particular that Parsonian Functionalism is more rigid than Sorokin's approach. When Parsons posits the normative order as '*constitutive*, rather than regulative, of the self; social actors (*qua* role bearers) as a reflex of the social system; and meaning, as a faithful imprint of the cultural pattern',[34] then the pluralistic alternatives and individual autonomy which Sorokin detected historically are in fact ruled out definitively by him.

Thirdly, the central value system which orchestrates Socio-Cultural integration enjoys an unquestioned position of dominance which is not seen as arising from power relations. Indeed because the power of human agency is itself denigrated, Parsons can never deal with the problem of why the values which are central also happen to be functional to the social system. Like Sorokin he can offer no mechanism *accounting* for the predominance of certain values.[35]

Instead they are simply posited as being central, binding and thus shared, but none of these three features are viewed as conditional on the exercise of power or any other aspect of social interaction. Consequently Parsons 'never seems to ask about the conditions under which moral values *will* be held in common: he never seems to notice that power differences (among others) are likely to be conducive to differences in moral values and will thus, within his own assumptions, undermine the stability of relationships in which they exist'.[36] Although Gouldner takes him to task severely for implicitly assuming a mutuality of gratification in the social system, such that the effects of exploitation are neglected, in order to stress the importance of conformity with a shared moral code, one thing is glaringly absent from his critique. Parsons is chastized for considering the Cultural System as shared (when much is imposed), as binding (when so many interpretations of convenience can always be made), and as producing consensus (when the differential accentuation of particular components can generate the most severe conflict), but Gouldner never – until his latter days as a 'Marxist outlaw' – challenges the existence of a *central* value system. Parsons was wrong not to have related domination *to* power but Gouldner, having changed sides, himself reduces the Cultural System to an epiphenomenon *of* power. In changing camps he had shifted from being an exponent of downwards conflation to become a proponent of upwards conflation (joining the protagonists of manipulated consensus and deserting the advocates of normative consensus). Only for the briefest period in *The Coming Crisis of Western Sociology* did he analytically separate the Systemic from the Social, showing how any moral code is a vehicle through which social tensions can be expressed as conflicts of interest and encourage divergent interpretations to develop. But even these fruitful sections, which include power-play and Systemic contradictions, are stymied by the Parsonian heritage which precludes the full-blooded clash of complete ideational alternatives. Gouldner's attack merely challenges the supposed *consequences* of central values at the *Socio-Cultural level*: it does not seriously question that these central values are indeed the *constituents* of the *System level* – and thus he, too, continues to prop up the basic tenet of the original Myth.

Fourthly, of all the problems in Sorokin's work, the adequacy of characterizing Cultural Systems by a highly subjective form of artistic hermeneutics is the one which receives most critical attention. However, this break is much less radical than it appears on the surface. Parsons proceeds analytically by delineating four 'problems' which any (functioning) social system has to solve – 'Goal Attainment', 'Adaptation', 'Integration' and 'Latency'. *How* these tasks are solved depends upon the values of the System – values which give meaning to the individual and order to society. The make-up of the value system is conceptualized as the pattern produced by opting for one side or the other of five 'basic' dilemmas. The choice between each pair *seriatim* (for example, Affectivity versus Affective Neutrality; Specificity versus Diffuseness etc.) produces a pattern of values – the 'pattern variables'. Different social systems may then be characterized and compared in terms of differing patternings within the matrix of the thirty-two possible combinations which represent different ways of solving the four functional imperatives. Superficially this reasoning seems to endow cultural patterning with functional necessity since it excludes any other view of the ways in which societies can be landed (or land themselves) with a value system. Nevertheless there is a covert hermeneutic aspect to these 'pattern' variables.

Sorokin proceeded unapologetically from his aesthetic grasp of the key premiss unifying each Cultural System to a typology of Cultural Systems (Sensate, Mixed, Ideational and all their subtypes) – his bunch of keys. Parsons, however, appears to work the other way round, generating a typology from the relationship between the four functional problems and the dilemmas which have to be faced in meeting them, in what seems to be a logical rather than an artistic manner. However, a strong element of interpretative licence still lurks here. The actual designation of the five dilemmas is not in fact derived *logically* from the functional imperatives in any way: fundamentally, this is the product of artistic grasp. They represent Parsons's understanding of the main dimensions along which Cultural Systems (particularly Western Systems) have opted and which, in combination, provide a 'satisfyingly' complete characterization of these values to him. Ultimately, however, Functionalists and non-Functionalists alike remain free to differ about, to delete from, or to extend on, the list of pattern variables in the light of their own understandings.

For example, some who were unwilling to go all the way with Parsons have simply used his pattern variables as a handy checklist for comparative purposes. This is unobjectionable *per se* (we can compare anything in terms of anything else if it serves some purpose), *but* the acceptance and retention of the schema then becomes a matter of proven empirical utility in particular cases, *not* a universal method of classification. Moreover once the pattern variables are employed purely as useful classificatory devices, the criterion of utility could well show them to be non-exhaustive – why stop at five dilemmas if a different list proves profitable in some respect? Parson's covert hermeneutics can thus be dethroned by any empirical demonstration of a better characterization, for ultimately his procedure rests on interpretative artistry and it is not logically sealed.

We have seen that the first three problems raised by Sorokin's work were systematically glossed over by Parsons: there was no serious exploration of the social role of inconsistency at the level of the Cultural System; there was an even stronger version of downwards conflation between this and the Socio-Cultural level; and there was no attention given to the role of power in establishing the domination of the central value system. All of these points attracted criticism from some neo-Functionalists as well as from the opponents of Functionalism. What was ironic was that the final methodological 'problem' left outstanding by Sorokin, which Parsons at least confronted and sought to contain, the issue of unlicenced, unjustified and untrammelled artistic grasp of Cultural Systems, was in fact to become the basis of structuralist anthropology. It was this approach which carried the flame of the original Myth into the second half of the twentieth century – at least in the downwards conflation version.

The structuralist version

While Functionalists had worked on the overt Socio-Cultural system, theorizing about the observable interconnections between its parts (individuals, groups, institutions) and had found the *key* to their overall patterning in the equally overt normative order, this procedure was reversed in the structuralist approach. Overt relations between parts did not present a clear patterning the explanation of which merely required identification of the particular component responsible for it. On the contrary, the superficial appearance which culture presented to its observers was closer to the old imagery of 'booming, buzzing confusion', but its hidden interconnections could be explicated by detection of an underlying and covert *code* which regulated them. The basic idea, stemming from linguistic structuralism, was that cultures could be decoded. The fundamental premiss here is obviously that Cultural Systems are in fact encoded (ontologically they are codes): the fundamental methodological implication for sociology is clearly that its task is to decipher them.

Structuralism had a lengthy historical background (in the work of Durkheim, Mauss, Saussure) but structuralists drew their main inspiration from Chomsky, seeking to apply his linguistic principles to wider Socio-Cultural phenomena. What was taken over and extended in application were two quite simple notions: that of a limited number of generative principles underlying any linguistic manifestation, and the associated idea of 'rule-governed creativity', that is the possible production of unlimited manifestations which were none the less obedient to the code. Already, in Chomsky's above notions, the germs of conflation abound. The generative principles (the linguistic code) regulate linguistic creativity (social usage of language). In other words, the independence of the latter (the Socio-Cultural level in our terms) is reduced to its ingenuity in elaborating permutations of the code (the Systemic level in our terms). As the users make and can make no reciprocal contribution to altering the code itself, the downwards inflection is also implicit. The merits or demerits of these notions in relation to language are not of concern here, what is at issue is their transfer to non-linguistic phenomena, that is to culture in general.

In endorsing and seeking to extend these notions, structuralism, particularly in Lévi-Strauss's most influential version, asserts not merely that the principles of linguistic structuralism can be adopted in the sociological domain but that cultural 'phenomena' are those 'whose inmost nature is the same as language'.[37] From adopting the linguistic analogy (or more strongly from assuming a homology between language and culture) the germs of conflation, which may or may not be justified in the original field, multiply and infect the new host. Indeed the linguistic analogy has had an even more powerful and baleful influence in buttressing the Myth of Cultural Integration in structuralism than did the organic analogy in Functionalism.

Essentially the very nature of the structuralist endeavour involves the assumption of *discoverable cultural coherence*. Structures for Lévi-Strauss are the models which we posit once we have delved below the surface features of social life and have detected the underlying hidden relations which order it. A model thus represents the recovery of 'intelligible reality' which had been overlain by superficial incoherence – that is, the massive variegation of cultural contents which defied surface ordering. The assumption is that there is always a code to be found. Moreover, the nature of this code (the hidden structure which interconnects the elements) is vastly more rigid than Sorokin's 'key'. Ideally the 'key' would fit together a whole welter of fragments but in reality it only unlocked some doors, since perfect coherence was admitted to be an empirical rarity. On the contrary the code, once elucidated, masters divergence, incoherence and inconsistency by deciphering them as transformations of the deeper-lying principles. Any non-detection of a code in particular empirical cases must logically be attributed to a failure of the investigator; for on structuralist premises it can never be the state of the case, since these premises have ruled out cultural incoherence in advance.

Not only is Cultural System integration deemed to be exceedingly high from the structuralist perspective but, in typical conflationist fashion, it is held to generate an equivalent degree of Socio-Cultural integration. This is not the circumstantial consequence of structuralists, as anthropologists, concentrating on well-knit 'cold' societies. It derives directly from the linguistic analogy. Actual language use does two things simultaneously: first, the production of a correct sentence in any language automatically embroils its user in the generative rules inescapably governing its formulation; and second, because this is so, pronouncing such a sentence helps to reproduce that language *in its entirety* (the sentence in question not only invokes the specific linguistic rules pertinent to it but also the total corpus of the rules of that language, since they are mutually invocating). Thus to pronounce a correct sentence in French entails the reproduction of the whole French language, although the latter was in no way part of the speaker's intention. This tight linkage between structure and user/usage is the kernel of downwards conflation. When carried over to the cultural realm it means that to employ any cultural element (cooking a meal, singing a song, gaining a living, explaining the cosmos) invokes the Systemic code and therefore enmeshes those engaging in such activities in its Socio-Cultural reproduction.

Hence downwards conflation is just as marked in structuralism as in Functionalism and represents their shared anthropological heritage. Both elaborate on the theme of society predominating over the individual, or, in our terms, of Cultural System integration enforcing Socio-Cultural integration. However

whereas the functionalists have concentrated upon practical activity, Lévi-Strauss concentrates on cognition; and while functionalism, especially as worked out by Parsons, has developed the theme of society as moral consensus, Lévi-Strauss has drawn primarily upon Durkheim's 'sociological Kantianism'. For each society 'has its reasons of which its members know little'. In the case of functionalism, these are the imperatives of societal co-ordination, the imperatives of normative order; for Lévi-Strauss they are the organizing mechanisms of the unconscious'.[38]

But this ultimate grounding of the code in psychic structures which remain unconscious is identical in depriving the Socio-Cultural level of any independent influence to Ruth Benedict's older form of mentalism, in which cultures were pictured as 'individual psychology thrown large upon the screen'.[39] The only difference is Systemic, not Socio-Cultural, namely that what appears on the screen does not make immediate sense since it is not manifestly patterned.

Let us now briefly see how structuralism, again like Functionalism, systematically evades the four problematic elements in the Myth of Cultural Integration which Sorokin's work had pin-pointed:

First, the adoption of the linguistic analogy completely precludes the empirical detection of any lack of cultural integration at the Systemic level, as we have seen, and this in turn forecloses the possibility of even raising the issue about the social role of Systemic inconsistency. Following structural linguistics, and treating cultural components as the equivalents of phonemes, Lévi-Strauss presents the Cultural System as a totally integrated code such that no element of it 'can undergo changes without effecting changes in all the other elements'.[40] Moreover, code-governed transformations are held to explicate any and all surface inconsistencies. Indeed, since the principle of binary opposition is considered by Lévi-Strauss to be the (mentalistic) origin of structures, then surface incoherence becomes the very meat of the code, not a problem with which it cannot deal but the grist of its mill. Contradictions and oppositions in fact express order via absent meanings: incoherence remains solely for those who work in terms of surface similarities and contiguities.

The task of 'socio-logic' is the disentangling of the *symbolist* consistency of mythical thought. What is discarded as of no social significance are the intellectual inconsistencies in mythology if myths are given a literal rather than a symbolic meaning or reading. Horton[41] has mounted a sustained defence of the intellectualist approach (that is, African religious belief systems should be treated as attempts to explain natural events), and although this has been criticized[42] for denying symbolism any importance at all, this criticism can be directed at Lévi-Strauss in reverse form. With what justification can he assume *a priori* that manifest intellectual contraditions in belief systems are never of social account, can never intrigue human actors, will never be grasped and exploited by some group, thus driving the Myth asunder or towards further elaboration? Of vital interest to the present argument is the fact that ultimately the justification for this is that of downwards conflation itself: the fact that the Socio-Cultural level is automatically deprived in this theory of any such *capacity* to manipulate intellectual inconsistency.

Secondly, within structuralism there is, then, a yawning void between the Systemic mythology at one extreme (a property of the collectivity) and, at the other, the structuring properties of the unconscious mind (a property of the individual of which he is unaware). Although these unconscious properties (pertaining to people) are the ultimate factors ordering the Cultural System level, nevertheless individual innovation or group interaction are denied any independent intermediary role, both individuals and groups being reduced to carriers of their unconscious cargo. In other words, the purposive human subject, his practical discourse and consciousness, his promotive interaction with others, are all absent in this theory. Taken together these constitute the Socio-Cultural level in our terms but to Lévi-Strauss they are epiphenomena and thus deprived of making any causal contribution. On the contrary, individual and group properties are themselves products of Systemic structuring: the reflexive understandings of individuals and the institutional organization of groups (for example kinship) are mere surface manifestations of deeper structures.

Downwards conflation is complete and in the following statement we see how social actors become conceptualized as 'passive' within structuralist analysis. In other words how is it that Lévi-Strauss solves the paradox of making the human mind the source of the Cultural System, while simultaneously denying human agency the capacity to 'change its mind' or the System? While he admits that every myth is ultimately an individual creation, nevertheless 'in order to move to the level of myth, it is necessary precisely that a creation does not remain individual; and that in the course of this transition it essentially discards those features with which it was contingently marked at the outset, and which can be attributed to the temperament, talent, imagination, and personal experience of the author'.[43] Here, as Giddens has stressed,[44] the activity of human subjects is 'individual' and 'contingent', compared to the supra-individual nature of the collective, represented by the Myth at the Systemic level. It is this subordination of the Socio-Cultural level which, fully encased as it is *by* the societal mythology, prevents it from exploiting the intellectual inconsistencies *of* the myths. Epiphenomena cannot act back to affect that which forms them. Indeed, any appearance of Socio-Cultural activity is just that – superficial innovations which are themselves decipherable by reference to the structural code. They are never novel interpretations capable of transforming the code. Simply because Lévi-Strauss stands Durkheim on his head and makes the mind the *logical* origin of the Cultural System, this does not prevent the two from standing shoulder to shoulder in asserting the *sociological* primacy of society over the individual, or the Cultural System over Socio-Cultural activities.

Thirdly, it is an obvious corollary of the above that power differentials and social differentiation in general are never examined as sources of symbolism. The very notion of symbolic strategies being employed to advance sectional interests implies some degree of autonomy at the Socio-Cultural level, which structuralist analysis categorically denies. The question which Sorokin's work raised about how a dominant Cultural System (if such there be) attained its dominance, is answered without addressing power relations by Lévi-Strauss as by Parsons. While Parsons side-stepped power by means of a holistic excursion (the central values of society are those needful to it), Lévi-Strauss evades power by the opposite route of mental reductionism (the human mind as an active grid which is the innate source of the deep grammar of culture). This concentration on basic unconscious mental operations which produce the mechanisms of signification underlying *all* conscious activities of human agents thus undergirds their institutions too, including those which institutionalize power relations.

Finally we come to the last problem posed by Sorokin, namely by what methodological procedure can we disclose the principles (if any) which articulate the Cultural System? Here the structuralist programme of carrying the 'phonological revolution' over to culture in general (that is, replete with its many non-linguistic elements) essentially prejudges the issue, in the same way that Sorokin was tempted to do when approaching all cultures as if they had an architectonic master key. By presuming that Cultural Systems are indeed coded phenomena, they are necessarily assumed to be susceptible of decoding. Hence deciphe*ring* becomes a technical problem; decipher*ability* is not questioned, even when it is beyond our present ingenuity. Thanks to this assumption, structural analysts can never find themselves in

Sorokin's difficulty – that of discovering that sometimes there just is no key, or that it only opens some of the doors.

Instead, for Lévi-Strauss, since all cultural phenomena are ones 'whose inmost nature is the same as that of language' we too can proceed to discover the underlying combinatory elements through which they are ordered. This enterprise is fundamentally dependent upon what many have rightly contested – the homology between culture and language. Such arguments have tended to start out by stressing the indubitably non-communicative role of certain cultural components, in contrast to language and its prime task of communication. This then leads such elements to be assigned to the symbolic realm, where the linguistic analogy ends up encountering further difficulties. For many, like Sperber,[45] doubt that symbolism constitutes a code, since the units comprising myths do not represent stable coded pairs of signifiers/signified capable of composing sentences according to the rules of a generative grammar. Hence mythology and language are not isomorphic. In more sociological terms it has thus been argued that cultural components lack the mutually implicative character of language. They are more loosely linked and susceptible of a freer combination which is not the equivalent of 'bad grammar' and might more properly be termed 'innovation'. If we accept *any* argument denying homological status to language and culture then we are led to question what in fact it is that structuralists are doing when they claim to be 'decoding'.

Basically they are constructing models which render observable phenomena intelligible and, outside positivism, there is nothing objectionable about positing structures as heuristic devices. The problems arise in relation to validating (rival) claims to having established 'intelligibility' and concerning the criteria of the latter – which or whose to use.

On the one hand, structuralist models are not hypotheses susceptible of refutation. Ultimately, structuralism is verificatory not falsificatory in character: its claim to acceptance rests on inner coherence and extensive, though illustrative, applications. Although the techniques are subtle and contain internal self-correcting devices they are insufficient to absolve the method from this charge. Thus Lévi-Strauss posits the principle of binary opposition as the origin of structures and then proceeds to decode myths by using it as a means for identifying their structural make-up. Then by a spiralling movement, the decoded myth yields clues for deciphering the structure of further myths, which fan out in opposition to it, and yet other myths, the axes of which are opposed to theirs in turn. These successive 'disclosures' are taken to substantiate the initial structural analysis. They do not, any more than the paranoid's latest 'evidence' of his persecution validates his fears. The only thing both reveal is a capacity for giving a coherent account on the basis of certain premises. The fundamental difficulty of the structuralist position arises from the fact that rival decodings can be advanced by starting from different premises (that is, binary opposition could be replaced by a 'trinitarian' principle or any other which can plausibly be attributed to our mental constitution): there is no way of adjudicating between them assuming they are all internally consistent. This is the classic problem of the absent context of justification.

On the other hand, the methodological problems are equally great from the point of view of the hermeneutic tradition. Since, as we have seen, any reflexive understanding is considered to be only a surface manifestation of deeper unconscious cognition, the road to any hermeneutic confirmation is closed. We can neither interrogate ourselves nor others as to whether the posited models 'ring true' as this would imply a widely dispersed ability to plumb the unconscious, which Lévi-Strauss denies.[46] Here again the gap between linguistic and structuralist analysis yawns, for the former utilized the competence of its practitioners as natural language speakers to devise and substantiate models of it. In structuralism there is no inter- or intra-communication: there is only one speaker, the analyst; the rest are listeners.

By cutting himself off from these two traditions of validation, Lévi-Strauss is forced into a 'lofty indifference towards the question of whether the structural interpretation ultimately amounts to the reality (however unconscious) of natives' minds or to a simple product of the structuralist's look'.[47] But such indifference can provide no defence against charges made that his interpretations merely impose categories of Western thought on other cultures. There is no way in which this charge can be rebutted, but in fact it is part of a larger charge: ethno-centrism is only a glaring example of what might be imposed, but the range stretches down to the most personal and idiosyncratic crotchets of the investigator. The simple answer, then, to the question of what the structuralist is doing when he claims to be decoding is that he is simply positing, full stop. Since the posited structure can receive neither public validation nor hermeneutic confirmation, its appeal rests on pure artistry.

3   'Upwards conflation': the manipulated consensus

Neo-Marxism gave the Myth of Cultural Integration a second youth. Its new vitality owed something to the use of a fresh point of departure rather than a parading of veteran anthropological arguments. For primitive society, in which the original Myth was grounded and from which it had been generalized to modern society, played no part in the genesis of 'upwards conflationism'. On the contrary, it was by examining the interregnum between primitive and modern societies (swept up, if not under the carpet, by downwards conflationists) that the notion of manipulated consensus germinated. This second version of the cohesion Myth went back, not to pre-literate society, but to the time of man's first glaring cultural imposition on other men – in Ancient Civilizations and the Middle Ages: not to the shared-cum-bindingness of traditional life, in its seamless totality but to the machinations of the first ideologists, that is, the clergy.[1]

The mystification and obfustication deliberately diffused by the 'legal–metaphysical class', to secure privileges for itself, had long been emphasized by Diderot, Rolland, La Chalotais, Condorcet and Sièyes[2] before it passed into Marx's own work (partly accounting for his early concentration on religion as a major form of alienation) and from there became one of the unifying themes in the diverse strands of neo-Marxist thought.

Thus many forms of neo-Marxism take as fundamental precisely that which the downwards conflationists had sedulously neglected – the role of power in the imposition of culture. What differentiates between the two versions of the Myth is not the end-product, which in both cases is a state of cultural integration, but how this is produced: here we are dealing with a manipulated consensus. But despite this major difference, the same error of conflating the Socio-Cultural level and the Cultural System level is committed, although in a different way. Here conflation is from the bottom upwards, since it is Socio-Cultural conflict which generates a common Cultural System – usually represented as 'the dominant ideology'.

Upwards conflation is not, of course, exclusive to Marxism (Comte and Mannheim were equally strong protagonists of it), nor are all Marxists of the upwards persuasion. Althusser provides one example of a downwards conflationist and his ultimate affinity with Parsons has often been noted.[3] Ideology is not generated by one class and imposed on others, for Althusser's whole conceptualization of social structure is not based on the interaction of social groups but upon the operation of the necessary conditions for the existence of the capitalist mode of production. Ideology, as a system of mass representations, is indeed indispensable if men are to be transformed to fit the conditions of their existence (thus constituting and reconstituting the non-material conditions of production), but it is an *objective* form arising from the requirements of production and not the creation of a particular class for the subordination of others. The drawbacks to this approach are similar to those of its Parsonian counterpart: there is no explanation of what generates the appropriate ideology but rather a lapse into the teleology of correspondence – there is no account of independent human agency, for the Socio-Cultural level is eternally encased in ideology which orchestrates it just as heavily as did the central value system. However, this is not the present concern.

What is germane to upwards conflation, and also much more pervasive in neo-Marxism, is what has been aptly termed the 'dominant ideology thesis'. In its essentials, the

thesis argues that in all societies based on class divisions there is a dominant class which enjoys control of both the means of material production and the means of mental production. Through its control of ideological production, the dominant class is able to supervise the construction of a set of coherent beliefs. These dominant beliefs of the dominant class are more powerful, dense and coherent than those of subordinate classes. The dominant ideology penetrates and infects the consciousness of the working class, because the working class comes to see and to experience reality through the conceptual categories of the dominant class. The dominant ideology functions to incorporate the working class within a system which is, in fact, operating against the material interests of labour. This incorporation in turn explains the coherence and integration of capitalist society.[4]

As such it is very much the product of Western Marxists. Their pessimism about the likelihood of a collapse of capitalism from its internal economic contradictions led them to shift their attention away from the infrastructure and towards the superstructure: their lack of political involvement displaced any 'Leninist' concern with the development of a revolutionary party and replaced it by a preoccupation with the cultural conditions of social transformation.[5] The latter element, of course, completes the upwards inflection of this approach. It is not merely that social relations supply the Cultural System but also that capitalism as a whole can only collapse through cultural undermining. Hence both cohesion and change at the Systematic level are generated upwards from the Socio-Cultural level.

The origins of this version of the Myth of Cultural Integration are undoubtedly rooted in a famous passage from *The German Ideology*. It is quoted at length because it is important to note both what has been taken from it and also what further assumptions have been added to it. For the latter appear to involve a much more categoric statement of upwards conflation than was held by Marx himself. In other passages and other writings he seems to have held that there were four problematic aspects to this relationship which have been brushed aside in the subsequent and facile elision of the two levels.

The ideas of the ruling class are in every epoch the ruling ideas, i.e. the class which is the ruling material force of society is at the same time its ruling intellectual force. The class which has the means of material production at its disposal, has control at the same time over the means of mental production, so that thereby, generally speaking, the ideas of those who lack the means of mental production are subject to it. The ruling ideas are nothing more than the ideal expression of the dominant material relationships, the dominant material relationships grasped as ideas; hence of the relationships which make the one class the ruling one, therefore, the ideas of its dominance. The individuals composing the ruling class possess among other things consciousness, and therefore think. In so far, therefore, as they rule as a class and determine the extent and compass of an epoch, it is self-evident that they do this in its whole range, hence among other things rule also as thinkers, as producers of ideas, and regulate the production and distribution of the ideas of their age: thus their ideas are the ruling ideas of the epoch.[6]

By comparing this and other statements made by Marx with the earlier characterization of the dominant ideology thesis (which I accept as a fair portrayal) the points at which the latter extrapolates, rather questionably, from the original can be identified. The object of doing this is not fidelistic. Being 'true to Marx' is no necessary criterion of acceptability in itself but rather like Sorokin, in relation to his successors, Marx honestly highlighted problems associated with upward conflation which his followers have glossed over.[7] To confront the latter with Marx's own writings constitutes a running critical commentary on the difficulties involved in a simplistic view of upwards conflation. The points involved can be summarized as follows and these will be examined in turn:

(1)   Is there a single dominant culture?
(2)   Is the dominant culture internally coherent?
(3)   Do subordinate cultures exist?
(4)   How is cultural domination produced?

(1) The first point concerns the major constituents of the Cultural System. From Marx, dominant ideology theorists take the basic notion that the Cultural System is articulated by the group which dominates at the Socio-Cultural level – the 'ideas of the ruling class are in every epoch the ruling ideas'. However, this key sentence contains an important ambiguity: since the 'ideas of the ruling class' are in the plural, these may refer either to a single set of ideas endorsed throughout the ruling class, or to several sets of ideas current within the ruling class. Reference to several sets implies ideational pluralism inside the ruling class; reference to a single set assumes the 'oneness' of the ruling ideas. While the dominant ideology theorists have collectively plumped for 'oneness', Marx himself concedes that there may be substantial pluralism within the corpus of ruling ideas themselves.

He discusses ideological dissension and even a division of mental versus material labour inside the ruling class. Here the activity of intellectuals develops and perfects illusions about the class, which may be at variance with the pragmatic activities of industrialists in pursuit of material class interests. Thus pluralism is clearly recognized by Marx but in the next breath he nullifies its significance. 'This cleavage within the ruling class may even develop into a certain opposition and hostility between the two parts, but in the event of a practical collision in which the class itself is endangered, it disappears of its own accord and with it also the

49

illusion that the ruling ideas were not the ideas of the ruling class *and had a power distinct from the power of this class*'[8] (my emphasis). Marx has thus conceded pluralism, only to dismiss it as unimportant. In contradistinction the dominant ideology theorists construe the denial of its importance as a denial of the phenomenon itself.

However, Marx has raised a genuine problem surrounding pluralism. Having acknowledged the existence of ideational alternatives he logically cannot sustain the notion of a dominant ideology in the singular. Although such differences *may* 'disappear of their own accord' in the face of some practical crunch, this can only be disappearance in a purely Socio-Cultural sense (the ruling class closing ideological ranks). As World Three entities, ideas cannot disappear – once voiced they are permanent denizens of the Cultural System. Any apparent disappearance must in reality be accomplished through suppression or syncretism at the level of social interaction, rather than being attributed to a metaphysical process of evaporation, which is an ontological impossibility for a Third World item. Thus our initial question about the 'oneness' of ruling ideas, eventually opens up the whole issue of the interplay between the Cultural System and social relations (of the connections between the 'logical' and the 'causal').

Marx in admitting to (logical) pluralism amongst the dominant ideas then tried to deprive them of any independent downward influence by signifying upward (causal) pressures which unify them. In the process he was in effect compelled to concede the analytical separateness of the 'logical' and the 'causal' (since there was a two-way interplay between them). Effectively this then imposed a task on neo-Marxists, namely to specify the actual mechanisms by which the Socio-Cultural level *socially* (not ontologically) nullifies part of the Cultural System (that is, when the latter threatens the former). Dominant ideology theorists have turned their backs on this task by simply denying pluralism and insisting on a single dominant culture. As upward conflationists they have made the logical depend exclusively and unproblematically on the causal, thus rendering the Cultural System as epiphenomenal as was the Socio-Cultural level to downward conflationists.

(2) From Marx is taken the generic stress on the social origins of men's ideas (the very formation of individual consciousness by social conditions) and the particular emphasis on the nexus between material interests and consonant ideas; the 'ruling ideas are nothing more than the ideal expression of the dominant material relationships grasped as ideas'. Here, then, we have the basic

notion of the *causal* level (material social relations) generating the *logical* level, the Cultural System. Yet simply to accentuate this nexus does not imply that what is generated is a consistent System which is (*pace* Abercrombie *et al.*) 'powerful, dense and coherent'. Again as a matter of logic, X may indeed be responsible for Y, without Y necessarily having the property of consistency. Instead the dominant ideology theorists reason that because a group has a coherent set of interests these will be given consistent ideational expression. This again is an additional assumption and one from which Marx frequently dissociated himself.

He appears to have been fully aware that to argue from the interests of one social group generating the ruling ideas to the consistency of these ideas themselves was a *non sequitur*. In other words, the logical properties of the Cultural System level could not be deduced direct from their unitary social origins. On the contrary Marx exemplifies the fact that the Systemic level may be characterized by precisely the opposite feature, namely inconsistency. Thus the scorn he pours on the classical economists rests on the manifest incoherence of their presentation of economic relations. These bourgeois ideologists *par excellence* set out such relations as

natural laws independent of the influence of time. They are eternal laws which must always govern society. Thus there has been history, but there is no longer any. There has been history, since there were the institutions of feudalism, and in these institutions of feudalism we find quite different relations of production from those of bourgeois society, which the economists try to pass off as natural and as such, eternal.[9]

Indeed part of the very instrumentality of ideology means that ideologies are matters of convenience, often hastily fabricated, rather than studiously elaborated and double-checked to eliminate contradiction. In this vein, Engels refers to the 'morality of the day, which the bourgeoisie has patched together in its own interests for its own protection'.[10] On the one hand, then, causal priorities and exigencies are seen to militate against logical coherence (indeed consistency is not at first a precondition of the social efficaciousness of ideology). On the other hand, however, since a vital part of the later demystification of bourgeois ideology *by* Marx consists of laying bare the social role of inconsistency in concealing ruling-class interests, then the part played by Systemic incoherence in spreading and later uprooting 'false consciousness' is acknowledged by him. It is nevertheless suppressed by many of his followers because of their assumption of consistency, which in turn absolves them of any need to examine the two-way interplay between the Cultural System and the Socio-Cultural level and thus allows them to engage in straightforward upward conflation.

(3) From Marx is taken the fundamental tenet that in each social formation are found 'the ruling ideas of the epoch'. Again, however, the original quotation is ambiguous. It can be given a 'softer' interpretation, that only the ruling ideas will be visible because any other group lacks the means of giving public expression to its culture, or a 'harder' interpretation, namely that there cannot be any subordinate culture since all classes are incorporated into one intellectual universe.[11] Adherents to the dominant ideology thesis endorse the 'harder' version. Conversely the weight of evidence suggests that Marx implied the 'softer' version for two reasons: first, his own work was predicated on cultural pluralism as a matter of logical necessity; and second, he was exercised by the problems raised by pluralism at the Socio-Cultural level.

First, then, Marx did not advance the 'exclusivity claim', that is that the Cultural System was made up of nothing but the ideas of the ruling class. This is an additional and a logically distinct proposition – the fact that certain things rule does not mean that they do so in splendid autarchic isolation, no more than the notion of 'political rule' carries this connotation. Not only is it an empirically unacceptable proposition, since changes in the ruling class (and ruling ideas) co-exist with continuities in language, mathematics, logic and other elements of the ideational realm, but also Marx had further good reason for not eliding the entire Cultural System with the ideas of the ruling class. Cultural monism had to be avoided in order to make room for alternative criteria through which validity claims could be established. At the very least, independent canons of logical argument, 'untainted' by 'ruling ideas' were essential to historian, sociologist or critic, but Marx required more than the universality of logic. When he warns against accepting the 'illusion of an epoch' (that is, accepting the evaluation of its conditioned actors that they were actuated by 'religious' or 'political' motives),[12] Marx thereby implies that *any* epoch can be examined from other than the dominant viewpoint and this in turn must mean that *every* Cultural System can itself furnish at least one alternative vantage point. Were this merely a historical argument, namely that only successive Cultural Systems (that is 'new' ruling ideas) could dispel the illusions of their antecedents, this would always leave the 'present epoch' (whenever it was situated in time) as unamenable to analysis, shrouded in impenetrable illusion. I take it that Marx would have been the last to assert that the 'present conjuncture' can only be understood after it has been superseded.

I am expressly *not* arguing that Marx solved the general problem of how knowledge is to outwit human interests and establish truth-claims (given his assertion that 'from the start "spirit" is afflicted with the curse of being "burdened" with matter'),[13] for whether he found an independent fulcrum from which to lever-out truth is not what is at issue here. I am simply distinguishing his views from the crude exclusivity claim of those who endorse complete cultural incorporation and thus suggest that because the Socio-Cultural level articulates the Cultural System, then the *dominance* of one set of ideas excludes the *presence* of other ideas.

Secondly, the existence of pluralism was acknowledged by Marx to be a source of Socio-Cultural problems. There were always more things in the cultural universe than any ruling class wanted to dream of but which could not be eradicated, either by manipulation or by coercion. Thus Marx accepts not merely the existence of counter-cultures, but also that they may be distributed quite extensively in society and that collectively they play a continuous role in social conflict. On the one hand, he mentions the survival of the ideas of previous ruling classes which are 'only subordinated to the prevailing interest and trail along beside the latter for centuries afterwards' and, on the other, the fact that 'consciousness can sometimes appear further advanced than the contemporary empirical relationships, so that in the struggles of a later epoch one can refer to earlier theoreticians as authorities'.[14] Hence there are at least two kinds of subordinate culture (ideas which once were dominant; ideas which may later become prominent) co-existing with the ruling ideas and making for significant pluralism at both the Socio-Cultural level and at the level of the Cultural System.

As with Sorokin this conclusion cries out for an examination of their interplay and (in exact reverse to Sorokin) for a questioning of the untrammelled predominance of the Socio-Cultural level over the Cultural System level. These issues were not rudely brushed aside by Marx, who allows that for the masses as for the intellectuals, oppositional ideas (from within the Cultural System) are selectively utilized to advance sectional interests (during Socio-Cultural conflict). Without this assumption, the transformation of a class 'in itself' into one 'for itself' would have to depend upon some source-less, spontaneous and instantaneous invention of ideas on the barricades – were there no oppositional trends of thought on which to build. However, although oppositional ideas make an independent contribution to the outcome of social conflict[15] this does not imply their free play. The reciprocal influence between 'philosophy' and the 'proletariat' (that is, between the Cultural System and the Socio-Cultural level) has stringent material conditions attached to it, and these serve for Marx to re-establish the predominance of the Socio-Cultural level since they define when and where counter-cultural elements (Systemic level) can enter seriously into play: 'But even if this theory, theology, philosophy, ethics etc., comes into contradiction with the existing relations, this can only occur because existing *social relations* have come into contradiction with existing forces of production'.[16]

Nevertheless this does leave us with two propositions which are not mutually implicative: the *admission* of continuous interplay between 'unmanipulated' sections of the population and parts of the Cultural System outside the dominant ideology; and the *assertion* that this is without practical significance except under pretty stringent conditions.[17] In exact parallel to point (1) the first proposition concedes the analytical separateness of the two levels whilst the second begs for a specification of *how* the Socio-Cultural level universally controls independent Systemic influences. Moreover, it should be noted that the limiting conditions outlined are those preventing transformation of the complete social formation. Thus Marx ultimately leaves open the question as to whether this continuous interplay between the two levels can affect *other* parts of society's superstructure, independent of and prior to such radical social change. Both issues lead on directly to (4).

(4) The account of how cultural domination is produced relies upon the key role assigned to power by Marx in bringing about a manipulated cultural consensus. Yet even in the original quotation Marx is cautious about the engineering of cultural integration being a foregone conclusion: 'The class which has the means of material production at its disposal, has control at the same time over the means of mental production, so that thereby, generally speaking, the ideas of those who lack the means of mental production are subject to it.' His insertion of the caveat 'generally speaking' indicates that to him such control is no absolute guarantee of the success of this enterprise. The additional assumption introduced by the dominant ideology theorists is that once power is used to manipulate the beliefs of others it will always be successful in generating cultural consensus.

Such an interpretation is based on Marx's statement about ruling-class objectives rather than achievements. Certainly Marx argued that 'each new ruling class which puts itself in the place of the one ruling before it, is compelled, simply in order to achieve its aims, to represent its interest as the common interest of all members of society, that is employing an ideal formula, to give its ideas the form of universality and represent them as the only rational and universally valid ones'.[18] Thus it attempts to bring about a state of 'mystification', but this outcome is never automatic. Although in the original quotation Marx wrote (too) confidently about the ruling class having control 'over the means of mental production', later passages cast some doubt on their unequivocal domination of the apparatus for the transmission of ideology. Especially when he proceeds to mention that 'an earlier interest, the peculiar form of intercourse of which has already been ousted by that belonging to a later interest, remains for a long time afterwards in possession of a traditional power'[19] and then specifies that this may be exercised in the law or the State, one is forced to ask why this may not also be the case in even more pertinent parts of the superstructure, namely religion and education. All that can be concluded is that the accessibility of the relevant apparatus is not unproblematic.

But not only may the ruling class have some difficulty over the *means* of ideological transmission, they may simply fail to be very good at, committed to or convinced of the enterprise which Marx believed they were under compulsion to accomplish. Thus, to Engels, 'so stupidly narrow-minded is the English bourgeoisie in its egotism, that it does not even take the trouble to impress upon the workers the morality of the day'.[20] Yet again we have another illustration of the importance of distinguishing between the two levels, for here the set of ideas elaborated at the Cultural System level by classical economists and utilitarian philosophers was simply not utilized at the Socio-Cultural level by practical industrialists. All of this makes the links between power *and* manipulation *and* the achievement of cultural consensus doubly problematic.

Marx's thought raises a series of problems in the context of recent versions of upward conflation which I have highlighted by singling out four points. The interesting thing about these is that Marx appears to have given the opposite answer to all four questions to those supplied by dominant ideology theorists. Thus with increasing trenchancy he denies the 'oneness' of the dominant culture, he refuses to view ruling ideas as internally consistent, and he categorically repudiates the notion of total cultural incorporation. Finally he insists that cultural domination is a socially 'accomplished' activity and not a mere epiphenomenon of power. Taken in conjunction his thought surrounding all four points indicates that Marx himself was a good deal more favourably disposed towards the analytical separation of the Cultural System from the Socio-Cultural level than were many of his later followers, who dismiss it out of hand in their four-square endorsement of upward conflation.

Furthermore Marx was at least willing to discuss the problems arising from each of the four points, whereas these have systematically been glossed over in most later versions of the dominant ideology thesis. There are three main varieties of this, only two of which will be examined here, as the third, structuralist Marxism, is aligned with downwards conflationism. The two versions of neo-Marxism which continue to endorse and indeed exaggerate upwards conflation do so in different ways and starting from different premises. The first has been dubbed as 'instrumentalism', because not only does it stress the common point that compliance is brought about by ideological control in capitalist societies[21] but it also emphasizes that this incorporation is achieved by one class *doing* something to another. Thus the manipulated consensus at the Cultural System level is produced through the action of one class on the other(s) at the Socio-Cultural level. The second, which emanates from the Frankfurt school, does not rely upon the indoctrination of one social group by another but rather on how the pursuit of technical interests in advanced industrial societies ultimately results in the mental distortion of the whole human race, that is, the universalization of a 'technocratic consciousness'. What makes it too an exemplar of upward conflation, is that this resulting Cultural System is rooted in interests which arise and are generalized at the Socio-Cultural level.

The instrumentalist version

Although this label groups together a fairly diverse collection of theorists they have in common: a 'class-theoretical' method of analysing culture (that is, classes are the origins of knowledge, belief or ideology); a joint conviction that ideological consensus arises from the activities of an identifiable group of actors; and a shared certainty that the ruling class is universally successful in employing ideology as an instrument which does incorporate all into a single Cultural System. Each of these common denominators involves neglecting the difficulties raised, and often confronted by Marx. They also entail an equally rough treatment of Gramsci's work, the bridge over which most of these theorists tramped or trampled to reach their present position. We will examine this by revisiting the four basic difficulties already outlined, starting with the issue of whether there is a single dominant culture.

(1) Oversimplification is nowhere more clear than in their treatment of the Socio-Cultural level as articulating the Cultural System. This turns out to be an unabashed adoption of cultural monism. Basically it is grounded in Gramsci's concept of hegemony, re-interpreted as a purely ideological notion. However, this interpretation seriously denudes the original: first, by stripping away Gramsci's conception of hegemony as a balance between persuasion and coercion and, second, by subtracting his awareness that to persuade people of something is usually to persuade against something else, that is, an implicit recognition of pluralism at the Cultural System level.

Despite his sophistication Gramsci nevertheless did furnish three crucial elements for the dominant ideology thesis: first, that hegemony was engineered, it was a matter of leadership and of 'doing'; second that Civil Society (the churches, unions and schools rather than the State) was the site of this cultural manipulation. The latter of course is crucial to the upwards inflection of the old Myth of Cultural Integration. 'Since hegemony pertains to civil society, and civil society prevails over the State, it is the cultural ascendency of the ruling class that essentially ensures the stability of the capitalist order. For in Gramsci's usage here, hegemony means the ideological subordination of the working class by the bourgeoisie, which enables it to rule by consent'.[22] Finally, although Gramsci, like Marx, had accepted pluralism at the Systemic level, for him this did not map onto the division between entrepreneurs and intellectuals within the ruling class. Instead, not only were intellectuals always attached to a class but, additionally, this role gave them no atom of cultural autonomy since it reduced them to cultural agents of their class. As part of the ruling class, the intellectual stratum both elaborated the world-view, thus supplying the ideational component of hegemony, and then transmitted it for the class as a whole: every relationship of hegemony was necessarily an educational relationship,[23] and this stratum did the educating. Thus Gramsci supplied three broad planks of the dominant ideology thesis – the conviction that hegemony was a matter of Socio-Cultural engineering, a specification of where it was engineered and an identification of who the engineers were.

From there on the descent into cultural conspiracy was precipitous. To Miliband, for example, an ideological acceptance of the capitalist order is deliberately fostered by 'massive indoctrination',[24] while in similar vein Marcuse argues that 'one-dimensional thought is systematically promoted by the makers of politics and their purveyors of mass information'.[25] The deficiencies of this crude version of upwards conflation are numerous. To begin with, what in fact is the dominant ideology now or at any time? If it is so purposefully and intensively disseminated then its contours and contents should be readily definable. Instead all that is forthcoming are *ad hoc* lists (*pace* Westergaard and Resler)[26] of beliefs about opportunity, property or social differentials. These are potentially infinite in length and open to empirical dispute on every item. Alternatively we are offered the personal synthesis, like the 'one-dimensional man' image, which evades Marx's problem of where the observer stands in order to see him without being him.

Next, how, when and amongst whom is the dominant ideology consolidated? This is not a naive request to view a control room where the indoctrination programme was hatched and monitored but a serious question about how we are to interpret the manifest ideological disputes within, say, the British Conservative Party, or between the British Labour Party and the unions, or between universities and governments? From within the dominant ideology thesis these are reduced to shadow-boxing, presumed to have no significant effect on social development and assumed to be unified by some broader ideological framework (which has so far defied adequate description). (Un)formulated in this way, the thesis defies counterfactuals, it is not really open to empirical dispute. Thus, for example, although I am convinced that Abercrombie *et al.* have demonstrated the absence of a dominant ideology in three different mature modes of production (feudal, early capitalist or late capitalist), their evidence can always be turned aside by others who claim that they were too riveted with the shadow-boxing to perceive the unifying framework. Thus every empirical assessment or 'attempt to falsify' has to furnish its *own* definition of the dominant ideology,[27] to which the original proponents then reply Rumpelstiltskin-like, 'no that is not my name', having the supreme advantage over him that they do not have one to be discovered.

(2) The dominant ideology is presented as having a unity which

far exceeds the coherence which Marx attributed to it. The independence, inconsistency and pluralism that could characterize the 'ruling ideas' for Marx are entirely eliminated from the modern thesis. Instead its proponents have so concentrated on the dominant ideology as complete delusion that they have failed to question its internal consistency: they have been more concerned with its 'wrongness' than with its contradictions. Furthermore, those Western Marxists who have immersed themselves in the intricacies of bourgeois culture have served to intensify belief in consistency at the Cultural System level. In general they have presented the interests of the bourgeoisie as giving coherence to art, literature and music[28] and significantly have relied on a re-vamping of artistic hermeneutics for their methodology. Although these continental excursions into 'high' culture are at some remove from the preoccupation with beliefs about property or opportunity of our dominant ideology theorists, the former do serve to reinforce the latter if only by telling them that the deeper you go *plus c'est la même chose*. In consequence there are no contradictions in the Cultural System which could operate as independent influences stemming from that level: indeed it has no autonomous properties but only the unity deriving from its unitary source. Marx may have argued that this pluralism and inconsistency were of little importance (since the former would 'disappear of its own accord' whilst the latter remained inefficacious until material conditions were propitious), but at least he granted their existence. Here there is nothing to disappear or to become amplified, as the case may be, for this extreme form of upward conflation turns the Cultural System into a mirror which can never be a social force in its own right.

Consequently the question of examining the interplay between the Socio-Cultural level and the Cultural System is ruled out of court, for it is a basic premiss of the dominant ideology thesis that this is a unidirectional relationship of simple reflection. Some degree of autonomy has to be assigned to both levels as a necessary condition of a two-way interplay but from this perspective it is denied either Systemically or, as we shall see, Socio-Culturally.

(3) Here the virtual denial of the existence of 'subordinate cultures' by dominant ideology theorists withholds that independence and pluralism from the Socio-Cultural level which are essential for domination to be challenged. Marx certainly made their efficacy dependent upon very stringent material conditions, as did Gramsci,[29] but while the former left open the question of whether this could contribute to superstructural change, the latter ultimately

pinned his hopes for the downfall of capitalism on ideological struggle, emanating from the working class but led by a revolutionary party. For Gramsci this was an eminently logical stance. If the stability of capitalism is founded on ideological domination, its downfall can only be produced by ideological undermining (in conjunction with appropriate material readiness). But to maintain this, he, even more than Marx, had to accommodate subordinate culture in his analysis and in such a way that it could co-exist with his notion of hegemony. This he did by asserting a dual consciousness within the working class. One part, grounded in common sense and practical activity, is at variance with the dominant ideas but rendered 'fragmentary, incoherent and inconsequential' as the result of hegemony; the other represents a superficial verbal conformity produced by ideological manipulation. The development of the former in direct opposition to the latter is the source of his hopes for social transformation.[30]

The dominant ideology theorists depart from both Marx and Gramsci on this issue. 'It is quite common for Marxists to write as if the working class were a *tabula rasa* on which the dominant class inscribed its ruling ideas. For example, the ideological institutions are so powerful in Miliband's discussion of the "process of legitimation" in *The State in Capitalist Society* (1969) that it is difficult to imagine how the system could ever be effectively opposed by the working class in terms of its own indigenous ideology.'[31] Yet the problem is even more severe, for, as has been seen, the same theorists disavow pluralism within ruling ideas too, thus leaving themselves without any source of ideational opposition. To a Marxist this has the depressing consequence of abandoning the hope of revolution; to the sociologist it has the distressing effect of abandoning hope of understanding manifest cultural conflict.

Many sociologists of course refuse to do so and simply reject the thesis on empirical grounds, that is the working class is not and never has been fully incorporated into the same Cultural System as the ruling class; sometimes it has even spoken a different language. Ironically others seek to save the main thrust of the thesis (ideological control by the ruling class) by jettisoning its negation of subordinate culture(s) and concentrating, rather, on their subordination itself. Yet here, paradoxically, the efficiency of ideological control is not attributed to successful cultural 'incoporation' but to the deliberate failure to incorporate culturally. This common thread runs through simple arguments about unequal educational opportunities to the sophisticated discussion of 'symbolic violence'[32]

– classes begin with cultural differences and unequal 'cultural capital', the educational institutions confirm the inferiority of the former without equalizing-out the latter, and so the class structure is reproduced. All that actually unites these theorists with proponents of the dominant ideology thesis is a joint belief in ineffable manipulation. However hard they press together in seeming solidarity, they are really a standing reproach to one another for their conceptualization of the Cultural System and its connections with Socio-Cultural relations could not be more different. Bourdieu's very choice of the term 'dominant cultural *arbitrary*' indicates a range of Systemic alternatives which the socially dominant use strategically as moving targets and that prevent the socially subordinate from overcoming their subordination by painfully mastering the original 'arbitrary' chunk of the Cultural System.[33]

(4) This leads directly to the monumentally deficient sociology of education associated with the dominant ideology thesis itself, which assumes automatic control by the ruling class over the apparatus for ideological transmission and guaranteed success in the mission. So unproblematic are these issues taken to be that the whole analysis of the machinery through which ideological domination is effected (which Gramsci saw as crucial) is dispensed with and replaced by a so-called 'correspondence theory' of relations between education and central features of capitalist development (of the Bowles and Gintis type).[34] The complex jargon in which this simple idea is expressed can conceal the fact that it basically begs the question – namely, what is it which first brings about and then maintains this 'complementarity'? At rock-bottom any correspondence 'theory' is merely a verbal statement that a positive correlation coefficient has been detected: it remains logically impossible to extract a causal explanation from the one as from the other.

At certain points those like Bowles appear to recognize the difficulty of treating the educational system as a completely permeable medium.[35] He admits for example that 'the perpetuation of inequality through the schooling system has been represented as an almost automatic, self-enforcing mechanism, operating only through the medium of class culture'. But his fall-back position is the simple assertion that the upper class does indeed command the educational apparatus and is able 'to control the ideological and institutional context in which educational decisions are made'.[36] What this does is simply to restate the bald premiss of upwards conflation in educational terms.

What it evades is the question of how institutional control is won (that is, omission of the Socio-Cultural dynamics involved – who won and how decisively, who lost out and how badly). What it entails, given that ruling-class control is assumed to be constant in capitalist societies, is a consistent failure to account for fluctuations in 'correspondence' (that is, no examination of the variability with which education faithfully, partially or inadequately inculcates ruling class ideas as co-terminous with the Cultural System). A satisfactory Marxist sociology of education cannot be predicated on upwards conflation as this will never give empirical purchase on the machinations for educational control (S-C level) or the mechanisms affecting curricular contents (CS level).[37]

The technocratic consciousness version

What Critical Theory shares with the dominant ideology thesis is the supreme importance attached to the subjective element of social life in providing the legitimation essential to capitalism. To the Frankfurt school, too, the continuation of advanced industrial societies depends on Socio-Cultural integration, for there is no sense in which capitalism is viewed as being self-sustaining through the functional adjustment and displacement of institutions, as in structuralist Marxism. Simultaneously it differs from both of these other theories in the conviction that people can be freed from the thrall of ideas which embody domination and, what is novel, that this emancipation is itself a *cultural process* dependent on the establishment of a new mode of discourse rather than on revolutionary class conflict. Here the bald upwards conflation contained in the dominant ideology thesis is embedded in a more subtle sociology of knowledge.[38] However, it also depends upon an explicit revision of Marx's economics rather than a simple rejection of 'economism'. In economic terms, advanced industrial societies are characterized in much the same way as by bourgeois economists:[39] in sociological terms they are represented as being increasingly purposive–rational in something of a Weberian manner. Both transformations, which constitute a fundamental break between early capitalism and the advanced industrial society, are the effects of science and technology which simultaneously transform the cultural realm: 'Hence the modern sciences produce knowledge which through its *form* (and not through the subjective intentions of scientists) is technically exploitable knowledge . . . Science and technology were not interdependent until late into the nineteenth century. Until then modern science did not contribute to the acceleration of technical development nor, consequently, to *the pressure towards rationalization from below'*[40] (my emphasis). In this quotation are most of the key elements, plus the first hint of the upwards inflection, of this approach.

The application of science and technology to production enters a continuous positive feed-back relationship until the leading productive force becomes not labour but controlled scientific and technical progress itself. The control is supplied by government – positively through its increased intervention for economic stabilization and negatively through its depoliticization of the population. But although welfare provisions, affluence and opportunity induce privatization, this is not tantamount to legitimation. A major problem remains: 'how will the depoliticization of the masses be made plausible to them?'[41]

The answer is that this new productive force now becomes the basis of its own legitimacy, bowling over the old mythical ideologies (based on religion etc.) and consigning them to the dead realm of tradition. In their place new sources of cultural legitimation arise from the integuments of technology and reach upwards to defend the institutional arrangements of advanced industrial societies:

In this universe, technology also provides the great rationalization of the unfreedom of man and demonstrates the 'technical' impossibility of being autonomous, of determining one's own life. For this unfreedom appears neither as irrational nor as political, but rather as submission to the technical apparatus which enlarges the comforts of life and increases the productivity of labor. Technological rationality thus protects rather than cancels the legitimacy of domination, and the instrumentalist horizon of reason opens on a rationally totalitarian society.[42]

Yet the spread of this 'technocratic consciousness', which is held to invade production, politics and personality alike, must never be attributed to the independent influence of science (which would make the theory a form of cultural idealism and also a case of downwards conflation). Science and technology may indeed appear to be quasi-autonomous but they remain firmly anchored in Socio-Cultural interests which instead determine the direction, functions and pace of their progress. Thus critical theory entails no departure from the basic notion that the Cultural System is articulated by the group which dominates at the Socio-Cultural level: all that has changed is that this group is much wider in conception than the traditional depiction of a 'ruling class' and it is no longer material necessity which drives it to commandeer the

Cultural System. Habermas continues to ram the point home when he argues that even if the interests maintaining this mode of production can no longer be 'clearly localized' in society as class interests, nevertheless 'the generalized interest in perpetuating the system is still anchored today, on the level of immediate life chances, in a structure of privilege. The concept of an interest which has become *completely* independent of living subjects would cancel itself out.'[43]

Interest, then, remains the root of Socio-Cultural domination which, in turn, is reproduced at the level of the Cultural System, with all the features of upward conflation – coercive imposition, comprehensive coverage and the manipulation of cultural consensus. Indeed the Myth of Cultural Integration is refuelled, for it is now mankind as a whole which becomes enmeshed in the scientific Cultural System through the systematic distortion of communication. Hence 'today's dominant, rather glassy background ideology, which makes a fetish of science, is more irresistible and farther-reaching than ideologies of the old type. For with the veiling of practical problems it not only justifies a *particular class's* interest in domination and represses *another class's* partial need for emancipation, but affects the human race's emancipatory interest as such.'[44] Given such 'revisionism' it now remains to be seen how Critical Theory deals with the four problems raised by Marx's original formulation and then glossed over in the dominant ideology thesis.

(1) As far as the 'oneness' of ruling ideas is concerned, Habermas joins ranks with the dominant ideology theorists. This accord is manifest in his characterization of the 'empirical–analytical sciences' as alone furnishing the dominant culture of advanced industrial societies (and generating the pervasive condition of 'technocratic consciousness'). Once again defence of this proposition rests on a fundamental conflation of the causal with the logical: on the basic argument that if dominant social interests are unitary so too is the dominant culture which they orchestrate. Essentially, to Critical Theorists, since the cognitive interest in technical control predominates at the Socio-Cultural level, it follows that the empirical–analytical sciences preponderate at the level of the Cultural System. The specific mechanism articulating the two levels derives from Habermas' key concept of 'knowledge constitutive interests' which inextricably conjoins 'knowledge' with 'interests'.

On the one hand it is interest (the social causal dimension) which prompts the consolidation of knowledge, for there is no possible mediation between subject and object (the knower and the known) without the impetus supplied by interest. Therefore in the empirical–analytical sciences the relevant facts receive an *a priori* organization from experiences acquired in *instrumental action* under the prompting of interest. The resultant scientific propositions are denied any ontological status independent of the knower, for the latter determines both the logical structure of admissible propositions and the conditions according to which they are held to be corroborated. Already the causal origins are engulfing the logical properties of the end-product.

On the other hand, not only do interests penetrate the logic of inquiry, but reality is *only* disclosed *subject* to the constitutive interest involved. Thus where the empirical–analytical sciences are concerned, these disclose reality subject to the constitutive interest in securing and expanding technical control over objectified processes. Hence the (logical) constitution of the emergent Cultural System *embodies* the (causal) influence of interests which govern which parts of reality shall be theoretically disclosed and which concealed (if only by neglect); what shall count as knowledge and what shall not; and how theory *can* be applied to society since this is established only by rules made in conformity with interest. To use Popper's phraseology, the properties of World Three (objective knowledge) are not just associated with World Two (subjectively grounded knowledge) but are completely confounded with them. The logical content, structure and potentiality of the Cultural System is granted no autonomy from the Socio-Cultural level which is causally responsible for it.[45]

In view of the foregoing Habermas has only to point to the *continuous* priority accorded to the interest in technical control on the part of the dominant group (due to the continuity of benefits and privileges accruing from its pursuit) in order to assert the *continuing* dominance of the empirical–analytical sciences in the Cultural System. The question of pluralistic sets of dominant ideas does not arise because of the dominant group's fixed set of priorities; given these the dominant speak with one voice in constant positivistic parlance.

Nevertheless, Marx's problem concerning ideational divergences between factions of the ruling stratum might still seem to hover in the wings, for if the other two cognitive interests (in inter-communication and emancipation) are indeed generic to humanity, then they must pertain to the dominant group too. But these sources of incipient pluralism are never actualized to threaten the unity of the ideas which dominate in the Cultural System: their prime concern for ever-expanding technical control effectively stills other inner voices amongst the socially dominant. In this way Critical Theory adheres to the notion of the 'oneness' of dominant ideas, in common with dominant ideology theorists but at the same time, like Marx, avoids the trap of cultural monism which would deprive it of an independent critical standpoint.

Thus the fact that Habermas holds one cognitive interest – the interest in technical control – as preoccupying the dominant group to the exclusion of others means that the Cultural System presents a unitary set of ideas constituted on this basis. Equally the fact that Habermas holds cognitive interests to be plural in society and includes two further ones – the practical interest in mutual understanding and the emancipatory interest in freedom from domination – prevents the Cultural System from being nothing but a saturate of ruling ideas. Pluralism exists, but as conflict between dominant and subordinate cultures not amongst ruling ideas themselves.

(2) Turning now to the problem of whether the Socio-Cultural interests which articulate the Cultural System do in fact generate one consistent body of 'ruling ideas', Critical Theory is again more closely aligned with the dominant ideology thesis than with Marx.

Habermas stresses that the modern scientific ideology is highly coherent and that much of it is indeed 'true'. 'Technocratic consciousness is . . . "less ideological" than all previous ideologies. For it does not have the opaque force of a delusion that only transfigures the implementation of interests . . . It is less vulnerable to reflection, because it is no longer *only* ideology.'[46] Components like the laws of planetary movements or the rules of bridge-building are not delusions. On the contrary Habermas asserts that given its premisses (that is, the constitutive interest in technical control) what follows is extremely consistent – indeed, too much so. When the technical ideology is extended to the social sciences it becomes 'repressive' because people and human relations are also treated as objectified processes over which technical control is to be gained (opening the door to behavioural manipulation). Here we do find the element of 'wrongness' but not of incoherence, for what is repressive is in fact grinding consistency – another name for the 'unity of method'.

The essence of the modern scientific ideology lies in misapplication rather than mendacity. When it embraces the social sciences then the knowing subject – man who can reflect on and change his action – is lost to sociology and to himself. Thus in the social sciences, observed regularities (like the connection between measured intelligence and school achievement or the persistence of gender roles) are taken as invariant, with no reflection about whether they merely express forms of social domination. Equally in personal life, self- understanding shadows scientific progress (we think of ourselves as 'extroverts', 'late-developers' or 'hyperactive'): we view ourselves as determined and objectified entities without self-mastery at the mercy of 'maternal deprivation', 'depression', or 'hormonal imbalance' and to solve our problems we swallow pills. Human communication is distorted because people think and talk about themselves in terms of scientific objectivity and make decisions about what are seen as purely technical problems, thus rendering moral debate inert.

Thus, once again, we find another strand of neo-Marxist thinking which remarks nothing but consistency amongst the dominant ideas, takes no account of internecine struggles within the elite and gives further credence to the coherence of bourgeois culture. All of this appears as the typical fallacy of upwards conflation which grants insufficient independence to the Cultural System for its internal contradictions ever to merit attention as autonomous sources of change. No aspect of cultural or social transformation is ever attributed to tensions between interdependent elements of the technocratic ideology: the possibility of change depends instead upon the rejection of this as the sole denizen or the only potent inhabitant of the Cultural System. It relies, in brief, on the existence or creation of *alternative* forms of knowledge – a denial of monistic culture.

Thus Habermas returns to Marx, if only briefly. The technocratic ideology must not be taken on its own evaluation, as the illusion of our epoch. ' "Scientism" means science's belief in itself: that is, the conviction that we can no longer understand science as *one* form of possible knowledge, but rather must identify knowledge with science.'[47] Thus there is nothing which endangers the dominant ideas from 'inside' (contradiction, schism, elaboration, modification) they can only be challenged from 'outside', that is by knowledge grounded in a different interest. The entire burden of change thus rests on cultural pluralism and more specifically on the activation of a subordinate counter-culture. In this, all links with both Marx and the dominant ideology theorists are finally severed:

a tenuous connection remains with Gramsci but whereas he considered a revolutionary party essential in such activation, Habermas advances a purely 'culturalist' theory of change.

(3) Thus supreme importance is attached to the emergence and development of a subordinate culture capable of challenging the 'technocratic ideology'. Obviously there are two problems here and Habermas deals with them sequentially. First, if all knowledge is based in some constitutive interest, then an alternative type of interest which is also hostile to the concern for technical control has to be clearly identified. Second, if this pluralism is not to degenerate into rival relativisms some method must be found to establish the validity claims of the subordinate culture.

The constitutive social interest which is both an alternative to and in opposition with 'technocratic consciousness' is located in *emancipation*, which produces knowledge based on *critical reflection*. Here the knowing subject is reintroduced. Those whom the empirical–analytical laws are about reflect on them critically and thus penetrate the interest structure which has joined subject and object together in a particular way. On seeing through the power embodied in such laws, the subject is released from thraldom. Hence the influence of the dominant culture on the subjective state is broken by reflection, following the psycho-analytical analogy that the powers of hidden background influences release their grip when we are brought to recognize them.

There is, however, a major problem here which attends any purely 'culturalist theory', namely that the subjective awareness of repression and domination does not in itself remove their objective effects. Just as in the structural realm, to be aware of the causes of inflation does not prevent it from reducing our standard of living, so in the cultural domain to know that schools do discriminate against the working class does nothing to alter educational opportunity. Habermas partly concedes this when admitting that self-reflection 'cannot cancel out interest, it can to a certain extent make up for it',[48] or again, in the 'end a critically mediated knowledge of laws cannot through reflection alone render a law itself inoperative, but it can render it inapplicable'.[49] Certainly, supportive illustrations can be adduced for this but they appear to be rather limited in scope. If as a female I become aware of the battery of socialization devices imposing a gender role upon me then I can largely repulse these forces and make them personally inapplicable, but unfortunately I cannot do the same thing about the arms race, nor if I were black could I exempt myself from racism. In other words, there are many objective cultural constraints which are not amenable to personal exemption. Some are not susceptible of change and certainly not immediate change, even if one assumes a collective critical determination to repel them.[50] However, Habermas is arguing that a changed subjective state (emancipation) can throw off existing *cultural* constraints (in particular legitimacy) and that if a legitimation crisis can be precipitated then all forms of structural transformation will be added to it. Thus he can pass directly on to the next question of how to free criticism from the charge of relativism and how to establish a genuine 'cultural break with nature' – in which knowledge finally outwits human interests.

The problem is that in critical knowledge validity is determined by the self-reflection of the subject who is the final arbiter (as in psycho-analysis, in which the patient decides whether the interpretation of his condition is valid). The difficulty is that while self-reflection may give people invincible theoretical certainty, it does not protect them against error or delusion or persuasion. Habermas therefore needs to defend the social efficacy of critical thought against the spectre of rampant irrationalism – ineffectual because it would loose self-cancelling and irresolvable points of view. Whereas Marx saw *stringent material conditions* as being necessary for the efficacy of counter-cultural ideas, Habermas attaches *speculative cultural conditions* to the emergence of effective critical thought.

Thus he elaborates the 'ideal speech situation', in which collective dialogue takes place under conditions which ensure that the consensus arrived at will represent a true statement rather than the effect of constraints on the discussion. Thus what are being specified are the *ideal* conditions for emancipation and not the *practical* or temporal conditions of it. Habermas recognizes the obvious difficulty of how to be sure that this communication is free from constraint, but his response merely highlights the difficulty of his attempt to dissociate the ideal from the practical, that is, free discourse exists when all participants enjoy effective equality of opportunity to participate in the dialogue. This is unsatisfactory because it assumes that the ideal form of life, on which the 'ideal speech situation' is predicated, has already come into being. Clearly Habermas is aware of this difficulty for he admits that 'only in an emancipated society, whose members' autonomy and responsibility had been realized, would communication have developed into the non-authoritarian and universally practiced dialogue . . . To this extent the truth of statements is based on anticipating the realization of the good life.'[51] The first part of this quotation appears to accept the charge of circular argument: we need an emancipated society before critical reflection can produce truth, so critical reflection alone cannot generate the emancipated society, since this is a condition of it itself, that is, the prime condition of undistorted communication. However, in the last sentence of the quotation Habermas makes a bid to escape from circularity, which depends on him locating a group of actors who have indeed 'anticipated the realization of the good life'.

This he finds in the community of critical intellectuals, themselves only a subgroup within university life. Thus Habermas seems finally to be driven to an admission that critical self-reflection will remain a *speciality* outside public consciousness as long as the positivistic heritage holds sway. However, to him critical academics are not merely models of the possible, they are a vanguard of the practical. This model of discourse could spread through the universities, suffuse the educational system and then lead society as a whole. Marx, as was seen, left open the question of whether subordinate cultures could affect other parts of the superstructure, while being certain that they alone could not transform society. Habermas is at least hopeful that Critical Theory can do both. In this he remains a complete 'culturalist' – societal transformation will come from within the superstructure; and equally he rests completely faithful to upwards conflation– cultural change originates from the bottom up. Any credibility that this view may carry, and many have dismissed it as completely utopian, depends upon assigning a role to the education system which constitutes a departure from the entire Marxist tradition.

(4) Although Marx was far from dogmatic about the ruling class having unquestionable control in the educational field or being universally successful in cultural transmission (and much less so than many of his followers), Habermas goes to the other extreme. The university is the apparatus of the minority, the protagonists of the subordinate culture, the Critical Theorists. These academics who have emancipated themselves within the university environment will do the same for those they teach: it is the students rather than the working class who are to be the agents of *cultural* transformation. At this point the 'deviationism' of the Frankfurt school in their analysis of economics and of education come together. Students, influenced by critical intellectuals, do not see why life amidst technological plenty should be governed by the dictates of careers, the norms of status competition, the values of possessive individualism or the repression of aesthetic and sensual gratification.

However, student protest

will give rise to a political force only if this sensibility comes into contact with a problem that the system cannot solve. For the future I see *one* such problem. The amount of social wealth produced by industrially advanced capitalism . . . make it ever more difficult to link status assignment in an even subjectively convincing manner to the mechanism for the evaluation of individual achievement. In the long run therefore, student protest could permanently destroy this crumbling achievement – ideology, and thus bring down the already fragile legitimating basis of advanced capitalism, which rests only on depoliticization.[52]

This role assigned in the late sixties to the student movement might be seen as an over-enthusiastic reading of the 'signs of the times'. Yet although the thesis becomes considerably more refined in Habermas's work in the seventies, the legitimation crisis of advanced capitalism is still attributed to the motivational system of 'familial–vocational' privatism which is becoming undermined by the forces of late capitalism and increasingly discrepant to it.[53] It is still the faulty 'supply of motivation offered by the socio-cultural system'[54] which represents the key to societal change. Habermas thus remains a consistent upwards conflationist: only fundamental changes at the Socio-Cultural level can transfer the Cultural System and, with it, the social system.

4   'Central conflation': the duality of culture

'Central conflation' is not the property of a clearly identifiable school and is still in the process of crystallization. The two theorists who will be taken as its major proponents are certainly far from being identical, except for marked formal similarities in their conceptualization of culture. Indeed, at a later date it may transpire that they spear-headed different subspecies of 'central' conflationism. Nevertheless it appears useful to discuss Bauman and Giddens together since our prime interest is with a general theoretical stance, not the comparison of individual thinkers. From a similar viewpoint both Bauman and Giddens look back on the epiphenomenal versions of cultural conflation with precisely the same ambivalence – outrightly rejecting them as they stand, yet seeking to retrieve something from both of them.

On the one hand they have nothing but censure for the central tenet of each version: for downwards conflation where the internal logical consistency of Cultural Systems generates uniformities in mentality and behaviour, thus reducing the actor to a Systemically programmed robot, *and* for upwards conflation where those dominant at the Socio-Cultural level produce a manipulated consensus, thus rendering most (if not all) actors the prisoners of hegemonic ideas. When culture is held to work surreptitiously 'behind the back' of every actor (downwards version), what is essentially lacking is the necessary role of human agency in actively constituting and reconstituting culture; when culture is seen as nothing but the imposition of one group's world-view on others (upwards version), what is systematically evaded is the necessity of culture as the stuff of any action at all, a fact that would have to be faced especially if domination and manipulation were ever overcome. In other words 'culture' should never be detached from human 'agency'. It is neither a floating property which becomes possessed through internalization, nor is it a property created by one group which then possesses others through incorporation. In place of both, central conflationists basically want a concept of culture in which *each and every actor is an active participant* – never a passive recipient or an enforced receiver.

On the other hand, both Bauman and Giddens are eclectic, they want to rescue a key element from each of the earlier versions and then to combine them into a concept of culture which is free from the above deficiencies. From the (downwards) Cultural System perspective they wish to salvage the notion of a semiotic order, supplying a corpus of meanings, which is the very medium of action – just as language is the medium which makes speech acts possible. However, what is accentuated here is not that this medium of action traps its users into regulated behaviour (through using it) but rather that it is a necessary resource in the production of *any* act which is to be meaningful.

From the (upwards) Socio-Cultural perspective they seek to resuscitate the notion of culture as praxis, 'an active constituting process, accomplished by, and consisting in, the doings of active subjects'.[1] Here again there is a considerable shift of emphasis, for this process never boils down to the doings of the dominant minority in mystifying the passive masses. Instead every social actor is held to know a great deal about the production and reproduction of his society and any culture must thus be viewed as resulting from the skilled performances of *each* of its members (not that they will always be able to express what those skills are and not that the results will usually be faithful to their intentions).

It is these two elements, rescued from the downwards and the upwards versions which, when recombined, make for and make up central conflation. The burden of the rest of this chapter is to demonstrate how this third type of elision (the 'central' inflection), produces just as defective a theory of cultural morphostasis and morphogenesis as did the previous two. To begin with, however, it is also important to underline how this final form of conflation yet again serves to buttress the Myth of Cultural Integration.

A new foundation for the Myth of Cultural Integration

It is largely due to a revamping of the 'linguistic analogy' that this line of thought becomes a new tributary to the old Myth of Cultural Integration. Although neither theorist views culture as directly *modelled* on language, the notion of linguistic order (an order reproduced through use and re-ordered in usage) is a potent analogue. Its main consequence is the conceptualization of 'culture-as-an-ordering-process', and this becomes the new foundation upon which the Myth of Cultural Integration is re-erected.

Here Bauman begins to conceptualize culture at the point where the critics of linguistic structuralism left off and does so by taking their criticisms on board. The main burden of these consisted in stressing the points where language could *not* be used as a model for culture as a whole. In particular critics accentuated the fact that the non-linguistic parts of human culture are sufficiently different in nature (they basically cannot be modelled around the information/communication function alone) that the methodology of structural linguistics cannot be extrapolated to general cultural analysis. Nevertheless this still left open a separate, because much larger, question, namely whether all aspects of culture are not obedient to the same general principles, of which language would be one specific case. Thus Bauman begins by posing precisely this question, by asking whether

all human culture, including language, stems from the same universal human effort to decipher the natural order of the world and to impose an artificial one on it, and whether in doing this all fields of culture are submitted to the same logical principles. . . and so whether we are justified in applying to the socio-cultural analysis the general methodological principles, which have achieved the highest level of elaboration and sophistication in structural linguistics.[2]

The answer is in the affirmative. Nevertheless, a little conceptual foot-work is needed to justify the application of the 'general methodological principles' of structural linguistics. After all, if language is a special case of something more general how do we know that its elaborate and sophisticated principles relate to these generalities and not to its own particularities? This is especially exercising given that the principles involved in language largely focus upon communication, yet the non-linguistic parts of culture have been held up as not primarily concerned with communication. Therefore it has often been argued that principles pertaining to the former cannot be transferred to the latter. The 'solution' or resolution consists in re-defining 'communication' itself, at a higher level of generality. Thus drawing freely on general systems theory where the notion of 'communication' is related to those of 'dependence', 'orderliness' and 'organization', and then noting that these concepts in turn have been defined as 'ordering activities', Bauman arrives at a re-definition of communication. We 'speak of communication whenever a set of events is ordered, which means to some extent predictable'.[3] This then acts as a stepping stone from which Bauman can leap to an audacious new position. It enables him to perform 'the switch'. The radical inversion which takes place provides a new foundation for the Myth of Cultural Integration.

If we now go *from the sociological perspective to structural linguistics and not the other way round, we look at the totality of human activity as an endeavour to order*, to organize, to make predictable and manageable the living space of human beings, and the language discloses itself to us *as one of the devices developed* to serve this overall aim: a device cut to the measure of communication in the narrower sense. *Instead of all the culture being a set of the particularizations of the communicative function embodied in language, the language turns into one of the many instruments of the generalized effort of ordering, laboured on by the culture as a whole.*[4] (my emphasis)

Once the switch has been accomplished, the stepping stone can be jettisoned, so henceforth 'to avoid misunderstandings caused by the equivocality of the term "communication" it is better to speak of "ordering" as the superior function of the culture as a whole'[5] In effect this is the reverse of the Indian rope trick: it is the rope that disappears having got its master safely off the ground complete with the linguistic baggage he will use later.

Giddens does not *invert* language and ordering in this way, but rather *induces* ordering from language, to arrive at much the same position. Hence to him speech and 'language provide us with a series of useful clues as to how to conceptualize processes of social production and reproduction – *not because society is like a language, but on the contrary because language as a practical activity is so central to social life that in* some *basic respects it can be treated as exemplifying social processes in general'* (my emphasis).[6] The logic here is far from impeccable but its purpose is the same as Bauman's highly dubious elastication of the term 'communication' – it justifies the use of the linguistic analogy. Yet just because language, or anything else, is 'central' to social life does *not* mean that all social processes are isomorphic to it. Moreover this leaves aside the contentious question of how 'centrality' is established for *any* factor in social life anyway. Generally a claim can only be established for 'indispensability', but the things which are indispensable (for example, biological reproduction and economic production) are not necessarily isomorphic with one another or with language.

Ultimately then Giddens's position is *not deduced from the centrality of language*, what he does instead is *to induce generality from language*. Thus, just as to speak I have to draw on language rules but, simultaneously, in uttering a grammatical English sentence, I contribute to the reproduction of the English language as a whole as an unintended consequence, so too with other aspects of culture. I have to use the ordered medium of language but in doing so I reproduce the linguistic order. It is the universalizing of this proposition, beyond the domain of language, which means that this approach is concerned with the same fundamental ordering activity as Bauman's. Hence to Giddens 'just as every sentence in English expresses within itself the totality which is the "language" as a whole, so every interaction bears the imprint of the global society'.[7] Thus the 'essential recursiveness of social life, as constituted in social practices'[8] represents an orderliness produced through social practice having to draw on the cultural order.

Thus culture-as-ordering becomes the new key concept and its affinities with the Myth of Cultural Integration are close indeed. Culture as a whole 'labours' on ordering the universe for mankind and without its success there would be no human actors or social interaction, for both are dependent upon a framework of meanings. Thus common ordering principles are moved to the centre of the cultural stage and the generic integration they provide is the essential condition of social life to Bauman[9] or its inescapable and constitutive feature to Giddens. This is far removed from the two previous notions of 'common culture' which involved the induction or imposition of a set of 'beliefs': here 'beliefs' may diverge but their articulation by knowledgeable human beings and their reception by others is grounded in a common medium of signification, a framework of meanings prior to both activities and without which neither would be possible. In this new version of the Myth, culture does not produce order by either socialization or indoctrination; it *is* both order and ordering.

Central conflation and mutual constitution

Central conflation is a position from which the Cultural System level and the Socio-Cultural level are held to be mutually constitutive. In its general, everyday applications, the notion of mutual constitution allows considerable relative autonomy for the elements involved in it. Thus mutually constitutive concepts like 'cycling', 'singing', 'haystack' or 'officer' are all cases where it is possible to examine the constituent components separately. Bicycles, songs, bales and armies can be inspected in their own right, independent of human agency, and regardless of their dispositional capacity for being ridden, sung, stacked or manned. In so doing, properties specific to these things can be identified which are quite independent of what people do to them (the colour of a bicycle, length of a song, composition of a bale and size of an army are all examples of such properties). The same goes for the human ingredient. We can, for instance, note differences between agents in the performance of those tasks (such as how well they do them) and in properties they possess which are unrelated to such tasks (such as their marital status). In other words the two constitutive components can be investigated 'dualistically'.

The point of this excursion into the everyday usage of mutually constitutive concepts is to note that central conflationists depart from it, because the constituent components *cannot* be examined separately, in their view. Culture is held to be such an all-embracing phenomenon, that it represents a kind of global matrix in which all facets of signification (CS) are intertwined with every feature of social practice (S–C). In this totalistic version of mutual constitution, those properties which are independent of one another *within* each mutually constituted element (as in the everyday examples), lose this status when inserted into the matrix and 'cross-referenced' with the totality of elements. Obviously this implies the immense coherence of the matrix itself, otherwise every social practice would not be embedded in the semiotic corpus and vice versa – an implication which itself constitutes the most extreme Myth of Cultural Integration to be encountered yet.

This of course prompts one to wonder why they promote such an *extreme form of mutual constitution*, rather than simply concluding that they are dealing with different aspects of a *single entity*? The answer seems to lie in their adoption of the linguistic analogy; for the corpus that is language cannot ultimately be reduced to the community of language users (or vice versa), despite their lack of autonomy from one another. Because this is the image behind the conceptualization of culture, a methodology reflecting its quintessential 'duality' is imperative. Correspondingly any attempt at 'dualistic' theorizing is repudiated as it presumes the influence of independent properties the very existence of which runs counter to the guiding analogue.

Thus the core of the central conflationist conception of culture concerns its essential *duality*. Culture is the product of human

agency but at the same time any form of social interaction is embedded in it: for Bauman 'being structured and being capable of
structuring seem to be the twin kernels of the human way of life,
known as culture';[10] to Giddens 'structure is both medium and outcome of the reproduction of practices'.[11] This central notion of
'duality' expressly refers to the mutual constitution of the Cultural
System level and the Socio-Cultural level. Indeed, so intimate is this
process that both authors do of course repudiate this very distinction and employ the concept of 'duality' precisely so as to reject and
to replace it.

Bauman starts from the credo that 'the peculiarity of man consists in his being a structure-generating and structure-oriented
creature'.[12] The notion of 'duality' is thus designed to capture this
generic bi-lateralism. On the one hand then, cultures are man-
made products, they are his own and not imposed on him by a
transcendental system and are never entities the fixity of which
defies further human elaboration or transformation. This is the
active voluntaristic side where agency creatively shapes culture. On
the other hand, since the life process of each generation only takes
place within earlier crystallized structures by which the long-dead
make the universe intelligible to the now-living, there is also the
determined aspect in which the actor, to be an actor, inevitably
becomes an 'epistemic subject'. As such contemporary existence is
immersed in a historically structured world.

So far Bauman has stressed 'duality', the Janus-face of culture,
without necessarily implying the *simultaneity* of mutual constitution.
This is a necessary predicate of 'conflation' for without it the
possibility remains of unravelling the interplay between the two
levels *over time*. However this compacting immediately follows as
Bauman proceeds to insist that culture is 'simultaneously, the
objective foundation of the subjectively meaningful experience and
the subjective "appropriation" of the otherwise inhumanly alien
world'.[13] Thus the Socio-Cultural level and the Cultural System
level are elided, for at any moment in time the formulation CS⇆S-C
holds good. It is this formula which essentially unites the theories of
Bauman and Giddens. Having endorsed it, Bauman then travels on
to give an account of *why* there is this mutuality of constitution
which he attributes to common grounding in a factor which
operates on both levels simultaneously – the ultimate source of all
culture-generating faculties is located in the ordering rules built
into the human mind,[14] and the unconscious mind at that. To

Giddens there is no call for a separate 'why' question: the reasons for mutual constitution are embedded in the very fact that 'the notions of action and structure presuppose one another'.[15] Digging any deeper is quite redundant.

For Giddens, then, mutual constitution derives from the fact that action inescapably has to draw upon 'standardized elements of stocks of knowledge, applied by actors in the production of interaction. Interpretative schemes form the core of the mutual knowledge whereby an accountable universe of meaning is sustained through and in processes of interaction.'[16] Here human agency is directly responsible for invoking part of this cultural corpus, and without this 'instantiation' in social practice then the bundle of knowledge/meanings/interpretations/rules is without social consequence; it remains socially inert.

By instantiating part of the bundle, actors will usually only be trying to 'know how to go on', but in Wittgensteinian fashion this involves knowing how to play 'according to the rule', and in so playing their practices are affected in conformity with it. This to Giddens is 'vital, because it connects rules and practices. Rules generate – or are the medium of the production and reproduction of – practices.'[17] Simultaneously, practices are the medium responsible for the reproduction of rules: instantiation is also revitalization of the rule (though it may also entail its modification).

Hence the essential bi-valence of the 'duality' notion and its twin assertions that agency both maintains and modifies culture whilst culture in turn enmeshes and shapes action. The following quotation clarifies how he conceives of this mutual constitution. (In it I have inserted my own notations: CS = Cultural System level; S-C = Socio-Cultural level.)

[The] standpoint I wish to suggest . . . regards rules as media and outcome of the reproduction of social systems. *Rules* [CS] *can only be grasped* in the context of the historical development of social totalities, *as recursively implicated in practices.* [S-C] . . . (a) There is *not a singular relation between an 'activity' and a 'rule'*, as is sometimes suggested or implied by appeal to statements like 'the rule governing the Queen's move' in chess. *Activities or practices* [S-C] *are brought into being in the context of overlapping and connected sets of rules* [CS], *given coherence* by their involvement in the constitution of social systems in the movement of time. (b) Rules cannot be exhaustively described or analysed in terms of their own content, as prescriptions, prohibitions, etc. [CS], precisely because, apart from those circumstances where a relevant lexicon exists, *rules and practices only exist in conjunction with one another* [CS⇄S-C].[18] (my emphasis)

This then indicates the route the terminus of which is the conflationary $CS \leftrightarrows S\text{-}C$ formula, which again supposedly holds good at any point in time.

Thus in Bauman's words, readily echoed by Giddens,[19] only *duality* can 'account for both, inextricably interwoven, facets of human existence: subjective and objective, determining and determined, creative and created, socializing and socialized. Then and only then can it be utilized in building models at once syn- and diachronical, and bridging the so far isolated levels of individual situation and social structure in a way which does not beg the phony question of the "priority" of one of the two modalities of human existence.'[20] But to me this is not a phony question, though it has been given some phony answers like the two examined in the upwards and downwards versions where one factor is assumed to have universal priority over the other. What is not phony is to question the *circumstances* or *conditions* under which one modality (*sic*) is more influential of the other, which is not to assume that the relationship always works in the same direction. In other words this would entail a genuine questioning of their interplay. Yet this is precisely what commitment to 'duality' proscribes, because it leads both theorists to withhold autonomy from both levels.

The denial of autonomy to the constituents of culture

It is entirely possible to adopt a position which could be called 'centrism' which indeed accepts that human agents shape culture but are themselves culturally moulded, *without* collapsing the two levels (Cultural System and Socio-Cultural) into one another. This is the stance I elaborate in the following chapters. However central conflation does confound the two, as just outlined. The notion of mutual constitution as a simultaneous process means that there is no way of 'untying' the constitutive elements. The intimacy of their interconnection denies even relative autonomy to the components involved. And in the absence of any degree of autonomy it becomes impossible to *examine* their *interplay*.

Although there are points at which it seems that Bauman allows of a relatively autonomous Cultural System, ultimately this cannot be disengaged from the Socio-Cultural level. Intimation of autonomy is contained in his statement that 'cultural data do enjoy existence in their own right, though of a kind different from the reality typical of the "natural universe". Culture is not only inter-subjective; *it is indeed objective in its own specific sense.*'[21] This quotation might look as though the Cultural System were being endowed with Third World status, in which case it would have independent properties of its own and would thus have been granted a significant degree of autonomy. However, Bauman persistently disavows *any* independent influence stemming from the Cultural System. *None* of its observable properties have any autonomous effect, including those two which are of particular interest in relation to the Myth of Cultural Integration, namely Systemic contradiction or complementarity. Any inconsistency (CS) is dismissed as it makes sense in its own context (S-C). Given Socio-Cultural contextualization, inconsistencies disperse for they are always found to embody the inherent logic of 'lived processes'. This argument rests on his affirmation of a use theory of meaning (the mutual constitution of meaning and use being another exemplification of 'duality'). Thus he insists 'on the intimate connection and *inter*dependence (in opposition to a one-way dependence only) between the contextual plane and the plane of meaning. *The two planes are inseparable and constitute each other*' (my emphasis).[22] Exit contradiction as an autonomous property of Cultural Systems and an independent influence upon the Socio-Cultural level. On the contrary, consideration of the Socio-Cultural level dispels inconsistencies and, by corollary, any question of their influence.

The status and effects of Systemic *consistency* are treated in the same way. An existing universe of discourse, established in a given community may *appear* as an external constraint foisting itself on each member and every act of communication. However, since communities can historically transmute the universe of discourse itself, it has no autonomous ordering properties since these are contingent upon the community sustaining them and lack independence since the community can change them.

Ultimately then the Cultural System is neither constraining by virtue of its consistency nor influential because of its contradictions. To Bauman it does not have the World Three properties of autonomous interconnections and independent influence because it is not a World Three entity. On the contrary he maintains that the 'only necessary and irreplaceable component of the concept is the *process of structuring*, together with its *objectified results* – man-made structures' (my emphasis).[23] This finally is the 'specific sense' in which culture is 'objective', a sense which reduces the Cultural System to an *objectified entity*, inextricably tied to the Socio-Cultural level. Its 'sovereignty' turns out to be the temporary rule of any given form of cultural objectification, and even an impermanent independent influence is denied to it (that is, autonomy while it lasts) since the community can effect transformation at any moment. In sum, there is no independent property or power granted to the Cultural System in this scheme, indeed its properties and effects can only be understood in conjunction with the Socio-Cultural level. However, this emphatically does not mean that the Cultural System is reducible to the Socio-Cultural level. As a theory premissed on 'duality', the two levels are treated completely symmetrically: if we now examine the treatment of Socio-Cultural interaction we find in parallel that no account of this can be given without constant reference to the meaning System.

Once again certain initial statements about the creativity of praxis appear to grant this level independence and autonomy via the human potential for creating new and different orders. This might seem to be conveyed in the approving quotation from Piaget: 'man can transform himself by transforming the world and can structure himself by constituting structures; and these structures are his own, for they are not eternally predestined from within or from without'.[24] However, if we ask the obvious questions (at the Socio-Cultural level) about how these structures are developed and imposed by some men on others, about how they are intertwined with interests and with power, it soon transpires that 'praxis' is distanced from the hurley-burley of social groups and loftily indifferent to the state and fate of individuals.

It is the 'community' which is the 'medium and the bearer of praxis'[25], never groups or individuals who are the creative fount of change. Indeed group antagonisms and alliances become as uninteresting at the Socio-Cultural level as were contradictions and compatibilities at the Cultural System level. The notion of community stands for a 'whole' which is somehow superordinate to the component social groups, their divisions and struggles. It harks back to the undifferentiated view of community presented by the early anthropologists – to one of the original mainstays of the Myth of Cultural Integration.

It is this view of community and praxis which leads him to deny autonomy to the Socio-Cultural level for all 'facets of human existence stem from the same root of human praxis'.[26] Just as the Cultural System could not be examined independently of social processes of objectification, so Socio-Cultural interaction cannot be analysed in isolation from the meaning System which impregnates it. Thus it is maintained that 'the same generative rules govern human praxis in politics, industry, agriculture, religion and whatever else'.[27] Clearly, the implication is that we cannot examine political or religious interaction apart from these rules as they have no autonomous features to investigate – there are no distinctive forms of political, religious or any other kind of action. In sum, then, social interaction cannot be examined independently of the principles ordering it, for it has no independence from them.

Consequently because the causal and the logical are systematically elided, then causal relations are logically ordered and logical properties are causally transmutable. Neither level is granted the relative autonomy necessary to examine their interplay or to theorize about it.

Precisely the same refusal to analyse the two levels separately is contained in Giddens's approach, and for the same reason. Only methodologically and never substantively can they be examined independently of one another. However, although the 'duality' notion militates against anything other than an analytical separation of convenience, Giddens does at least attempt to deal with the *articulation* of the Systemic and Socio-Cultural levels, that is *how* it works. This involves separating out the two levels by a methodological bracketing procedure which artificially enables one to conceptualize the way in which Systemic factors (treated as chronically reproduced features of societies) and Socio-Cultural relations (treated as the strategic mobilization of cultural properties) are inter-linked through the intermediary of 'interpretative schemes', as in the diagram below.

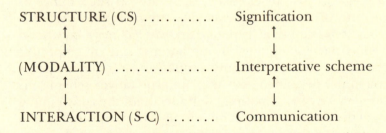

STRUCTURE (CS) . . . .   Signification

(MODALITY) . . . .   Interpretative scheme

INTERACTION (S-C) . . . .   Communication

The intermediary level (or more strictly 'dimension') is both drawn upon strategically by actors in the generation of their social practices but at the same time embodies institutional features of the system. 'The level of modality thus provides the coupling elements whereby the bracketing of strategic or institutional analysis is dissolved in favour of an acknowledgement of their interrelation'.[28] My criticism is that this scheme merely boils down to a re-statement of mutual constitution: it is fundamentally unpropositional about the conditions patterning different relationships. Again this is because no genuine relative autonomy is granted to either level so what results is merely a re-assertion of their interpenetration, not an examination of their interplay.

The study of 'signification' as a structural feature of social systems concerns rules, or aspects of rules embodied in 'codes'. Initially it might seem that such codes are endowed with a relative autonomy which would permit examination of their independent influence upon interaction. This impression is conveyed in the approving quotation from Eco: 'A signification system is an autonomous semiotic construct that has an abstract mode of existence independent of any possible communicative act it makes possible.'[29] Thus signification systems exist but, and here comes the first caveat, only as produced and reproduced in the instantiation of codes. Nevertheless, once instantiated, drawn on and reproduced by actors in the form of 'interpretative schemes', their properties could still exert an independent influence on 'communication'. And this too appears to be the case at first, since Giddens argues that 'signification' can be understood in terms of the *mediations* and *transformations* it makes possible. This would then imply that *some* mediations and transformations are not possible, they cannot be derived from within the code and this constraint would also necessarily figure in the 'interpretative scheme'.

However, this independent constraining influence emanating from the Cultural System is immediately diluted to the point of insignificance, because to Giddens 'there are no such things as "rules of transformation"; *all social rules are transformational*'.[30] It follows that codes can thus 'generate an *indefinite range of empirical contents*, which have identity with one another only in respect of their relation to those rules' (my emphasis).[31] If the range of transformations permitted by the 'interpretative scheme' is indefinite then we can say nothing definite about the constraining influence of the Systemic code. It merely gives the empirical range a common denominator because related to the rules but does not deny that it may have other and higher common denominators stemming from the interactional level, where agency may consistently exploit its transformational freedoms in connection with social interests (through ideological manipulation for example).

Here however comes the Catch-22, for although actors may indeed seek to, and succeed in, transforming 'interpretative schemes' in such fashion, this very accomplishment (to repeat) 'presupposes a signification system as its necessary condition'. Thus agency is also deprived of significant autonomy for it is Systemically fettered in its very acts of Socio-Cultural manipulation. In other words the 'modality' which articulates the two levels merely lumps together the dual aspects of transformation – code-related but socially manipulated. It asserts their interrelationship but tells one nothing about their interplay.

The following statement therefore stands as his conclusion on this matter: 'We cannot identify pre-existing codes which generate messages, since the "messages" also enter into the reconstruction of "codes" in the duality of structure in interaction; but, more than this, in social interaction, the "messages" are always "texts" in the sense in which they are generated from, and express a plurality of codes.'[32] The relationship between the levels is thus analytically intractable, for there is no way in which we can break into the circuit. The levels themselves lack too little autonomy from one other to start from either and slowly disentangle its interplay with the other – for the terminus is already present in the point of departure. Nor can we distinguish cycles of encoding and re-encoding, for since the flow of practice is continuous, there is only a ceaseless tide of 'becoming' and never of 'being' – all is process, nothing is ever, even temporarily, end-product.

The problem is thus how to gain purchase on this interrelationship, given that the above methods have been proscribed by the premises of the 'duality of culture'. In practice, Giddens attempts to grasp what takes place in the whirlpool of transformations by interpolating central 'modalities' in order to disengage 'structural principles' from them. But as I have discussed elsewhere[33] there are serious (I believe unsolvable) difficulties attaching to this, the most important being the absent context of justification, the fact that there is ultimately no way of validating one interpolation, imputation or interpretation. In many ways this procedure remains redolent of grasping cultural patterning by recourse to artistic hermeneutics.

The 'duality of culture' and conceptualizing cultural stability or change

What both Bauman and Giddens want to unite through the 'duality of culture' notion is both the creativity of actors in introducing cultural metamorphosis (employing their transformative capacity to produce change of real magnitude) and its opposite, the 'ruttedness' of recursively produced actions (generated by drawing on and thus reproducing cultural rules), as in bureaucracy where life is constantly breathed into inert regulations which then deaden their animators through routinization. In other words they attempt to use their key concept of 'duality' to transcend the traditional dichotomy between voluntarism and determinism, for they want (quite rightly) to retain something of both.

However, the difficulty is that this central notion effectively precludes a specification of when there will be 'more Voluntarism' or 'more Determinism'. In fact, the 'duality of culture' *itself* oscillates between the two divergent images it bestrides: between (i) the hyperactivity of agency, the corollary of which is the innate volatility of the cultural realm; and (ii) the rigid coherence of ordering rules, associated instead with the essential recursiveness of Socio-Cultural life.

(i) In Giddens's work hyperactivity is an ineluctable consequence of all rules being defined as *transformative*, in contradistinction to the rigid transformational grammar of linguistics. Here rules are endlessly interpretable, thus transfiguring codes and norms. However, it follows that if rules are inherently transformative then actors generically enjoy very high degrees of freedom – at any time they could have acted otherwise, intervening for change or for maintenance of the cultural status quo. Hence the counterfactual image of hyperactivity in which actors explore and exploit these generous degrees of freedom. Hence, too, the outcomes must be correspondingly variegated – culture becomes highly volatile if 'the possibility of change is recognised as inherent in every circumstance of social reproduction'.[34] (A case of S-C$\longrightarrow$CS in our notation.)

(ii) The other side of the 'duality of culture' is intended to rectify the image and introduce a more recognizable picture of social life. Instead I believe over-correction takes place, generating a counter-image of 'chronic recursiveness' in society. Basically this arises because actors have to draw upon rules in social interchange and these are thus reconstituted through such interaction. However, Giddens goes further than this, now endorsing the kind of linguistic analogy disavowed in (i). Thus when actors do draw on rules they necessarily invoke the whole matrix of differences which constitute structures, 'in the sense in which the utterances of a grammatical sentence presupposes the absent corpus of syntactical rules that constitute the language as a totality'.[35]

In this way Giddens commits himself to the enormous coherence of the signification system, such that actors' inescapable use of it embroils everyone in its stable reproduction. The pendulum swings so far the other way that we are now presented with another over-integrated view of man, for the 'duality of culture' relates the smallest item of day-to-day behaviour to attributes of far more inclusive codes: 'when I utter a grammatical English sentence in casual conversation, I contribute to the reproduction of the English language as a whole. This is an unintended consequence of my speaking the sentence, but one that is bound indirectly to the recursiveness of the duality of structure.'[36] (A case of CS——▶S-C in our notation.)

What is wrong with this image, as with the previous one, is that it does not allow for *some* behaviour engendering replication whilst *other* action initiates transformation. Rather than transcending the voluntarism/determinism dichotomy, the two sides of the 'duality of culture' embody them respectively: they are simply clamped together in a conceptual vice.

This oscillation between contradictory images derives from Giddens not answering 'when' questions – when can actors be transformative (which involves specification of degrees of freedom) and when are they trapped into replication (which involves specification of the stringency of constraints)? Bauman's work is identical in these respects. Thus, instead of examining the preconditions of transformative interaction, he insists on the *unconditional* nature of transformation. Since that key feature of praxis is its 'essential unpredictability',[37] it can happen at *any* moment and, therefore, it follows under *any* conditions. Since nothing could be much less helpful than a conceptualization of change as permanently imminent yet defiantly unpredictable, it is important to see that this is a direct consequence of the 'duality' approach itself.

To do this involves unpacking the 'duality of culture' to examine its constituents in terms of my own dualistic categories – the Cultural System and the Socio-Cultural levels. When unpackaged in this way, we re-encounter a pair of now-familiar errors, (1) and (4) below, shared with downwards and upwards conflation respectively, and a couple of new difficulties, (2) and (3) below, originating from the attempt to reconcile this mixed heritage.

(1) At the Systemic level the enormous coherence attributed to the signification system and its supposed penetration into the minutiae of daily life has been met with before, in the version of downwards conflation advanced by linguistic structuralists. To central con-

flationists too, every daily instantiation of a code serves to reveal the nature of coding as a whole but simultaneously it works to reproduce the code itself, thus contributing to recursiveness in social life. But the rigidity of this recursive image (as presented under (ii) above) is open to criticism on two counts. First, cultural rules are not so coherently organized as grammar, often lacking the mutually invoking character of syntax (to speak standard English does not imply the 'correct' use of cutlery or of French, nor does it invoke parental responsibility, rectitude in completing income tax returns or the closing of lavatory doors). Second, action is not really so tightly integrated by these social codes: not only may some of the smallest items of behaviour be irrelevant to 'the code', certain larger ones may also be trivial, mutually cancelling or self-contained in their effects, while still other actions can produce far-reaching aggregate or emergent consequences – yet these different possibilities remain undifferentiated in this approach. The common denominator of both criticisms is that the 'duality' perspective has remained over-faithful to the linguistic analogy in its presentation of the Cultural System. In turn this results in a refusal to specify the *variable* degrees of freedom of which actors could avail themselves in different contexts, for these are invariably low when the System itself is endowed with such coherence.

(2) The second difficulty surrounding this treatment of the Cultural System is that the presentation of its constituents precludes any specification of variations in their constraining power. It stems from the assumption that all its components are equally susceptible of change. None of them are held to be more resiliant or resistant to change than others, at any given time. Indeed this postulate is *intended* to get away from the whole notion of Systemic constraints.

The assumption that there is no differential changeability amongst the constituents of the Cultural System derives from the latter being viewed as only an 'objectified' entity (Bauman) or having merely a 'virtual existence' (Giddens),[38] outside time and space, operative only when instantiated by actors. Since what is instantiated depends on the power of agency and not the nature of the property, then properties themselves are not differentially mutable. This ontological 'diminution' of the Cultural System is the device by which the freedom of action, seemingly withheld under (1) is now returned to human agency. Yes, they seem to be saying, the System has the force of coherence but it affects action only in so far as and as long as actors summon up and sustain its various elements. The powers of Mephistopheles ultimately depend on Faustus continuing to invoke them.

However, why should one accept this peculiar ontological status for all cultural properties in the first place? Why should World Three knowledge, even if it lives on only in libraries, be regarded as outside time and space? It is there continuously and thus awaits not instantiation but activation. Yet when it is activated it contains its own potentials and limitations, independent of the constructions and regulations imposed upon it.

Furthermore, even if the two authors in question are not willing to accord the Cultural System Third World status, they are still engaging in an act of pure theoretical *fiat* when maintaining that each of its constituents is as changeable as every other. After all, many of these are unintended consequences of action, yet is there any other area in sociology where we would feel confident in making such a blanket *a prioristic* judgement about these results of interaction? Surely not: proper caution would prompt proper scrutiny, and closer examination usually reveals empirical variation – some such consequences are irreversible, while others show differing degrees of susceptibility to change. So here, it appears to me that the quality of the cultural properties (CS) makes its own contribution to differential malleability, independent of the amount of power actors bring to bear (S-C). Some properties can be changed relatively quickly (tax rules), some take longer to change (knowledge distributions), some prove highly resistant to change (bureaucracy, ethnicity, gender distinctions), and some are unchangeable (historical information lost or irretrievably destroyed). Even more importantly, central configurations of rules (the Law or the Constitution) display this differential mutability *among* their internal components.

The key point here is not that (most of) these elements are ultimately unalterable: only that it takes different amounts of effort and time to modify them. And during the time it takes to change something, then that thing continues to exert a constraint which cannot be assumed to be insignificant in its social consequences. Nations can fall, polities be deposed and economies bankrupted, *while* efforts are being made to change the factors responsible (for example, birth rates, despotism, illiteracy, ethno-centrism). As a general theoretical proposition this holds good however short the time interval involved. Yet this is what Giddens spirits away by making all cultural properties atemporal and according them only a pale 'virtual existence' and what Bauman likewise banishes by holding all to be 'objectified' and assigning them an immanent but unpredictable changeability. Fundamentally both theorists prevent us from talking about the stringency of constraints or the existence of facilitating factors at the Systemic level – because they will not accord 'full' ontological status to the Cultural System.

(3) The foregoing assumption that all components of the Cultural System are *equally* changeable has its direct equivalent at the Socio-Cultural level where it is assumed that actors enjoy a *constant* degree of transformative freedom. This is embedded in Giddens's assertion that 'change, or its potentiality is thus inherent in all moments of social reproduction'.[39] It is also embodied in Bauman's argument that 'essential unpredictability' is the key feature of transformatory praxis.

It thus represents a further 'correction', this time at the Socio-Cultural level, of the seeming enmeshment of all actors in the chronic reproduction of Systemic features under (1). Point (2) began this process of restoration by the argument that nothing in the Cultural System was more resistant to change than anything else: point (3) completes it with the proposition that *nothing else* trammels the transformative capacity of agency at the Socio-Cultural level. Hence this 'corrective' move emphasizes not just knowledgeability of actors in the accomplishment and repair of Cultural Systems but also the *unconditional* transformative capacity of agency over System.

Once again, upon what grounds can the degrees of freedom for action be assumed to be constant from one Socio-Cultural context to another? This assumption is completely *a prioristic* and can be confronted with plenty of empirical counter-evidence. Much of the time this combined accentuation of actors' knowledgeability and underemphasis of how culture does work 'behind our backs' (or before our faces for that matter) produces a complementary neglect of characteristics about which people may well be aware (such as racism, parenthood or the highway code) but which limit their degrees of freedom none the less. They do so quite objectively by imposing limitations on opportunities for certain actions (for example racial barriers to social promotion, or the restrictions child-care entails over free time and disposable income), or by attaching equally objective penalties to actions which traduce them (for example legal prosecution for motoring offences or neglect of children). Similarly, there is a range of cultural factors, which limit freedom of action, without the vast majority of us having much discursive penetration of them; the archetype of which is the censored withholding of information itself, but would also include the effects of high science on what Habermas calls the human race's emancipatory interest in general.[40]

From this perspective these factors are always seen as what people produce and never as what they confront – and have to grapple with in ways which are themselves conditioned by the cultural features involved. Certainly these features are the results of anterior social actions (which historically shaped prejudices, norms, rules and knowledge) and in all likelihood they will be modified by posterior interaction, but in the present, wherever it is situated historically, they constitute an objective if temporary limitation on degrees of freedom. Yet an examination of this interplay over time, of how our open future is the next generation's constraints, just as the things restricting us are the product of the previous generation's use of its degrees of freedom, is precisely what the 'duality' approach prevents. This is particularly evident in Giddens's bracketing exercise where institutional analysis and strategic conduct are separated out by placing a methodological *epoché* upon each in turn. But because they are the two sides of the same thing, the pocketed elements must thus be co-terminous in time (the symmetry of the *epochés* confines analysis to the same *époque*); and it follows from this that temporal relations between institutional structure and strategic action *logically cannot be examined*. (Yet ironically, what does the bracketing device do other than traduce the very principle of duality, since it merely transposes dual*ism* from the theoretical to the methodological level – thus conceding its analytical indispensibility?)

In short this means that the concept of duality can never acknowledge that the Cultural System and the Socio-Cultural levels work on different time intervals (however small the gap between them). It can therefore never theoretically incorporate the two most important *dualistic* assumptions: (i) that Systemic features (CS) logically predate the action(s) (S-C) which transform them; (ii) that elaboration of the Cultural System logically post-dates those actions at the Socio-Cultural level.[41] Yet recognition of both points is fundamental to any theory of Cultural Elaboration as a process occurring over time. (4) Finally, then, does this approach fare any better if we look at it the other way round, that is, not focusing on what curtails freedom but on the conditions under which 'transformative potential' (constant at any moment of interaction) in fact constitutes real 'transformative capacity' (enabling this potential to be utilized)? Unfortunately, such is not the case, the reason being that the 'transformative capacity' of actors is immediately conflated with the concept of power. Then certain difficulties of relying exclusively on power, as encountered in upward conflationist accounts of change, resurface here.

In direct opposition to Giddens, I would maintain that this capacity to transform is logically independent of the power of agents, the relationship between them being one of contingency. Let us take a simple example, in order to establish this point. Any 'discovery' which has the capacity for introducing social change would serve the purpose: contraception will be used for illustration. It seems to be the case that this discovery and the changes it could produce:

(i)　May not be capitalized upon by those with the power to do so. (Often political or religious considerations meant the dismissal or rejection of a family-planning policy by those groups with the power to make contraception available throughout society.)

(ii)　Do not necessarily involve power. (Contraception may enter social usage through example and persuasion without any use of power. Yet always to Giddens 'transformative capacity is harnessed to actors' attempts to get others *to comply with their wants*'.[42] This was not the case with the slow spread of family planning in England, where the social learning process could only be termed compliance by rendering that term vacuous (that is, to accept anything is to comply with it.)

(iii)　May mean that considerable power can be deployed in this context without producing any transformation. (Much effort has been devoted to universalizing contraception in some countries with very little effect: in others it has been the source of struggle between powerful contestants, like Church and State, which have locked in immobilism and blocked transformation.)

This example highlights several problems attaching to Giddens's elision of 'transformative capacity' and power.

The first problems pertain to the Socio-Cultural level where change has been made logically dependent upon the power of agency. Yet, on the one hand, as the above example illustrates, the fact that the capacity to introduce change does not necessarily involve power (ii), while the use of power is no guarantee of change (iii) points to a constricted view of the forms of Socio-Cultural interaction producing modifications of Systemic magnitude. At the very least it omits those processes by which large-scale change can stem from a confluence of desires or reciprocal exchange without any coercively induced compliance. On the other hand it would also seem to share with conflict theory the basic difficulty of accounting for why intense power play sometimes fails to generate change (as in (iii)), while at other times an exercise of power produces far reaching modifications. All that can be advanced to account for this variety are *ad hoc* lists of variable empirical conditions which influence the balance of power or the efficacy of power itself.[43] Explanatory purchase on change peters out at this point if the account of transformation is restricted to the Socio-Cultural level alone: as in structural analysis, our theoretical grasp can only be extended by examining social interaction in conjunction with Systemic features.

Giddens is well aware of this trap but seeks to evade it by making his concept of 'power as transformative capacity'[44] straddle the two levels: Systemic features are implicated in power relations and power relations are implicated in the Cultural System. What this does in effect is to recapitulate the problems of duality notion, basic to central conflation. Since the two aspects of power, the institutionalized and the strategic, become inseparably intertwined, it also becomes impossible to understand their *independent variation* – as in instances like (i), in the above example, where available Systemic potential for change (CS) was not utilized by powerful actors (S-C). Once again, this signals a need to examine the interplay between Systemic facilitation or constraint and the pushes and pulls of social interaction, which is precluded whenever the components of duality cannot be unravelled – in the case of power, as in general.

Fundamentally Lukes's conceptualization of power appears more profitable because he maintains analytical dualism by seeking to draw a line between Systemic determination and the use of power. Hence he talks of 'where structural determinism ends and power begins'[45] and is predictably chastized by Giddens for tending to 'repeat the dualism of agency and structure'.[46] Lukes does not deny interconnections between the two but he avoids Giddens's compacting of these elements, which blurs the distinction between responsible action and determined action, thus severing the essential tie between power and responsibility. On the contrary, Lukes tries to discover, explain and assess the weight of Systemic limitations on actions which delimit the zone in which it is proper to speak of power relations: 'although the agents operate within structurally defined limits, they nonetheless have a certain relative autonomy and could have acted differently'.[47] What is then required 'is a sustained discussion of the nature of, and conditions for, autonomy (and its relation to social determination)'.[48] In other words, we need a specification of the degrees of freedom *within which* power can be exercised, and this in turn is dependent upon employing analytical dualism and rejecting the notion of duality.

Theorizing about stability and change

The implication of the foregoing discussion is that neither Giddens nor Bauman can advance a satisfactory theory of cultural stability or change because central conflation necessarily compacts together those elements the interplay of which is essential to such a theory. Indeed, both appear to be aware of the cul-de-sac into which the duality of culture has led them in this connection. Thus Giddens confesses that there is 'little point in looking for an overall theory of stability and change in social systems, since conditions of social reproduction vary so widely between different types of society'.[49] Equally, since Bauman has argued that transformation is quintessentially unpredictable, he too has obviously abandoned hope of theorizing about the conditions of its presence or absence. The basic tenets of the 'duality of culture' thus press both authors towards an acceptance of historical specificity. Both in turn resist this effectual abandonment of sociological theorizing. They attempt to evade this implication in identical fashion by *positing one general social process as universally associated* with either stability or change, given that they cannot unravel the conditions of stability and change from the standpoint of central conflation.

Thus Bauman adduces the importance of the process leading to 'uncertainty' and 'insecurity' in relation to change – in which, as old signs lose their signifying power, they loose intolerable 'ambiguity' on society. It is worth noting that these states are often externally induced – by threat, aggression, the invasion of boundaries or the opening-up of new frontiers. Unfortunately it then transpires that the social tolerance of ambiguity defies operationalization. Bauman admits that he 'doubts whether groups, or categories of individuals, can be classified at all according to their global resentment of all kinds of equivocality alike. It is rather that (owing to the peculiarities of the group praxis or to individual idiosyncrasies) the foci of ambiguity most intensively resented or the types of sliminess most obsessively feared are differently located'.[50] Consequently, there is no way of validating the hypothesized association between the process generating 'uncertainty' and cultural change and, in turn, no hope of building an adequate *theory* of change on such shaky foundations or even of construing stability as ensuing in the absence of this process.

However, instead of taking a sustained interest in this problem, Bauman falls back on his undergirding principles of order to assert continuities in social ordering *despite* the plethora of cultural changes characterizing different societies at different times. 'Nothing but the formal universal of praxis, its "generative rules", constitutes the tough, invariant core of human history'.[51] Even if this could be substantiated, it would leave us incapable of explaining variations and change in non-core aspects of culture, and as it stands, we are left without an unequivocal method of identifying core-elements – if such there be.

While Bauman posited 'uncertainty' and 'ambiguity' as associated with cultural change, Giddens advances 'habitual action' as the process enhancing cultural stability. To correct the voluntaristic bias in his work, Giddens counterposes two factors which temper hyperactivity and volatility, that is his 'attempt to show the essential importance of tradition and routinization in social life'.[52] However, while a proper specification of constraints details who is limited, when and how, distinguishing these people from others with a vested interest in stability, Giddens only stresses that society forms actors in general terms by inducing habitual action. Yet 'habit' lumps together a variety of conditions promoting stability in a way which is not only methodologically unhelpful but is also positively misleading in its implication that *all* that is required for destabilization is a change of habit.

Thus, instead of a specification of degrees of freedom related to features of the Cultural System and the Socio-Cultural action contexts they create, Giddens provides a general account of 'deroutinization' detached from variations in cultural configurations. Primarily it is treated as a passive process in which external events (war, cultural contact, industrialization) disrupt ingrained habits. At most Giddens allows that there are 'critical situations' or 'critical phases' where the drastic disruption of routine corrodes the customary behaviour of actors and heightens susceptibility to alternatives. Then 'there is established a kind of "spot welding" of institutions that forms modes of integration which may subsequently become resistant to further change'.[53] Not only is the notion of a 'critical situation' dubious because of its *post hoc* designation but also this formulation begs more questions than it answers. What makes a phase 'critical' – does this not have to be described in terms of Systemic features and Socio-Cultural factors and are these not always germane to it? What produces subsequent resistance? Logically *this itself* cannot be attributed to the long term sedimentation of habits.

Ultimately it is the inability to untie the two levels constituting the duality of culture which prevents anyone employing this concept from grounding a theory of cultural stability and change in the interplay between properties of the Cultural System and characteristics of Socio-Cultural interaction. Protagonists of central conflation thus have to resort to rather vague universal processes whose presence or absence is broadly associated with stability or change rather than being able to come to grips with the conditions and mechanisms involved.

The different forms of conflation and their deficiencies: a summary of Part I

Conflation of the two levels of analysis – of the properties of the Cultural System with Socio-Cultural activities – always takes place in a particular *direction*. Chapters 2 and 3 dealt with two out of the three possible methods of conflation. This pair were the antithesis of one another for in them conflation took place in precisely the opposite direction: in the one the Cultural System was held to organize the Socio-Cultural level, while in the other Socio-Cultural interaction orchestrated the Cultural System. Thus in the downwards version, Cultural Systems engulfed the Socio-Cultural domain through the basic processes of regulation and socialization, while in the upwards version, the Socio-Cultural level swallowed up the Cultural System as the result of domination and manipulation. In brief, both versions treated one level as an epiphenomenon of the other level – they differed about which of the levels was held to be epiphenomenal.

However, epiphenomenalism is not the only way in which the more general process of conflation operates. It takes up two of the directions in which the 'logical' can be confounded with the 'causal', but this does not exhaust the methods available. There remains the third possibility, that of central conflation, where the two levels are held to be inseparable because they *mutually constitute one another*. We have, of course, already met with this version in the first chapter, for central conflation was the direction followed by the anthropological founders of the Myth of Cultural Integration. However, this does not mean that the central method of confounding the logical with the causal, in the cultural field, has become anachronistic and superseded by the two epiphenomenal versions. On the contrary, not only must elision at the centre remain a perennial logical possibility, it is also one which enjoys considerable sociological vitality at the moment.

In examining the upwards and downwards versions it was seen that the fundamental drawback to both was that by making the Socio-Cultural level *dependent* upon the Cultural System, or vice versa, they automatically precluded any two-way interplay between the levels. In both, this was because one level was rendered inert: instead of interplay there was the one-way domination of either the logical (downwards account) or the causal (upwards account). Consequently, the dependent element was robbed of the capacity to exploit or to influence the determining element, for it lacked the autonomy or independence to do so. This it was argued then blocked an adequate conceptualization of cultural dynamics and cultural conflict upon which a theory of cultural stability and change depends. Instead, as both approaches developed, their adherents produced increasingly crude unilateral accounts. The resultant theories had equal but opposite defects. In the one, the properties of the Cultural System were simply pushed around by the dominant group or interests in society; in the other, the cultural interaction of social groups danced to the Cultural System as puppet-master. If an adequate theory depends on examining the *interplay* between logical properties and causal processes, then this is predicated on some autonomy or independence being assigned to both Cultural System and Socio-Cultural levels. Failure to meet this predicate was considered to be the major error of both versions and one which became more glaring in the two as they progressively glossed over the entire issue which at least had been recognized at the origin of each version – by Sorokin and Marx respectively.

However, the errors attaching to conflation do not *depend* on epiphenomenalism, on rendering one level of the cultural field inert. Epiphenomenalism is not the only way in which logical properties or causal relations are deprived of autonomy and thus their interplay is denied. Any form of conflation has the same two consequences. In other words, conflation is the more generic error and epiphenomenalism is merely a form of it, or rather two particular cases of it. This is demonstrated by the remaining possibility, namely central conflation, where elision occurs in the 'middle'. This directional approach, which is reflowering at the moment, interprets neither the Cultural System nor the Socio-Cultural levels as epiphenomena of one another. Indeed this is a prime article of faith among modern proponents of central conflationism. Instead what happens here is that autonomy is withheld from *both levels* and has precisely the same result of precluding any examination of their interplay. Here properties of the Cultural System and Socio-Cultural activities are conflated because the logical and the causal are presented as mutually constitutive. As such, the two elements cannot be untied and therefore their reciprocal influences cannot be teased out in cultural analysis.

Thus, these deficiencies can be attributed to the conceptual act of conflation *per se*, regardless of the direction it takes. When examining the downward and upward versions of conflation it was consistently noted that they served to buttress the Myth of Cultural

Integration and it turned out that the new central variant was no exception to this. The Myth itself is never completely derivative from the method of conflation, rather methodology supports mythology *once* certain assumptions have been made about coherence itself. Thus, for example in both the epiphenomenal versions, rendering one level completely passive does eliminate half of the problem, for the inert side cannot be the *source* of incoherence. Nevertheless an independent assumption has to be introduced about the nature of the dominant level. Whichever it is, the property of coherence has to be attributed to it. Without this, epiphenomenalism merely points to co-variance between the degree of Cultural System integration and Socio-Cultural integration, it does not guarantee consistency. But once either the Key, the code or the dominant ideology was postulated as being free from significant contradictions, then conflation did indeed ensure that societal coherence followed, for the dependent level, because of its dependence, could not endanger it.

Exactly the same was true of the early anthropological accounts of cultural coherence. Once culture had been defined as a community of shared meanings, thus eliding the 'community' with the 'meanings', it really did not matter whether the assumption about coherence was attached to the consistency of meanings or the integration of the community, for the other element was not capable of independent variation – thanks to the notion of mutual constitution. The fact that both of these assumptions were endorsed in relation to 'cold' societies simply rendered one of them redundant and made the resulting cultural integration of primitive society an over-determined phenomenon. However, to state the case in this way is to use my conceptual framework, which insists on keeping the two levels, the logical and the causal, distinct and therefore allows one to speak of making two assumptions (whether the same or different) about them. It is not to use theirs. For if the Cultural System level and the Socio-Cultural level are indeed inextricably constitutive of one another, then only a single assumption can be made about the whole bundle – 'it' either is or is not consistent. Most early anthropologists were in no doubt about which.

The situation is identical in the contemporary version of central conflation. Because of the intimacy of their mutual constitution it is impossible to speak of high Cultural System integration and low Socio-Cultural cohesion or vice versa. Again, *if* an assumption is made, then it applies to the lot: the entire cultural corpus constitutes either order or chaos. It should be underlined that there is no compulsion whatsoever to make this kind of assumption in advance of empirical investigation (on the contrary, it is an unwarranted prejudgement, just as it is to construe this as an either/ or issue). Nevertheless the assumption of order (the emphasis on chronic recursiveness and the accentuation of speedy re-ordering), in modern societies, is indeed found in the thought of central conflationists and from there this (pre)judgement is supported by conflation itself. Hence we return full circle to the Myth of Cultural Integration. And, once back in its confines, there is no place for considerations about cultural disorder – its causes, its constitution or its consequences. These have been ruled out of court by theoretical *fiat*, but along with them has also departed any adequate theory of cultural change. Instead, as has been seen, we were left with holistic adaptations (downwards version) or manipulated alterations (upwards version) or unpredictable transformations (central version).

Part II works towards a theory of cultural dynamics by abandoning the basic assumptions underlying the Myth of Cultural Integration and underpinning the process of conflation. Turning one's back on the notion that culture is always and everywhere an integrated phenomenon then allows the concept of *cultural contradictions* to come into play. Replacing conflation by analytical dualism then permits contradictions and complementarities in the Cultural System to be examined in their interplay with different states of Socio-Cultural affairs. Together these reversals facilitate a reconceptualization of cultural dynamics which culminates in a theory of cultural morphogenesis.

Part II
Reconceptualizing cultural dynamics

5 Addressing the Cultural System

This chapter is devoted to the argument that a dualistic approach to cultural analysis can deliver the theoretical goods which conflationism failed to produce. Eventually I hope to show that the advantages of approaching the structural domain by distinguishing analytically between System and social integration also accrue in the cultural realm, yielding similar improvements in the explanation of stability and change. The whole enterprise thus looks towards a promising land where the theoretical unification of structural and cultural analysis might be accomplished.

This promise was one which none of the theorists already examined ever under-valued. It was the golden apple which the downwards and upwards conflationists thought they could grab by their familiar tactic of rendering one the virtual epiphenomenon of the other and which the central conflationists thought they could graft by their usual strategy of elision. But in theoretical development there are never easy pickings: like those who borrowed the mechanical analogy, the organic analogy or even the cybernetic analogy, the conflationists are punters with their 'formula' for breaking the bank. Thus my hope for unification is just that– not an expectation – and my procedure is correspondingly different. It is not an argument *by analogy* with a particularly fruitful form of structural analysis; it merely starts by making an analogous analytical distinction. The elements so distinguished then have to be conceptualized in their own terms and a set of theoretical propositions formulated about their interconnections. Succeeding chapters thus grope towards a reconceptualization of the cultural domain, utilizing analytical dualism, but until this has been completed it is impossible to determine whether the resulting propositions will parallel those advanced by Lockwood in the structural realm.

To approach the Cultural System (CS) from a dualistic perspective means talking about characteristics proper to it but distinct from the Socio-Cultural (S-C) level. Of course almost every word in that sentence is contentious. First, 'what is a Cultural System'? At this stage complex definitions with intricate subdivisions (for example, language, knowledge, beliefs, theories, semiotic patterns, conceptual schemes, signification systems, socio-symbolics and so forth) serve no point. At this point it is only necessary to know what kind of animal we are dealing with in order to make clear how we propose handling it.

To get off the ground it is sufficient to say that a Cultural System is held to be roughly co-terminous with what Popper called Third World Knowledge. At any given time a Cultural System is constituted by the corpus of existing intelligibilia – by all things capable of being grasped, deciphered, understood or known by someone. (The inclusion of components depends on this dispositional capacity alone, and not on whether contemporary social actors are willing or able to grasp, know or understand them, which are matters of Socio-Cultural contingency.) By definition the cultural intelligibilia form a system, for all items must be expressed in a common language (or be translatable in principle) since this is a precondition of their being intelligible. In other words they have at least one characteristic shared with at least one other component (language) which is also the precondition of them being a system.[1]

It follows that if Cultural Systems are defined in this way, then there is ultimately only one such System *at any time*.[2] For at any particular point in time, if an intelligible exists someone may come across it in a sense quite akin to (or actually involving) geographical or archeological discovery. By corollary, the use of Cultural Systems in the plural strictly refers to different time periods, such that the System at T_2 compared with T_1 is different because of the growth of knowledge, elaboration of beliefs, accumulation of literature and so forth.[3] Obviously this answer to the question 'one System or many?' will have to be strenuously defended against those who maintain that people of different cultures live in different worlds and who go on to deny the possibility of successful translation between them.

Equally it will be necessary to defend the existence of invariant logical principles for describing the 'characteristics proper to a

Cultural System'. If analytical dualism is to be sustained, let alone prove fruitful, then we need to be able to ascribe properties to Systemic relations themselves and in such a way that they do not collapse into the judgements of social actors. Otherwise Systemic properties would not remain 'distinct from the Socio-Cultural level'.

The procedure adopted again takes off from a Popperian springboard, namely his distinction between subjective mental experiences, on the one hand, and objective ideas on the other. That the ideas of, say, Buddha agree with those of, say, Schopenhauer is to say nothing about the subjective mental experiences of the two people – it is a *logical* statement: to say that the ideas of Schopenhauer were influenced by those of Buddha is to assert something about subjective mental experience – it is a *causal* statement. 'So we have actually these two different worlds, the world of *thought-processes*, and the world of the *products* of thought-processes. While the former may stand in *causal* relationships, the latter stand in *logical* relationships'.[4] The precise formulation of the above should be underlined: causal relationships are contingent (they 'may' pertain) whereas logical relationships *do* obtain. In other words, items in society's 'propositional register' *have to stand in some logical relationship* to one another. This is the case even if the relation between propositions[5] is one of independence: for this is logical independence ascribed in conformity with the same principles of logic.

Thus the Cultural System is composed of entia which stand in logical relations to one another – the most important of which are those of consistency or contradiction between items since *both* are vital elements in an adequate theory of cultural stability and change. Obviously no version of the Myth of Cultural Integration addressed logical relationships separately precisely because each elided the CS and the S-C levels.

Conflationists always talk about logical and causal connections simultaneously and judge the pair to make a coherent whole. The approach adopted here challenges all three elements which contribute to that judgement – that the Cultural System is free from logical contradiction; that the Socio-Cultural level exists in causal harmony; and that relations between the two are universally integrative. On the contrary, by distinguishing logical relations (pertaining to the CS level) from causal ones (pertaining to the S-C level) I want to make the interface between them an area of intensive exploration and theorization, the results of which should say much about the *conditions* of integration, without taking this state to be a foregone conclusion in the cultural realm. Cultural integration is demythologized by rendering it contingent upon the particular pattern of interconnections *at* the two different levels and *between* the two different levels.

The approach to cultural analysis which will be developed throughout Part II can thus be summarized in the following propositions:

(i) There are logical relationships between components of the Cultural System (CS).

(ii) There are causal influences exerted by the CS on the Socio-Cultural (S-C) level.

(iii) There are causal relationships between groups and individuals at the S-C level.

(iv) There is elaboration of the CS due to the S-C level modifying current logical relationships and introducing new ones.

Taken together they sketch in a morphogenetic cycle of Cultural Conditioning→Cultural Interaction→Cultural Elaboration. Cycles are continuous: the end-product of (iv) then constitutes the new (i) and begins another cycle of cultural change. Separating out the propositions in this way is prompted by the adoption of analytical dualism: its profitability must be judged by the explanation of cultural dynamics which results from it.

This chapter will concentrate exclusively upon proposition (i). To recap: A dualistic approach is being advocated for cultural analysis, such that only logical relationships pertain to the Cultural System and only causal ones obtain within Socio-Cultural interaction. The following discussion concentrates upon the CS level and its logical characteristics alone. Here *the prime concern is to establish the existence of objective contradictions and complementarities within a Cultural System, independent of any reference to the S-C level.* This is crucial given the working hypothesis that these Systemic features exert important influences *on* the Socio-Cultural level (point (ii) above) and, through it, on cultural dynamics in general. However, if exploring the effects of CS properties, like contradiction and consistency, appears profitable for explaining cultural stability and change, then it is necessary to conceptualize them in a particular way. It must be possible to talk about their existence cross-culturally, that is in formal rather than substantive terms. For if formal properties are inextricable from parochial contents, it will remain impossible to test the social significance of these Systemic features. Even if an effect was associated with the presence of a contradiction in a certain society, there would be no way of establishing whether the result derived from the particularistic contents of the inconsistency rather than being consequential upon contradiction itself. Since the aim is to advance more audacious hypotheses about the general (and neglected) effects of logical relations between CS components, these themselves will constitute the major concepts at this level.

Using the concept of 'contradiction' as the touchstone for discussion of CS properties, it is as well to clarify three claims about their status which are made here, but have proved extremely contentious in other quarters: (1) Ontologically it is maintained that there are objective relations of contradiction whose existence is not dependent on people's awareness of them; (2) epistemologically it is claimed that these can be known by reference to invariant logical principles the applicability of which is not relative to time or place; (3) methodologically it is argued that the problems involved in their cross-cultural identification are not intractable. Each claim will be spelled out briefly and in relation to the opposition that it has attracted. In every case these objections are so fundamental that were they to be sustained our four-point project for reconceptualizing cultural dynamics would have to be abandoned, having foundered on its first proposition.

(1) As an emergent entity the Cultural System has an objective existence and autonomous relations amongst its components (theories, beliefs, values, arguments, or more strictly between the propositional formulations of them) in the sense that these are independent of anyone's claim to know, to believe, to assert or to assent to them. At any moment the CS is the product of historical Socio-Cultural interaction, but having emerged (emergence being a continuous process) then *qua* product, it has properties of its own. Like structure, culture is man-made but escapes its makers to act back upon them. The CS contains constraints (like the things that can and cannot be said in a particular natural language), it embodies new possibilities (such as technical applications undreamed of in the pure theory on which they are based), and it introduces new problems through the relationships between the emergent entities themselves (the clash of theories), between these and the physical environment (mastery and ruin), between these and human actors (proud makers and brave openers of a Pandora's box).

Consequently contradictions exist independently of people noticing them or caring about them – indeed since there are an infinite number of situations upon which any theory may bear, it might well contain logical contradictions of which no one is aware. (Similarly, the relationship between a problem and a solution, which is an example of a compatibility, is ultimately divorced from whether anyone *does* understand it, though not from the capacity of someone *to do so*. Thus a soufflé recipe might not have been used by anybody living, but it would still work for the cook who eventually tried it.)[6]

The fundamental objection to this view comes from those who deny the very existence of Systemic (CS) properties like contradictions. What some of us present as such are held instead to be entirely derivative from the Socio-Cultural level, inadmissibly dissociated from it and only knowable through it. Winch provides a basic statement of this objection in his formula that the 'logical relations between propositions . . . depend on social relations between men'.[7] (This is of course a philosophical version of upward conflation, taking the typical S-C→CS form, and depending here on the elision of 'meaning' with 'use'.) Hence to Winch 'what is real and what is unreal shows itself *in* the sense that language has . . . we could not in fact distinguish the real from the unreal without understanding the way this distinction operates in the language'.[8] Therefore the last thing that we can do is to stand outside any community and aside from its linguistic conventions and then 'legislate about what is real for them or what counts as a contradiction in their beliefs'.[9] Thus Winch begins to pull the ontological rug from under the Cultural System, making it collapse into the Socio-Cultural realm. Later, more trenchant relativists seek to complete the process.

By now a repertoire of responses to this fundamental objection has been well rehearsed. To begin with, critics have regularly pointed out that although there is undoubtedly plenty of variation in the social relations between men, no one has provided a convincing demonstration that logical relations are capable of the same variability. Next, the use theory of meaning on which philosophical conflationism depends has attracted considerable criticism and the final indignity of being stood on its head – that is, the counter-claim that often the usage of concepts depends upon exploiting their lack of meaning, double meaning or ambiguous meanings.[10] In other words the intelligibilia are not always or even usually the dependent variable as the S-C→CS formula assumes *a prioristically*. Finally, anyone who repudiates the use theory of meaning cannot then allow meanings to be relocated in some other use context (like the works of the 'metaphorical' interpreter or the mystificatory practices of the dominant group), for the original objection would (re)apply. Thus if meaning can be separated from use, rather than just from the use of certain people, then meanings have to be granted ontological status. Such arguments provide support in *principle* for the approach adopted here which claims this status for *Systemic* contradictions and complementarities. However, they themselves have not been proof against comeback, as will be examined in the next section.

(2) Epistemologically it is assumed here that the question 'what counts as a contradiction?' can be answered by reference to the same criteria everywhere, namely those of formal logic:

Internal consistency is probably the most important and evident of these. The numerous 'laws' of mathematics and logic may be viewed as various elaborations on this most central rule of the symbolic world. We refer here not to a psychological need for consistency on the part of the person or persons who hold symbolic statements . . . but to the relationship among the symbols themselves which can be characterized and rearranged, drawing on the laws of consistency intrinsic to the symbolic world.[11]

Providing that the identity of the components can be established (that is, neither is too vague for us to know what p stands for) then the principle or law of contradiction asserts that nothing can be both p and *not-p*. Whether a particular relationship between CS items is found to be contradictory, consistent or independent in no way rests on claims made about it on the part of any group (for example the 'certainty' of a community of believers or the theoretical prejudgements of a body of investigators).

This notion of an invariant logical principle, which is universally serviceable for identifying cultural contradictions, came up against the basic objection that what *counts* locally as being contradictory is fundamentally relative. This arose partly from encounters with extremely 'alien' beliefs the very obscurity and peculiarity of which fuelled the idea that 'intelligibility takes many and varied forms.'[12] From this it has been argued that the same logical criteria cannot be used universally to identify contradiction and consistency, because there are varieties of logic ('different mentalities' are a variant of this). Broadly this objection makes contradiction a matter of local convention. So the objection runs, the 'criteria of logic' advanced here are not 'a direct gift of God, but arise out of, and are only intelligible in the context of, ways of living or modes of social life as such. For instance, science is one such mode and religion is another; and each has criteria of intelligibility peculiar to itself.'[13] Hence *within* science or religion, beliefs can be logical or illogical, as understood from inside that form of life, but because standards of logic vary with the context there is no question of making such judgements across the two domains. Consequently the cross-cultural designation of contradictions is not on because our logical terms of reference are ethno-centric.

Again a series of ripostes have been marshalled to undercut this objection. Basically these insist upon the necessary universality of logical principles and deny that they can be construed as matters of local linguistic convention. The first reason for this concerns their indispensability to alien thought itself and is summarized in Lukes's argument that were the concept of negation and the laws of identity and non-contradiction not operative in S's language then how could 'they even be credited with the possibility of inferring, arguing or even thinking? If, for example, they were unable to see that the truth of p excludes the truth of its denial, how could they even communicate truths to one another and reason from them to other truths?'[14]

The related line of defence stresses the necessary invariance of logic if any outsider is ever to grasp what is being asserted in alien thought and speech. Here Hollis has developed his well-known argument about the need for a 'bridgehead' of logic plus low-level perceptual beliefs in order to get translation going. A fundamental condition of identifying the most everyday belief is to find the local word for 'no', for only if we can establish to what they will assent and from what they dissent can we make the great leap to agreeing that the cow is indeed in the corn. A language has a word for negation only if those who speak it hold the truth of a statement to entail the falsity of a denial of that statement – that is if its speakers share the same formal principles. But if it is essential to suppose that they do for identifying their most mundane beliefs, then the same argument holds for grasping their more and most exotic ones. 'If the natives reason logically at all, then they reason as we do.'[15]

Such arguments provide support *in principle* for the cross-cultural conceptualization of contradictions through the use of invariant logical principles. Winch, to whom most of these replies were addressed, half concedes their force when admitting that 'the possibilities of our grasping other forms of rationality different from ours in an alien culture ... are limited by certain formal requirements centring around the demand for consistency'.[16] However, the relativist camp, far from being concessionary, has made a new and forceful case for the social co-variance of alternative logics which will require further examination.

(3) Undoubtedly there are methodological problems involved in the cross-cultural identification of Systemic properties like contradiction; the question is whether these are manageable or intractable. Obviously in advocating analytical dualism I shall be arguing for manageability (and putting forward management methods). What is worrying are the methodological reservations of thinkers like Gellner and Lukes who, having made so much of the running against relativism, then see practical difficulties in escaping from local context – dependence. Basically they consider the Cultural System to be so firmly embedded in its Socio-Cultural context that although the two levels may be accepted as analytically distinct, this is a theoretical abstraction and they cannot, or cannot usefully, be studied dualistically. The generic problem is that CS intelligibilia are considered to become vague, denuded and open to misconstruction if prised out of their local S-C setting. Generalizations based on formal similarities tend to be avoided because of the danger of substantive distortion involved. Consequently cross-cultural comparisons are severely limited though not entirely precluded.

Thus the procedure I am advocating faces some hefty opposition from those who argue respectively that Cultural Systems, first, have no independent existence to study; second, are socially relative and only understandable in their own terms; and, third, cannot in practice be examined separately from the S-C level. Although these objections are in descending order of antagonism to the position adopted here, they really represent an ascending order of difficulties to be confronted. In other words, despite the intransigent hostility of 'philosophical conflationism', I believe it can be defused by reference to the same manifest deficiencies which completely flaw its sociological equivalents. Conversely, methodological reservations based on the 'contextual-dependence' of Systemic properties cannot readily be brushed aside. These require a sustained argument that the problems involved in studying the CS in analytical separation from the S-C are solvable; that the profitability of solving them and then proceeding to theorize dualistically are much greater than was thought. Hence the next two sections are concerned with establishing, first, the legitimacy and, second, the viability of analysing the Cultural System as distinct from the Socio-Cultural level.

Resisting the revival of relativism

The revival of relativism by Bloor and Barnes[17] constitutes an imperialistic 'strong programme' which stakes an explanatory claim for the sociology of knowledge to the entire cultural domain. As with some forms of imperialism, its first task is to boot out the present inhabitants and the candidates for immediate extradition are those philosophers who have misled generations into believing that the truth, rationality, success or progressiveness of knowledge (colloquially known as TRASP)[18] had quite a lot to do with people holding it. The strong programme is therefore the anti-TRASP charter. War is declared on the latter in order to defend the fundamental principle of *symmetrical* explanation, namely that the 'same types of cause would explain, say, true and false beliefs'.[19] What is strong, therefore, about this programme is that it asserts the *social* character and *social* causation of *all* knowledge. Nothing about beliefs themselves plays any part in accounting for why they are held (or not) and this includes their relational properties like consistency or contradiction.[20] It advocates a total relativism – totally hostile to the present undertaking.

If this is so, if all beliefs are relative, then it follows that those held at different times and places are incommensurable. They have no common measure in terms of percepts, concepts, truth, reason or logic, for these are all matters of local idiomatic evaluation. 'The words "true" and "false" provide the idiom in which . . . evaluations are expressed, and the words "rational" and "irrational" will have a similar function . . . The crucial point is that the relativist accepts that his preferences and evaluations are as context-bound as those of the tribes T1 and T2. Similarly he accepts that none of the justifications of his preferences can be formulated in absolute or context-independent terms.'[21] There are *no* such terms. Consequently two components (propositions) from two different contexts can never be said to stand in a contradictory or complementary relationship to one another; nor can consistency within one cultural context be assessed from the standpoint of another. According to this programme we can really only talk about local preference for the non-contradictory – in local terms. To do otherwise, as in this work, entails two propositions which are firmly rejected by the strong programme:

(1)   It implies the existence of some non-conventional and trans-contextual criterion by reference to which contradiction or con-

sistency could be assigned to the relationship between CS items. The law of contradiction is used as that criterion in the present work, precisely because of the invariance of this logical principle. However, its universality is categorically denied from within the 'strong programme' and is indeed incompatible with thorough-going relativism.

(2)   It implies the ability to ascribe beliefs to social groups across time and space successfully. Both the necessity and the possibility of determinate translation are thus assumed, for they are preconditions of employing logical principles to attribute contradiction or consistency amongst or between alien beliefs. Translatability, however, is also strenuously repudiated by upholders of the 'strong programme': anything more than rough translation for rude purposes is inconsistent with relativism itself.

In order to justify my mode of addressing the Cultural System I have therefore to uphold the following two propositions against the arguments of radical relativism – first, the invariance of the law of contradiction; and, second, the possibility of successful translation.

The invariance of the law of contradiction

Obviously I believe that Mannheim kept his head rather than losing his nerve[22] when acknowledging that the universality of mathematics and logic was such that neither could be explained by reference to anything about the specific cultures in which they were adopted. In view of this, he quite rightly forewent a thorough-going sociology of knowledge. However, my particular concern is to restore certain logical principles to where Mannheim left them, thus retaining their serviceability in the attribution of properties like 'contradiction', 'consistency' and 'independence' to CS items located anywhere in time or space.

Bloor has provided a detailed attempt to demonstrate that 'mathematics is within the scope of the strong programme, and consequently that all beliefs whatever are within its scope'.[23] With Barnes identical arguments were later extended to logic, re-emphasizing the view 'that logical necessity is a species of moral obligation'.[24] The basic argument consists in denying any invariable principles within mathematics and it is held to be equally applicable to logic: instead both disciplines are socially co-variant.

Bloor gains elbow-room for socially caused variations in

mathematical thinking by noting (*contra* J. S. Mill) that maths is not a direct 'abstraction' from physical reality because any concrete situation (like pebble sorting) can be 'abstracted' in any number of ways. He then insists (*contra* Frege) that the gap between the amorphous physical situation and its 'characteristic' ordering is filled not by *universal* ideas but by a variety of social conventions which renders these patterns of ordering 'characteristic' to a given society in exactly the same way as traditional patterns of rug-weaving[25] and therefore equally variable between societies.[26]

The onus is thus on protagonists of the strong programme who conceive of mathematical necessity and, by extension, logical necessity, as social institutions, to supply us with convincing examples of 'alternative mathematics' and 'alternative logics'. Alternatives would be ones in which practitioners share a consensus on something we deem erroneous and where they engage in forms of reasoning which 'would have to violate our sense of logical and cognitive propriety'.[27] The problem with their examples, in both fields, is that these are intended to illustrate *variability*, which they always fail to sustain, while simultaneously these cases display brute *regularities*, which they never can explain.

Historically the fund of mathematical variation does not begin to match the range of socio-cultural variability, yet the former should parallel the latter if indeed it is socially determined – the original objection (p. 108) retains its force. Indeed, Freudenthal's detailed dissection[28] of the examples offered shows that rather than facing the prospect of returning empty-handed, the concept of an 'alternative' is elasticated in advance[29] and stretches well outside the realm of mathematical necessity to encircle various conventional differences which have no bearing on it.

One instance of this, particularly relevant to the law of contradiction, is Bloor's discussion of early Greek number theory since he concludes that this illustrates the relativistic status of the whole notion of contradiction. It is considered an 'alternative' because, as the generator of all numbers, 'one' was not regarded as a number itself – consequently resulting in claims about the oddness and evenness of numbers which today would be regarded as false. From this it is concluded that in the Greek classification '(d)ifferent things will therefore count as violations of order and coherence, *and so different things will count as confusions or contradiction*' (my emphasis).[30] But this only follows if the example constitutes a genuine alternative, which it does not. The question at stake here is one of *definitions* and their 'otherness' can readily be accepted as a matter of community consensus the local negotiation of which involves all sorts of non-mathematical considerations. What he is advancing are the different elements that can figure in arguments over the adoption of definitions and not alternative conceptions of the validity of mathematical proofs, entailing a reasoning which repudiates 'our' deductive logic but was deemed valid by the Greeks.[31]

Secondly, if we consider proofs themselves, then Bloor's concern to highlight stylistic variations in reaching conclusions only serves to obscure their common core: while he expatiates on the variability of methods used, he ignores the stunning *regularity* of the solutions produced by them. For instance, because Diophantus provided specific algebraic solutions rather than general methods of solution, his is hailed as a form of mathematical thinking that is as different from ours 'as the morality or religion of another culture is different to our morality or religion'.[32] Yet Diophantian solutions entail no violations of logic whatsoever and involve no error. Bloor ignores the latter point by 'not recognizing the simple fact that Diophantus's solutions to his problems, however he may have produced them, and although not general, are *correct*: the numbers cited satisfy the posed conditions'. On his account 'the occurrence of the same results within "alternative mathematics" – e.g. Diophantus's and ours – that are all "about" different societies, should appear as nothing short of a miracle'.[33]

In brief, since neither of these examples falls within the realm of mathematical necessity (which imposes no particular definitions as mandatory and no set style in which problems must be tackled), they cannot be construed as alternative conceptions of it. Consequently the original corollary to variability, namely that different things will count as contradictions to those like the early Greeks who were credited with an 'alternative mathematics', has not been sustained either.

Thus it becomes crucial whether Bloor's later work with Barnes is any more successful in breaking down either of the main barriers restraining relativism. In other words, can they deal with the apparent absence of a fund of 'alternative logics' which their strong programme requires, and with the presence of stubborn regularities in the principles of logic which seem to deny co-variance with social differences?

As a matter of fact, they claim, people do violate supposedly universal principles (like the law of contradiction) all the time. And these actions therefore withhold universality, compelling necessity or even practical utility from this rule of logic. Thus Barnes and

Bloor invite us to '(c)onsider all the familiar locutions we find of pragmatic value in informal speech which appear to do violence to formal logical rules'.[34] By implication logical variations are everyday occurrences, so thick on the ground that there is no need to appeal to obscure systems of formal logic, invented by academic logicians, as their source of 'alternatives'.

The examples specifically adduced in supposed violation of the law of contradiction are the following locutions: 'Yes and no'; 'It was, and yet it wasn't', 'The whole was greater than its parts'; and 'There is some truth in that statement'.[35] These instances, presented as the tip of an iceberg on which the law of contradiction breaks up daily, must be genuine cases where two propositions, p and not-p are simultaneously asserted to be true. Spurious instances of apparent contradictions have always been easy to generate by simply failing to specify crucial elements like time and place (when supplied, propositions like 'the sun is shining' and 'the sun is not shining' are not contradictories). As everyday locutions, all of those above are verbal shorthand, each of them is incomplete and therefore none of them is fully propositional. Barnes and Bloor argue that their occurrence in discourse is only intelligible in terms of contingent local determinants, as relativism demands, for as deviations from the rules of logic they cannot be explicated by reference to supposedly universal rules. On the contrary, inspection of the four instances cited shows that 'local contingency' or 'context-specificity' boil down to no more than the specification of omissions, mentioned above, as necessary *before* the universal rule can be applied at all *and* prior to knowing *whether* it is applicable.

The first two exemplars, 'Yes and no' and 'It was, and yet it wasn't', obviously had the appeal of (apparently) reproducing the classical form of a logical contradiction – the assertion of p and not-p. However, both are incomplete because they are shorthand responses in a dialogue which has been suppressed. Ask speakers to transcribe their replies into longhand and they may well supply their own specification, thus obviating any violation of the logical rule. Consider the following three questions which could have elicited either locution:

Q1   'Was a letter expected from your lawyer?'
Q2   'Is he an architect?'
Q3   'Was the show a success?'

Now allow the respondent the use of longhand and the contradictories can disappear:

R1   'Yes, my lawyer's letter was expected in the near future, but no I
        didn't expect it to get here by today.'
R2   'He is a qualified architect, but not a practising one.'
R3   'It was a very successful production but a commercial disaster.'

It is not only valid but essential to have shorthand locutions
transcribed, for only by examining the longhand version *can it be
known whether a rule like the law of non-contradiction is applicable to them.*
Often people will use formulae like 'Yes and no' or 'It was, and yet it
wasn't' to express their inability, unwillingness or unreadiness to
advance a propositional statement at all. They are other ways of
saying 'I'm not sure' and clearly when a locution expresses nothing
but uncertainty it cannot count as an instance of contradiction between two propositions, which is what violation of the law
entails.

The last instance, 'There is some truth in that statement' could be
applied to 'The whole was greater than its parts', and raises the old
problem that we often do talk of propositions being sometimes true
and sometimes false whereas the very definition of a proposition
excludes this possibility. Traditionally this difficulty is removed by
recognizing that if a proposition like 'The whole is greater than its
parts' asserts that this is *universally* the case, then the existence of any
exception to it serves to prove that it is false – *not* contradictory.
However, to produce an exception we have to complete the proposition by specifying what kind of whole we are talking about – for
example, a book is not of greater length than the sum of its pages – a
completion showing the falsity of the *universal* proposition.
Nevertheless it is true that the volume of frozen water is greater
than that of melted ice. Thus when it is said that a statement is
sometimes true and sometimes false, what is meant is that expres-
sions like 'the whole' may be completed in some ways which
express true propositions and in other ways which express false
ones. To say 'there is some truth in that statement' is to volunteer to
complete it in both of these ways!

Once again the strong programme confronts its dual difficulty –
the absence of common-or-garden variability and the indubitable
presence of regularity. On the one hand Barnes and Bloor do concede the general unacceptability of contradictions across the 'alternatives' examined and acknowledge the 'widespread acceptance of
deductive inference forms and the avoidance of inconsistency'.[36]
Immediately, however, they ask what *causes* people to avoid inconsistency and never whether anything regularly happens when they
are *confronted by* contradictions, as one would expect from a

trenchant version of upwards conflationism.[37] Thus biology is wheeled in to take care of these obtrusive regularities, working in tandem with sociology[38] which explains the variations. The social element is still considered vital because 'no account of our biologically-based reasoning propensities will justify a unique system of logical conventions'.[39] On the other hand, the varieties of logical system now appealed to are the various forms of non-standard logic developed in specialized academic contexts and not everyday abrogations of the law of contradiction. Moreover, these instances like intuitionist logic in the foundations of mathematics, proposals for three-valued logic in quantum physics and the four-valued logic of De Morgan implication, fail to impress a firm partisan of the strong programme, such as Mary Hesse, as *alternatives*. She freely admits that 'the possibility of different basic logics is not by itself very cogent, because it may be said that the examples we know of are all parasitic on standard logic.'[40]

Consequently Hesse supplements the programme with her own argument against any logical principle being a necessary condition of a belief system, without however significantly strengthening the relativists' case against the universality of the law of contradiction. Basically she asks how can the rationalist account for cases 'where we *have* found sign systems unintelligible(as in many anthropological and theological examples where the criteria of identity, for example, of men with birds, three persons in one, etc., do not answer to our criteria)',[41] but which we have eventually come to understand? So the argument goes, here are instances of contradictory beliefs which according to the rationalist should be unintelligible, yet we can come to understand them, but without resort to the rules which rationalists claim are indispensable to intelligibility, that is, utilizing the yes/no distinction. I shall argue that the two examples like the Brazilian Bororo's assertion that they are red macaws or the Trinitarian doctrine, do nothing to support her view that our understanding of these cases does not conform in obvious ways to the application of propositional logic or indeed, in the case of metaphors compares with the non-propositional use of language in poetry, that is an advocacy of artistic hermeneutics. On the contrary, the extent to which we can achieve an understanding of either belief is precisely the degree to which they remain obedient to the law of contradiction.[42]

Crocker's re-investigation of the Bororo[43] found that the male statement 'we are red macaws' hinged on the facts that these birds are kept as pets by Bororo women and that men are dependent on women, given matrilineal descent and uxorilocal residence. The statement is thus an ironic comment upon the masculine condition,[44] the understanding of which involved no extension of 'our language in unpredictable ways'[45] for we say much the same in English with the words 'hen-pecked'.

More generally, a claim to have rendered any metaphor or simile intelligible always depends upon 'cashing it in'[46] propositionally. It means identifying at least one aspect of something which is consistent with something otherwise unlike it. Hence the explication of poetry is *not* non-propositional – Burns asserts the truth of his love sharing attractive properties with the rose but also, we can feel confident, the falsity of her 'being prone to black spot' or 'benefitting from mulching'.

Trinitarian doctrine has a vast propositional history and unlike Hesse I maintain that it is only *publicly* understandable through it and not beyond it. The desperate struggles within the early Church (Doceticism or Gnosticism versus Arianism or Sabellianism)[47] are perfectly comprehensible as attempts to advance consistent doctrine which avoided the *perceived contradiction* of asserting 'three persons in one'. Precisely because the Bishops of the first centuries were clear about the logical rules of intelligibility, they were equally aware that each of the above propositional interpretations, though logically consistent, had unacceptable implications (for example, the Gnostic christological doctrine reduced the second person to a phantasm *because* of its consistency – 'if he suffered he was not God; and if he was God he did not suffer'). Thus rather than accept any of the doctrines mentioned, the Councils took their stand on a semi-propositional belief, namely a mystery whose 'meaning (i.e. the proper propositional interpretation) is beyond human grasp'.[48]

So, what sense can be made of Hesse's claim that we can extend our understanding and give intelligibility to that which the faithful themselves deem a mystery? Certainly not through treating the Trinity to any metaphorical or symbolist interpretation, for such were formally repudiated from the Creed of Nicea onwards. Just possibly (though most improbably in this case) an outsider may occasionally come up with a propositional interpretation previously unthought of but acceptable to 'the natives'. But when this is so, it is a point in favour of logical invariance.

Thus I am arguing that *public* understandability of Trinitarian doctrine is exactly co-extensive with the law of non-contradiction being upheld within it and lapses with its suspension. We can all comprehend the doctrine 'before' it is deemed mysterious, but when faith sets in there is no means of comprehension for the outsider other than by becoming of the faith and sharing its mysteries. We can all comprehend 'afterwards', that is when the authority of the Apostolic church becomes the basis of the belief. For then the rules of contradiction and consistency came back into play, to identify heterodoxy and define orthodoxy[49] and these applications of authoritative doctrine are matters again generally understandable. Public intelligibility, then, is a thread which breaks with the suspension of the law of contradiction. The suggestion that faith is penetrable is, of course, true because it can be embraced, but this does not advance Hesse's case. Since it is nonsense to claim that one professes more than one faith, it is even more nonsensical to predicate an extension of our understanding upon this state of affairs.

Nevertheless Hesse considers that she still has a decisive argument in hand against the proponents of invariance, namely that all they 'could possibly prove would be a purely formal similarity of logical structure between belief systems. If language is to convey information, then it does necessarily follow that it contains at least some binary distinction corresponding to yes/no, agreement/disagreement, true/false, that is, it contains elementary "bits" of information. But this says nothing whatever about the *content* of formal logical principles.'[50] But my foregoing argument requires nothing more than the acceptance of this purely *formal* similarity of logical structure between belief systems. For *substantive* cross-cultural differences may also be superficial; their mere existence provides no direct evidence for relativism. On the other hand, their *formal* similarities may give considerable theoretical purchase on the major question of whether there is any connection between the incidence of consistency or contradiction among CS items and patterns of cultural stability and change.

In her above conclusion Hesse believes that she has only given away something 'empty'.[51] Similarly, advocates of the strong programme doubtless believe that their major weapon remains in reserve. They, too, could indeed – again courtesy of biology – allow the invariance of the law of contradiction feeling secure that the last thing I could do is employ it as a tool in comparative cultural analysis. For its use is predicated upon the ability to ascribe beliefs to social groups across time and space which depends upon their translatability. Since the relativist denies the possibility of successfully ascribing beliefs through translation, he could grant me my universal rule safe in the conviction that I will only be able to use it locally. There is no harm in handing out a tool box, or benefit in receiving one, if the raw materials are then withheld.

The necessity of translation

Successful translation is a precondition of employing logical principles to attribute contradiction or consistency amongst alien beliefs or between those and our own. Unless we can feel confident in the beliefs we ascribe cross-culturally, nothing can be said about their relations. This confidence rests on the conviction that it is possible to produce adequate translations of the alien beliefs. Yet it is considered misplaced by founders of the strong programme, who are well aware that 'an anti-relativist argument' could 'be based simply upon the possibility of successful translation'.[52] For it is a necessary condition of a translation being correct that it matches sentences between languages with regard to truth-conditions, but for relativists of course this condition can never be met since what is true for the Nuer is not true for us. Thus as Newton-Smith puts it economically, 'the possibility of translation entails the falsehood of relativism. By contraposition, the truth of relativism entails the impossibility of translation.'[53]

The standard rationalist approach to translation, as formulated by Hollis, depends on the establishment of a bridgehead between two languages, that is 'a set of utterances definitive of the standard meanings of words'.[54] The investigator has to assume that 'he and the native share the same perceptions and make the same empirical judgements in simple situations', such as the cow being in the corn. These simple perceptual situations serve to anchor communication and to get translation going by allowing the researcher to identify standard meanings for everyday native terms, uncomplicated by cultural variables. Each of these key assumptions is denied in the strong programme, which seeks to blow up the pass between one language and another. Thus to Barnes and Bloor, 'learning even the most elementary of terms is a slow process that involves the acquisition from the culture of specific *conventions*. This makes apparently simple empirical words no different from others that are perhaps more obviously culturally influenced. There are no privileged occasions for the use of terms – no "simple perceptual situations" – which provide the researcher with "standard meanings" uncomplicated by cultural variables. In short, there is no bridgehead in Hollis's sense.'

Hence, advocates of the strong programme conclude 'perfect translation cannot exist: there can only be translation acceptable for practical purposes, as judged by contingent local standards'.[55] Were the common-sense protest made that the bridgehead serves perfectly well for getting over the channel and into agreement with any French farmer that 'the cow is in the cowshed'/'la vache est dans l'étable', this kind of relativist could respond *either* by questioning the perfection of the translation *or* by stressing conventions shared by the speakers.

In the first case he could insist that these two sentences were only *pragmatic* equivalents by underlining the lack of precise equivalence between, perhaps, 'cowshed' and 'l'étable', or 'byre' and 'vacherie'. However, this reply does not carry any particular force in relation to *translation* since these terms show regional variations of equal magnitude within the 'same' language (English 'cowshed', Scottish 'byre' and American 'cowhouse'). This fact does not perturb Hollis's argument which is about the 'conditions of the possibility of language in general'[56] – so what is true for two languages applies equally to one. But it does raise problems for the strong programme, for it carries relativism beyond the endorsement of 'many worlds', each with its own truths, towards an infinite regress of decreasingly small worlds, also incapable of exchanging truths.[57]

Alternatively, the relativist might suggest that the Common Market is really very parochial: an Englishman, a Scotsman and a Frenchman are all locals (joking cousins) but the strong programme acquires its teeth when it has something on which to cut them, such as really alien concepts couched in thoroughly foreign conventions. This seems to be the preferred line of attack since Barnes and Bloor maintain that 'the bridgehead argument fails as soon as it is measured against the realities of . . . anthropological practice'.[58] How?

They cite the case of Bulmer's work among the Karam of New Guinea where 'he found that many of the instances of what we would call "bird" were referred to as "yakt". He also found that instances of bats were included amongst the "yakt", while instances of cassowaries were scrupulously denied admittance to the taxon.'[59] These discoveries are taken to mean that the anthropologist had acquired the local culture of specific conventions. In other words, what Bulmer was doing was not the impossible act of translating: instead he was learning Karam conventions until he could pick out 'yakt' as well as they did.

Quite the reverse; the anthropologist had made standard use of the bridgehead in his fieldwork and without it could not have come up with the above translation, which is a quite different achievement from becoming a Karam amongst Karam. Bulmer started by going into the field through his first language (for as we will see a little later, he could not do otherwise), sensibly selected a simple perceptual object, 'bird', and soon established a rough correspondence between it and 'yakt'. He could then pin-point where the two terms did not overlap by proceeding just as Hollis suggests – pointing to a cassowary, saying 'yakt' and receiving a dissent sign, pointing to a bat, saying 'yakt' and commanding assent from the natives. All of which is *only* possible through the use of ostension and correction *in* 'simple perceptual situations'.[60]

The fact that there was imperfect equivalence between the two terms did *not* rule out use of the bridgehead, for there were enough of 'our' birds which were also 'yakt' to get the translation going and take it beyond the point sufficient for 'practical purposes', cropping up in the field, to a specification of the non-overlapping areas between the two classificatory terms. From there the anthropologist could move on to a task – open to the translator but not to the Karam amongst Karam – of trying to explain why there is cross-cultural variation in a classification. Note that Bulmer's paper which the relativists chose to use is entitled '*Why* is the cassowary not a bird?'.[61] Classifications in our own language change (whales were fish; whales are mammals), but changes in them are not matters of *mere* convention, there are always theoretical reasons for them. Far from the bridgehead argument being 'a plea for a single pure observation language' as the relativists claim,[62] it is the translator who takes Hesse's 'theory-dependence' of descriptive predicates[63] seriously, for only through translation can the theories be explicated and an account of why different ones are held by different language groups be offered; the relativist merely lives with the theory, mono-linguistically. He is finally shown up as the real parochial pragmatist. But the possibility of addressing these crucial *comparative* questions, as of translation itself, depends on the existence of a bridgehead – its roughness and readiness are quite immaterial.[64]

Not only will the bridgehead be rough and ready, it will also be floating rather than fixed. We advance with it in crab-like fashion, prepared to accept that the seemingly obvious truths we impute to aliens, in order to make sense of their behaviour, will undergo endless correction in the light of the evidential consequences of making such assumptions. The bridgehead is made and remade plank by plank – but which planks we change and which assumptions we alter is prompted by the resultant translations now making better sense than did their predecessors based on assumptions just discarded. Success in predicting the words and actions of those being translated confirms that the bridgehead can carry our weight. This is an empirical procedure validated by an empirical criterion.[65]

Indeed, one of the most persuasive forms of substantiation is supremely empirical, namely that we have not yet failed. No anthropologist has yet come home to report the aliens 'incomprehensible' and the supply of tribes is drying up. Yet it remains conceivable that one day we may fail, if not on this earth, at least with extra-terrestrials. Quite rightly this is of no great concern, for the unknown is the unknown and its relationship with *any* theory is identical – simply unknown. Moreover, the appeal to life on other planets performs no critical knife-work. Take for instance, Hesse's argument, intended to buttress the strong programme; to the effect that all cognitive terminology is 'relative to some set or sets of cultural norms' and that these 'might even *be as wide as biological humankind*, but if so, they would *still not* be rendered absolute or transcendentally *necessary in themselves*' (my emphasis).[66] This is completely off-target because the rationalist case is expressly and ineluctably predicated upon some version of the 'principle of Humanity'.[67] Rationalism is indeed earth-bound but this does not mean that it has feet of clay – even were it unable to translate standard inter-galactic. (Either the latter would remain incomprehensible or its translation would rely on the generalizability of some 'principle of intelligent life,' from or to humanity, which thus demonstrated its necessity.)

Translation is necessary to my undertaking because without it beliefs cannot be ascribed to people of other places and times, in which case nothing can be said about the formal logical relations between these beliefs. Yet relativists also want to assert things about alien beliefs – very different things like their relationship to local conditions and conventions, but assertions nevertheless – so why is translation not equally necessary to them? How can theories be identified as alternatives or indeed be known to be incommensurable if translating them is an impossibility? Their answer consists in circumventing the entire translation enterprise and making a direct assault on alien language and culture. As a strategy it could be called 'become as a child' or 'go native'. I shall argue that there are insuperable difficulties preventing the fulfilment of either injunction and that even if these could be spirited away it would not answer the above requirements and obviate the necessity for translation.

Before doing either, however, it is important to stress that quite regardless of whether my arguments prove convincing, their strategy *cannot* be a complete alternative to translation for it can only be attempted with other living people. Of its nature it deals only with the contemporary, with inserting oneself into some current alien context in order to assert its difference. By its nature it cannot then dispose of the necessity of translation when attempting to ascribe beliefs to the majority of cultural agents – for these are the dead. Furthermore although the strategy is doomed to incompleteness from the outset this does not make protagonists of the strong programme feel bound, in consistency, to eschew pronouncements on the mathematical thought of ancient Greeks, Enlightenment and Romanticism in eighteenth-century Europe, the politics of Second Empire France and so forth. However great the combined linguistic skills of these relativist authors, they could not have been exercised in discourse with the long dead.[68]

However let us now turn (1) to the strategy, (2) to its defects, and (3) to the reassertion of the necessity of translation.

(1) Hollis had defended the necessity of translation and developed his method of getting it going because where alien beliefs are concerned 'there is no more direct attack on meaning available'.[69] Barnes and Bloor question his premiss and seek a substitute for his procedure. To them

the fact is that translation is *not* the most direct attack on meaning that is available. It was not available, nor did it play any part at all, in the first and major attack that any of us made upon meaning when we acquired language in childhood. First-language acquisition is not a translation process, and nothing that is absent here can be a necessary ingredient in subsequent learning. To understand an alien culture the anthropologist can proceed in the way that native speakers do. Any difficulties in achieving this stance will be pragmatic rather than *a priori*.[70]

Problems now arise because the fact that nothing which is absent in first-language learning can be a necessary ingredient of learning a second one may be a true statement (though it is neither obvious nor testable), but it is then allowed to obfuscate the undoubted truth that the presence of a first language is an ingredient, willy nilly, in subsequent language learning. This leads to difficulties which are indeed *a prioristic* and not just pragmatic.

(2) As language speakers we simply are unable to become as pre-

linguistic children. One's mother-tongue cannot be cast aside, as your shoes can be left at the mosque door. Since all knowledge is conceptually formed (and therefore linguistically enshrined) then acquisition of a second language will inescapably be filtered through the first. Pragmatically, as anyone learning a foreign language knows, the ability to think in it comes fairly late on, *after* one has become proficient enough to stop translating-in-one's-head! Theoretically the idea of becoming like the pre-linguistic child is uncomfortably close to the mythological being whom Gellner dubbed the 'Pure Visitor', creatures capable of divesting themselves of their conceptual clothing[71] and surveying the cultural horizon from a decontaminated vantage point. Since linguistic strip-tease is not on, then it is an impossibility to 'go native' as the strategy recommends. It follows that, *a priori*, there is no alinguistic *entrée* accessible to existing language speakers.

Second, even were we to suspend these points for the purpose of argument, it is also the case that given the premises of the strong programme, there could be no 'return of the native'. For without the possibility of translation there is no way in which the investigator of alien beliefs who had gone through the business of 'becoming as a child' could then report back what the natives did believe. In other words, not only is there no *entrée*, there would also be no *exit*.

Anthropology would then become a curious study indeed. The role of its professors would reduce to saying: 'If you want to understand the X, then go and live with them for five years as I did and then we will talk about the X in the X's language, replete with its conventions, reasons, truths, that is we will then talk together as natives.' It would remain impossible to ascribe beliefs to the natives and communicate these to others – and things get curiouser yet. For if one tries to imagine this capacity to move from one linguistic skin to another, stating and believing one thing in one language and something incompatible in another, then if translation is indeed an impossibility, one could not know that one was doing this oneself. In short, on the strong programme, *nothing relational* can be either privately known or publicly communicated about alien beliefs.

(3) Hence we come full-circle back to the necessity of translation. For as Newton-Smith argues 'if translation lapses so does the ascription of beliefs and the explanation of behaviour in action terms'.[72] It becomes impossible to describe the behaviour of aliens as constituting particular actions or to explain it by reference to the beliefs and desires producing them. Translation cannot be set 'aside as

something problematic for a relativist while going on to talk about beliefs and actions as if these notions would remain unproblematic'.[73] If we cannot ascribe beliefs the end-result is that sociology has *no* role to play in explaining action. This must be handed over to behaviourism, materialism or indeed biology – in short, anything which excludes reference to the determinate beliefs of human subjects. Thus the strong programme ends up as the vanishing programme.

The problem of contextual dependence

However it is admittedly the case that some of those whose work has been drawn on to criticize the conflationists and the relativists also draw back from the notion of advancing formal cross-cultural propositions about the existence, inter-play and effects of contradiction and consistency. The reason for this is because, without retracting anything about the objectivity or knowability of contradictions, generalizations are resisted because the *methodological identification of a contradiction is held to be context-dependent.* Stated crudely, they are saying there is nothing much wrong with my enterprise except that it cannot be done. So the next question is whether contextual dependence does indeed constitute a total road-block? By an irony which is sweet, if it works, I will argue that this is only the case if the Cultural System and Socio-Cultural levels are not kept analytically distinct – the vindication of my position depends on sticking to it.

The crux of this problem is *how* methodologically one can 'assert the existence of a contradiction'. It arises from the simple and uncontestable fact that two cultural items (at the CS level) may appear contradictory in isolation but may not be so if considered in context. One reason why unease flares about projects like my own is that if evoking the context can remove the contradiction and yet the context itself is socially specific, how can anyone advance cross-contextual propositions? In other words, contextual dependence threatens to drive a different wedge, but still a wedge, between 'asserting the existence of a contradiction' (universally) and 'what counts as a contradiction' (locally). The problem unfolds as follows:

(i)   Some contextual reference is needed precisely because cultural components are interrelated with one another. Usually their interlacement with others has to be addressed in the very process of identifying them and this is necessarily prior to saying anything about the nature of inter-connections with yet other components. Thus for instance, the religious notion of 'salvation' is only identifiable in the context of related concepts like 'sin', 'redemption', 'grace' etc. Consequently, for any two cultural items under consideration, we have to take into account the respective contexts of both and *also* the context *against which* they are judged to be contradictory or consistent. Too much local context and there ends up being so little in common that comparability goes out of the window.

(ii)   Gellner is undoubtedly right that the difficulty of letting the context in, as one must, is the absence of flood gates. For there is nothing in the context itself which dictates just how much of it is relevant to any proposition, concept or unit, or which regulates how we should select from it. The problem is that how much is taken in can be decisive for our judgements: too little contextual reference and many pairs of items appear absurdly contradictory (just as ripping two statements out of context in a book and then juxtaposing them can be used by a reviewer to make any author look ridiculous). Conversely, too much contextual charity and almost anything can be freed from the charge of inconsistency. The problem thus is that we need to make reference to the context but appear to lack rules specifying what can properly be let in and what can justifiably be kept out. In Gellner's words '(c)ontextual interpretation is in some respects like the invocation of *ad hoc* additional hypotheses in science: it is inevitable, proper, often very valuable, and at the same time dangerous and liable to disastrous abuse. It is probably impossible in either case to draw up general rules for delimiting the legitimate and the illegitimate uses of it.'[74]

(iii)   Finally, the death-trap opens up. Without rules delineating which part of the context may be taken into account, then everything can be rendered consistent simply by invoking the convenient part or enough of it. Consequently contradictions make their exit, the social role of inconsistency disappears and with it much of our understanding of cultural change which 'may occur through the replacement of an inconsistent doctrine or ethic by a better one, or through a more consistent application of either. It equally blinds us to the possibility of, for instance, social control through the employment of absurd, ambiguous, inconsistent or unintelligible doctrines.'[75] Certainly in specific cases it may be possible to *argue* that the over-charitable interpreter, committed to absolving the concepts he is examining from the charge of logical incoherence, is either misdescribing the social context or manipulating the context in order to make sense of the beliefs.

Sometimes, as Gellner illustrates, to make sense of the concept is to make manifest nonsense of the society, the functioning of which may indeed depend upon the use of incoherent 'bobility' type concepts. At other times it may be possible to show that the context wheeled in to make sense of beliefs actually makes a mockery of them. Take a case where social explanations are adduced to remove inconsistencies in beliefs: contradictions in Zande accounts of witchcraft. Some maintain these can be disposed of by placing them in the context of their social effects (ritual statements are 'about' the power structure of Zande society). But, as Hollis argues, since a bewitched Zande does *not* simply believe that he has offended a higher authority, he believes he is the victim of witchcraft, this use of context implies that believers do not know what their beliefs are about and that what they think they believe is misguided.[76]

The problem with contextual charity is partly that cases of mismanagement are not always so blatant as the above. Overcharitability may *not* be detectable through the mangling of social practice or the misconstruction of beliefs, for the above is as much an instance of bad sociology as it is an illustration of the point in question. A good but charitable sociologist may get away with murder but he will not leave incriminating evidence behind. And if he does not, then on what can he be indicted? For, more profoundly, the problem is that in the absence of rules governing appeal to the context there *is* no dividing line between excessive benevolence and legitimate reference. This is the ultimate death-trap: anything can be rendered consistent provided only that it is well done. The expulsion of contradiction from sociology merely depends on a high quality manipulation of context; and since charity and quality are not mutually exclusive, the flood gates stand ajar.

I want to suggest that this problem basically arises from the failure to maintain a working distinction between the logical and the causal, and that it is capable of solution. These arguments will be explored by returning to Gellner's paper on 'Concepts and society', in which he battles with the problem of too much contextual charity, seeks laudably to rescue the notion of cultural contradictions, but in the end cannot yield up a cast-iron restraint for over-benevolence which would prevent inconsistencies from being plausibly explained away. It seems to me that the reason why he cannot erect an effective flood wall is that, like the theorists taken to task, he too does not differentiate analytically between properties of the Cultural System and those belonging to the Socio-Cultural level.

(1) Gellner begins with the perfectly valid point that 'concepts and beliefs do not exist in isolation, in texts or in individual minds, but

in the life of men and societies'.[77] However, this fact does not itself enjoin us to analyse cultural items in any particular way. It contains no methodological injunction either

(i)   proscribing their examination 'in isolation' from life (CS level), or

(ii)   insisting that they be examined at their nexus with social life (CS + S-C levels).

(2) However, Gellner seems to think that it does, or at least that there are good reasons for abjuring (i) and pursuing (ii). Thus he talks of avoiding (i) because of the 'unrealistic literal-minded scholasticism' of 'textual' (that is, CS) analysis, in contrast with 'the unfortunate need to *interpret* just what the concepts in question meant to the participants', which implies endorsing (ii) (that is, the CS + S-C approach).[78] This need apparently arises from the fact that texts and sayings may be broad, vague and fragmentary with ill-defined logical implications for conduct. Its corollary is taken to be that we therefore must interpret the meanings they have for people since these are the key to their conduct. I cannot contest what Gellner says about many 'texts' but I do challenge his implicit contrast with 'meanings'. It simply cannot be assumed that because some or many 'texts' are vague that meanings *must* be more precise. They can be vague too. Nor is 'precision' the preserve of the Socio-Cultural level; a geometry text is just the opposite of being broad, vague or fragmentary and has the clearest implications for conducting geometrical exercises, but its meaning to the average schoolboy is probably the messiest hodge-podge. It is therefore at the very least a matter of *methodological choice* to eschew the analysis of 'texts', procedure (i); and not a question of *methodological necessity* to plunge into the interpretation of 'meanings', procedure (ii). However Gellner does dispense with (i) and proceeds with (ii).

(3) In then interpreting what concepts meant to participants Gellner invokes *two different aspects of context* in elucidating their concepts and beliefs. These are the social context as:

– other ideas (CS logical relations)
– other people (S-C causal relations)

This of course is an inevitable corollary of adopting procedure (ii) which deals with both CS + S-C levels for this makes the two kinds of context pertinent.

In turn I want to make three points against this methodological procedure: that it is *unnecessary* to Gellner himself for the arguments he wants to advance about the existence of contradictions; that it

impoverishes the sociological examination of the role played by contradictions; and, most seriously of all, that this is what *prevents him
from firmly closing the door on over-charitable contextual interpretation.* First,
then, in so far as Gellner is seeking to show the existence of conceptual contradictions (in opposition to the charitable contextualists
who always end up asserting the consistency of beliefs), I consider
procedure (ii) unnecessary, for the demonstration of the contradictions in question only depends on contextual reference to *other
ideas.* Thus, for example, the Berber concept of *igurramen*, people
blessed with prosperity and capable of conferring this on others by
supernatural means, attributes a clutch of characteristics to its
possessors 'including magical powers, and great generosity, prosperity, a consider-the-lilies attitude, pacifism and so forth'.[79]
Clearly contradiction exists here, but purely because these properties are *logically* incompatible with one another. As Gellner
comments 'an *agurram* who was extremely generous in a consider-
the-lilies spirit would soon be impoverished and, as such, fail by
another crucial test, that of prosperity'.[80] Equally it is merely a logical
corollary that those credited with the full clutch of characteristics
cannot possess all of them if they are to get by. Here a consultation of
the 'texts' is not unrealistic scholasticism; it is all that is necessary to
demonstrate 'contradiction'. In other words, this can be done
exclusively at the Cultural System level. It is true that Gellner is
interested in some other related questions, such as the divergence
between concept and reality in relation to *agurram*-hood being
essential for the working of the social system, but this would seem
to depend upon precisely the CS/S-C distinction that I am advocating. For the 'reality' of being an *agurram* is a matter of causal relations with other people and these effects therefore can be analysed
at the Socio-Cultural level.

Secondly, it follows that this treatment of the cultural context is
one which *impoverishes* the problems that can be addressed (that is,
the *relation* between Gellner's own above two concerns— the existence
and the effects of contradiction). By including in the context what it
means in practical life to be an *agurram* (bearer of a social role replete
with logical contradictions) is in fact methodologically to run
together the concept and reality— that is the co-existence of inconsistent demands and the entirely different question of how people
live with them. Thus Gellner writes that 'fieldwork observation of
igurramen and the social context in which they operate has convinced me that, whilst indeed *igurramen* must entertain lavishly and
with an air of insouciance, they *must* also at least balance their

income from donations from pilgrims with the outgoings from entertaining them, for a poor *agurram* is a no-good *agurram*'.[81] But by making the (S-C) need to cope part of the context of *agurram*-hood (they *must* balance their books), this contextual imperative removes some extremely interesting Socio-Cultural questions. It prevents the examination of *how*, by what strategies, ploys and financial chicanery the successful *agurram* manages to balance his accounts, and by doing or not doing *what* the no-good *agurram* fails.

In essence we do not want to lose the problem of how the same inconsistency is coped with by different sets of people, for this denudes understanding of Socio-Cultural mechanisms and machin-ations. But this is lost if strategic action is mixed up with logical rela-tions as part of the bundle called 'context' (that is, logical relations–problem situation–practical solutions). This bundle is indeed its 'meaning to participants', but we should unpack it. Cer-tainly when a contradiction is detected it becomes a key task to explain how it is possible that this inconsistency does not appear as such or is made tolerable in daily life. This is a vital issue but its detection and exploration depend on maintaining analytical dualism in one's methodological approach. Furthermore, as is always the case, interplay between the levels gets lost too. For ex-ample, it appears an intriguing question how the (S-C) failure of an *agurram* to cope is squared with his supposed (CS) selection by God and also how many no-good *igurramen* (S-C) it takes for divine provi-dence to be queried (CS)?

Thirdly, and most important of all, I think that what stops him from shutting the floodgates on overwhelming charity really and effectively is this attempt to distinguish what people 'really mean' (by reference to a conjoint CS/S-C context) from what they 'text-ually' say they mean. What Gellner himself is 'anxious to argue is that contextual interpretation, which offers an account of what assertions "really mean" in opposition to what they seem to mean in isolation, does not by itself clinch matters. I cannot arrive at determinate answers (concerning "what they mean") without doing a number of things which may in fact pre-judge the question: without delimiting just which context is to be taken into consider-ation, without crediting the people concerned with consistency . . . or without assumptions concerning what they can mean.'[82] Yet hav-ing argued this he also argues for a fuller use of the contextual method of interpretation, fuller in the sense that it allows for the possibility that what people mean may sometimes be absurd. But in the absence of rules governing contextual invocation what protection does this offer against the above charitable deficiencies? Only, ultimately to Gellner, the maintenance of a 'vivid sense of the possibility that the interpreted statement may contain absurdity'.[83] But if, as seems likely, charity atrophies this 'vivid sense', what then? Merely an irresolvable haggle over interpretation between the universally benevolent and those who have kept a certain acerbity – when this happens we are all of us in the pit. For if there are no rules about what parts of the context it is legitimate to invoke there is no court of appeal against improper usage.

A suggested solution to the problem of contextual dependence

What the last few pages were concerned to establish was basically that it is only possible to have a workable concept of 'cultural contradiction' if the distinction between the Cultural System and the Socio-Cultural level is maintained sociologically and sustained methodologically. Gellner, it seems, did come to hold a very similar sociological distinction indeed, for later on he writes that: 'Despite these difficulties inherent in using the notion of a "system of belief" instead of the individual or group credited with holding it – difficulties for which there may be no formal solution – I nevertheless think it essential that the great Dividing Line be drawn in some such terms.'[84] My suggestion is that the problem of drawing the dividing line is made out to be worse than it is because Gellner's *méfiance* of 'texts'[85] rules out a practicable *method* for using analytical dualism.

In 'Concepts and society' this resulted from the first step – rejecting 'textual' analysis in isolation from life in favour of interpreting 'meanings' in social life. For 'meanings' invoke both levels (CS + S-C) and therefore the context of interpretation also involves both levels. The rest of the problem stems from that: from the mixing of the logical and the causal. Logical contradictions become confused with and concealed by social strategies for coping with them when they are treated as a bundle – social explanations can be trundled in to dispel seeming logical inconsistencies and there is no effective way of shoving them out.

Put even more succinctly the 'problem' of contextual-dependence arose from trying to do too much at once. It stemmed from attempting to deal with the Cultural System and Socio-Cultural life simultaneously *because* they *are* intertwined. Instead I suggest that the death-trap can be skirted by proceeding more slowly.

Specifically this involves examining the Cultural System first, in isolation from social life, before addressing the Socio-Cultural level and then the relations between them. By doing this, by separating 'sayings' and 'meanings' in Gellner's terms, it does seem that we can solve the problem posed by contextual-dependence, namely what part of the context can be legitimately brought in and what portion justifiably kept out. The difficulty which Gellner was left with was due to the absence of any such general rules; but in this he gives us the hint that the way out of the difficulty is to find a rule.

My next step is thus to adduce such a rule. But I must make it crystal clear that this only applies to the Cultural System level and only works if this level is rigidly, though only analytically, separated from Socio-Cultural life. Quite simply, if the Cultural System (CS) is held to be constituted of nothing but objective items, 'texts' and the *logical relations* between them, then the only part of the context which is relevant to them, because of their dependence on it, are the *'other ideas'* to which they are related. In sum, if we clearly distinguish between the two cultural levels, the Systemic and the Socio-Cultural, then we can also differentiate between the aspects of context – 'other ideas' and 'other people' – on which the former and latter depend respectively. Schematically this can be represented as shown in Table 1, the key point being that the logical and the causal are systematically separated.

Table 1

Cultural level	Context on which dependent	Relations between them
Cultural System	Other ideas	Logical
Socio-Cultural	Other people	Causal

Resistance might be expected from others who maintain that the two levels are so inextricably intertwined, because of the constant interchange between them, that their separation is not on even as a matter of methodological convenience. That this view is ill-founded can be shown by a side-glance at those insisting most strongly on the tightest bonding between 'sayings' and 'meanings', that is, proponents of the 'family resemblance' approach to human categorization who insist on the continuous role of natural-language speakers (S-C) in defining what 'spread of resemblances' is carved out by a particular word, concept or idea (CS). Their reaction should presumably be along the following lines: the constituents of 'texts', indeed one of their most basic, namely words themselves, are constantly changed through usage – by the erosion of old and the accumulation of new attributes picked out by them. Thus words (regarded as CS entities here) are subject to ceaseless grinding at their margins by (S-C) use and this incessantly dissects the world in new ways and hence continuously inscribes these changed meanings on the CS register. Since the latter is never free from (S-C) buffeting, it would therefore be artificially frozen by any methodological attempt to examine it separately.

However, none of this actually precludes the analytical separation of levels which is fundamental to the rule I am seeking to advance, provided that two features of the process they describe are fully recognized by those who approach lexical categorization in this way. The first involves acceptance of the accumulating body of evidence that categories do have 'core features', for example, 'focal colours', 'natural prototypes', 'best examples' or 'basic-level objects',[86] which have now been investigated in relation to a wide range of taxonomies. The implication of this work is the existence of anchorages constraining the potential 'spread of resemblances' to movements akin to a boat on its mooring, rather than the volatile lexical dissections suggested, for example, by the original Whorfian hypothesis.[87]

The second concerns the equally important point that changes in the 'spread of resemblances' named by a particular word not only 'revolve' around core attributes but also 'evolve' over time. Consequently it is only necessary to insist upon the temporality of our analytical separation (word X covers Y attributes at T_1), for any incompatibility to disappear, since our methodological procedure in no way denies changes through usage – it only stresses that they take time. In general the continuousness of a process must *not* be confused with the instantaneous registration of its effects (for confusion itself, resistance or thresholds may be involved) and this is especially so since speakers often disagree over changes of usage.

Indeed, though this is not our main concern, we are now well on the way towards a micro-morphogenetic framework for analysing interplay at the lexical level. Thus 'one influence on how attributes will be defined by humans is clearly the category system already existent in the culture at a given time'.[88] This would constitute the CS conditioning which confronted natural-language speakers, whose subsequent S-C disagreements about word usages could then result at T_2 in a new 'spread of resemblances', provided that these lexical changes did not tug too hard at their moorings, that is did not negate the co-occurrence of attributes in the perceived world.

In sum, the macroscopic effrontery of our proposal to separate textual ideas (CS) from people's meanings (S-C) turns out to be of utility to the micro-concerns of those whose first reaction was to flinch away from it. However, let us now return to the main issue, namely the question of generating a rule to regulate contextual-reference, which does indeed depend upon separating the two aspects of any ideational context – the CS and the S-C.

When 'asserting the existence of a contradiction' (CS) the rule which is invoked is that *only* reference to 'other ideas' upon which the items in question logically depend, or to which they can be shown to be logically related may be admitted to dispel the contradiction which appears when the said items are taken in isolation. Thus a contradiction exists if two CS items are logically inconsistent with one another and this inconsistency cannot be removed (reduced to an apparent contradiction) by elucidating their logical connection to another/other CS item(s). A simple example is the apparent contradiction between the proposition that water boils at 100°C and the observation that it does not do so at the top of a mountain or the bottom of a valley, which is resolved by showing that both are logically related to two contextual items, temperature and pressure. Then the first proposition is rewritten as 'water boils at 100°C, standard temperature and pressure', and this specification of the law then embodies the observations which appeared to contradict it.

To be more precise, the rule entails that not all 'other ideas', but propositions alone are relevant when 'asserting the existence of a contradiction'. For contradiction or consistency can only be attributed to propositions, that is to sets of statements which are either true or false (though with metaphysical propositions like 'there is a God', we may never be able to prove that it is one or the other, only that it cannot be both). *Propositions, as opposed to sentences or utterances or many of our thoughts, cannot be ambiguous, that is true in some interpretations and false in others. Thus where the attribution of contradictions is concerned, the only pertinent part of the cultural context is the propositional itself.*[89]

Clearly, however, we want this part to be as big as possible, because it is the pool from which items are drawn to resolve apparent contradictions and therefore the undesirable effect of settling for a smaller reservoir is that other 'societies' will be made out to be (i) more prone to inconsistency than they are, and, (ii) than we are – since we all know our own pools best. Thus one methodological objection to adopting our rule is that by limiting reference to the CS context of 'other ideas', and propositional ones at that, we have automatically and artificially reduced the type and number of items which can legitimately be consulted – because many of them do not come in the form of propositions. In short, a critic might say that our rule produces a job specification for a small pool which will boost inconsistencies and give a boost to ethno-centricism.

I agree that much of the time 'other ideas' are not presented and packaged to meet the logician's requirements (that is, scientific texts and religious creeds probably are exceptional). More usually we do confront them as sentences, utterances and recorded fragments but in fact the last thing that our rule enjoins is that they should be sent packing immediately because they are not fully propositional (that is they are capable of being interpreted in several ways and therefore appear to assert several things at once, or one of several things without it being clear which). On the contrary, the methodological injunction associated with our rule is 'make the fullest possible reference to the admissible context in an attempt to complete propositions'. Although this context remains firmly restricted to 'other ideas', it is recognized that any approach leading to errors (i) and (ii) above is both self-vitiating and socially vicious and therefore the rule is completely resistant to decontextualization.[90]

Ironically the same cannot be said for many who would oppose our rule, and particularly those adept at extricating intelligibility from the oddest sayings. For these are the arch-decontextualisers – absorbed in displaying their own cryptographic virtuosity (despite the odds) rather than demonstrating the common sense of others (despite oddities of expression). Witness here the common abuse of anthropology by certain philosophers who perversely pluck an enigmatic saying from an exotic text and then speculate freely on what the natives could conceivably have been getting at. Here we should note that the context evoked to disclose intelligibility is the philosophers' own and not the natives', for the procedure is to make the armchair creak under the pressure of speculation rather than to get out of it and consult every available text of native sayings, or if need be, go into the field and ask if the locals can supply contextual clarification (that is, more sayings). Indeed this is the main attraction of using anthropology – full reference to the complete ideational context is often ruled out because it is impossibly expensive to track down or, even better, is irretrievably lost. (Thus the prizes go to speculative ingenuity which 'shows' that all native talk about contents of cooking pots is really the statement of cosmological recipes, or better still that cosmologies are actually about raw carrots.) But puzzles can always be invented by decontextualization from the 'other ideas' which give them sense (see note 44), and to many of 'us' most statements in modern science seem just as enigmatic because their ideational context is unfamiliar. Yet in that area, fullest reference to the 'other ideas' available at the time is what makes sense of (false) assertions about the existence of 'phlogiston' or the 'embryo as homunculus', *not* their transposition into a modern context where the only way of saving their perpetrators from the charge of inanity is to foist some meaning on them which cannot be disavowed from the grave.

In sum, the fullest possible application should be made to the CS context in order to rescue intelligibility from ambiguity and to obtain the highest warranted ratio of propositions to utterances. Methodologically this may mean asking the subjects to supply contextual clarification by amplifying on previous sayings or commenting on existing texts. Where the subjects are not extant this implies an even closer scrutiny of texts with the same aim in view – an explication of what else they knew and what other information was available to them – for this was the only material from which they could fabricate both true and false propositions and therefore from which contradictions and consistencies could arise.

Exactly the same is the case for subjects *own* sayings about their Socio-Cultural environment which are as admissible as contextual referents as any 'other ideas' about anything else (and can be used in the same way to complete one another). The fact that what was known to them or what they could find out about their social environment might (and this is not at all self-evident) more obviously have been manipulated by 'other people' than what they could know about their physical environment is of no concern in the assertion of a contradiction. For all propositions are based on restricted material and all restrictions were caused by something, but the logical relations which ensue between them are emergent properties and thus irreducible to the biological, geographical or Socio-Cultural causation involved. We are dealing with the *results* of limited knowledge and it is therefore the fact of the limitation which counts, not its source.

Thus the methodological injunction remains – 'incorporate from the ideational context only that which is needful to complete propositions or to demonstrate that a given "saying" is non-propositional. If this is successfully performed for two items, then, assuming the adequacy of translation and the invariance of logic, it becomes possible to characterize the relations between them as contradictory or consistent. In the process we must thus expect to encounter some items, which although meaningful to (certain) subjects, are not of propositional status. These have been the main source of the great interpretative debate between the 'intellectualists' and the 'symbolists'[91] which is of relevance here in so far as both sides have assumed that they are indeed dealing with native propositions, but what is being asserted as true or false is a matter for theoretical determination by the investigator. (This is yet another instance where 'sayings' and 'meanings' are compacted, with the familiar unhelpful consequences.)

Instead I would follow those who have maintained that we confront a difficult methodological problem rather than a choice between theoretical alternatives. In this connection Sperber has argued very persuasively that people hold their *factual* beliefs (which are true or false) quite differently from their *representational* beliefs (which do not pretend to propositional status). Neglect of this distinction is a systematic methodological deficiency:

Most accounts of beliefs are written as if the utterances of so-called informants should all be taken on the same level, irrespective of whether they are produced in answer to the ethnographer's queries, during ordinary social intercourse, on ritual occasions, in judicial proceedings, etc. All native utterances get distilled together; their quintessence is then displayed as an homogeneous world-view where, indeed, no epistemological differentiation of beliefs occurs. This, however, is a fact of ethnography, not of culture.[92]

Lukes also presses his argument to the same conclusion. The problems of how beliefs are held and should be interpreted involve methodological difficulties but this does not render them matters for theoretical arbitration. Instead these questions 'are susceptible to empirical investigation. And if no given piece of evidence is decisive between alternative interpretations, some crucial mass of it will not fail to be so.'[93] Methodologically, then, it is not easy to get at the propositional uncluttered by a mass of Socio-Cultural overlay belonging both to those investigated and imported by investigators as part of their theoretical baggage. But this only makes the process of disentanglement, which is a necessary precondition for using our rule, a matter of methodological ingenuity not of theoretical intractability. In the process one will have learned a good deal about 'meanings' as well as 'sayings', about the S-C as well as the CS, but an approach based upon analytical dualism enjoins that the two should be kept separate in order to examine their interplay. Two implications of following this rule are worth drawing out in conclusion.

First, it involves always taking what people say/write seriously and doing this *even* when we are sure that they mean something different. To anticipate an obvious objection, I do agree that there are *certain circumstances* in which we can know unequivocally that public 'sayings' and private 'meanings' are at variance with one another, for example, formal speeches in Parliament, the writings of those living under dictatorships, or some of the things we say to our children. In all these cases the speaker/writer can tell us (and give good reason) why what they said or wrote was not what, or exactly what, they meant. Nevertheless the distinction is worth maintaining because here the 'sayings' tell us a good deal about their interconnections with the rest of the Cultural System – about what is logically entailed by parliamentary procedure (which is a completely different question from why people subscribe to it); what the logical consequences are of doing something unlawful (which again is entirely distinct from the acceptability of the laws in question); or about the logical restrictions on communication – we tell a four-year-old that it rains 'because the clouds open' since the child is incapable of grasping all the links in a full account of precipitation. Correspondingly our 'meanings' in these circumstances indicate a good deal about our Socio-Cultural attitudes towards the Cultural System – whether we feel bound to it or constrained by it, or, in the last case, of how we live with it and transmit it to others. Once again the vital interplay between them would be lost if 'sayings' and 'meanings' were run together or (when possible) if the valid meaning were substituted for the public 'text'.

Secondly, following this rule, two items are contradictory if no other CS item can reduce them to an apparent contradiction. And the implication is that this remains the case whether or not the population involved is aware of the inconsistency. An objective contradiction remains just that at the level of the Cultural System, even if it never troubles anyone in his Socio-Cultural life. Thus Gellner's *igurramen* must themselves be aware of the contradictory requirements of their roles, even if other Berbers are not, but this awareness is not what makes *agurram*-hood inconsistent. Equally, Evans-Pritchard's account of witchcraft among the Azande, which he holds to involve logical contradictions, continues to embody these (if his account is correct), despite the twenty-two Socio-Cultural reasons he advances to explain why this incoherence never bothers them and is not in fact recognized by them.[94] This points to a very important category of cases where the objective Systemic contradiction (CS) has no (S-C) meaning and would therefore be missed by those who rejected 'sayings' in favour of 'meanings', but which may still be socially influential, since we do not have to be aware of all the things that impinge upon us or may come to do so.

What this rule proscribes is any appeal to the social environment in which contradictions manifest themselves and are lived out in one way or another – in unawareness, by strategic coping, or direct confrontation, etc. Considered as a *context*, the Socio-Cultural level can do *absolutely nothing* to resolve a logical contradiction (by showing it to be only apparent). Another way of putting this is that *contextually* contradictions at the CS level are *not dependent* on any of the goings on at the S-C level, since logical relations are independent of causal ones at T_1 (though not vice versa – a very important asymmetry as will be seen later). Again let us be crystal clear what is being asserted: I am not claiming that the two levels are independent of one another; the whole point of analytical dualism is to be able to investigate the relations between them. Obviously the S-C level crucially effects the CS level – after all, the latter originates from the former, from ideas, beliefs, 'texts' dreamed up by people and people continue to form theories, formulate novel creeds and write new texts, which become part of the CS level and may indeed transform it at T_2. But all this concerns the interplay over time of the two levels. Analytically, at any given point in time, the items populating the CS realm have escaped their creators and have logical relationships among one another which are totally independent, at that time, of what the population notices, knows, feels, or believes about them. At future time what people do about them *may* be highly significant for the CS universe, but only if the things done in turn enter the CS register (as a new theory superseding an old one, a new ethic replacing a previous one and so forth) in which case they, in turn, escape their progenitors and immediately assume logical relations amongst themselves and with prior ideas. The crucial point therefore is that analytically, for the time being, that is at any given T_1, Cultural System relations are not context-dependent upon Socio-Cultural relations.

Consequently in 'asserting the existence of a contradiction', we never need and never should descend from the logical to the causal level, for of all the interesting bearings that Socio-Cultural interaction has upon the Cultural System, the ability of the former to arbitrate on the logical status of the latter is not one of them.

Those who attempt to treat the Socio-Cultural level as the context of the Cultural System can learn nothing more about existing logical relations from existing causal ones. Instead, all they do is to blur the issue because in fact they are embarking on a separate enterprise, that of understanding or explaining. They enter the realm of trying to understand the meaning of X and Y to participants, of attempting to explain how a population can hold X and Y simultaneously, or why other people consider X and Y antipathetic. These are vital questions (which will be addressed when we examine the Socio-Cultural level), but they are quite distinct from whether X and Y are in contradiction according to the canons of logic. What they are in fact about is how people live with logical contradiction or logical consistency in their Cultural system. Yet this is precisely what we want to explore; to make it part of our tools of identification is to rob us of our topic.

6   Contradictions and complementarities in the Cultural System

This chapter focuses on the second of the four propositions which are explored throughout Part II:

(i)   There are logical relationships between components of the Cultural System (CS).

(ii) *There are causal influences exerted by the CS on the Socio-Cultural (S-C) level.*

(iii) There are causal relationships between groups and individuals at the S-C level.

(iv) There is elaboration of the CS due to the S-C level modifying current logical relationships and introducing new ones.

As will be shown in this chapter, the result of adopting a dualistic approach is that when examining the effects of the Cultural System (CS) the analysis still remains largely 'unpeopled'. Nevertheless our prime interest in the Cultural System lies precisely in its two-fold relationship with human agency; that is with its effects upon us (those logical properties which affect people) and our effects on it (how people form and transform its logical properties). In the first case, analytical dualism means that we will be discussing the conditional effects (on people) of the System; in the second case, the logical consequences (of people) on the System. Analytical, as opposed to philosophical, dualism is an artifice of convenience. Even artificially it cannot completely depopulate the cultural world and sociologically it would not be advantageous to do so. Thus when we examine Systemic influences upon us, human agency appears as a ghost in the machine; on the other hand, the investigation of our cultural products views ghostly agents as creating the machine. And this is how it should be, for without this constant if pallid reminder of the interface between the two levels (CS and S-C) we would lose touch with our main problem of cultural dynamics and wander aimlessly around the Encyclopedic Library of the deserted planet.

Consequently, analytical dualism is, first, based on the premises that the CS originates from the S-C level (culture is man-made), but, second, that over time a stream of intelligibilia escape their progenitors and acquire autonomy as denizens of World Three, after which time we can examine how they act back on subsequent generations of people. Third, that since people go on making culture we can investigate how new items enter the CS and old ones are displaced, providing again that the timing is specified. Of course both CS and S-C effects are at work simultaneously throughout history, but it is impossible to unpack their morphogenetic or morphostatic contributions without making use of analytical dualism to disengage temporal cycles of Cultural Conditioning → Cultural interaction → Cultural Elaboration.

This chapter is thus devoted to the first phase of the cycle. It is concerned with specifying which Systemic relationships condition action, how they do so and the range of possible reactions to such constraints. It does not deal with the actual responses themselves, which are Socio-Culturally determined and therefore constitute the second phase which is examined in Chapter 7. The final part of the morphogenetic cycle involves identifying the systemic consequences *of* action and the processes by which these modify the system in turn – both being discussed in Chapter 8. For present purposes, however, only the CS conditioning of the S-C level is investigated; the actual Socio-Cultural 'guts' of stability or change are not addressed yet. In other words, the causal relationships between groups and individuals (S-C) are put aside for the time being in order to disengage the conditional influences which shape them and stem from logical properties of the CS.

Hence this chapter is focused on the effects of *holding* theories or beliefs which stand in particular logical relationships to other theories or beliefs – that is, relations of contradiction or complementarity. The express concern is with the influence of these CS properties on those who uphold ideas possessing them. It explicitly does *not* purport to explain *why* people endorsed such ideas in the first place, since this is predominantly a S-C question – the answer to which would require historical recourse to anterior morphogenetic cycles.

The crucial effects to be discussed are causal ones. It will be

144

argued that the maintenance of ideas which stand in manifest logical contradiction or complementarity to others, places their
holders in different ideational positions. The logical properties of
their theories or beliefs create entirely different situational logics
for them. These effects mould the context of cultural action and in
turn condition different patterns of ideational development. Subsequent Socio-Cultural interaction is marked in entirely different
ways by these differences in situational logic as are the eventual
modification sof the Cultural System which are generated at the
S-C level.

Detection of these regularities in ideational development, which
derive from particular patterns of CS conditioning, is debarred by
any theory committing the fallacy of conflation which analytical
dualism resolutely denies. This is the case, for example, in the
relativistic strong programme just discussed which shares the
familiar defects of upward conflationism – the upward version
nevertheless being the only one of the three which is firmly wedded
to the causal explanation of cultural phenomena. Although such
relativists constantly talk of beliefs in the plural, *all* relations between them are construed as matters of local social convention (S-C
properties). Consequently there can be no comparative work on the
patterning or effects of these relations given the principled absence
of invariant criteria in terms of which they could be compared.[1]
Thus any regularities which are detected in this work as stemming
from different logical patterns of relations – defined by reference to
their contradictory or consistent character – will be nothing but
inexplicable coincidences from the standpoint of the strong programme. Obviously since the causation of belief is the relativists'
prime concern, it is maintained here that they have deliberately
excluded an indispensable explanatory component – by denying
invariant logical properties pertaining to the CS and dissipating
them away as S-C variables.[2]

Hence, in direct contrast, analytical dualism prompts a prior
inspection of the relational properties of theories and beliefs (condemned by relativists as parochial evaluation: but justified in the
previous chapter by reference to the invariance of logic) *before*
explaining the consequences for people of holding such theories or
beliefs. It is, of course, the *latter* part of the exercise which is redundant to the downward conflationist, for if Socio-Cultural life is
defined as epiphenomenal then it is already explained.

However, since our concern is ultimately with cultural dynamics
and change, then only selected logical properties of the CS are dealt

with, while many cultural components which impinge upon different groups and individuals are left aside. Specifically the analysis will neglect those cultural items which are logically unrelated (or more precisely, those which are not 'known' to sustain logical relations with others at some determinate time). For, in fact, an exhaustive compilation of contradictions, complementarities or autonomous elements in the Cultural System is impossible. If, as Popper has argued, we can never fully appraise the implications of *one* theory (because this would entail anticipating all its future applications and anomalies),[3] then by corollary we can never itemize all the potential contradictions between *two* theories or beliefs. At any given time innumerable contradictions will go unknown, pass unperceived, rest undetected. Every society at T_1 represents a 'library' in which numerous contradictory items remain 'unspotted' by anyone and where the most exhaustive cross-referencing system that is technically conceivable could never approximate to a complete listing of them. (Partly because between the time it was produced and digested, knowledge would have moved on, but more importantly because such a method could only deal with formal propositions and recorded implications, while in any field contradictory implications are not disclosed until its various items are worked on – yet it is far from being the case that every 'pair' of items has been subject to this process.) Precisely the same is true of complementarities or of seemingly autonomous items.

Moreover, in instances where they have captured the attention of investigators, it is obvious that many of the perceived contradictions are a matter of supreme indifference to most people. For example, only a few specialists working on comparative belief systems either know or care about which Melanesian beliefs contradict those of Greek Orthodoxy. Furthermore their knowledge and interest is entirely academic, their detection is that of outside observers uncommitted to either set of beliefs, and the consequences (if any) are distanced from both sites, being situated instead in academic journals where the original contradiction might acquire significance if recontextualized in an intellectual debate, perhaps by being inserted as a 'counterfactual' against an established theory. *If* this occurs, it is the secondary (academic) contradiction which would form part of our concern here, not the primary one.

In other words, at any time *part* of the known contradictions or complementarities in the CS can leave *everyone* unmoved. Our interest is exclusively with those contradictions or complementarities which do 'move' people precisely because, for reasons outside our purview, they uphold ideas which have these particular relational properties. The task is to uncover by what practical mechanisms of constraint or facilitation these condition distinctive patterns of cultural action and development. Talk of such regularities should be taken literally to mean a patterning which is discernable, not one that is rambling or inconsequential, that is, random in nature and effect. It must not be confused with a pattern of conflict-free change – which pertains to the Myth of Cultural Integration and not to the present analysis. Here I am concerned to unravel the pattern (the contours of morphogenesis and morphostasis), but begin from the opposite assumption that this is woven from contradictions and complementaries which constitute its woof and its weft.[4]

Quite apart from the conceptual difficulties surrounding these two terms, which were taken up in Chapter 5, there are enormous substantive problems deriving from the empirical complexities of contradictions and complementarities themselves which snake and intertwine through the cultural tissue. Consequently the following discussion will be pared to the bone by formulating it simply in terms of the logical relationship between two cultural items 'A' and 'B'. In this way the propositions advanced are intended to be of sufficient generality to apply equally at any given T_1 to:

- logical relationships within a system;
- logical relationships between two empirically separate systems (see p. 104);
- logical relationships between two subsystems;[5]
- logical relationships between a subsystem and its ideational environment.

This does not imply a displacement of cultural scope, for the actual items examined at a macroscopic level may well be emergent properties in relation to smaller scale cultural phenomena.

Any of the above relations between a given A and a given B will first be examined for logical contradiction, consistency or independence. Consequently none of the sets of relationships listed above are presumed in advance to be more of one kind than another. This of course is the difference in theoretical starting-point from the Myth of Cultural Integration – any version of which took harmony to be *a prioristic* for all the above sets.

It must be recalled that the procedure adopted is to break into the analytical cycle of cultural dynamics by examining the Systemic conditioning of subsequent interaction. Therefore it follows that we begin only with those CS relationships of contradiction and complementarity which respectively constrain or facilitate cultural agents – thus exerting a causal influence on their later actions. The rest of the chapter derives its organization from this and falls into three parts: definition of when constraints and facilitations arise from contradictions and complementarities; delineation of how these exert operative effects on agency; and detection of what patterns of interaction result from the original Systemic conditioning.

Formal features

The distinction which follows is a formal one; it has nothing whatever to do with the different kinds of components which may make up the Cultural System but operates over the entire range of intelligibilia. Demarcations between contents which may be vital for other concerns, like the demarcation of science from metaphysics, are not important here. (Indeed I will later argue that one of the general effects of contradictions is to shift science into metaphysics and metaphysics into science, as part of the morphogenetic sequence.)

Constraining contradictions

Here the contradiction is a property of the CS (A and B are logically inconsistent): it exerts a constraint upon the S-C level if any actor(s) wish to maintain A (whether a theory or a belief). This is the only S-C assumption that will be made. Throughout we will presume that someone or some group does seek to sustain A (for reasons unknown but residing at the S-C level). The whole effect of the constraining contradiction is entirely conditional upon this assumption, for the existence of the incompatibility between A and B is of no social consequence if no one asserts or advocates A, even if it is well-known.

Assuming then that protagonists of A exist, the key point there is that their action in invoking A also ineluctably evokes B and with it the logical contradiction between them ('concomitant compatabilities' share exactly the same features, the key difference being that they evoke logical consistency). The reason for this is some necessary connection between A and B, that is, the 'dependence' of A on part of the general preserve of B. In this type of contradiction, B constitutes the hostile environment in which A is embedded and from which it cannot be removed. For A cannot stand alone; it is compelled to call upon B, to operate in terms of B, to address B, in order to work at all. This is part and parcel of the *theoretical* constitution of A; but part of the parcel that is B constitutes a threat to A because it simultaneously contravenes it. Emphatically this is not to assert the existence of a 'real contradiction', on the contrary, like all logical contradictions it cannot be tolerated by the protagonists of A or anyone else.

But those seeking to sustain A are heavily constrained. They cannot simply repudiate B for they must invoke part of it, but if B is fully actualized it threatens to render A untenable. They are, we assume (for S-C reasons), unwilling to abandon A as long as tenability is rationally possible. (Irrational dogmatism is an S-C problem; being psychological it does not pertain to the CS, any more than do the actual social reasons *for* holding A. It is the logical consequences *of* A being held which are CS affairs.) Therefore those adhering to A are in a situation where *the survival of A depends upon their repairing the inconsistency with B.* Since the relationship between A and B is a genuine logical contradiction then its *direct* resolution is logically impossible. Corrective manoeuvres are mandatory, but they require substantial theoretical work, even in the scientific domain where it may be possible to reduce the original contradiction to an apparent contradiction. Another name for the phenomena with which we are dealing could be 'corrective contradictions'.

However, this is to get too far ahead, for the phenomenon itself remains excessively abstract without illustration. I have deliberately selected two examples which differ monumentally in substance but share the same gigantic importance in the history of thought – the development of Christian beliefs and the advancement of scientific theories. Both are cases of birth into a hostile ideational environment, with which they had to cope if they were to survive but which constituted an unending threat to their survival. To claim that both surface(d) in inhospitable surroundings is not like saying they had the misfortune of bad 'home backgrounds' (and could otherwise have been other than they were), for without their respective environments we simply cannot conceive of them at all. Thus Christianity had to tangle with Antiquity because it emerged enmeshed in it, just as scientific propositions have to tackle observational data because the (f)act of stating a hypothesis entangles it in them. The key feature shared by these disparate instances of constraining contradictions is that both are concerned with the logical relationship between *ideas* (with a belief in relation to other beliefs, with a theory in relation to other theories). In science it is never the case that nature (hard fact) steps in and arbitrates directly in scientific disputes, any more than God manifestly intervenes in mundane religious struggles. Given this formal common denominator (despite the enormity of the substantive differences) some of the parallels which emerge between the two examples will be less surprising.

One of Durkheim's best and most neglected studies[6] *The Evolution of Educational Thought*[7] provides a superb gist of the contradiction in which Christianity was embroiled. Halbwachs called it a 'kind of sustained discourse on the progress of the human mind in France', but an even greater generality can be claimed for this work which tackles the interface between Christianity and classicism 'in the development of the peoples of Europe'.[8] Paradoxically, given Durkheim's reputation as a consensus theorist, this book is a towering contribution which goes at least as far as Weber's *Ancient Judaism* in elaborating the notion of cultural contradictions.[9]

The root of this constraining contradiction was that Christianity's 'origins were Graeco-Latin and it could not but remain more or less faithful to its origins. It had acquired its form and organization in the Roman world, the Latin language was its language, it was thoroughly impregnated with Roman civilization.'[10] In turn this confronted the Church with 'a contradiction against which it has fought for centuries without ever achieving a resolution. For the fact was that in the literary and artistic monuments of Antiquity there lived and breathed the very same pagan spirit which the Church had set itself the task of destroying.'[11] The contradiction between this particular A and B was profound and extensive: 'we have here two quite different and even mutually contradictory moral systems',[12] 'the one thoroughly impregnated with the eudaemonistic ethic, the other steeped in the contrary principle; the one regarding happiness as another aspect of virtue, the other sanctifying and glorifying suffering'.[13] But the incompatibility exceeds the ethical domain and spills over to affect conduct in the temporal world and conceptions both of man and of mundane reality; 'the Christian way of life . . . depends on the idea of man rising above his nature and freeing himself from it by taming and subjugating it to the spiritual laws whose object is, in a word, sanctity. By contrast, the ideal of antiquity is harmony with nature; nature is regarded as the source of information about the laws of human life.'[14]

Simultaneously this initial logical contradiction was accompanied by the lasting dependence of Christianity on classicism: 'The single fact that Christian doctrine is complexly involved in books, that it expresses itself daily in prayers which are said by each of the faithful and which are required to be known not only in the letter but also in the spirit, rendered it necessary not only for the priest but also even for the layman to acquire a certain amount of culture.'[15] Thus for the divines, like St Augustine, the understanding of Holy Scripture was primary but it could only be achieved by steeping themselves deeper and deeper in profane literature. Here, comprehending the Christian God entailed acquaintance with the pagan deities; grasping the symbols of the New Testament spelled immersion in classical languages; clarifying Christian theology meant journeying so far into hostile territory that its denizens may have remained enemies but ceased to be aliens.

Moreover, if the elaboration of the faith could be left to the divines, its propagation involved teaching the people. Hence the religious origins of education in Europe, which more than anything else displayed the inextricable dependency of A on B and the incompatibilities which this invoked, institutionalized and reproduced. From the start,

this embryo of education *contained within itself a sort of contradiction. It was composed of two elements, which no doubt, in some sense, complemented and completed one another but which were at the same time mutually exclusive.* There was on the one hand the religious element, the Christian doctrine; on the other, there was classical civilization and *all the borrowings which the Church was obliged to make from it*, that is to say the profane element . . . But the ideas which emerged from it *patently conflicted* with those which were at the basis of Christianity. Between the one and the other there stretched the whole of that abyss which separates the sacred from the profane, the secular from the religious.[16] (my emphasis)

With this vivid picture in mind of the inescapability of the constraining logical contradiction, its torturing nature and the inexorable antinomies it harbours but which cannot be eradicated at will, let us immediately compare it with a very different substantive case.

Likewise any scientific theory is launched into a rough sea of 'empirical evidence' which is its one and only environment. It is buoyed up by corroborative instances, which do not serve to *prove* it, as the justificationists or verificationists believed, but which make journeying on seem worthwhile. Also it usually wallows in 'counterfactuals' (which no more *disprove* it, contrary to the view of dogmatic falsificationists) yet these rocky anomalies cause our theoretical adventurers to ponder about returning to port for a complete refit or sailing on doing running repairs. Even if a theory gets off to a good start, the tossing about between substantiation and anomaly is inescapable like the weather and just as variable. Constraints thus arise when theories have collected some corroboration *together with* some counterfactuals – the usual fate of all scientific theories given that at best corroboration is only *pro tem*.

Thus constraining contradictions are part and parcel of the scientific enterprise. They are ineluctable because any theory which bids to explain something must necessarily face up to the evidence available in the environment. However, our fledgling theory never meets the so-called 'hard facts' head-on: its environment is *not* natural but is made up of observations which *purport* to capture it. Little could be further from the case than Braithwaite's characterization in which 'Man proposes a system of hypotheses: Nature disposes of its truth or falsity. Man invents a scientific system, and then discovers whether or not it accords with observed fact.'[17] This assumes a firm, accessible, uncontrovertible *empirical basis*; natural rocks on which theories break up.

Yet this notion of a strict dividing line between the theoretician and the experimenter where 'the theoretician proposes, the experimenter – in the name of Nature – disposes'[18] is itself untenable. Observations are not demarcated or separated from theoretical propositions, the former being unproblematic and the latter being problem-ridden. There are no pure observations, all facts are conceptually formed[19] and they never speak for themselves – this is the fallacy of empiricism. In other words, if every fact is theory-impregnated then what any 'explanatory theory' confronts are not pure observations but 'observational theories'. The latter is advisedly put in the plural, for most 'explanatory theories' *also* advance their *own* 'observational theory' (for example, Galileo's 'observations' were stated in the light of his optical theory; the genetic theory of intelligence was advanced in conjunction with the observational theory embodied in the Intelligence Test). Simultaneously they contravene *alternative* constructions of the facts which are incompatible with the 'observational theory' attached to the new 'explanatory theory' (as well, perhaps, as with the guts of the theory itself). For instance, Galileo's observations' confronted those of the Aristotelians, construed in the light of their theory of the heavens; the Intelligence Test was challenged for measuring nurture as much as nature by sociologists stressing the social determination of manifest ability.

In brief, this means that all factual propositions are only a special kind of theoretical proposition (they constitute 'observational theories') and hence are just as *unprovable* as the 'explanatory theory' itself. It follows that if 'factual propositions are unprovable then they are fallible. If they are fallible then clashes between theories and factual propositions are not "falsifications" *but merely inconsistencies*'[20] (my emphasis). It would be hard to improve on Lakatos's formulation of that which lies at the heart of the constraining contradiction in science: 'it is not that we propose a theory and Nature may shout NO; rather, we propose a maze of theories, and Nature may shout INCONSISTENT.'[21]

Thus nature (hard fact) pronounces no death-sentences, instead it sentences the majority of theories (which do not achieve immediate or lasting corroboration) for life – a life of coping with inconsistency. This is inescapable, for any aspiration to scientific status depends on a theory addressing the empirical world and since this world is not one of pure hard fact, its protagonists are driven to address the theories purporting to portray it. The points where the two patently conflict represent environmental threats which the theory cannot evade, for the nature of the scientific enterprise remains empirical even if it cannot be construed in empiricist terms.

Concomitant complementarities

Before going on to examine the operative effects of constraining contradictions, like those just discussed, it is useful to contrast them with the opposite concept. At the Systemic (CS) level, the direct counterpart of the constraining contradiction is what I have termed the 'concomitant compatibility', for this bears the same formal features in reverse. In other words invoking A also ineluctably evokes B, but since the B upon which this A depends is consistent with it, then B buttresses adherence to A. Consequently A occupies a congenial environment of ideas, the exploration of which, far from being fraught with danger, yields a treasure trove of reinforcement, clarification, confirmation and vindication – because of the logical consistency of the items involved. This, for example, was the generic feature which Weber analysed as linking together the religious beliefs, the rationale for status distribution and the economic ethos in Ancient India and China.

However, concomitant compatibilities are by no means the prerogative of traditional culture (nor, as I have emphasized, were all traditional cultures seamless webs of consistency); a similar relationship maintained, for instance, between classical economics and utilitarian philosophy. Indeed modern examples are so abundant in natural science that Kuhn was tempted into portraying the entire enterprise as a succession of paradigms, each of which constituted a cluster of concomitant compatibilities in our terminology.[22]

Nevertheless, just because A and B manifestly go together, the one being the logical accompaniment of the other, this should not conceal the fact that the concomitant compatibility, like the constraining contradiction, is a logical relationship which also conditions action (causally) at the Socio-Cultural level. To the actors involved this may seem nothing more than a felicitous facilitating influence, but facilitation is a constraint too. It guides thought and action along a smooth path, away from stony ground, but over time this wears a deeper and deeper groove in which thoughts and deeds become enrutted.

Operative effects

Constraining contradictions

In the cultural realm, as in the structural domain, contradictions only exert a conditional influence upon the course of events and only then by shaping the action contexts in which people find themselves.[23] Structural contradictions represent obstructions for certain institutional operations and these translate themselves into problem-ridden situations for the actors associated with them. Very much the same is true here. A constraining contradiction is the site of cultural tension. That part of the system in which A and B are located is characterized by a form of 'strain' which arises from their incompatibility in the context of dependency. There is nothing metaphysical about this, no Hegelian overtones of superordinate battles between ideas: pure ideas purely sleep on in books until awoken by actors. It is dependence which generates the 'strain', which enforces the fraught relationship between A and B yet simultaneously prevents their divorce or separation.

What the constraining contradiction does in practice is to confront those committed to A who also have no option but to live with B as well, with a particular *situational logic*. According to this logic, given their initial commitment to A, they are driven to engage with

154

something both antithetical but also indispensable to it – which therefore they can neither embrace as it stands nor reject out of hand. They must struggle to extract what is necessary from B, warding off B's counter-attractions or counter-claims and avoiding the seductive labyrinth of doubt, to return to A bearing their offering.

This situational logic spells mental torment, social subterfuge or technical contortions: it produces at worst a divided self denied refuge in schizophrenia. Of course, its precise nature differs with the composition of A and B, but the situational logic is identical. It is the same for Gellner's *igurramen* driven to palm the cash with one hand and to distribute largesse insouciantly with the other, who have to be scrupulously calculative in order to balance the books whilst maintaining the image of serene confidence in divine providence. It is the same for Durkheim's doctors of the Church, forced to keep company with paganism whilst maintaining and in order to maintain the faith. And it is the same for the scientist who is compelled by the need to substantiate his hypothesis to confront the 'facts' in the form of the observational theories available, however hostile they may be.

There is no effective method of containing the problematic relationship between A and B and there is no way of evading the problem by the simple repudiation of B. This is precisely the force of the constraint characterizing this type of contradiction. It relentlessly fosters the ultimate clash between the two contradictory components and does so through the situational logic it creates for the actors involved. Certainly human agency often tries to get off this hook by the use of Socio-Cultural containment strategies, that is, causal manipulation of other people to prevent either the realization or the voicing of the logical difficulty. These are purely 'social solutions' which may be quite efficacious for a time at the Socio-Cultural level but do not ultimately dispose of the constraining influences exerted by the Cultural System on the Socio-Cultural level. The situational logic emanating from them bears down inexorably: actors have no choice about this, their only choice is whether or not they will try to cope with it. The constraining contradiction is never a determinant, for at any point in time, actors can make their exit, turning away from a belief or theory in scepticism or turning towards an alternative which appears less problematic or more profitable. However, for those who remain steadfast in their adherence to A, then the situational logic firmly directs the way in which they deal with the contradiction.

If A and B are logically inconsistent then no genuine resolution is possible between them (unless it can be shown that this is an apparent contradiction), but if B remains unaltered it threatens the credibility or tenability of A. Consequently the situational logic dictates that continued adherence to A makes a *correction* of its relationship with B mandatory (which is why the name 'corrective contradiction' would be equally appropriate for these Systemic properties, as mentioned earlier). Corrective action involves addressing the contradiction and seeking to *repair* it by re-interpretation of the components involved. Obviously since I have cast the presentation in terms of partisanship of A, then the re-interpretative efforts will be directed at adjusting B, though, as will be seen later, they do not necessarily stop there.

In science, when a hypothesis clashes with 'the facts' corrective action consists in instituting an *appeal* against the 'observational theory' which stood for 'the facts', and, on that basis, purported to refute A empirically. In other words, B itself is rendered problematic, it is not allowed to count as unquestioned, naive, background knowledge, but its genuine though sometimes implicit theoretical character is brought to the fore and challenged. The experimental techniques, the measurement instruments, the operational indices, the statistical data base – any of those items which constituted the inimical 'observation' are appealed against on the grounds of their *theoretical* inadequacy. Thus those advancing the original hypothesis do not accept that the contradiction was ' "between theories and facts" but between two high-level theories: between an *interpretative theory* to provide the facts and an *explanatory theory* to explain them . . . The problem should not be put in terms of whether a "*refutation*" is real or not. The problem is how to repair an *inconsistency* between the "explanatory theory" under test and the – explicit or hidden – "interpretative theories." '[24]

Under an appeal procedure the theoretician always demands that the 'observational theory' is clearly specified and opened up for criticism. If the appeal is supremely successful, then the contradictory 'interpretative theory' is replaced by one providing corroboration for the explanatory theory which had originally been 'refuted'. Usually the outcome is not so neat – B is not readily replaced by B^1, with the contradiction dissolving in its wake – instead a variety of corrective manoeuvres ensue with variable outcomes (discussed in the next section). Nevertheless in all such cases the concern has '*shifted* from the old problem of replacing a theory refuted by "facts" to the new problem of how to resolve inconsistencies between closely associated theories'.[25]

Corrective repairs are equally mandatory in the realm of belief and the processes involved have formal similarities with the 'appeal procedure' in science. Again it is the interpretation of B which is at stake, again the objective is to tame it through re-interpretation and again the stakes are identical – correct B or go under, make the ideational environment more hospitable or perish in it. The 'faithful' must in some way domesticate the cultural monsters confronting them. Pagan ideas were much more of a threat to Christianity than the Roman lions, for with the latter passive resignation could be seen as a sign of grace whilst with the former it could only be viewed as a sign of inadequacy. Instead the inconsistency has to be tackled, repaired and the correction made to stick. This is the task that the situational logic enforces on all those who neither make their exit nor change sides in the context of a constraining contradiction.

Concomitant complementarities

In contrast, the situational logic generated by the concomitant compatibility is problem-free to the actors involved. The consistency of its components makes exploring B rewarding for protagonists of A – the source of ideational bonuses like psychological reassurance, technical back-up, corroboration of theories and confirmation of beliefs. Thus, instead of the restricted access to B associated with the constraining contradiction, the situational logic of the concomitant compatibility fosters no limitation whatsoever on that part of B which is accessible to partisans of A.

Not only are Socio-Cultural containment strategies unnecessary, they would represent self-inflicted injuries – a deliberate spurning of the rewards mentioned above. A prime indicator of this difference engendered by the two very different forms of situational logic, is the much longer and more open 'education' associated with the concomitant compatibility where nothing is risked the deeper and further adherents plunge into the ideational environment constituted by the A B complex.

Nevertheless this situational logic is exerting a causal influence on the Socio-Cultural level and not one which is the unmixed blessing it might appear. Its initial operative effect is the direct product of its felicitous consequences for the actors involved. It reinforces their adherence to A, for the absence of exigencies leads to less turning away. Certainly, exit remains possible but desertion is not a product of the logic; this pushes no one to the door for it makes staying inside seem cosily inviting. However, cosiness is the close ally of closure. Over time the situational logic fosters a negative feed-back loop which discourages alterations in the felicitous cluster of items making for concomitant consistency. Hence the *exemplary* nature of cultural leadership whose effect is to repress internal innovation – Mandarin, Guru, Maestro or Mentor – identified by Weber and over-generalized by Kuhn.

Consequently the adherents of A are enmeshed in the cluster forming the concomitant compatibility and insulated against those outside it. Yet because their 'truths' are not challenged but only reinforced from the proximate environment, then actors confront no ideational problems, are propelled to no daring feats of intellectual elaboration, but work according to a situational logic which stimulates nothing beyond cultural embroidery. The net effect of this is to reduce Systemic diversity to variations on a theme (which do however increase its density) and to intensify Socio-Cultural uniformity (through the absence of alternatives). In brief the situational logic of concomitant compatibility conduces towards *protection* (the maintenance of purity), not *correction*.

Divergent results

The rest of the chapter will be concerned with tracing through the characteristic results of the two different kinds of situational logic stemming from the Cultural System. Suffice it to say that with each pains will be taken to show that human actors can evade the situational logic (they are never determined by it, though *how* they avoid it is also influenced by it). Also what they make of it is not pre-figured by it except in the most formal terms. Substantive matters like progressive or degenerating problem-shifts are the responsibility of agency: Systemic influences only shape the form of ideational enterprise. The remaining discussion deals with quite how different the two forms are and with the yawningly divergent results they produce.

Constraining contradictions

The basic proposition advanced is that the situational logic generated by the constraining contradiction, which is concerned with the *correction* of inconsistency, generically results in ideational *syncretism* (that is, the attempt to sink differences and effect union between the contradictory elements concerned).

Since the relation between A and B is that of a genuine logical contradiction, which is therefore incapable of direct resolution, then the corrective exercise which aims to repair the inconsistency necessarily involves some redefinition of one or both elements. Correction can thus follow three paths:

(1)   A ⟵ B, i.e. correcting B so it becomes consistent with A.
(2)   A ⟷ B, i.e. correcting both A and B so they become mutually consistent.
(3)   A ⟶ B, i.e. correcting A so it becomes consistent with B.

All three paths lead to syncretism, but they differ considerably in terms of which element changes and how much it alters in the course of the repair-work.

Obviously for adherents to A, the preferred solution is (1) since here it is B which undergoes the revision, then leaving A both intact and in congruence with its immediate environment. The middle solution represents the only form of symmetrical syncretism, as both A and B jointly undergo reinterpretation. As such it is less desirable to adherents of A than (1), but clearly protagonists of A will find (2) preferable to (3) if repair cannot be effected by method (1). For those faithful to A, the final path is a last resort because it is their theories and beliefs which have to do all the adjusting in order to survive. The situational logic of correction fosters use of this last redoubt, since the alternative is the unbridled counter-actualization of B.

Although we will work through each syncretic path in turn (using the examples of constraining contradictions which have already been introduced) there is no presumption that they are followed sequentially in every instance. On the contrary if an inconsistency can be corrected by method (1), the situational logic provides no impetus whatsoever towards more 'generous' syncretic moves. Sequential movement is noticeable however in cases of successive failure to effect repairs through both the preferred method (1) and the compromise method (2).

(1) Correcting B so that it becomes consistent with A

Here, the situational logic of correction places the onus on those who adhere to A to engage in the active project of eliminating the contradiction by furnishing a re-interpretation of B (sufficient minimally to remove their inconsistency and maximally to present B as doing nothing but serve A). This constitutes a real assault on the logical problem at the CS level, for basically it seeks to substitute a re-interpreted B^1, which is compatible with A, for the original B which was in contradiction with A. This of course is predicated on the successful invention/interpretation of a B^1 which logically can replace original B (hence the reason for calling this an active enterprise). In addition the success of this method also depends on getting B^1 to stick Socio-Culturally (on people accepting B^1 in place of B). However the fact that there is a substitute B^1 on offer shows that this is never a simple exercise of Socio-Cultural manipulation (where resort is made to power) since prior to any such activity the new interpretation of the item has had to be registered in the Cultural System.

Formally this method and the difficulties it can encounter are very similar in the scientific and metaphysical domains. In science we have already mentioned the 'appeal procedure' when the theorist questions the negative verdict of the experimentalist by asking him to specify his original B, to lay bare his 'interpretative theory' for inspection. When in certain cases it transpires that this constituted nothing but unquestioned though erroneous 'common-sense' assumptions it proves relatively easy for the theorist to replace it by B^1, his improved 'interpretative theory', which now corroborates his 'explanatory' theory, overruling the original 'refutation' by B and thus repairing the inconsistency. Such, at a more sophisticated level, was the relationship between Newton and the first Astronomer Royal: on the basis of his own lunar theory Newton not only told Flamsteed that his observational data (which contradicted Newtonian theory) needed re-interpreting but also how to perform the correction from B to B^1.[26]

A parade of successful appeals, in which inconsistencies are repaired in the above manner, makes correction seem a simple procedure in the natural sciences (I am not talking about the theoretical and technical complexities involved). It might then appear there is no reason why scientific theorists should settle for less than full satisfaction through method (1) – where the syncretic element only entails producing B^1, which resolves the inconsistency and leaves A triumphant. Nevertheless there are powerful reasons which can propel them towards a greater syncretism.

The first is that 'full satisfaction' is not to be had (even when temporarily and psychologically it may seem to have been given), for 'the verdict of the appeal court is not infallible either'.[27] Thus when it decides whether it is the replacement of the 'interpretative' theory or of the 'explanatory' theory that produces novel facts it still must take a conventional decision about the acceptance or rejection of basic statements. As a conventional decision this cannot incorporate all 'background knowledge', every factor which could conceivably (or inconceivably at the time) be in play. Consequently such verdicts are strictly *pro tem*: the court must always be ready to reconvene, for the issue is reopenable by either side. Hence 'satisfaction' may later be withdrawn. Alternatively, the theorist who had contested 'interpretative' theory B, suggested the re-interpretation B^1 but had this turned down on appeal, may yet seek to uphold his theory in a further attempt to repair the inconsistency by trying to advance a B^2. In short, theorists indeed have the right to be contumacious litigants, but, and this is often the key point, they may have great problems in exercising these rights.

Basically the difficulty for many who have good reason to fight for their theories, is that a workable B^1, let alone a B^2, simply cannot be found by them. Since they know therefore that original B will retain its force in court, they are constrained not to go to appeal. What course is then open to them other than abandoning ship? The example of Prout is illuminating here. In 1815 he claimed that the atomic weights of all pure chemicals were whole numbers but planted this theory in the hostile environment of nineteenth-century analytical chemistry, when the techniques for the purification of chemical substances consistently produced results contrary to the theory. Those adhering to it contended that these anomalies resulted from defective experimental techniques of the time which did not produce pure elements and therefore were inadequate to dispose of the truth value of the theory. Their basic difficulty, however, was in coming up with a convincing B^1, a new experimental technique in analytical chemistry by which pure elements could be separated, which should then prove congruent with the theory.

Despite some progress, anomalous instances remained, the recalcitrance of which had two consequences by the mid-century. On the one hand there was desertion by those tired of pursuing the elusive B^1, who concluded that since corrective repair was an impossibility the theory was without foundation.[28] On the other hand a reduced band soldiered on in the belief that there must be *further* hidden assumptions in the techniques for chemical purification leading to the miscalculation of atomic weights which were still discrepant with the theory. By 1886 Crookes was proposing a new B^2, a kind of 'sorting Demon', but this novel corrective technique in turn proved deficient thus leaving the inconsistency unrepaired.

This again depleted the army still battling on in the hope of identifying yet further hidden assumptions which would enable them to advance the conclusive B^n. But as long as they remained shackled to the core technical assumption of the century, namely that two pure elements must be separated by *chemical* methods, then original B (discrepant atomic weights) resurfaced time and time again to contradict the theory. That their case was eventually upheld was not due to the redefinition of a corrective B^n from within analytical chemistry but from a syncretic move (method (2)) involving 'conceptual stretching' of both the 'explanatory' theory and the 'observational' theory. Since precisely the same may be required of those who once thought they had received full satisfaction, later were overruled, but still want to attempt a come-back, then syncretism in natural science does not always stop at method (1) – where the syncretic element is reduced to the drive to produce B^1 which, in resolving the inconsistency, leaves A triumphant.

In the light of these considerations we can see that the same kind of difficulties characterize the metaphysical domain when the method of correction consists in the re-interpretation of B alone. Successively B^1, B^2, B^n, fail to eliminate the contradiction (though they may suppress its social effects for centuries) because the original B resurfaces to discountenance the B^n substitutes. Basically, then, A is threatened by its dependence on some form of B which precludes a complete rewrite of it, just as our proto-atomic theorists were constrained to attempt the resolution of their inconsistencies from *within* analytic chemistry. The parallels can be illustrated by returning to our original example of the contradictory relations between Christianity and Hellenism. However, this unfamiliar parallelism may feel closer if we use our 'scientific' vocabulary to describe the theologians' task. Their basic aim was to produce an 'interpretative theory' of classicism (given that there is no more 'hard thought' than 'hard fact') – a corrected method of observing the classical heritage which repaired its inconsistencies with Christian beliefs. Durkheim's study of educational thought contains a magnificent dissection of the internal dynamics of 'one-sided syncretism' from the pre-Medieval Catholic Church to the end of the eighteenth century.

Thus from the eighth century onwards he charts three major phases in the re-interpretation of classicism for Christian consumption; a movement from B^1 to B^2 to B^3. These followed on one another's heels historically as each attempt broke down sequentially because the corrected versions did not succeed in expunging the inconsistent elements and effecting lasting repair. These failures in correction were of course prior to the reanimation of the original heritage of classical civilization by social groups outside the Church and antagonistic to the syncretic enterprise during the Renaissance. Until then the difficulties were not Socio-Cultural ones of getting a revised formula to stick, they were due to deficiencies in the re-interpretative repairs themselves.[29] Generically all such interpretations accentuated *formalistic* skills as the element of classicism both essential and assimilable to Christianity, not *positive* knowledge giving a window on the world of things.[30]

First then, from the ninth to the twelfth centuries, the *verbal formalism* of the ecclesiastical Grammarians accentuated only the linguistic element of Hellenism. This constituted the sparest re-interpretation which stripped it of its substance (the preoccupation with things) and stressed only its form (the supreme importance of words *because* of their intimate association with the Word). Yet even this was insufficient to dispel its contradictory potential. Purely grammatical study lead inexorably to problems of logic: through considering simple grammatical classifications (should white be classed as a substance like table?), thinkers were propelled to ask ontological questions.[31] And from these seemingly abstruse arguments about words and substances, by the end of this era the contradiction re-emerged in the form of faith versus reason.

Thus, crucially, if it was admitted

that there exists no other substance than individual substances and that this genus consists of nothing other than the individuals which compose it, that it is a word used to designate the agglomoration of these individuals or the collectivity of their common characteristics. *In this case the most crucial teachings of the Church become unintelligible.* How, for example, are we to conceive of the divine Trinity? If it is true that the individual by himself, taken in his totality and in his unity, is a substance, if the diverse elements of which he is made up have no substantial reality, then it follows that the three divine persons of the Trinity are three distinct and irreducible substances. Consequently we concede a thorough-going polytheism which is repugnant to the Christian mind; or alternatively we maintain that the three persons are really only one; and that they are different aspects of one and the same substance having no distinct individuality of their own. Then we wind up with a unitarianism *which is no less contrary to the teachings of the Church.*[32] (my emphasis)

Since the same difficulties attended the Christian doctrines of the real presence in the Eucharist and of Original Sin, the husk of classicism which had been retained in the expectation that this eliminated its germinative capacity, in fact proved sufficient to re-animate the contradiction – by making controversial the central beliefs of the Church.

Consequently the Scholastic philosophers of the Medieval university were driven to a new syncretic re-interpretation of classicism embracing its irrepressible rationalism but presenting it in such a way that it served the faith rather than representing an alternative to it. Formalism was again the key to correction: the exigencies appearing at the end of the first period being tackled by a shift from verbal to *logical formalism* – the new B². Logic and dialectical reasoning were presented as the core of the classical heritage but stripped from their context, the subjects with which they were originally preoccupied and ends to which they were then applied. This decontextualized logic could then work in harness with Christianity to buttress the intellectual credentials of dogma, clarify the intelligibility of doctrine and adduce good reason for belief. Thus it 'was not a question of juxtaposing reason and doctrine but rather of introducing reason into doctrine, of rendering faith rational'.³³

The result was indeed greater doctrinal coherence but as a corrective formula it did more damage than it repaired, for 'the moment one introduces reason, criticism and the spirit of reflectiveness into a set of ideas which up to that time has appeared unchallengeable it is the beginning of the end; the enemy has gained foothold'.³⁴ Both the Reformation and the Renaissance were the *pas de géant* of this enemy – the threatening harbingers of counter-actualization. In this context what Durkheim is concerned to demonstrate is how the Jesuit Order deliberately sought a way 'of extricating themselves from the contradictory situation'.³⁵ Hence the bold attempt to harness unbridled humanism to the propagation of the faith by a third re-definition, which took on board the classical literature, dear to arisocratic frivolity, but made pagan sources serve the Christian ethic.

When members of the Order elaborated the new B³, then because

classical literature enjoyed the favour of the cultivated public they turned themselves into devotees of it; but they only expounded Humanism in order *to be able to contain it to channel it, to prevent it from issuing in its natural consequences*. Humanism, unfettered, was in the process of bringing about a revival of the pagan spirit; the Jesuits undertook to transform it into an instrument of Christian education. To do this, however, they had to expunge virtually all positive content from the works of the classical authors: they had to rid them of their paganism and to retain only their form so that this form might be inspired by the spirit of Christianity. Their Humanism was thus doomed to the most absolute formalism imaginable.[36]

And one which was not to last, for one-sided syncretism had already failed in French society: with the Revolution its time was up in education too.

It is not the case that method (1) is bound to fail in either domain. Indeed, much of the progress in science, though certainly not all, consists in the successful repair of inconsistencies as in the model Newtonian case. Equally there would have been no Church, at least as we know it, had it been unable to repair many of its other contradictions with the multi-cultural beliefs in which it was embedded. Instead two examples were deliberately employed where both science and metaphysics could not produce a triumphant A through the 'simple' syncretic manoeuvre of correcting B so that the two became congruent — precisely in order to demonstrate why actors may engage in a more thorough-going form of syncretism. For, on the face of it, this is contrary to their initial ideational interests. But if and when method (1) fails, not only is there a stimulus to further syncretic endeavour, but some of the tools for it have also been forged in the process of failing — criticism which progressively assumes a deductive structure and critics who are as familiar with the enemy terrain as with their own.

(2) Correcting both A and B so they become mutually consistent

Fundamentally this form of syncretism is achieved through A and B both undergoing re-interpretation or 'concept-stretching' such that A^1 or A^n becomes consistent with B^1 or B^n, the two new versions having shed the contradiction which dogged their ancestors. At the Systemic (CS) level, the fact that a shift occurs in the nature of A and B alike should not lead syncretism to be construed as a process of convergence or to be pictured as a discovery that 'the truth lies in the middle'. Correction has nothing to do with finding a *via media*. On the contrary, this form of syncretism is morphogenetic, it amplifies deviations from both points of departure and the syncretic repair performed on their derivatives signals a new arrival point — cultural elaboration at the CS level. In general method (2) leads to progressive problem-shifts in the Cultural System.

When method (1) has failed, then the situational logic of correction constitutes an on-going drive which conditions greater syncretic efforts because of the exigencies experienced by those whose ideas still wallow in inconsistency. Thus not only does failure propel committed actors towards bolder syncretism, it also equips them for the task. Those who had failed to produce a 'goodness of fit' by tampering with B alone, become a body of adept tamperers, who having cut their critical teeth on B are now more ready to resolve their problems by baring them at A too. As Durkheim noted, once reason, criticism and the spirit of reflectiveness develop, A itself is no longer safe from mutation – simple fidelism is destroyed by the development of techniques to defend the faith.

It is not necessarily the case that the successful syncretic technique is propounded by the original adherents of A: indeed what increases is the critical readiness of later advocates to identify and incorporate techniques appropriate to the task. Thus in the case of Prout's theory the repair kit emerged a century later from Rutherford's school of atomic physics. This vindicated the sustaining conviction of the Proutians that there had remained a hidden assumption which vitiated the chemical purification of elements and continued to produce experimental results contrary to the theory. This it transpired was the most fundamental assumption of all, namely that two pure elements must be separable by *chemical* methods, and it accounted for the nineteenth-century failure of these proto-atomic theorists to repair the inconsistency by method (1) – which had sought to correct analytical chemistry itself. Instead the latter needed to be overthrown and left behind. The successful syncretic formula which developed early in the twentieth century entailed the 'idea that two different pure elements may behave identically in all *chemical* reactions but can be separated by *physical* methods'. This in turn 'required a change, a "*stretching*", of the concept of "pure element" which constituted a change – a *concept-stretching expansion* – of the research programme itself'.[37]

An analogous path winding towards the eventual redefinition of A as well as B was eventually followed in our example of the development of Catholic thinking. Unwilling to endorse the Reformation formula that faith was justifiable by private feelings and therefore incapable of conflict with scientific findings, those like Lammenais[38] in France and Newman in England engaged in a Kantian enterprise of distinguishing two realms of facts (for the truths of Revelation were never to be at the whim of private judgement; never to be ceded to the vagaries of emotionally veridical experiences), but with the realms re-defined in a non-contradictory fashion.

Newman's syncretism, which is gradually elaborated in his *Idea of a University*,[39] starts from the basic proposition that 'Religious doctrine is Knowledge, in as full a sense as Newton's doctrine is Knowledge', [40] and then asserts Revelation and Reason to be different but not incompatible sources of fact. Classical learning, the product of reason, can be accepted as good in itself with the sole proviso that it is not conducive to virtue. 'Knowledge is one thing, virtue is another; good sense is not conscience, refinement is not humility, nor is largeness or justness of view faith.' [41] This proviso that classical cultivation is good in itself, like health, but amoral constitutes the guts of the re-defined B^1.

Contradiction is banished through the demarcation of the two realms, which in turn places a parallel restriction on theology, for in its A^1 version it must abjure any search for naturalistic evidence supporting Christianity. Whereas physics keeps 'within the material system with which it began . . . with matter it began and with matter it will end', [42] so '(T)heology begins, as its name denotes, not with any sensible facts, phenomena or results, not with nature at all'. [43] Consequently the new A^1 debars attempts, like Paley's 'natural theology', to cross the two domains which 'cannot be Christian in any true sense at all'. [44]

This demarcation of two different universes of discourse, and the consequent impossibility of either usurping the other, means that Newman's A^1 and B^1 are incapable of logical incompatibility because they are now defined as being *incommensurate*. Precisely because of their incommensurability, peaceful co-existence between them becomes possible. 'If then, Theology be the philosophy of the supernatural world, and Science the Philosophy of the Natural, Theology and Science, whether in their respective ideas, or again in their own fields, on the whole are incommunicable, incapable of collision and needing, at most to be connected, never to be reconciled.' [45]

These forms of syncretism are morphogenetic. On the one hand the old contradiction between A and B is repaired by an *entente* between A^1 and B^1. Although the latter are distant relatives of the former they are so far removed from them that the family feud cannot be sustained. Instead the tortuous manoeuvres of the nineteenth-century chemists, struggling for mensural precision within the now-discarded framework of analytical chemistry, are a source of wry amusement: the mental contortions of the Jesuits become a by-word for casuistry, once the classical heritage no longer has to be sieved through formalism before it is fit for Christian consumption. This is the result of the shift from B to B^1. On the other hand the complementary move from A to A^1 generally constitutes a progressive problem-shift. A century later the original idea of Prout had become the corner-stone of theory about atomic structure, developed outside the narrow disciplinary boundaries of chemistry. In parallel, the old theological problem of how to subordinate classical rationality to ecclesiastical authority had given way to the much bigger problem of reconciling intellectual freedom with religious obligation, which similarly burst its original institutional boundaries.

Syncretism is morphogenetic because through it a new item enters the intelligibilia – a new theory or a new doctrine – but it is not always possible. A syncretic formula rendering an A^1 and a B^1 congruent may simply not be found, and it is not always the end of the story, for syncretism is often a rolling stone rather than a fixed resting place providing lasting shelter for adherents to A^1. It is in such cases that resort is made to method (3) as the sole means of survival left for those still wanting to uphold something of A.

(3) Correcting A so it becomes consistent with B

Basically this type of syncretism consists in the accommodation of A to B in order for the former to survive at all. In contrast then with the two methods already discussed, it is A which bears the brunt of re-interpretation in the process of corrective adjustment to B. The conditional influence prompting recourse to be made to method (3) becomes operative under two conditions. First, when every version of A to be advanced (A^1, A^2, A^n etc.) has met with B (or B^1 etc.) which remains in contradiction with it. Here those protagonists of A who are unwilling to abandon it entirely are compelled to adjust it much more substantially. Second, the same pressure exists when a syncretic formula (some $A^1 B^1$ elaborated under method (2)) cannot be made to stick. As was argued above, such new theories or doctrines are morphogenetic, representing deviations from their starting points and ones which may continue to amplify to the detriment of either component (or sometimes both), eventually leading to the collapse of the $A^1 B^1$ formula. Once again the survival of A can only be at the price of its adaptive mutation.

In short this corrective adjustment of A to some version of B spells a radical change in its character: a shift to an A^n which often indicates the social demise of the theory or belief in relation to the salience originally achieved for A and a degenerating problem-shift within the theory or belief itself. The change in character can be profound when an idea is on the run. It is here that scientific theories take on an increasingly metaphysical nature to avoid extinction, while beliefs become progressively rationalized for the same reason.

In science any theory can be saved from counter-instances, or to put this another way, theories and factual propositions can always be harmonized, by the introduction of auxiliary hypotheses. Contrary to the view of naive falsificationists there is nothing in natural science which forces a theory to go under and compels its protagonists to admit defeat. Survival is always possible, the question is, on what terms? To Popper, saving a theory with the aid of auxiliary hypotheses can be acceptable procedure if the auxiliary clauses, added to the original theory to accommodate some inconsistency, have at least as much content as the unrefuted element of their predecessor: they may even be progressive in problem-shift if they also predict novel facts and thus require testing afresh as a new theory. In other words, accommodation does not automatically spell degeneration. However, salvage may consist in pseudo-scientific adjustments, the addition of *ad hoc* hypotheses or the linguistic re-interpretation of theoretical terms. Such corrections are derived in the wake of facts, without anticipating new ones. *Ad hoc* corrections thus accommodate the theory to the 'facts' (the latter are not questioned as in the appeal procedure) and are purely linguistic strategies which prevent extinction.

Survival through *ad hoc* devices means that a theory loses its empirical character. Adherence to it is no longer because of the theoretical purchase gained on the empirical world: instead it is a matter of commitment where the empirical domain is drawn upon to prop up the theoretical structure. This spells degeneration but not extinction. However, the price of survival through pseudo-scientific means is that the theory increasingly assumes a metaphysical character; since ultimately every new anomaly encountered can be accommodated by a suitable re-interpretation of its terms or an extension of the *ad hoc* clauses, then eventually no state of affairs is incompatible with it. Why some people are willing to pay this price is, of course, a Socio-Cultural question.

In the realm of belief itself, precisely the same scenario may result especially if the syncretic formula begins to come unstuck Socio-Culturally. Thus, for example, Newman's type of syncretism had removed any religious attempt to contain reason on the grounds that the two domains were incapable of collision because of their eternal incommensurability. The fact that he was entirely correct did not, however, stave off the progressive disenchantment of the world as rational man became scientific man and eventually social-scientific man – with each move representing both a bigger chunk of the universe amenable to naturalistic explanation and a larger proportion of the population engaging in rationalistic discourse. In other words the scope of B appeared to be increasing at the expense of A and religious adherents (no longer people of simple or even complex faith alone but men of rational education too) increasingly attempted a rationalistic reconciliation of the two domains – overthrowing the shelter of Newman's syncretic formula and throwing in their lot with demagification in order to keep in the swim.

Often the same degenerative sequence is followed as was traced in natural science, but entailing an opposite change in character – a rationalization of metaphysics. For once the 'believer' begins playing this game, belief itself is on a slippery slope. The progressive redefinitions of A, intended to bring it into greater congruence with developments in B, gradually led to its miracles becoming metaphors, its sacraments becoming symbols, spirituality becoming depth-psychology, its priests becoming social workers and its ethics becoming a code of social fraternity. In sum, this represented a shift towards naturalistic explanation, mundane application and this-worldly justification. In practice it replaced the Apostolic Church by the World Council of Churches.

Again, however, as in science accommodation does not necessarily equal degeneration. Here too non-regressive shifts can characterize adjustment, but just as in science these entailed the advancement of a new theory (salvaging something of the old but superseding it) so in metaphysics the new belief only rescues part of the old by substituting something new. Thus in either the scientific or the metaphysical field such syncretic shifts actually signal the demise of original A in terms of the area over which it claimed mastery. In natural science only the unrefuted content of the initial theory survives, which ironically is smaller the more progressive the new theory proves to be! Similarly in metaphysics – only the old facts of theology are retained which prove pliant to the new symbolics. And the more potent the new symbolism, the more the old beliefs are relegated to the status of facticity.

This corrective strategy can finally allow the distant ancestors of A and B literally to sink their differences. For morphogenetic syncretism, as opposed to the defensive degenerating syncretism which we have also seen to be a frequent end-product of method (3), continues to roll on with gathering momentum. The reason being that as re-definition progresses it is less and less constrained by the original dependence of A on B. Since the new accommodative definitions of A (A^1, A^2, A^n) have shed so much of their original core in response to the difficulties created by B (B^1, B^2, B^n), they become so different that both the dependency and the contradiction are left behind. What then takes place is cultural morphogenesis, the syncretic elaboration of a new item which enters the intelligibilia. Thus, humanism for example, as de-deified as it is de-Hellenized, commits itself to a 'caring society' which is as far removed from the City of God as the City of Rome. For protagonists of A however, the use of method (3) is generally seen as the road to slow inglorious demise or to more rapid and dishonourable degeneration: quite rightly, from their point of view, they will only follow this route when the situational logic leaves them no other means of correction available.

In conclusion, whichever method is used to correct a constraining contradiction the generic result is some form of syncretism. The main thrust emanating from its situational logic is the sinking of differences and the effecting of union between its components. In other words, the existence of constraining contradictions within the Cultural System conditions *ideational unification*. However, neither this Systemic impetus towards unification nor its end-products, unified theories or beliefs, should be viewed as forces or results which guarantee proportional consensus in the relevant part of Socio-Cultural life. The unificatory thrust can be deflected in various ways by its Socio-Cultural reception. Everything depends on whether it happens to coincide with a prolonged lack of antagonism in society or whether it collides with structured cleavages between social groups. Nevertheless both the morphogenetic syncretism at the CS level and the pressure towards ideational unification at the S-C level which result from the constraining contradiction stand in complete contrast to the equivalent resultants of the other key concept – the concomitant complementarity.

Concomitant complementarities

The basic proposition advanced is that the situational logic generated by the concomitant compatibility, which is concerned with the *protection* of consistency, generically results in ideational *systematization* (that is, the 'strengthening of pre-existing relations among the parts, the development of relations among parts previously unrelated, the gradual addition of parts and relations to a system, or some combination of these changes').[46] This is the technical term which will stand for what was earlier mentioned as 'cultural embroidery' because it directs attention more pointedly to the kinds of relationship to be investigated.

It has already been argued that the cluster of interdependent but compatible propositions represents a kind of adventure playground, a congenial environment which can be explored with profit (for it reinforces the original idea) and without danger (since it presents no threat to it). Examples of such clusters include certain primitive 'collective representations', the Weberian other-worldly religions but especially Hinduism, classical political economy and political philosophy, and the high tide of a victorious research programme (the closest this analysis will come to acknowledging Kuhn's paradigms). These have been deliberately chosen for their historical span, since if we can establish common results stemming from the situational logic they share we might finally have succeeded in putting the Myth of Cultural Integration in its place, by showing that the concomitant complementarity is its real empirical home but also that it is not nearly so homely as the Myth depicts.

The trouble with 'early' examples has always been that the anthropologist or historian confronts them as finished products. Necessarily, through looking backwards, one sees a fully Systematized endeavour. Thus contemporary inspection of certain primitive belief systems does indeed show kinship, headship, commensality, cuisine and cosmology to be closely interwoven. What cannot be revealed retrospectively is the temporal activity by which strand was knitted with strand.

The results of concomitant compatibilities may form an integrated whole, but they do not get born in one piece. Formally they arise from the exploration of a pair of interdependent and mutually compatible notions, the extrapolations, implications and ramifications of which are then dovetailed together. In the process the ties linking the initial compatible items strengthen considerably and a corpus of cognate notions are progressively incorporated. The latter represent a kind of in-filling of the environment staked out by the original compatibility, which encourages great wholeness over time. But both time and intellectual endeavour are essential.

Weber was acutely aware of the active mental nature of the enterprise but given his historical sources, was less able to deal with its temporal unfolding. Thus for him, in 'religious matters "consistency" has been the exception and not the rule':[47] its achievement is an intellectual product rather than any kind of given. It entails a rational process of 'systematic arrangement',[48] which contrary to the views of the over-charitable anthropologists is both hard-won and correspondingly rare. Thus in contrast to the other-world religions reviewed, he considers the Hindu doctrine of Karma to represent the most consistent theodicity ever produced in history[49] – articulated around the interdependent notions of caste and reincarnation but consistently incorporating allied concepts of commensality, connubiality, education, politics and economic activity. Nevertheless Weber confronted it not only in its developed form but overlayed by centuries of traditionalistic veneer, obscuring the process of doctrinal genesis. For example, the social origins of the Brahmans associated with the early Vedic literature were historically clouded – some apparently stemmed from sons of the priestly nobility, in which case the Karma doctrine reinforced their social position; others probably originated from a guild of sorcerers, the doctrine here presumably allowing them to join those of exalted rank. All that can confidently be stated is the concomitant compatibility *of* caste and Karma, their interdependence and interlinkage with cognate concepts.

This is the advantage of more modern examples: we can document how they did get pieced together. If we take the relationship between political economy and political philosophy then the steps involved in systematization are retraceable. In particular the origins of the compatibility can be pin-pointed, the strengthening of this pre-existing relationship can be documented, and the inclusion of additional interconnections can be traced through. Here the original concomitant compatibility between economics and ethics is embedded in the Physiocratic concept of 'natural order'. On the one hand this is a descriptive notion about the interdependence of all groups in society, which stresses their ultimate dependence on nature replete with existing property relations; on the other, it is also a normative concept since it is held to be the embodiment of a divine order pre-ordained for the human happiness of all.[50] From the beginning then *laissez-faire* was both a practical and a moral injunction. To Adam Smith the Physiocratic system was 'the nearest approximation to the truth that has yet been published',[51] but the 'full truth' entailed a much more sophisticated linkage between the economic and the moral order.

In classical economics a 'spontaneous order', working for the general good, would automatically stem from the 'uniform, constant, and uninterrupted effort of every man to better his condition'[52] were it not for governmental intervention (which does not concern us here) and the perversion of individual hedonism such that many failed to perceive that their true interests were indeed fulfilled by the existing order (which is of major concern since it is an admission that self-interest required 'enlightening'). Thus before Utilitarian theories were developed, the classical economists had 'demonstrated' that the self-interest of the middle class was tantamount to the general interest, but that the general interest would be harmed unless corrective measures were taken through moral education of the people.

The complementarity of Utilitarianism with both the basic postulates of political economy and as a solution to its major problem of 'unenlightened' self-interest was complete. It immediately displaced references to the divine origin of laws regulating society. This system of secular ethics supplied a primary definition of the motivation by which the natural order was guaranteed (the secular pleasure principle) and an equally basic tenet by which the maximum concordance between the individual and the general good was ensured, that is, morality consisted in promoting 'the greatest happiness of the greatest number'. In order to implement this ideal it was not necessary to convert people to the Utilitarian ethic; it sufficed to engineer a correspondence between their desires and the maximization of general happiness, through education. Such instruction was not to counteract hedonism, but merely to inform it of the most advantageous individual goals, thereby channelling behaviour towards the general good.[53] This education was seen as indispensable to increasing productivity by the economists and essential for increasing morality to the Utilitarians: to these thinkers it therefore underpinned both the general economic interest and the general good. Thus historically we can see here the tight bonding of political economy and political philosophy and that the complementarity of these two major bodies of thought immediately encouraged their protagonists to reach out and attempt to incorporate another domain, that of education, thus adding a new part to their already coherent system. Simultaneously this extends both its range and its 'wholeness'[54] thus constituting the first of various efforts to systematize other parts of the social environment on cognate lines.

Precisely the same scenario typifies the consolidation of a successful research programme or 'paradigm' – a period of euphoria as the complementarity is first detected and explored; then each new positive interconnection discovered adds to its sophistication and reinforces the conviction of scientists that they are really 'on to something'. In turn this gives them the confidence to reach out to embrace and incorporate adjacent problems. It is not that no difficulties are encountered *en route*. Anomalies always attend scientific development, just as aesthetics were problematic for Utilitarianism, which never gave a very convincing argument for the superiority of poetry over pushpin. Nor is it the case that a hundred per cent consistency is achieved. But the great feeling of inner security bred by the concomitant complementarity fosters a belief in the resolvability of discrepancies. Thus puzzles titillate; they do not dismay. What has been described so far is a rather exuberant process akin to striking gold, digging deeply enough to find big nuggets, but then realizing that it forms a gold field with other seams running from it. Like a gold rush, this is the time too when hoards of prospectors flood in (a Socio-Cultural result which is the direct opposite of the desertion attending every constraining contradiction). Instead of free and easy pickings, the claims are then staked out, digging in depth begins and the treasure is carefully banked. This signals the stage of systematization proper.

Systematization and cultural density

What then follows is a phase of internal preoccupation with working out the inclusive linkages and tying them into the original core to form a comprehensive conspectus. With his usual perspicacity Weber appreciated these two strands of extensive exploration and inclusive formalization, which the world religions welded together.[55] Again, however, only the modern examples allow us to disengage the temporal staging – how the initial compatibility encourages an imperialistic exploration of the surrounding environment and these gains then undergo systematic incorporation. Thus Mill, Bentham and their successors pressed on to annex theories of government, administration, politics, law, penology and knowledge itself, which were linked back to the core complementarity between economics and ethics, then refined and tabulated to constitute the liberal conspectus.

Much the same is detailed by Kuhn as the process making for paradigmatic science. The paradigm is temporally prior to theory (hence his need of the concept), while laws, applications and instrumentation are posterior to it. However, his multiple definitions of 'paradigms' serve to confuse the habits and commitments of people (S-C) with the framework of compatible assumptions

(CS). Obviously it is unacceptable to confound the two, since it is impossible for anyone habitually to follow anything which did not pre-date their actions or be committed to a non-existent framework. But were the 'framework of language and assumptions' (that is, the bedrock of the paradigm) to be construed 'historically' as a newly discovered CS complementarity, then the formation of a set of habits in research and the intensification of commitment to the framework can easily be interpreted as consequences of its situational logic. His subsequent analysis of how new developments and parts are added to the paradigm by 'Normal Science' exploiting a 'network of over-lapping and crisscross'[56] is then fully consonant with our dynamics of incorporation and formalization.

Thus it is being argued that, Systemically, the core complementarity becomes increasingly sophisticated, extends outwards to embrace further readily compatible elements and the whole bundle then undergoes intensive systematization. This entails the tabulation of cross-linkages, the specification of how part dovetails with part, the identification of lacunae and missing relations – in short a detailed ordering of the ideational environment which surrounded the original complementarity and is now brought within its bounds.

The systematization process is augmented by the Socio-Cultural consequences of a buoyant complementarity. More and more people are drawn to it, as we have seen, and intensified work upon it is what completes the 'in-filling of the environment'. Although there are no necessary limits on how far any conspectus can be extended, easy imperialism is followed by a gradient leading into areas which provide diminishing returns. As the environment ceases to yield new fundamental discoveries, the enlarged body of workers turns to tilling the field, which has now been staked out, yet more intensively – exploring its nooks and crannies, tackling its tractable 'puzzles', undertaking the 'mopping up' operations which to Kuhn constitute 'Normal Science', and furnishing the exegeses and commentaries which attend the consolidation of any corpus of ideas.

None of these activities is exclusive to the concomitant complementarity but the fact that they are all conducted from and contribute to a consistent conspectus does produce a distinctive end-product. There is a substantial increase in 'cultural density', by which this sector of the Cultural System becomes particularly rich in fine and subtle distinctions, possesses an elaborate and often technical vocabulary to describe them and a complex body of concepts to manipulate or capture them. The development of a thousand words for cattle, the intricacies of caste rights and prohibitions, the bulging libraries of exegetical literature are all products of the same situational logic.

Systematization and boundary formation

In turn, growing cultural density through which systematization is accomplished, has as its corollary the formation of a natural boundary. Quite literally there are more internal interconnections within the field of the conspectus than external relations with components outside it. This is an objective feature of the Cultural System which is independent of, though not unrelated to, the formation of Socio-Cultural communities the cognitive field of which remains within these bounds. Logically the more complex the internal structure becomes, the more difficult it is to assimilate new items without major disruption of the delicately articulated interconnections. 'The more oppositions an organism is capable of distinguishing meaningfully, the "richer" becomes its assimilated environment, the more involved the corresponding structure of internal organization; but the less tolerant is the organism of even subtle vacillations of environmental state.'[57] In other words, tight and sophisticated linkages eventually repel innovation because of its disruptive capacity.

This has implications *within* the conspectus, which progressively accommodates less and less radical innovations and can reach the stage where in Kuhn's word it 'suppresses fundamental novelties because they are necessarily subversive of its basic commitments'.[58] Precisely the same point is made by Weber about the effects of complex ritualization in Hinduism: 'A ritual law in which every change of occupation, every change in work technique, could result in ritual degradation is certainly not capable of giving birth to economic and technical revolutions from within itself, or even of facilitating the first germination of capitalism in its midst.'[59] Equally there are repercussions for the relationship between the conspectus and its *external* environment. Innovations from across the boundary do not knit in easily either. Increasingly the systematized conspectus can only tolerate a stable, non-intrusive environment and since the world of ideas is generically lacking in these features, the solution is artificial stabilization by closure against the outside. The situational logic of protection means brooking no rivals from outside and repressing rivalry inside.

In so far as protective insulation is successful, then closure represents a negative feed-back loop in which any morphogenetic amplication of deviations is eliminated. Instead protective closure induces morphostasis and reduces cultural development to the embellishment of the conspectus. Only embroidery is possible once a static problematic has been enforced and then it is the kind of *petit-point* the stitchwork of which takes years to finish a cushion cover.

Finally, we should note the Systemic consequences over time if a period of closure does ensue. When cultural activity is reduced to embellishment, then cultural density deepens proportionately. Finer and finer distinctions of ritual, language and concepts produce the most closely woven texture of thought, speech and writing. Whether this is held to constitute 'cultural richness' or 'cultural degeneracy', it incontrovertibly strengthens boundary-maintenance itself.

Protection and reproduction

The generic Socio-Cultural thrust of protection is the social reproduction of the conspectus. To begin with this, too, is naturalistic rather than in any sense conspiratorial. The concomitant complementarity is usually unfurled from a loose community, for example, Adam Smith was friendly with the French Physiocrats, Quesnay and Turgot; David Ricardo with later liberal economists; Jeremy Bentham with the Mills, and so forth. And as the programme progresses, so the community grows and strengthens, leading Kuhn to compare the research team with the religious order. Once it enjoys some success an assault is then made on the next generation through the rewriting of text-books, a 'process of professional initiation' preparing 'for membership in the particular scientific community'[60] and a selective distribution of rewards for promising novitiates. In short, the immediate incursion of political economy into the educational field was no accident.

Nevertheless, we must not fall into the trap of certain sociologists of education and presuppose that because reproduction is attempted, then its success is a foregone conclusion. It is fundamentally a device for extending cultural control and as such its effectiveness can be deflected by two factors governing its Socio-Cultural reception. First, the S-C level will prove less amenable to passive reproduction the more ideational alternatives are socially available: since the monopoly of opinion is the goal of reproduction then the elimination of all competing ideas cannot be taken as its starting point. Secondly, the degree to which Socio-Cultural cleavages map onto these ideational divides will decrease the effectiveness of reproduction amongst part of the relevant population. All the same, this steady impetus towards the stable reproduction of a cultural status quo represents a major contrast with the attempts to correct people's ideas which emanate from constraining contradictions.

Thus the generic result at the Cultural System level of the concomitant complementarity is systematization, the formation of a dense, tightly articulated set of ideas. Its main thrust at the Socio-Cultural level is reproduction, that is the distribution of *similarities* throughout the population. In so far as reproduction is successful it engenders shared ideas and common practices thus forming 'islands of order'[61] which are also integrated communities. These results of the concomitant complementarity, and particularly the general scenario of systematization–density–protection–reproduction will probably have struck readers as redolent of semiotic anthropology. In fact the concept of the concomitant complementarity, as explored here, represents a criticism of that approach which is not without interest for both the depiction and explanation of cultural dynamics.

Descriptively the most important difference is that the scenario associated with the concomitant complementarity, as just presented, *is one among two* – or rather as will be seen in Chapter 8, one among four. At certain times and in certain areas it may have been the systemic feature of prime importance, but analytically it has no primacy over the other configuration(s) of intelligibilia. By contrast the semiotic approach takes these 'islands of order' as prototypical of all cultural phenomena and interprets their results as being generic to all cultural dynamics. Thus to begin with I would resist an approach which by definition either ignored any other kind of systemic patterning or engulfed them, on the presumption that their logical differences made no difference.

Secondly, as far as the concomitant complementarity itself is concerned, the scenario which I have sketched as resulting from it is temporally reversed in semiotic anthropology and this reversal introduces explanatory difficulties, which from my point of view need never arise. In their different ways Lévi-Strauss, Barthes, Douglas and Bauman see the *fons et origo* of all culture in a basic semiotic act of 'separation' (that is, an act of signification that splits a domain into a class and its *negative* complement thus creating meaning which is 'above all a cutting-out of shapes').[62] Thus Barthes posits such 'rules of exclusion' as fundamental to the creation of a cultural order because they specify the domain in which a universe of discourse applies by delimiting it from the unregulated realm of chaos. Bauman sums up the general case as follows: 'The ordained oppositions are meaningful only within the limits drawn by the rule of exclusion; more important, the rules of association retain their regulative power only when employed well inside the circumscribed area; and, finally, rules of ritual are useless in efficiently organizing the domain unless transgression of its boundaries is effectively barred. From whatever corner we start, we arrive inevitably at the same conclusion: the role of rules of exclusion is crucial indeed fundamental, pre-conditioning applicability of all other rules.'[63] There are three difficulties with this temporal sequence, one of which is the treatment of time itself. However, to begin at their beginning shows the problem of starting there.

To posit 'rules of exclusion' as prior to any cultural order whatsoever, means that semiotic anthropologists then have to account for the existence of such rules themselves. This they can only do by reference to culturally independent factors – the universal properties of the human mind (Lévi-Strauss) or the perennial requisites of social solidarity (Mary Douglas)[64] – thus endorsing either psychologism or holism. Second, the instant effect of a 'rule of exclusion' is boundary-creation and therefore boundary-maintenance immediately becomes crucial to the continuation of the meaningful, predictable and secure arrangement of events. The two elements are thus mutually constitutive; rules establish boundaries and boundaries are essential to the continuation of rules. Consequently, from this perspective, boundaries are theoretically derived as corollaries of the (psychologistic or holistic) properties governing rule formation and are empirically assumed to be in place from the start. This is the source of the final difficulty, namely that a temporal sequence is repressed in the semiotic account. If rules of exclusion–inclusion instantly set up boundaries and boundary-maintenance is simultaneously held to be the pre-condition of cultural order, then such an order is necessarily viewed as being born in a piece. The suppression of time is, of course, a prime reason why these theorists denounce cause and effect analysis as inappropriate when dealing with culture – since causality is only operative over time.

In comparison, the reverse sequence proposed here has the following contrapuntal advantages. First, it eliminates any need for postulating the prior existence of 'rules'. (Of course it also avoids attendant difficulties about the ontological status of the kinds of 'rules' stipulated above and the methodological problems raised in the absence of a context of justification for them.) Thus in place of these dubious psychologistic or holistic entities we need employ only two logical universals: the capacity to recognize 'identity' and 'complementarity'. Our starter-motor consists in nothing but these, confronting the cultural terrain, or culturally unprocessed nature for that matter, since if we credit actors with thinking at all we have to grant that they have already cut their logical teeth.[65] Thus given these two properties all we need to assume is that some of the time some actors will eventually *notice* some of the concomitant variations in their environment and include them in their cultural repertoire because of their felicitous character– on the simple model of noting that water stimulates plant growth then encourages the watering of plants. The key point here is that neither the noting, nor the marking, nor the including are done 'in opposition' to anything– there is no fundamental principled act of separation. Exclusion is no 'rule', except in the trivial and truistic sense that to include a figure is to exclude its background.

The background is not excluded on principle because it is threatening but is left outside because it is (temporarily) uninteresting. This Bauman is willing to concede but only for parts of reality in their 'pristine', pre-cultural state, unnamed and culturally irrelevant and neglected. 'These parts, until processed by the semiotic procedure of cultural praxis, as good as do not exist for human beings . . . these conceptual unbeings cannot possibly jeopardize the orderliness of the culturally tamed and assimilated part of the universe. . . They supply, instead the inexhaustibly vast virgin land for prospective cultural assimilation.'[66] Indeed they do, but why should we assume that the noting of complementarities between items already 'marked' defies the same process of assimilation? The answer is we would only if we buy the semioticians account of boundary and boundary-maintenance.

And the second point about my revised sequence is that it rejects this interpretation of immediate rule-generated boundaries, necessary to the operation of rules themselves and their protection from external threat. Instead boundary formation comes much later in the day after what can be prolonged exploration of congenial parts of the environment. Moreover, its development is a natural consequence of preoccupation with handling, arranging and systematizing the discoveries made rather than being the predicate of any cultural activity at all. In other words it is not from external threats but from internal preoccupations that boundaries start to arise, due to the preponderance of internal linkages over external relations. This alternative 'naturalistic' interpretation can be supported both positively and negatively.

On the one hand the historical development of *density* in a set of beliefs (richly and highly articulated) was often prior to the manifestation or perception of external threats to them. Indeed the focusing of attention on internal issues seems to be what is of primary importance given, for example Weber's demonstration of the remarkable tolerance of Hinduism to a variety of alternative beliefs. Similarly Lakatos stresses that the self-absorption of those involved in the construction of a research programme leads to the 'relative autonomy of theoretical science'. Far from being detained and distracted by criticism, 'the positive heuristic forges ahead with almost complete disregard to "refutations": it may seem that it is the "*verifications*" rather than the refutations *which provide the contact points with reality . . . it is the "verifications which keep the programme going"* (my emphasis).[67] In other words, the autonomous and preoccupyng activity of systematization has its own dynamics which engage in the absence of external threats or regardless of them.

On the other hand, closure (procedures for exclusion) appears in this analysis as the last element in the sequence and never the first. Again it is naturalistic and not *a prioristic* in character. For only when a body of ideas has achieved such internal complexity that new items cannot be assimilated without major disruption, is innovation then met with aggression and opposition with counterattack. Weber thus appears correct in viewing the taboo as belonging to a fairly well-developed stage in the process of rationalization since the basic purpose of such prohibitions was the protection of something already gained or achieved. 'In a word, the *taboo in his view was a secondary phenomenon*' (my emphasis).[68] Thus we can derive closure from the situational logic of protection where it represents the final part of a temporal sequence typifying concomitant complementarities: from this perspective there is no need to build it into the grid of the human mind or elevate it to a prerequisite of cultural praxis.

Finally our accentuation of the temporal sequence, in contrast to its repression in semiotics, enables us to retain cause and effect analysis. Here the different phases during which logical relations condition social responses which then react back on the former can be teased out, while the semioticians deprive themselves of explanatory purchase because they are committed to the 'mutual constitution' of the above components as their key premiss.

Moreover we can identify a *morphostatic* sequence, operating via the establishment of a negative feed-back loop, as the particular characteristic of one part of the Cultural System (the logical relations of which constitute concomitant complementarities) whereas semiotics would have us take a part for the whole.

This chapter has been concerned with the effects upon people of contradictions and complementarities in the Cultural System. In it social actors only entered the picture as those who held ideas and who were conditioned in various ways if they went on holding them, for without people doing so there would be no picture at all. Emphatically this is not to reduce human agents to *träger*: it is a methodological artifice, deriving from analytical dualism, which directs us to look at how the cultural context is shaped *for* actors *before* examining what they do in it or what they can do about it.

The types of ideas they held could vary enormously, for the conditional influences of interest here stemmed from relations between ideas and did not reside in their specifically scientific or metaphysical or poetic character. These substantive differences were irrelevant to the main argument – namely that it was formal (logical) relations of contradiction or complementarity with other ideas which (causally) placed actors in entirely different positions, whatever the nature of their theories or beliefs.

In turn these logical relationships were seen to create different situational logics for their holders, by moulding the context of cultural action in two distinctive ways. The relational properties of a constraining contradiction enmeshed those upholding its constituent ideas in a problem-ridden situation. The causal influence of the situational logic was one encouraging correction since opportunity costs attached to failure in repairing inconsistencies. The reverse was the case for the concomitant complementarity which placed its advocates in a problem-free situation and presented them with ideational bonuses for continued advocacy. Here the causal influence of the situational logic fostered protection of benefits received from the cultural status quo. Consequently the two situational logics conditioned different patterns of ideational development – syncretism (a sinking of differences) in the case of correction, and systematization (a consolidation of gains) in the case of protection.

However these were the systemic consequences: there was no presumption whatsoever that they had similar Socio-Cultural effects. Syncretic endeavours to effect ideational union are doubtless undertaken in the hope of also producing ideational unification amongst the relevant population, just as the promotion of systematization aims to induce the ideational closure of a particular community against alternatives. Neither are necessarily successful in generating the appropriate form of Socio-Cultural consensus – indeed these CS influences are at the mercy of their S-C reception, for a conditional effect is never a determinant.

Thus to understand what happens next it is necessary to bring the people back in, not merely as static upholders of this or that idea, but as active makers and re-makers of their culture – in pursuit of their interests, by use of their power and through social alliances or group antagonism. In short, we need to move on to the second phase of the morphogenetic cycle – Cultural Interaction – to see how relations between people are capable of changing or maintaining the relations between ideas. More generally this is also the next step in linking the CS and the S-C, the logical and the causal, or most basically of all, culture and agency.

7 Socio-Cultural interaction

This chapter focuses on the third of the four propositions which are explored throughout Part II:

(i) There are logical relationships between components of the Cultural System (CS).
(ii) There are causal influences exerted by the CS on the Socio-Cultural (S-C) level.
(iii) *There are causal relationships between groups and individuals at the S-C level.*
(iv) There is elaboration of the CS due to the S-C level modifying current logical relationships and introducing new ones.

The previous chapter was not entirely unpeopled but it was completely lacking in social interaction. It dealt only with the relations between groups and the ideas they held and not their relationships with other people. The main concern was to demonstrate that social groups confronted two completely different kinds of situational logic depending on the Systemic properties of their beliefs, that is, their contradictoriness or complementarity. In other words the existence of orderly or conflictual relations at the CS level was held to condition S-C action in very distinctive ways.

However, it was never suggested that the logical state of affairs in the Cultural System causally determined the extent of Socio-Cultural integration – a proposition only a downwards conflationist could endorse. On the contrary it is maintained that orderly or conflictual relations at the S-C level can show a significant degree of *independent variation* from those characterizing the CS at any time. In short, S-C integration does not mirror CS integration. Although the former is indeed conditioned by the latter, it also has its own dynamics which need to be examined.

These are the subject of the present chapter: however, I am going to be theoretically selective about them. Because my concern is to explain cultural stability and change, least interest attaches to times and places in which S-C orderliness simply co-varies with CS orderliness, as the former cannot then be held to make its own independent contribution to change or lack of it. Instead the focus will be upon significant *discrepancies* between the degree of integration at the two levels and the reasons for them. In particular this entails a close examination of, first, why S-C relations can be either more orderly or much more disorderly than a CS which is characterized by contradiction, at the same point in time; and also, second, why S-C relationships can manifest disorder when the CS displays great internal consistency. Obviously to focus intensively on these discrepancies between the two levels is to be guided by the theoretical hunch that if culture behaves at all like structure then these deviations are crucial in accounting for future stability or change. Equally obviously, this theoretical preoccupation means that in all likelihood, the bulk of S-C business is being left entirely out of account. In no sense does this chapter attempt to capture the main lineaments of causal relations between cultural actors: its concern with S-C interaction is exclusively as the *middle element* in a three-part morphogenetic cycle: Cultural conditioning (CS) $\longrightarrow$ Cultural interaction (S-C) $\longrightarrow$ Cultural Elaboration (CS).[1]

Thus the last chapter broke into the analytic cycle by outlining the conditional influence exerted by logical properties of the CS. The justification for starting there was simply that any given time Socio-Cultural interaction is put on a spot by the Cultural System, since the latter pre-dates the former *even if* actors promptly demolish their cultural heritage upon its reception. (A theory has to be advanced before it can be rejected; a language to be spoken prior to being modified; a practice to have been in use before it can fall into desuetude.)

This, of course, is an analytic not a genetic starting point. All the examples of Cultural Conditioning employed in Chapter 6 were ones where the social advocacy of some beliefs could be taken as given. Anterior analytical cycles would need examining to provide a historical account of how certain people had become the protagonists of certain ideas. Indeed this work makes no contribution whatsoever to answering the fundamental genetic question of how belief(s) are possible at all. Instead the same appears to be the case for culture as for structure, where an account of structural elaboration can be advanced without engaging in ultimate regress or answering the question of how social organization was possible in the first place.

If it is accepted that all S-C action takes place in a CS context and is ineluctably shaped by it, nevertheless only the first part of the cycle has been completed when these conditional influences are fully specified. Second, a complete account of cultural morphostasis and morphogenesis has to incorporate those internal relations at the Socio-Cultural level which determine what the relevant actors do on the spot. For factors like Socio-Cultural homogeneity or heterogeneity, consensus or cleavage, are not simple reflections of the state of affairs in the Cultural System but also embody structured antagonisms based on material interests and the quintessential power of human agency to react with originality whatever its circumstances. (The last may be regarded as a theological lapse by some readers; if so it is one for which I make no apology – the apologia is ecumenical enough to commend itself to the Marxist who believes that 'men make history'.)

Ultimately these Socio-Cultural factors determine:

- what responses are forged under the pressure of the situational logic emanating from the Cultural System;
- which of these can be made to stick Socio-Culturally; and
- whether that which passes back from the S-C to the CS restarts a new cycle or repeats the old one again.

As in structural analysis, it is how the contradictory or complementary relations between parts of the Cultural System map onto orderly or conflictual Socio-Cultural relationships which determine morphostasis or morphogenesis. Cultural Elaboration is therefore completely at the mercy of the *combination* between the two levels of analysis. Detailed consideration of *what* is culturally elaborated and *how* this modifies the CS will be taken up in Chapter 8.

Variations in Socio-Cultural integration

What then does account for Socio-Cultural variations, that is for the occurrence of more orderly or conflictual cultural relations between people than between ideas themselves in the same society[2] at the same time? Social interaction at the S-C level is a network of causal influences involving things like being influenced by ideas from others, imposing ideas on others and challenging the ideas of others. All of these are complex social processes and our task is to explain their basic contours and contents. The raw materials for such an account are the social groups, intermediate between the Cultural System on the one hand and the social structure on the other, yet shaped by both, with their differences in material and ideal interests and their differential power and resources *vis à vis* one another. The problem is how to disentangle the interplay of interests, power and ideas between them and to explain its patterning. *It appears to me that the key to explaining independent Socio-Cultural variations lies in how the social (or sectional) distribution of interests and of power actually gel with the situational logic of the Cultural System (or subsystem) at any given time.*

Obviously the basic question in relation to cultural power is who wields it in an attempt to advance their interests. For the sake of continuity the discussion will be continued with reference to a social group 'a' who are the protagonists of theory or belief A. It will be assumed that they have attained sufficient power in the structural domain to attempt exercises of cultural manipulation the objective of which is S-C orderliness. This is merely a convenient but artificial way into analysis, since, of course, nothing ensures that the social structure uniformly stacks influential power on the side of the advocates rather than the opponents of ideas. It is a helpful starting-point however since two key propositions can be established from it:

(i) That the use of cultural power is indeed accountable for long periods of S-C orderliness, when wielded effectively by those seeking cultural quietism, even if the CS is riven with inconsistency. This is its short and mid-term consequence.

(ii) That the employment of cultural power is an active process which eventually results in both confrontation with and the actual creation of oppositional interests. In the long-term, then, social interaction has far-reaching unintended consequences at both S-C and CS levels – even under this most unfavourable analytical assumption that power initially attaches to the group seeking to *contain* a contradiction or to *maintain* complementarity.

The use of power in the ideational manipulation of social quietism is a well-established theme and recently several theorists have noted the utility of applying Lukes's three-dimensional view of power to the cultural domain.[3] This will be utilized here, but the same methodological problems have to be faced as in the structural realm. Specifically it is inadequate merely to point to the vested interests (in this case both material and ideal) of a particular group in the universalization of its ideas or in ideational control; it is necessary to identify the mechanisms through which cultural power is exerted. Although a more complex exercise it has the advantages that (i) a desire for social or sectional hegemony does not make its success a foregone conclusion, (ii) nor do imbalances in power, lack of reciprocity and dependence in social relations automatically ensure cultural control unless the appropriate means are used, and (iii) that what power is being used for is not treated as self-evident, but can be unpackaged into strategies for different kinds of cultural containment – a very important corrective to the common-sense assumption that the objective of ideational control *is* always the universalization of a group's views.

However, let us now turn to each instance of a significant discrepancy between S-C and CS integration to see, first, how the interplay of situational logic, power and interests worked together to produce it and, second, to examine the consequences of different combinations of orderliness and disorderliness between the CS and S-C levels for cultural morphostasis and morphogenesis.

S-C variations with CS contradictions

The S-C level is more orderly than the CS level

It was argued in the last chapter that the effect of a constraining contradiction was to drive the protagonists of the beliefs or theories which confronted it to syncretic endeavours with the joint aims of CS correction and S-C unification. What we are examining now are instances which exceed these aspirations – cases where Socio-Cultural life appears unruffled by the Systemic perturbations. Why this should be so is often unhelpfully construed as a question of understanding how people can tolerate or even hold contradictory items of belief. This gets off to a bad start because it makes a highly questionable assumption about there being general awareness *of* the contradiction and it comes to a bad end, namely the imputation of primitive mentality, popular irrationality or logical relativity. Instead, the fact of Socio-Cultural orderliness neither implies tolerance of contradiction nor acquaintance with its constituents. For a contradiction to be extensively noticed then it must be noticeable throughout the S-C level; for it to be of concern to numerous social actors then it must impinge upon their action contexts. *The use of power to control the social visibility of contradiction and the presence of interests which mitigate its impact, together account for manifestations of greater orderliness at the S-C compared with the CS level.*

The prime concern of those advocating theory or belief A, which is embroiled in a CS contradiction, is to prevent it from erupting into an S-C controversy. Strategically top priority goes to concealment of the contradiction itself. Indeed such concealment is a pre-condition of group 'a' defending A itself, for unless B is hidden from social view it remains a permanent source of S-C pluralism and confrontation. Given this priority then it is not surprising to find that the strategic maintenance of ignorance amongst vast tracts of the relevant population is regarded as a better method of securing S-C orderliness than intensive indoctrination. Consequently this is the main use made of third-dimensional power under the situational logic of contradictions. For any attempt to universalize beliefs in all their fullness would simultaneously familiarize people with them and hence be counter-productive in introducing those with different material interests to an armoury of ideational difficulties, susceptible of elaboration into a counter ideology.

This is in striking contrast to the uses made of cultural power where the situational logic of reproduction, associated with the concomitant complementarity prevails. Here, as we shall see, is found the true locale for the universalization of beliefs which are inserted into all interstices of social life, like foam-injected damp-proofing.

However, while the social maintenance of ignorance plays a significant background role (in keeping the quiet that way), the general use of various 'containment strategies' directed towards the concealment of contradictory elements is the real hallmark of cultural power when associated with contradictions. Where successfully deployed they are the major factor responsible for a long-lasting period of discrepancy between low system integration and high social integration. In short, containment strategies are largely accountable for a lack of cultural change despite the existence of a fault-line running through the System.

First-dimensional power here entails cultural repression. I have termed it 'authoritarian containment' for generically it works through the *strategic limitation of what part of B is available to A* (that is, to group 'a' who profess A). Orthodoxy is shored up by limiting access to the heterodox. A fairly standard repertoire of tactics is associated with this strategy, whether it is used in the religious, political or academic fields: selective censorship, the banning of books, and the branding of heresies or 'deviations', to prevent contamination; the use of sanctions, enforced recantation or confession of error, excommunication, transportation or incarceration, to remove the contaminated elements.

Their net effect, if they are socially efficacious, is to suppress part of B through the repression of sources of that part of B, whether these are 'texts' or 'dissidents'.

But there are three drawbacks to authoritarian containment, all of which derive from the situational logic of the constraining contradiction, and each of which nullifies it even as a purely social solution – in the long run though not the short. First, this strategy is necessarily limited by the very dependence of A upon B: not everything pertaining to B *can* be burned or banned. Thus the dilemma which Durkheim portrayed: 'Hence the insistence of the early fathers on the dangers to which the Christian is exposed when he gives himself immoderately over to profane studies. They multiply their proscriptions in order to reduce such studies to the minimum. *On the other hand, they could not do without them altogether. In spite of themselves they were forced not to proscribe them*' (my emphasis).[4] Selective access to part must be allowed to some, but where is the guarantee that this will be used to the right end or interpreted in the right light? And even, or perhaps especially, if it is, what if 'conventional' exegesis requires further reference to the forbidden parts of B to back it up: social efficacy of the strategy would presumably dictate that it should not undermine itself by self-defeating prohibitions.

Hence the available zone of B would enlarge. Thus, for example, the sixth-century Benedictines enjoined the reading of Holy books but

amongst holy books it was necessary to include, in addition to the Old and New Testaments, all the commentaries and all the expositions which had been made by the most reputed of the early fathers . . . But this alone was enough to open the door to study and reflection. For who can say where the list of early fathers who were the most orthodox and reputable begins? Then in order to understand their commentaries and their controversies it was necessary to know the theories which they were discussing and which they rejected. This is how profane literature inevitably found its way into the monasteries.[5]

But once the available part of B has been enlarged, what then ensures that it too is used right-mindedly? Nothing – except 'right-mindedness' itself, yet this was supposed to be the result of authoritarian containment though in fact it turns out to be its precondition.

Secondly, once a heresy exists (like the Manichaean doctrine) no authoritative pronouncement can eliminate it from the CS level: ontologically it has been born and at the Systemic level items cannot die, they can only fade into obscurity. No authoritarian tactic can deprive them of eternal life. The burning of books is a ritual Socio-Cultural lesson: the Systemic level is proofed against 'Fahrenheit 451', for ideas survive mentally and orally to be re-recorded after every *auto da fé*. Nor are such tactics socially very effective, they can do nothing against the quiet cherishing of heresy or deviationism which merely await weakened authority to re-surface; while active persecution or purge produces martyrs and is counter-productive in that it increases the visibility of alternatives to the authoritative rulings. All of this is the stuff from which schismatism is made at the Socio-Cultural level – exiling the schismatics does not eliminate the source of schism and socially it merely moves them to a new breeding ground.

In natural science the same strategy may be deployed but its outcomes are similar to the above and just as inefficacious. 'Authoritarian containment', that is, the concealment of counter-evidence, is doomed by precisely the same 'seepage effect' as in the Durkheimian illustrations, not that this deters various closed societies from attempting to use it. Once again it is strictly a feeble means of social control for the scientific masses, since meanwhile, in self-defence, the elite must immerse itself (scientific espionage) in the banned zone in order to anticipate counter-attacks and prepare new authoritative U-turns to deal with them. Indeed it has often been noted that Kuhn's picture of the (authoritarian) scientific community 'contains many suggestions . . . of a significant parallelism between science, especially Normal Science, and theology'.[6] Thus he states that 'Normal Science' 'often suppresses fundamental novelties because they are necessarily subversive of its basic commitments'.[7] Yet even in Kuhn's account, the evil day of the accumulation of anomalies cannot be indefinitely postponed – and when it occurs, on his own account, the fragility of authoritarian containment shatters in the face of contradiction.

It is where the inadequacy of 'authoritarian containment' is acknowledged that the second-dimensional strategy of 'sectional containment' really comes into its own, using non-decision-making to repel dangerous ideational contacts. In the realm of belief, while the first strategy limited the part of B available to upholders of A, the second works the other way round, restricting the section of those holding to A who may have access to B. More generically, 'sectional containment' aims to keep the 'faithful' insulated from B and its dangers, but particularly to prevent the discursive penetration of the contradiction by those whose interests are not concordant with those of group 'a'. Strategic insulation can secure Socio-Cultural orderliness where indoctrination produces resistance to the abuse of preceptual power.

In science, insulation is a supreme example of non-decision-making for it involves holding back the bid for scientific status, protecting both theory and theorists from contact with the danger zone. This spells a self-enforced sojourning in the metaphysical domain (whilst clarifying concepts and building up theoretical interconnections) but refusing, for the time being, to advance propositions susceptible of 'observational' testing. Nevertheless Judgement Day has to come: the venturing of some proposition(s) for testing is the initiation right into the scientific enterprise. This Day comes quickly for what are sometimes called low-level 'trial and error' hypotheses, that is, simple propositions the very aim of which is to say something direct about 'the facts'. Thus in the case of a hypothesis like 'social class is the main determinant of school achievement', sociologists of education could have gone into a metaphysical retreat while 'social class', 'main determinant' and 'school achievement' remained ill-defined and disputed concepts in need of considerable clarification. But precisely because the bid *is* for scientific status, the retreat cannot be indefinite: eventually some operational concepts have to be inserted into the explanatory hypothesis which must then stand up to be scrutinized by 'observations'. (Often the retreat is cut too short. In the desire to establish a primacy claim or scramble into the scientific mantle someone will stick his neck out – thus detonating the contradiction and demonstrating that sectional strategies of Socio-Cultural containment are ultimately at the mercy of social agency.) The Day may be longer in coming for a complex corpus of theory but even it must touch the ground at some point (usually venturing its least central hypotheses first) in order to be deemed part of science at all. (Complex theories like psychoanalysis which persistently refuse to venture any propositions for test – that is for potential contradiction with 'observations' – may have eternal life in the metaphysical realm but they never enter the scientific domain.) The Day of Judgement is of course only the first of an indefinite number of succeeding Days in science and if the hypothesis or theory does not gain immediate and sustained corroboration, then the contradiction is unleashed and once again its protagonists have to engage with it for as always it has crashed through the Socio-Cultural defences.

All the same containment strategies can buy months, years or centuries of peace from social controversy for a theory or belief. Nevertheless as S-C contributions to cultural stability they only secure temporary reprieve. Repression and segregation are incomplete both *in urbi et orbi* and the manipulated consensus is shaken if internal doubts begin to resonate with external incredulity.

The fundamental defect of containment is that its effectiveness is confined to the 'lower orders' or 'underworkers': it never does anything for the fidelistic elite itself who are left face to face with the Systemic inconsistency. The authoritarian version raises but cannot settle the problem of 'Who censors the Censors?' Since they need full access to B in order to sift it for others, then they necessarily confront the full force of the logical contradiction, and there is nothing which guarantees their own immunity from contagion or their unerring judgement about safe materials. Similarly in the sectional version, nothing again is solved for the fidelistic elite. The exigencies created for them by the situational logic continue, and what is to say that their faith or theoretical convictions will not collapse in the face of such problems? The incursion of the outside world, in the form of other interest groups, vaunting precisely that which should remain concealed but cannot be hermetically sealed – like the Renaissance aristocracy brandishing their own version of pagan rationalism – shows the impotence of these S-C strategies when changes in the social structure remove dependence in social relations. Equally, over-hasty precipitation into the hurly-burly of empirical testing, in the hope of advancing material interests by grabbing some scientific palm, makes the theory public property and pushes aside the protective shield which contained the free play of information on it.

And once the city walls are down – pushed from within and battered from without – then ineluctably 'believers' or 'theorists' must face up to the full blast of contradictory ideas. Containment strategies are shown in their true light as a series of temporizing S-C manoeuvres which merely delay looking reality in the face. This, of course, is the point at which the defenders of A are compelled to address the CS problem and produce syncretic corrections, if they do not throw in the sponge. The aim of syncretism at the Systemic level is the effecting of union or sinking of differences. Thus, if and when a coherent syncretic formula is forged, this introduces a higher degree of integration into belief systems and scientific theories than when the contradiction was being concealed and tackled only through S-C containment.

However, to remain with containment strategies for a moment, we have been looking at these exercises of cultural power as sources responsible for producing orderliness in S-C relations – which indeed they are. Nevertheless, this raises the question of whether they are exclusively responsible for all quiet on the Socio-Cultural front. In other words, every time a high level of S-C integration is found in conjunction with a low level of CS integration, can this state of affairs be explained as the product of cultural power alone (in particular the use of containment strategies) or are different causes sometimes at work?

Important as cultural power turns out to be in the engineering of S-C orderliness, it would still be a serious mistake to attribute every manifestation of the latter to an application of the former. (This would transfer to cultural relations the fallacious view that all social relations are power-governed – a proposition which makes no allowance for reciprocity or autonomy in either domain.) Consequently, if we do not want to say that the incidence of S-C orderliness is entirely due to cultural power, or that when it is not, this is because some groups have a high tolerance of contradiction,[8] then we have to answer the question, 'under what conditions can some people be immune from the effects of cultural manipulation?'

The short-hand reply is 'those whose lifeworld is unaffected by an issue and who also abjure involvement'. This attempt to specify the general conditions for exemption from cultural power contains both an objective and a subjective element. Where both obtain simultaneously we have a specification not only of those who will play no part in the controversy surrounding a particular contradiction, but also whose non-involvement has not been strategically manipulated.

Thus, on the one hand, it must be ascertained that a group(s) has interests (material and ideal) which are independent of the issues at stake and has no relations of dependence on the party which is attempting to manipulate consensus in this connection. Power theorists will often object that the self-absorption of a social group in the proximate interests of its life-world is precisely the result of manipulation. The latter induces a group to ignore its broader or longer term interests and to concentrate on privatized concerns; here, getting on with its own business becomes the same thing as minding its own business. Frequently this argument is quite correct and it is therefore always necessary to check whether anything is being done, or deliberately not done, or whether social arrangements are being maintained the effect of which is to block 'the egalitarian effort of understanding'.[9] But if none of this is the case and if we can also point to independent interests upon which the contradiction does not impinge, then it should be granted that such a group has the necessary objective conditions for non-involvement.[10]

On the other hand, since the strategic manipulation of ignorance plays such a conspicuous role in the exercise of cultural power, it does seem safer to concede to the power theorist that evidence must be produced to support any assertion about the subjective irrelevance of a given issue to a particular group, before its immunity is granted. Methodologically it is indeed difficult to accord exemption with conviction. This is mainly because when we are both uninterested and disinterested in something we do not bother to find out much about it. Nevertheless, there is a significant difference between dismissing a theological or scientific question as being of no concern and not knowing that the issue even exists. The difference lies precisely in a subjective determination not to find out more, while objectively being able to do so. Undoubtedly subjective preoccupations also produce selective ignorance, such as people who never glance at the sports pages of newspapers, but the methodological decision has to turn on the objective capacity of a group to be informed and the fact that it has turned down this option.

Thus the orderliness of certain groups at the S-C level will have little or nothing to do with the cultural power-play of those embroiled in the containment of contradiction. Groups which self-consciously abjure involvement and pursue their own self-sufficient interests effectively resist cultural manipulation, without correspondingly raising the level of cultural antagonism. What is being accentuated here, for groups whose hands are not tied by relations of social dependence, is the capacity of human agency to withstand manipulation on two fronts: the cultural raiding and the cultural censorship of the life-world. The ability, in other words, to undertake an autonomous research programme; to entertain an independent belief or stick to common-sense concerns; to leave the current academic controversy alone; to remain aloof from the toils of any particular crisis of conviction; and to let the self-appointed intellectuals and pundits stew in their own juices. Indispensable as all this is to human intellectual freedom it is not necessarily inimical to those seeking to stage-manage a contradiction and produce S-C consensus in the face of CS inconsistency. If groups with autonomy and autarky want to engage in some quiet lateral thinking, their orderly withdrawal can even be a net benefit. Effort and resources can then be concentrated on the points of incipient CS disorderliness.

Thus, when the social distribution of power and interests favour the advocates of A, their use of containment strategies is furthered and these foster a higher level of S-C integration by concealing the low levels of CS integration – indicated by the very existence of contradiction itself. Nevertheless the use of cultural power to manipulate social quietism is still a temporizing manoeuvre even if containment proves long-lasting: things work out very differently if we now suspend our initial assumption that the distribution of power and interests are stacked to the advantage of group 'a'.

The S-C level is more disorderly than the CS level

It has been argued that the situational logic of the constraining contradiction fosters corrective CS syncretism with the S-C goal of unification. This entails (i) the elaboration of a syncretic formula, and (ii) its Socio-Cultural acceptance, as the nuts and bolts of successful unification. None of this is automatic or unproblematic: the nuts have to be culturally made and then socially bolted into place. Both involve a vast amount of work by human actors. Forgeing the nuts is not a task carried out by systemically programmed robots, even though the CS lays down the job specification, nor is securing them a matter of spot-welding.

In exact parallel to the social production of order, the emergence of social disorder depends upon how the initial distribution of interests and of power gel with the situational logic of correction at any time – either societally or sectionally. Where divisions of interests are pronounced, there is a predisposition towards disorderliness – to naked group antagonism at the S-C level – which is prior to anything that the proponents of correction may try to do. (This is the counterpart of that orderliness which stems from the autonomous activities of self-absorbed and self-sufficient groups, as discussed in the last section.)

Where the distribution of resources does not place the advocates of A in a position of social (or sectional) supremacy, then antagonistic interests prove unamenable to social control through the use of containment strategies. The deployment of cultural power to conceal a contradiction is impotent against those whose interests and social position enable them to repudiate authoritarian rulings and to achieve discursive penetration of the controversial. In short, first-and second-dimensional power simply do not work against the opposition of, for example, a cosmopolitan aristocracy or free-travelling intellectuals. This is serious, because no containment strategy addresses or resolves the CS issue but only attempts to conceal it, yet here are groups capable of publicizing the contradiction.

Indeed this is one of the factors (the external pressure rather than the internal impetus) which prompts the shift towards syncretism itself and away from shifty practices. However, the effect of a continued division of interests, either societally or sectionally, is that those with divergent concerns refuse to let any syncretic formula stick Socio-Culturally. It is their antagonistic response, their continuing S-C disorderliness which drives the protagonists of A to more and more generous forms of syncretic accommodation in order to make the Systemic correction socially acceptable. This S-C resistance is therefore part of the dynamics which prevent the syncretic endeavour from stopping short at re-defining B to make it consistent with A.

The general unificatory thrust of the CS enterprise can be deflected in three main ways, each of which propels the advocates of A to make further accommodative corrections. The three forms of deflection spell a progressive increase in S-C disorder and are of ascending order of importance in bringing about CS elaboration. By tracing them through in turn we will be following a rough sequence (for the forms are overlapping) in which high and growing disorderliness in the cultural relations between people ultimately precipitates a corresponding clash in the realm of ideas.

Desertion

The first major manifestation of the failure of unification takes the form of an individual response – personal disenchantment with A and consequent disaffiliation. This tends to be more marked the longer it takes to forge a syncretic formula and the more the latter is a cosmetic job which meets a serious anomaly with superficial casuistry.

At the Socio-Cultural level no one is compelled to take part in the syncretic enterprise. Exit remains a permanent possibility and indeed a steady stream of deserters attends the unfolding of any constraining contradiction. In the scientific domain the attendant 'hitches inevitably induce many individual scientists to shelve or altogether jettison the programme and join other research programmes where the positive heuristic happens to offer at the time cheaper successes: the history of science cannot be *fully* understood without mob-psychology'.[11] In the metaphysical domain the parallel effect is that wranglings breed sceptics. (Also private dogmatism represents a kind of Socio-Cultural dug-out where the flat-earthers and various 'old believers' bury their heads in a sand which blankets them from further changes in the Cultural System.)

Although desertion may be an individual response it has important aggregate effects at both levels of analysis. First, disaffiliation can be of such magnitude that the numbers streaming through the exit progressively denude a cause of supporters. Consequently a cultural contradiction which was a central social concern or a crucial preoccupation in some discipline, gradually drifts out of the mainstream of thought. When this loss of salience occurs, then CS attempts at unification necessarily fail to promote significant S-C consensus because the issue itself has become so marginal that it has lost the attention of most people.

Equally their departure is more than a negative index of disillusionment, signalling loss of monopoly or reduced prominence for some body of ideas. Deserters must also be viewed in their positive role as emigrants; not merely as those divested of their old faith or theoretical convictions but simultaneously as a collectivity freed to join other causes, often ones orthogonal to their source of disenchantment. These they immediately endow with their enhanced deductive powers, sharpened by the necessity of examining the implications of B for A and heightened by the effort of working through the proposed correction and finding it intellectually wanting. Exit is then more than numerical depletion: it is the aggregative transfer of adept deductive reasoning power to external alternatives. Attitudinally it has often been remarked that the ex-member of a school of thought frequently becomes its most virulent critic, but it is equally important to note how involvement in the constraining contradiction fits both apologists and opponents with the same cognitive equipment.

Schismatism and sectarianism

The manifest slipping of containment strategies and the consequential threat of growing disorder provide the impetus for a bolder syncretic manoeuvre – a more thorough-going correction, a

Systemic accommodation, not undertaken solely for the purpose of social control but certainly in the expectation that Socio-Cultural unification will be part of the pay-off. Ironically these more radical attempts at accommodation and unification themselves become bones of contention amongst the faithful: those who were once united in their difficulties often fall into schismatism when they try to solve them.

Here the unificatory thrust is undermined by in-fighting the consequence of which is an unintended exacerbation of Socio-Cultural conflict. A copy-book example of this process was the interplay of Reformation and Counter-Reformation thought which generated lasting sectarian conflict rather than restoring social consensus in post-Renaissance Europe. Despite the fact that the two movements were equally concerned to prevent the actualization of classical rationalism – Luther at one extreme commending an irrational faith which 'wrings the neck of reason and strangles the beast', and Ignatius de Loyola at the other upholding an irrational traditionalism through which 'we ought always to be ready to believe that what seems to us white is black, if the hierarchical Church so define it'[12] – this formal similarity was of no social significance compared with the ferocious schismatism they unleashed. Here is not the place to enter the intricacies of theological controversy and religious politics, except to extract two points about the intensification of S-C conflict.

On the one hand the interests of nascent nationalism battened on to whichever side of the religious divide was most conducive to monarchical aspirations, thus shattering the old international unity of Christendom for good. Moreover, Protestant licensing of private judgement led to the ransacking of tradition and produced not only the better-known divides – Calvinism, Pietism, Socianism, Anabaptism, Unitarianism, Puritanism, Pantheism and so forth – but fostered a narcissism of small sectarian differences, providing potent reinforcement for progressive social differentiation. Nor were those nations retaining their traditional allegiance to Rome assured of a source of Socio-Cultural unification: the frequency with which the Jesuits were expelled and re-admitted is indicative of the split between the ultramontane and gallican Orders within the Catholic Church which exacerbated as well as reflected social divisions.

On the other hand since all the religious grouping mentioned above claimed the right to authoritative pronouncement in religious matters yet appealed to the same body of scripture (in ever-new vernacular translations), the Church universal had animated another constraining contradiction in its midst which was to preoccupy it to this day. And when ever the manifest Systemic unity of ideas is disturbed, their unificatory role in society is reduced: a once-united source of cultural power gives way to a dispute over cultural authority. What sectarianism had done was to remove the opprobrium of heresy and heterodoxy from deviant opinions and re-label deviationists as claimants to sectional authority. The unintended consequence of unleashing private judgement, which made what syncretic adjustments it would, was that it bred a new generation of private judges who turned away damning the entire enterprise, thus augmenting the ranks of the deserters. As Gramsci perceptively noted, '(r)eligion, or a particular church, maintains its community of faithful ... in so far as it nourishes its faith permanently and in an organised fashion, indefatigably repeating its apologetics, struggling at all times and always with the same kinds of arguments'.[13]

Counter-actualization

Desertion and schismatism together constitute a positive feed-back loop. They culminate in a high level of CS disorder, as internecine divisions intensify, and this is outstripped by the S-C disorderliness associated with it. The deserter does not quietly go away. Some of those who had been passively manipulated by a unitary power now actively withhold authority from all parties seeking syncretic unification. It is in this context that those with an interest in so doing can harness S-C disorder to bring about the full actualization of B. In other words they leap-frog over the whole syncretic undertaking to take up their cudgels on the other side.

For one of the unintended consequences of syncretic accommodation is that the contradictory component comes out of concealment, in which it has been kept, and breaks the surface of S-C awareness. Even if one group alone were responsible for presenting a re-interpretation (like the Jesuit repackaging of classical humanism for aristocratic consumption, that is their CS accommodation to the S-C pressures of privilege), still the contents of B become better known and sources of B more available. Obviously availability is restrained in this case precisely because B would be sieved, doctored and monitored. However, given schismatism and sectarianism, then *different* parts of B become accessible *simultaneously* – presented and packaged in different syncretic formulae. Those whose interests are at variance with correction itself gain the wherewithal to deny Systemic corrigibility by becoming fully familiar with B. They also acquire the cognitive skills to advance its claims, for they need only to change the object which the subtleties of the deductive mode of reasoning is used to serve – it is commonplace to note continuities in mode of formal argument which passed from the theological disputation into secular university practice.

Once the Systemic barriers are down, only profound imbalances in social relations to the detriment of our oppositional group can prevent it from pressing forward to the counter-actualization of B, for purposes of self-advancement. In this case a new item is elaborated (not 'original' B, which was the starting point, but 'modernized' B, re-tooled for whatever contemporary tasks are dictated by current interests). If this occurs then the S-C disorder which initially prompted accommodation is now paralleled by a CS split. In fact the social group which accomplishes the Systemic split may not be the one which had first stimulated a move away from simple strategies of containment. What is crucial about the social group which introduces cultural change by inducing a split along the Systemic fault-line is that it has no cross-cutting allegiances with other groups to restrain it from promoting counter-actualization. Accommodative syncretism is thus a hostage to the fate of subsequent social change: present exigencies foster corrective concessions but future developments in society determine whether they stick or become a stick with which to beat their progenitors.

Thus the movement away from simple containment in France was initiated by the emergence of the frivolous leisured aristocracy, but while the clergy and nobility were increasingly to close ranks as the two privileged estates in eighteenth-century society, it was the bourgeoisie who sponsored the secular rationalism of the Enlightenment, pressed it through the provincial parliaments and elaborated it in opposition to privilege itself in the lead-up to the Revolution. France is cited as a particularly straightforward case where no reciprocity stabilized social relations between the Third Estate and privilege which, as Gouldner argued,[14] serves to moderate both social and ideational conflict. Instead the assaults of the Revolutionary Assemblies on the Catholic Church are a replication in the cultural domain of the conditions Lockwood set out for profound structural change, that is, where social disintegration finally superimposes itself on Systemic malintegration, forcing the latter asunder and actualizing the changes which had previously been strategically contained.

When this happens then cultural pluralism has finally defeated the pressures towards ideational unification stemming from attempted corrections of the constraining contradiction. Pluralism is entrenched because the protagonists of A do not simply bow out conceding the cultural field. They fight on, but they have now lost many of the faithful whom they can never recover, and they constantly confront the faithless; not those who have lost their faith to doubt but promotive interest groups who have repudiated it in favour of a new certainty which contradicts it. Hence in this instance we have the counter-actualization of secular scientific man, a being whose genesis was rooted in the constraining contradiction, though he would probably only have recognized that it delayed his emergence and then fought back to dethrone his goddess of supreme reason.

The emergence of the competitive contradiction

When Pluralism wins out through counter-actualization, and the protagonists of A face the advocates of B, though their Socio-Cultural antagonism is mutual, they do not share the same situational logic stemming from the CS level. The essential difference is that those retaining adherence to A are still in the business of correction because nothing had altered their tension with but dependence on B: the game has become harder, winning it more unlikely, but its name remains unchanged – syncretism. In some cases no more than the defensive syncretism of survival – the accommodation of A to B in order to stay alive. In complete contrast, the group now advocating B is utterly unrestrained by interdependence: the cultural stance adopted is independent of any revised version of A whatsoever. Far from pursuing union or attempting to sink their differences, the new proponents of B are in *competition* with adherents of A – a pure unbridled competitiveness at the Systemic level which parallels their total Socio-Cultural hostility. What has emerged from the failure to bring about syncretic unification by successfully correcting the constraining contradiction is an entirely new contribution to cultural dynamics – the *competitive contradiction*.

Although the competitive contradiction enjoys a Systemic existence once it has been fully actualized, it depends upon some group continuously asserting its claims at the S-C level, for nothing else keeps it in social currency. The new 'modernized B' does not (initially at least) derive perpetual salience from the fact that other beliefs and theories are dependent on it and therefore constantly evoke it – even if this is done unwillingly or unwittingly by their advocates. 'New B' may achieve this status, eventually spawning its own ideational dependants, but it will never do so until and unless it becomes Socio-Culturally entrenched. To begin with it is not in the least like 'original B' which had to be compulsively if revulsively handled and re-handled by the 'faithful'.

Moreover, when the competitive contradiction emerges through the corrective vicissitudes associated with a constraining contradiction, then the protagonists of A will be quick to recontain it if no group stands up and keeps on championing it. Those still adhering to A have every interest in this course of action which would obviate or at least postpone the depressing prospect of last-ditch syncretism. The repugnant A $\longrightarrow$ B move is a form of accommodation which they will use any S-C strategy to resist, but to which they fear being driven if competition gets off the ground and has the best of the CS argument. Thus to pursue our French example, both the Catholic Church and bourgeois governments fought throughout the nineteenth century to prevent the crystallization of 'les deux jeunesses' which would signify that the two outlooks had entrenched themselves Socio-Culturally among the new generation and would signal that the CS dispute was going to be protracted. In other words an intensification of S-C conflict necessarily attends the competitive contradiction – whatever the outcome. Those whose interests are served by the new item have to stand up and fight for it; those whose traditional sway is threatened by its actualization have to weigh in and fight against it.

In the above discussion I have been concerned with the *derivation* of the competitive contradiction from the constraining contradiction, for this constitutes a vital morphogenetic mechanism resulting in elaboration of the Cultural System. However, the derived sequence is not the only source of the competitive contradiction. Just as in the previous section, S-C orderliness in its entirety could not be credited to the effective use of cultural power – for some of it was due to the autonomous pursuit of unrelated interests – so here, all observable S-C disorderliness cannot be attributed to the ineffectual use of cultural power and the failure to contain counteractualization. Again importance has to be attached to actors who autonomously accentuate *independent* but contradictory items by ransacking the CS stock in order to advance their S-C interests. These we will return to soon.

The significance of *the competitive contradiction as a derived phenomenon*, however, is that the dynamics of its emergence are self-contained. In other words it is not necessary to posit independent sources of ideational variation or even pluralistic interests, for both of these conditions can be generated by the 'faithful' themselves as they unfurl the constraining contradiction whilst trying to contain or correct it. Nevertheless we have frequently noted instances where social changes in material circumstances or available ideas have served to speed up the morphogenetic process, so independent sources of the competitive contradiction deserve serious attention. The ultimate significance, then, of derivation is that cultural morphogenesis can take place *regardless* of whether there are precipitating material conditions or independent ideational sources of competitiveness at work.

Independent sources of competitive contradictions

Where pure derivation is concerned, then those who unleash the competititve contradiction constitute a subgroup which progressively disengages itself from the main body supporting A, as schismatic hostilities intensify. Here in contrast, we are talking about a socially independent group promoting its separate material interest, which will be termed group 'c' in order to avoid confusion. Were this a collectivity advancing material interests *alone* in opposition to the defenders of A, then the ensuing disorder would take the form of a naked conflict of interests, that is, a form of social antagonism unproductive of change in the Cultural System. Instead, if it is to play a part in cultural morphogenesis through the medium of the competitive contradiction, then it needs to develop a set of ideas, C, which are in competition with and contradictory to A.

The conditions for this occurring are, first, the social availability of a pool of ideas which stand in logical contradiction to A and which therefore can serve in legitimating opposition to the protagonists and beneficiaries of A. While at the CS level this reservoir can be large, S-C access to it may be heavily restricted due to concealment strategies if those defending A are culturally powerful. At other times, however, a Systemic fund of competing ideas has not been culturally constituted – formal contradictions may abound between existing corpuses of ideas but these await detection and what can be termed 'registration' at the CS level, preferably being lodged there in writing if groups elsewhere in space or time are to have much chance of gaining access to them. If this is the case then our independent oppositional group will be condemned to brute social or intellectual antagonism for some time to come. It is a frequent occurrence in all forms of science to observe groups which are hostile to a certain body of well-established theory but which are unable, for the time being, to do more than provide a negative critique of its internal inconsistencies, methodological inadequacies, normative implications etc., since as yet they have no positive alternative to offer.

Providing that this first condition is met, the next requirements for the independent development of the competitive contradiction all revolve around group 'c' actually adopting an ideational C which stands in particular CS relations *vis à vis* A and S-C relations *vis à vis* 'a'. There has been an unfortunate tendency in social theory for such considerations to be bundled together under the blanket of 'elective affinities'. This is unhelpful because simply to stipulate that there must be 'congruence' between a group and the ideas it adopts can be construed in so many ways that at any one time a given group will have multiple 'affinities' (several sets of ideas which meet this loose requirement). The process of 'election' between them is generally then left as an atheoretical matter of local contingency. Consequently many of the relationships between groups and ideas, or material and ideal interests, which can be said to display 'elective affinity' fail to meet the much more stringent conditions for constituting a competitive contradiction. Analytical dualism helps to carry forward this task of further specification.

At the CS level there must be logical consistency between the avowed interest of group 'c' and the ideas C which it adopts from those which are both objectively available and socially accessible. Equally important, there must be logical *in*consistency between the two sets of ideas A and C. This of course is where the notion of an 'elective affinity' turns out to be much wider than the concept of a competitive contradiction. For example the corpus of belief or theory representing C may merely constitute a logical compromise in relation to A. This would not rob it of 'congruence' with the interests of group 'c', for if brought about the compromise might be more favourable to them than the status quo. But just as a wage increase does not challenge the principle of pay distribution, so A stands uncontradicted here.

However, even if the logical CS requirements are met, additional S-C conditions must also maintain if a competitive contradiction is to be unleashed. Next, then, C must be 'non-contaminated' through undue proximity to A. This is a purely social requirement which has to do with being seen to be distinctive, above and beyond the fact of being in contradiction, for we are dealing here with the question of marshalling S-C support. The latter is absolutely crucial, for unless support can readily be mobilized and maintained for C then nothing else ensures its lasting social salience and consequently its endurance as a competitor. Since a support base is so vital for C, it thus comes close to being a condition of competitiveness that the ideas making up C can batten on to, or are developed out of, ones which already enjoy acceptance and prominence amongst the relevant social group. Such S-C entrenchment also provides some protective resistance against the S-C repression which is encountered by competitive contradictions.

S-C responses to nascent competitive contradictions

All protagonists of competitive contradictions (whether of derivative or independent origin) come up against attempts to still their oppositional voice. As purely Socio-Cultural efforts these again prove deficient, but now because of the *competitive* nature of the contradiction itself. When a logical inconsistency of this kind attains social salience it is predicated on two groups actively accentuating its contradictory components. In terms of the situational logic then created, it follows that one group is never capable of untrammelled Socio-Cultural manipulation since its opponent will always fight back.

Confronted with a contradiction which has achieved some degree of social prominence, the basic reaction of those adhering to A is indeed to seek the elimination of opposition. As Durkheim put it 'simple antagonism breeds rejection'.[15] But although the repudiation of uncongenial, inconvenient, hostile or threatening ideas may be a viable personal solution, it does nothing to remove the contradiction as a social problem.

Nevertheless some of the everyday rationales which enable individuals to spurn contradictory items can also be marshalled into a social strategy for discrediting them. By branding certain ideas as ludicrous the individual justifies having nothing more to do with them, thus eliminating one of the contradicting elements by denying it tenability, validity or veracity. The same technique of denigration can be used collectively, but its efficacity has more stringent conditions attached to it. While each of us can privately label anyone else a fool, lunatic or charlatan, it takes a pretty hefty social imbalance between opponents to make such labels stick societally. However, given that social imbalances are the rule rather than the exception, a refined version of the above, that is, dismissal-by-devaluation, is a frequent tactic used by the socially dominant in any field.[16] Thus the subordination of another group's ideas is engineered by covert uses of power in communication systems (ideological or scientific), to mark them as 'primitive beliefs', 'folklore', 'superstitions', 'false consciousness', 'old wives' tales', 'pseudo-science' or just 'far out'. From our point of view the real problem with this tactic is not that it is ineffectual but rather that it is maximally effective against the weakest social groups – that is, just those whose position prevented them from attaining high Socio-Cultural salience for their ideas in the first place.

Without dismissing the social importance of this tactic, it is basically a method of using power to organize potential contradictions out of the Socio-Cultural arena,[17] rather than a means of tackling the pressing problem of those which have already achieved prominence. Here the armoury of everyday rationales cannot be re-tooled for 'strong' opponents, because what results is a crossfire of mutual abuse with all the effectiveness of ritual incantations. Repudiation of opponents may suffice for an individual to get by, but it goes no way towards eliminating the opposition at the Socio-Cultural level – once the (relevant) population has divided into strong partisans of A and strong protagonists of B or C. In other words, as a competitive strategy, repudiation is only thoroughly effective when wielded against the weakest competitors. It is far more interesting to view discrediting in the light of a preventive measure rather than a conflictual strategy, and to examine its longitudinal effects in *precluding* the articulation of certain antitheses associated with subordinate interests at the Socio-Cultural level. As in structural analysis, the silent areas of organized cultural inaction can prove more important over time than where the shouting was loudest at any particular moment.

Nevertheless if the shouting continues then contradictory ideas remain salient, fuelled by the divergent interests of proponents of A and of B or C. What this means is that neither group can rest with impunity on tactics directed merely at discrediting the other: a rougher strategy is needed if alternative interests are to be repressed. At this point in the competition resort may well be made to coercion which is the strategic counterpart of 'authoritive containment' in relation to constraining contradictions. In a sense the use of coercion acknowledges that it is an ontological impossibility to eradicate unwanted elements from the Cultural System and implies that the alternative is an epistemological assault – aimed at preventing others from bringing them to our attention. The objective then is not to eliminate the oppositional ideas but to wipe out or permanently gag their upholders – at its most extreme it means killing the infidel, the political purge, or the ideological witch-hunt. Less brutally, it can mean refusing research grants, academic or public appointments, publication in academic journals, access to the media or professional recognition.

Again this is a purely Socio-Cultural solution which does and can do nothing to eliminate the contradictory element from the Systemic level. A revealing illustration is provided by the mid-nineteenth-century controversy between Pasteur and Pouchet on whether the micro-organisms responsible for putrefaction, fermentation, the appearance of moulds etc., were introduced from the air (Pasteur) or were spontaneously generated in certain substances (Pouchet). After various (inconclusive) experimental contests and vitriolic public debate, the *Académie des sciences* at Pasteur's request formed a commission which pronounced in his favour. This 'effectively supressed opinions in support of spontaneous generation for some years, especially in France. A decade later, however, Bastian, an English physician, put forward the thesis once more in extreme form. As Bastian received support from both scientists and laymen, Pasteur and others were forced to undertake further research, in the course of which many new problems were revealed and several old problems reopened.'[18]

Obviously then S-C coercion is not a watertight strategy as people can still encounter competitive ideas in all their entirety, reactivating them at the first let up of authoritarian pressures or undermining these from afar. At its most successful, and given a substantial imbalance of power favouring one side, then competition may *temporarily* be deprived of *overt* salience in society. In fact, even at the Socio-Cultural level, it is rarely fully effective (as the underground press, circulation of banned books and stimulation of dissident literature bear witness). Moreover it is frequently counter-productive since its backlash is often an intensified Socio-Cultural antagonism and a reinforced attachment to oppositional beliefs – the strength of Catholicism in Poland being a prime example.

S-C variations with CS complementarities

In turning to examine times and places where relationships of complementarity prevailed at the CS level, one is now dealing with an orderly Cultural System. This 'high' CS integration represents a very different starting point from the contradictions which have just been discussed and constituted, by definition, a state of 'low' System integration. There the factor crucial for change was when the Socio-Cultural relations between people became even more disorderly than those between ideas. Thus the conjunction between low CS and low S-C integration was the formula for morphogenesis; morphostasis coincided with the existence of a higher degree of S-C orderliness, largely engineered through the use of cultural power, which enabled contradictions to be concealed and contained. Once again, where the complementarity is concerned, the key factor for introducing cultural change is a substantial drop in S-C integration. Here, however, the development of low S-C orderliness is the exclusive motor of change, for there is no accompanying tension within the Cultural System which encourages the former or can be exacerbated by it. On the contrary it is malintegration at the S-C level which has to disrupt the dense and resilient constitution of a well-dovetailed CS.

In other words the sequence leading to cultural change is the opposite in the two cases: with contradictions, the fault-line is present from the start in the CS and has to be split open by S-C struggle, but with complementarities, S-C disorder has to develop until it can damage the smooth face of the CS. The real problem here is *how* can Socio-Cultural relations actually become so disorderly? Because systematization is extremely thorough then social groups appear to have no internal elements to exploit as oppositional ideas; and because boundary-maintenance also gets tougher, they appear to have no external ideational sources to explore in opposition either.

So where does S-C disorder come from? Some find it tempting to offer a Gramsci-style explanation. This would dismiss the notion of orderly S-C relations, generated by a genuine acceptance of the CS, as binding on a population whose interests are undifferentiated enough for it to be universally congruent with them, as nothing but pure myth. Instead, power relations would be advanced as the quintessential causal element in consensus building – responsible for the enforced submergence of certain interests (sectional or regional, etc.) from the start. This, it would be argued, is what underlies the long periods, characteristic of the concomitant complementarity, where the outward manifestation is of high CS integration paralleled by high S-C integration. One of the attractions of such an account is that it then only needs point to contingencies which result in a relaxation of power for the submerged interests to surface and order to be destroyed.

Now although I would not want to dismiss such considerations out of hand, this seems to have several deficiencies as a theory of cultural dynamics. First, it is doubtful whether it is indeed a theoretical account since it is entirely dependent upon the empirical ebb and flow of power, and moreover a power the suspension of which depends on a variety of *ad hoc* circumstances. Alternatively it can only escape from being wholly empirical by endowing the state of affairs described above with an *a prioristic* character – which is unwarranted for exactly the same reasons that upwards conflation is unacceptable.

Moreover it is quite unnecessary when accounting for S-C disorder to postulate a pre-existing differentiation of interests which have, until a given moment, been effectively subordinated by cultural power. Nor is there any need to deny the point, which is only wrong when the downwards conflationist universalizes it, that sometimes a high level of S-C integration can arise from the reproduction of CS similarities among a population. In sum, it is not necessary to make either conflationary assumption universal. The reason for this is that the concomitant complementarity *itself* generates a sufficient differentiation of interests to unleash S-C disorder eventually. Once again the dynamics of cultural morphogenesis can be *derived* from within the concomitant complementarity – which is not to deny the contribution of independent sources of differentiation to its emergence.

Density and differentiation

Here I am going to argue that just as the constraining contradiction contained the seeds of its own opposition, so too does the concomitant complementarity. Although the social processes involved are completely different, both ultimately depend upon cultural power for germination to take place. The root-cause in this case is the increase in CS *density* which, as has been seen, intensifies greatly as the complementarity is explored and systematized. Density, in turn, is incompatible with complete sharing and the development of hierarchy is its inescapable S-C accompaniment. Hierarchy constitutes differentiated interests which are hostile to S-C order. In other words, it is argued that density and differentiation create a positive reinforcement loop which introduces disorderliness – whether or not there were any independent interests submerged from 'the start' by the use of cultural power.

To see how this self-undermining sequence works, let us first examine why density is generically inegalitarian. This is not self-evident for the situational logic of the concomitant complementarity, being one of reproduction, conduces to the diffusion of the CS in all its fullness. No recourse is made to strategic concealment as there is nothing to hide. A prime indicator of this difference from the containment strategies associated with the constraining contradiction is the much more open 'education' typical of the complementarity. Here nothing is risked the deeper and further adherents plunge into the ideational environment constituted by the A B complex – witness Weber's classic examples of the protracted Chinese literary instruction and of the life-long Hindu quest to perfect spiritual techniques. Such 'education', however, may be formally open but it is also formidably long; the more density grows, the longer still it becomes. Eventually Systemic density becomes so great that it cannot be reproduced throughout society for it has become too elaborate for all to share in all its detail.

Consequently CS density becomes the enemy of S-C equality. For who has the time and the resources to acquire it? Obviously not everyone and as time goes on with density ever-increasing and induction lengthening proportionately, then an increasingly smaller section of the relevant population can become conversant with the CS in all its fullness. A hierarchy of knowledgeability based on S-C self-selection thus emerges as the first unintended consequence of density. It means that S-C integration-through-sharing declines as the thing to be shared becomes too elaborate for all to assimilate. Any resemblance (societal or sectional) to a state of co-thought and co-action has gone for good. From now on fissiparousness at the S-C level eats deeper and deeper into the 'sharedness' which was the mainstay of S-C order. Its final effect is substantially to weaken S-C integration.

Specifically the hierarchy of knowledgeability creates three clearly differentiated interest groups in relation to the CS and these become ever more distinct at the Socio-Cultural level:

(1) A socio-intellectual elite crystallizes from those whose prerogative it is to know the CS in all its logical coherence. Elite formation intensifies as cultural density is progressively formalized and institutionalized – formalization generally establishes a new social distinction between the literate and the illiterate (or those who have time to learn to read and those who lack the facilities), while institutionalization creates further distinctions between standards of mastery and new role-divisions between masters, journeymen and the rest. These elites – the Brahmins, literati, intellectuals and academic barons – become the social beneficiaries of their high

level of cultural proficiency and the more so as such attainments also become less accessible to the population at large. Consequently they acquire a vested interest in protecting the systematized whole against any form of CS simplification or disruption: their S-C interests are in complete harmony with the situational logic of protection.

(2) However as the cultural conspectus is progressively filled in and work on its systematization shrinks to mere embellishment, an important S-C consequence comes into play. The cultural 'honours' go first and foremost to the ancestors or founders (much intellectual work being devoted to tending their literary shrines) and, second, to their contemporary 'representatives', who, having undergone the longest or most arduous process of reproduction now constitute the line of intellectual succession. What this means is that the next generations, even of the culturally privileged, are by definition 'moppers-up'. In brief, there is a progressive reduction in ideational rewards to be had over time and usually longer to wait in the individuals' lifetime or work-time even for these. Thus the concentration of rewards and benefits in the hands of an S-C elite (archetypically the intellectual hegemony of conservative old men) means that more and more of the 'educated' find the state of affairs in their country, specialism or field of activity stifling, stultifying or stagnating rather than satisfyingly absorbing. From them a category of social marginals is created, of those who have made a major personal investment *vis à vis* the Cultural System but who are denied much return from it as it stands, and yet who are firmly discouraged from making cultural innovations to increase their rewards. If it is permissable to speak of opportunism as an interest then it is theirs.

(3) The masses emerge residually as the products of an incomplete S-C induction into the full CS. Integration-through-sharing no longer enfolds them, their cultural benefits are the lowest going, and their S-C bonding weakens as full CS citizenship is gradually withdrawn from them. That they do not immediately manifest disorderliness is pre-eminently due to the cultural power which is brought into play against them, on the emergence of hierarchy in S-C life.

Uses of cultural power

The differentiation of interests and rewards creates the conditions for the use of cultural power by elites to maintain S-C order amongst the masses and the marginals. Different strategies are deployed in the two cases.

The masses are the recipients of third-dimensional cultural manipulation – of the mobilization of bias, the structuring of wants and the shaping of motives in relation to the concomitant complementarity which the elite seeks to protect. Generically I have termed these 'naturalization strategies' for they work through the presentation of the CS as the natural order of affairs which, it is conveyed, will carry its own penalty if traduced.

The basic theme is laid down in Brahmin teaching which motivates adherence to caste rules among the lower castes for fear of imperilling other-wordly opportunities, despite this group having everything material to gain by rejecting them here and now. The same tune blares through political economy with its paradoxical message that though natural, the laws of nature need teaching, but because natural can be acquired by any labouring man (see James Mill),[19] and must be before unenlightened self-interest falls prey to the 'complaints of faction and sedition' (see Adam Smith),[20] damaging itself as well as endangering the general good. Hence the development by the Utilitarians of an associational method of teaching for the overt purpose of moulding attitudes. The naturalization theme re-echoes more subtley in Kuhn's account of the high-tide of a research paradigm where, since the theory is naturally right, then the younger practitioner is cowed into intra-punitiveness when his puzzle solution is not ingenious enough. He does not blame the theory, attitudinally he has been rendered incapable of this: 'only his own ability not the corpus of current science is impugned . . . in the final analysis it is the individual scientist rather than the current theory which is tested'.[21]

The orderliness produced amongst the masses and under-workers is thus manipulated by what Bourdieu calls the 'naturalization of arbitrariness'.[22] However, it is not necessary to assume that the groups on which cultural power is used become fidelistic believers, even if they display social quietism. Their acceptance is largely gained by keeping alternatives inarticulate, insisting that there is but one natural order, that anything other is a dangerous departure and thereby insidiously depriving the masses of the tools for dissent. Thus it would be wrong to construe passive acceptance as active assent. For S-C order among the masses is no longer the product of the bindingness of ideas or their being binding because they are shared – it is due to preceptual power. This may not be recognized either by those applying it (their religious, political or scientific convictions can veil their interests to themselves rather than necessarily being a conspiratorial mask donned to dupe others[23]), or by those at the receiving end whose detection of the interest nexus may be blocked by the opacity of irrational practices – deferential rites, status symbols, professional etiquette or academic protocol. Nevertheless where order is based on preceptual power it rests on shaky foundations: here I must disagree with Bourdieu that the logic of symbolic violence is such that it universally produces the conditions which prevent groups from ever seeing through it.[24]

For in any case such tactics are inefficacious against the marginals, because culturally they are in the know and one of the things they know about their culture is that it is not rewarding them. If the elite is unwilling to redistribute benefits more generously amongst the marginals then since it is unable to shape their attitudes, its only recourse is to deploy power so as to shape their intellectual environment. This has the dual objective of cutting off access to ideational alternatives from outside, and cutting out any signs of their internal elaboration. Strategies based on the use of first- and second-dimensional power are thus employed to protect systematization against internal or external sources of disruption at the hands of marginal groups. When effective, the latter may continue to grumble or even display a certain S-C antagonism, but marginality does no Systemic damage.

Internally, the powers of the hierarchy are used to sanction and subordinate innovatory ideas and particularly any deviant interpretations of the CS which threaten to crystallize into heresy or heterodoxy. Gouldner's attack on Parsons' treatment of the normative order is particularly relevant to the concomitant complementarity. The latter approximates to the Parsonian notion of one central value system (an *a prioristic* condition for a functioning social system to him, but merely one of four cultural states of affairs here, though the one under discussion at the moment). Gouldner argued[25] that if there is no 'mutuality of gratifications' (which is the case for those I have termed 'marginals'), then different interpretations may well be placed on central values which are conducive to the furthering of differentiated interests. In brief, discontent can find disruptive ideational expression by accentuating those aspects of a theory or set of beliefs which are most congenial to it. Sometimes, as Gellner suggests,[26] this may take the form of discomforting the elite by the proposal of a more consistent application of a hallowed principle (for example, a thoroughly meritocratic literati).

Inconvenient interpretations obtruded by marginal groups are usually treated to first-dimensional repression – the stripping of honours, professional demotion, expulsion or extradition. Signs of interpretative innovation among the masses are generally more amenable to second-dimensional techniques of non-decision-making. Since their restricted access to the cultural stock will induce them to generate defective syntheses of ideas, these interpretations are more controllable through social dismissal, public ridicule and other methods of exclusion from serious consideration. An interesting variant is where the 'mass' interpretation is imitative of elite beliefs but geared to improving their own lot (as in Sanskritization or practices of the '*blancs–noirs*'). For providing their S-C pretentions are not too great (or numerous), this version of fidelity to the CS is rewarded by silent incorporation, or what some might call 'repressive tolerance'.

If the above uses of cultural power are internally effective, then the 'outside' becomes the great source of ideational alternatives. This is the point at which exchange with the environment becomes reconstrued as external incursion. Power strategies (first- and second-dimensional) are now directed towards social or sectional boundary-maintenance with the object of *closure* against the exterior. In other words, we are no longer dealing with a 'natural' boundary, created by preoccupation with internal affairs, but with a defensive barrier constructed by the elite against external threats to their interests.

Since access to some source of variety (new information, signals, symbols, messages) is essential to cultural innovation, then if power strategies prevent it from being generated internally or imported from outside they indeed succeed in protecting the status quo in the CS. The 'marginals' have, through the use of power, been denied access to the raw material of cultural change. They are placed in a prison from which all instruments for inflicting damage have been removed, but in this case it is the environment which is being protected against the inmate. Under these circumstances marginal groups are given every incentive to return to authorized cultural activities and are denied the equipment to do otherwise. To Popper this picture of prisoners condemned to gilding the prison walls is defective since they could instead employ themselves in digging their way out.[27] In fact I am going to argue that he is absolutely correct, but only if his argument is given the completely literal meaning of physical escape, which was not, I think, what he had in mind.

In sum, the successful use of cultural power can protect the CS in basically unchanged form, for long periods of time (of course what is a long time in science is but a moment in a world religion). Nevertheless the problem of order at the S-C level has not been solved. There remains a pool of disaffected marginals, ready to exploit any opportunity to their advantage, and a reservoir of disgruntlement among the masses who at best display quietism rather than the outward signs of inner conviction. In short, CS integration remains high but the degree of S-C integration is now considerably lower.

What this means is that one of the two conditions specified in information theory as necessary to cultural innovation has developed as an unintended consequence of the concomitant complementarity – namely, sufficient S-C differentiation of interests such that there are now groups of 'receivers' ready to capitalize on new cultural items.[28] And these groups tend to become even readier over time, as their frustrations grow and their benefits decline while sanctions accumulate and restrictions rankle. But the fact that S-C integration is imperfect, or, as others put it, that there is some structural slack present, is a situation which can continue without CS issue unless the second condition is met – namely the availability of some alternative source of Systemic variety. Yet as we have seen power prevents the internal generation or the external importation of just this. So if variety is denied to our marginal groups for fear of its disruptive potential, then marginality will only generate morphogenesis if it migrates towards variety.

Marginality and migration

Cultural morphogenesis *derives* from the concomitant complementarity only when the marginal groups become migrants. The potential 'receivers', that is, the educated yet frustrated opportunists, venture to the source of new variety in order to increase their benefits. And this source now lies outside the boundary, artificially maintained by power, which must therefore be crossed. They go willingly, impelled by their interests, and no power restrains the departure of such disruptive S-C elements. Marginal groups at the S-C level thus push open the door to cultural change quite literally, and go out through it. The changes that their opportunism may eventually lead them to produce 'outside' are independent of any co-terminous alteration in the CS which they have left behind. For the time being this 'profits' from their departure precisely by remaining unchanged and its elite may believe that it has solved the problem of S-C order through having rid itself of the most disorderly. Migration might be made more difficult were it not for this alluring prospect of re-establishing a state of affairs where high CS integration was again matched by high S-C integration. However, our concern for the moment is with the fortunes of the migrants.

The push of power and the pull of their interests has prepared a category of opportunists ready for ideational innovation outside their existing purview. As marginals they are not vowed to repairing some position, not committed to one side in some competition, and are no longer wedded to embellishing a tradition. As migrants they are open to new ideas, especially those which fall, at least partially, within their field of competence, and are on the look-out for novel components which will advance their interests. Thus for an item to be taken up by them it has to have two basic properties: be prominent enough to come to our group's attention and be promising enough in terms of compatibility with its ideal interests.

Migration *per se* promotes none of these. It simply makes new necessarily prompt the exploration and exploitation of the complementarities encountered. Indeed most gross generalizations about cultural contact (CS) fail to work precisely because they omit any reference to the S-C motivation of those involved. The first common error is to stress 'culture clash' as almost synonymous with cultural contact, but the fact that independent though compatible items come into contact does not objectively spell clash at all, nor does it automatically result in subjective antagonism to the novel or unknown. Second, and equally erroneously, contact has also been played down in some quarters as being of no general consequence because there are instances of it being inconsequential. Episodic evidence, that for example, travellers to the Holy Land in the Middle Ages 'expressed little or no curiosity about their fellows, little interest in alien ways, little reaction to cultural diversities'[29] cannot be magnified into universal indifference towards 'Curiosa'. Third, contact can be overplayed as a recipe for instant innovation, as with the once-fashionable belief that interdisciplinarity was some kind of 'open sesame' to invention.

Migration *per se* promotes one of these. It simply makes new items available to the host and the migrant populations and these can be welcomed, ignored or attacked by either. What is more they can simply be registered or utilized *as* alternatives. Thus in developing societies many quite regularly patronize the health centre and the witch doctor, the priest and the sooth-sayer, the agricultural advisor and the rain-maker, the trained midwife or the obeyah woman, without questioning the complementarity or contradictory nature of these practices, let alone trying to synthesize them. And this is not a point about 'primitive peoples' for precisely the same is true of what is actually called 'alternative medicine' now in the West. In other words, objective (CS) contact by itself is not enough; it must be accompanied by a particular kind of (S-C) motivation on the part of the migrants.

Migration acts as a catalyst to cultural change when the migrants have become such because of dissatisfaction with cultural developments in their own 'area'. Their discontent is not a purely subjective phenomenon, equivalent to 'wanting a change', but occurs when internal resources are inadequate for pushing forward some line of thought or developing some kind of skill which they do not want to abandon entirely. The everyday equivalent, when one gets stuck over an idea, is to reach for a new book in the hope of finding a new lead. In short, the migrant goes out looking for a *complementary* stimulus which will further his project. Because the search is for CS items which have this particular logical property – of consistency with existing ideas, interests, skills, techniques etc. – a distinctive type of cultural change emerges from it.

The emergence of the contingent complementarity

I have called this product the contingent complementarity, for cultural innovations of this kind are composed of items which are at the same time logically consistent but independent of one another. These are its Systemic properties and neither the element which the migrant group contributes nor the item which it appropriates through encounter, are of its own making (never the latter; never all of the former). That for which the marginal migrants are alone responsible however, is *bringing the two items into active conjunction*. Since the CS compatibility of the elements is a matter of contingency and not concomitant variation, then the promotive S-C efforts of such interest groups are solely accountable for bringing them together and making something of them. Without S-C action in pursuit of interests these CS complementarities could pass unnoticed indefinitely.

Fundamentally a contingent complementarity is detected (on the derived scenario) because somebody has gone out of their way to look for one and with some idea of what they were looking for. Quite literally they were searching for a 'foreign' complement to a 'domestic' item. Instances can be as disparate as Peter the Great and Catherine I inspecting Europe for naval, military or educational techniques which would match Russian resources and promote Westernization, at variance with sclerotic domestic practice, but congruent with enlightened plans for national development. Very different, except in formal terms, was the small group of disenchanted physicists, described by Mulkay, who began work on bacterial viruses (phages) in the 1930s. 'These men concluded that research in physics was unlikely to reveal any interesting problems for some time to come; that biology seemed to offer the most promising opportunities for using the physical methods with which they were familiar; and that the application of these methods to living matter might generate not only significant biological findings, but also new laws of physics.'[30] (These examples also serve to show that the social conditions of marginality by no means apply to nonentities.)

So far we have looked at *why* these people are motivated to undertake their migratory quest but not at *what* they are doing cognitively *when* they bring two complementary items into conjunction. Nor have we questioned *how* it is that they regularly explore the contingencies encountered rather than undergoing conversion to some oppositional cause. The marginals are heavily conditioned in their responses by their prior investment in acquiring a complex body of knowledge and by the modes of cognition which became habitual to them in the process. (It is the 'masses' who make the converts to foreign religions, for example, if and when the opportunity arises. Groups such as the Indian unscheduled castes with nothing to lose have thus displayed mass conversions to the more egalitarian beliefs of Islam, Christianity and Buddhism at different times.[31]) The marginals, too, want a way out but their reaction differs for they both have something to lose and they have also been schooled in a mode of thought, not just drilled into outward ritual performance.

Thus what our migrants are doing when they bring two complementary items into active conjunction is actually behaving quite 'traditionally' – in cognitive terms. As has already been discussed (pp. 171–8) the *concomitant* complementarity represented a conspectus which was formed by exploring the friendly environment of ideas, the interdependencies of which encouraged inductive generalizations for the simple reason that induction works in such an ideational context. In fact the *contingent* complementarity is developed in precisely the same way. Through migration the marginals find what they were looking for; they hit upon some item in their new environment which happens to complement their existing knowledge, although the two components are independent and previously no connection had been noted between them. Our opportunists then make the inductive leap from the old environment to the new, encouraged by verificatory evidence which is their directional guidance instrument. Precisely the same euphoria attends the preliminary working out of the contingent complementarity as in the golden days of exploring concomitance. The pay-offs at the point of breakthrough are often enormous and prove enormously attractive. Innovation surges forward over this *terra incognita* without any resistance to its inductive advance since there is no orthodox consensus and there are no defensive interests in no-man's land.

Consequently migrant groups make what they will out of their newly discovered contingent complementarities. Since they are innovating they are neither held up by the restraining powers of entrenched elites nor are they diverted from their novel course by established expertise which draws them aside to address difficulties or answer criticisms. Initially, at least, they veer away from the anomalous until they have consolidated a body of inductive generalizations which appears to meet their prime requirement – they constitute a profitable alternative to the point of departure. In short, the problems come later, not necessarily much later, but after cultural morphogenesis has taken place – such that the innovation is 'solid' enough to be criticized and a body of critics has had time to consolidate itself. Meanwhile a new source of societal or sectional *variety* has both been registered at the CS level and has also begun to achieve social prominence.

Once again cultural change has been *derived* from the S-C dynamics set in train by the status quo at the CS level – that is, by the unintended social consequences of the concomitant complementarity. Of course, this derived sequence parallels the emergence of the competitive contradiction from within the confines of the constraining contradiction. The significance of the parallel is identical, for in this case too, change derives from internal dynamics. Once again these societies are *not* condemned to morphostasis or dependent upon external intervention for morphogenesis. Yet it should be noted that many authors who stress the cultural stability of 'cold' societies are referring to exactly those cultures characterized by concomitant complementarities. What the internal derivation of morphogenesis shows is that such arguments are unlikely to be sustained if 'traditionalism' is dissociated from 'timelessness' – as it is the atemporal view of tradition which artificially conceals the derived sequence of change. Equally, however, it is true that the derivation discussed is not the only source of the contingent complementarity.

Independent sources of the contingent complementarity

There are two basic kinds of encounter with compatible items, the sought and the unsought, and so far we have dealt only with the former. Unsought encounters affect those working at the margins of an area – those outside the mainstream of their discipline, on the fringes of the orthodox consensus, or at the borders of standard professional practice. There is no sense in which they are necessarily disenchanted with their present position or activities, but as they come into contact with the new item and begin to explore it, they become progressively *distanced* from their origins. Morphogenesis takes place as the contingent complementarity is elaborated and as those engaged in this process become more and more absorbed by it. When they follow it up and go where the new ideas lead, then their own migration ends up being the unintended consequence of the original fortuitous contact. The series of steps involved is the reverse of the derived sequence, where migration was the last thing to happen; here it is the product of morphogenesis rather than vice versa.

Contact with variety is again essential: the reason why the items in question are not subject to any embargo by the powerful is that their significance for change is simply not recognized by them until it is too late. Fortuitous contact between compatible items is common; in all fields the research initiated for one purpose regularly produces unexpected findings. It briefly illuminates a whole range of issues previously ignored or unperceived, but the beam passes on over them unless someone spotlights it on a particular item. When this happens and something productive emerges from the connection then the term 'spin-off' has been coined in experimental science, while the arts tend to use more occult phraseology and talk of 'sources of inspiration'. Both compact the process and present its end-product as an unexpected gift; all the recipient has to do is unwrap it.

If we take another example discussed by Mulkay, the origins of radio astronomy, we can begin to unpackage the process and see that at most the gift was a construction kit with the instructions missing. Although the notion of extra-terrestrial objects emitting radio as well as light waves had been advanced by Clerk Maxwell and Hertz in the nineteenth century, no attempt at receiving electromagnetic emission was successful. The method was finally stumbled upon in 1932 as an accidental by-product of industrial research. Jansky, working for the Bell laboratories on the noise level in directional short-wave radio-receivers, discovered constant radio emission which he concluded were signals coming from the Milky Way. His findings 'were quickly published in an engineering journal and widely publicized by the American mass media'.[32] In other words a contact mechanism, publication, existed but only one 'opportunist' was forthcoming. While the academic community did not respond, an amateur astronomer, Karl Reber, built a steerable parabolic reflector in his backyard and immediately established that the optical sky and the radio sky were very different. Without the increase in salience which Reber's work gave to detectable radio emissions, Jansky's discovery may have led nowhere. Without the war-time constitution of a body of 'opportunists' by the British government, who decided that research into radar was likely to be most militarily productive, both Jansky's and Reber's work might not have been pursued.

As it was the new branch of study was slowly consolidated from the post-war work of the radar physicists. Those who continued to work on radio transmission were *not* a group of dissatisfied migrants and they did not immediately form a new specialism concerned with radio astronomy: 'On the whole they regarded themselves still as physicists and their subject as "radio physics". They took up such problems as the reflection of radio waves from meteor trails and the physical character of the upper atmosphere. Only slowly did they become aware of the immense possibilities involved in detailed study of the radio universe. Gradually, purely physical problems were dropped in favour of astronomical problems.'[33] Migration had finally taken place and was associated with the two consequences typical of the contingent complementarity – an S-C re-grouping of people on specialist lines and an increased specialization of ideas at the CS level.

S-C responses to nascent contingent complementarities

In so far as specialization increases, this spells a reduction in uniformity at the S-C level. Once variety has been detected, explored and elaborated it reacts on density at the CS level. The objective growth in variety in turn constitutes an equally objective increase in choices, available alternatives and ideational opportunities for the population in general. These may be particularly attractive to the disgruntled, especially those whose previous 'assent' was manipulated by power. Obviously the S-C elites still attempt to filter, monitor or censor which alternatives are taken up and what use is made of them, but again objectively these changes in the CS represent a shifting environment and an extension of horizons which account for changes in cultural interaction because some social actors will take account of them. And whether many take active account or not, the environment has altered radically for all since increasingly they cannot fail to be aware that alternatives exist – and such an awareness is death to tradition.

However, because the alternatives people adopt are not necessarily contradictory, the S-C consequences of their diffusion often represent a decline in consensus without any proportional increase in conflict. Instead of the reproduction of a shared conspectus which is promoted by the concomitant complementarity, the proliferation of contingent complementarities chips away at any conspectus, whether societal or sectional carving off new particularistic specialisms, slicing out novel avenues to be explored and recombining familiar elements in a new way which negates their familiarity. The result is Socio-Cultural differentiation rather than social conflict. Its positive face is choice, freedom and progressive individuation; its negative face is dislocation, problems of identity and sectionalism. The latter issues never arose when cultural density was high and shared, for then people knew where they belonged, to what they belonged, possessed a sophisticated language for talking about it and internalized an intricate map of their cultural environment. When variety becomes pronounced, choice replaces certainty, specialist vocabularies are exchanged for a rich mode of common communication, and a large-scale map marking routes to foreign parts is substituted for the detailed street-plan of the walled city.

In dealing with the middle element of the morphogenetic cycle, this chapter attempted to disentangle the independent contribution made by S-C interaction to cultural stability and change. Social actors were viewed as both conditioned by the Cultural System but also as possessing degrees of cultural freedom which could be used to reinforce or to resist these CS influences. The questions were: which they would do, why and with what consequences.

The decisive factor determining whether actors backed or

bucked the Cultural System was how their power and interests matched the situational logic they confronted. In other words if the cultural contexts in which people found themselves were riven with inconsistency and in consequent need of repair, the power and interests of those involved could lead them either to carry out correction or to exploit the contradiction. Alternatively if actors confronted a smooth, highly consistent set of ideas, then their power could be devoted to protecting this conspectus if it promoted group interests or promotive interests could induce people to work against this particular configuration of Cultural System.

Thus the interface between the CS and the S-C was the site where pressures for cultural stability or change were first defined and where groups first became aligned for these purposes. Here if those capable of wielding cultural power harnessed it to the systemic tasks of correction or protection then they furthered these two morphostatic processes: indeed the more effectively such power was wielded in society, the more pronounced and prolonged was cultural stasis. Proposition (i) (p. 188) thus appeared substantially correct, that is, the use of cultural power is indeed accountable for long periods of S-C orderliness when effectively deployed by those seeking cultural quietism, even if the CS is riven by inconsistency. Conversely, however, if S-C powers and interests set themselves against the situational logic, correction cannot be made to stick nor protection to last. Moreover it was the very use of cultural power itself which in the longer term often stimulated these oppositional activities, as proposition (ii) (p. 188) originally asserted, that is that the employment of cultural power is an active process which eventually results in both confrontation with and the actual creation of hostile interests.

It follows from this that decisive as the states of affairs prevailing at the interface always are, it would be disastrous to endow them with permanence and to advance a series of generalizations on that timeless assumption. Thus the temptation to present the summary diagram (Figure 1) on the basis of proposition (i) alone, should be resisted, *unless* shifts over time are strongly emphasized. Otherwise it implies the existence of settled relationships between the two levels with fixed results and nothing could be more misleading than that. In fact the most crucial element in Figure 1 is the arrow on the right-hand side, signifying the passage of time. For the use of cultural power has *both* intended Systemic consequences (CS) in the short-term and unintended social results (S-C) in the long run. Thus even where the power of social groups was marshalled to the

		HIGH	LOW		
	HIGH	Concomitant complementarity	Constraining contradiction	MORPHOSTASIS	T
S-C				↓	i
integration		Contingent complementarity	Competitive contradiction		m
	LOW			MORPHOGENESIS	e

Figure 1   *CS Integration*

cause of correction or protection, its very use (and frequent abuse) eventually resulted in the creation of oppositional interests, hostile to the cultural status quo, its repair, or reproduction.

Hence proposition (ii) turned out to be of equal interest because it uncovered the mechanisms by which forces for cultural change *derived* from social action geared to producing cultural stability. In both cases whenever cultural power was used, over time it resulted in cultural morphogenesis. On the one hand, corrective manoeuvres to repair constraining contradictions represented a motor generating the precise opposite, namely competitive contradictions, with groups wedded to these antagonistic causes and intransigently opposed to letting corrections stick – as interaction brought contradictions out into the daylight and desertion, schismatism and counter-actualization gathered momentum. On the other hand, protective restrictions to insulate concomitant complementarities from disruption by internal innovation or external intrusion also had the opposite effect, in this case stimulating the emigration of marginal groups who followed up contingent complementarities and ended up repudiating stable cultural reproduction – as they cashed in their cultural capital in a more open market by trading on what they knew by applying it to something new somewhere else. Thus, although in the two cases the CS contained the seeds of its own opposition, only S-C action working over tracts of time was ultimately responsible for their germination.

What exactly was germinated through S-C interaction is the subject of the next chapter. There we will consider how cultural interaction acts back upon the CS, modifying its composition and resulting in Cultural Elaboration. In other words the state of play at the end of Chapter 8 will bear little resemblance to that with which we began the morphogenetic cycle in Chapter 6 – precisely because of the Cultural Elaboration unleashed by the Socio-Cultural interaction that has just been examined.

8   Elaboration of the Cultural System

This chapter focuses on the last of the four propositions which are explored throughout Part II:

(i)   There are logical relationships between components of the Cultural System (CS).

(ii) There are causal influences exerted by the CS on the Socio-Cultural (S-C) level.

(iii) There are causal relationships between groups and individuals at the S-C level.

(iv) *There is elaboration of the CS due to the S-C level modifying current logical relationships and introducing new ones.*

The last stage of the morphogenetic cycle has now been reached. Chapter 7 ended with the derivation of two cultural innovations from the interplay between Cultural System conditioning and Socio-Cultural interaction. It remains to examine these derivations *as* elaborations of the CS, that is in terms of being:

substantively different inhabitants of the Systemic domain;

with their own situational logics conditioning subsequent interaction; and

their own distinctive end-products which modify cultural dynamics.

Since it has never been maintained that 'derivation' is the only source of these elaborated features (the last chapter touched briefly upon how they could arise independently), then what is being prof-fered here is a theoretical account of the sufficient rather than the necessary conditions for cultural morphogenesis. Nevertheless, even if the two elaborated properties do have independent origins, they share the features listed above and thus there is no call for separate treatment.

With the introduction of these innovations – the competitive contradiction and the contingent complementarity – a more complete and more recognizable picture of the cultural domain should immediately emerge. This will represent a large-scale map on which can now be placed most of the macroscopic cultural phenomena which spring to mind, or are encountered in the field or the literature, and which may earlier have caused anxiety amongst readers because of the signal absence of a place for them.

However, in completing this skeletal morphogenetic account, a more complex picture of cultural dynamics is the final result. The methodology of analytical dualism which made its construction possible, also allowed it to be done in easy stages. The curtain was raised and lowered so the cultural play could be presented in separate acts. Of course in reality, which generally means history, the full range of complexity is in play throughout. This means that once the elaborated features have been presented we will finally have to consider the interplay between the four major cultural components which have been conceptualized sequentially because of the dualistic perspective adopted.

Analytic dualism *is* an artifice of methodological convenience for the components which it disentangles overlap and intertwine in reality. Far from this constituting a limitation of the approach, it is precisely what gives this method of analysis its utility. On the one hand, it is only the use of this perspective which has permitted the main phases of cultural morphogenesis to be disengaged, the *grandes lignes* of cultural development to be sketched in and the whole process of cultural dynamics to be given some shape. On the other hand, its usefulness is not restricted to such an abstract and macroscopic task. Analytical dualism can be used by any researcher to gain theoretical purchase on much smaller problems where the major difficulty of seeing the wood from the trees becomes much more tractable if they can be sorted out into the components of temporal cycles of morphogenesis – however short the time-span involved may be.

Further consideration of these theoretical implications and applications will be postponed until the two new concepts have been fully explored. The format followed will be identical to that used in Chapter 6, when the first pair of logical properties of the CS were introduced as conditional influences upon cultural interaction. For although the innovations under discussion at the moment have been presented as derivative phenomena this in no way implies their inferior importance. As in history, biology, chemistry or any other discipline, a derived phenomenon can be more important than its sources of origin or less so: this is not an issue amenable to generalization, for all else apart, the significance of any derivation is not fixed but varies over time with changing circumstances.

Substantive differences

Competitive contradictions

The simplest way of delineating this new addition to the Cultural System, which has been shown to emerge from the toils of the constraining contradiction, is by comparing the two. Formally what these different kinds of contradiction share is the logical property of inconsistency: again there is a basic incompatibility between the premises, contents or implications of two items, A and B, which means that both cannot be upheld simultaneously. The two differ, however, in that where constraining contradictions are concerned the upholders of A cannot get away from B because these components are inescapably conjoined and therefore the full brunt of their incompatibility imposes itself as a problem on the partisans of A: in contradistinction, the competitive contradiction is not a matter of Systemic *constraint* for the new item is not dependent on the old. Here, to advocate this A in no sense invokes some B. For example, secular rationalism does not entail constant reference to religious beliefs. The rationalist may set his face against these once and for all by a declaration of his atheism, or, more coherently, by opting for agnosticism and asserting that a matter which cannot be proved or disproved, for which good reason cannot be adduced, need not detain him. Instead this kind of contradiction is only activated if someone else insists on counterposing B and goes on doing so – thus enforcing debate between the two groups. In short, competitive contradictions, though systemic in substance, require Socio-Cultural activation. However, active opposition is a matter of Socio-Cultural contingency and not of Systemic inescapability.

Thus the existence of opposing groups is an essential precondition of a competitive contradiction. To highlight the fact that the competititve contradiction depends upon the Socio-Cultural 'decision' to counterpose two contradictory Systemic items, let us recall that at any time the CS contains an unlimited number of contradictions – ranging from incompatible proverbs ('it's never too late to learn' 'you can't teach an old dog new tricks'), through irreconcilable scientific theories to antithetic beliefs. Indeed, 'independent' contradictions have the dispositional tendency to go 'unnumbered' precisely *because* when invoking, advocating, enjoining, advising or proclaiming A, these activities do not simultaneously summon up not-A as a shadow which threatens to overshadow it and is therefore noted. Empirically, it would be an interesting exercise to ask those who recite the Church of England's creed, as an explicit endorsement of a doctrine, to list the Bs – theological, cosmological, biological, physical, chemical, ethical, historical, etc. – from which they were implicitly dissenting. Not only would these listings probably be very brief in relation to the most careful compilation of antinomies, but (as has been seen) the latter too would of necessity be incomplete. And even if such contradictions are known they can leave *everyone* unmoved since they exert no constraining influence. Were we to communicate the points at which Melanesian beliefs contravene those of Greek orthodoxy to the respective bodies of believers, we would not be embroiling them in an implacable problem which they were then driven to address – more likely the contradiction would simply be shrugged off.

In contrast to the constraining contradiction, where the alternative to a given set of ideas is also inextricably linked to them and thus constantly threatens them with its own counter-actualization, here the *accentuation* of an 'independent' contradiction is a supremely social matter. Accentuation depends on groups, actuated by interests, *making* a contradiction competitive, by taking sides over it and by trying to make other people take their side. In short, these oppositional interest groups *cause* the contradiction to impinge on broader sections of the (relevant) population: it does not impose itself as the ineluctable force of ideas as is the case with constraining contradictions, the moment anyone asserts A.

Even then only their continued antagonism keeps this particular issue socially alive. Withdraw Socio-Cultural accentuation and such an issue fades back into the Systemic reservoir of contradictions, socially deemed unnoteworthy, and noted only by an additional 'entry' in the history of thought at the CS level (which may or may not ever be re-read). Moreover, deprive the new idea of its advocates, and the likelihood is that it will be strategically recontained by its antagonists – not that they can any longer prevent its actualization but they can still control its social availability if S-C circumstances permit. The potential for reactivation is, of course, ever-present, but always contingent on new S-C antagonists to re-animate it.

By contrast the unfolding of a constraining contradiction does not require S-C opposition, the protagonists of A and those of B. One group alone can set it in train – alone, that is, at the Socio-Cultural level but in continual discourse with the (CS) ideas which threaten them but upon which their beliefs depend. The faithful can ultimately destroy the faith in the very process of trying to ground it more firmly, just as the scientist can refute his own theory in attempting to corroborate it. Durkheim's analysis of early Christianity is particularly helpful here, for no single surviving Greek or Roman and no social protagonists of paganism were responsible for the intellectual toils in which the divines enmeshed themselves over the centuries.

In sum, then, a competitive contradiction only becomes salient in society if two opposing groups simultaneously assert its incompatible constituents; Socio-Cultural alignment thus mapping onto one of the innumerable discontinuities in the Cultural System, and, in the process, endowing it with a social significance lacking in the pool of unaccentuated contradictions. What has been pin-pointed in the derived sequence, via the process of counter-actualization, is *which* of the items in the Systemic pool attract social attention. The activation of competitive contradictions is then the direct responsibility of human agency, though this does not render the incompatibility itself one whit less Systemic. In other words, we are discussing the relationship between the S-C level and CS properties (causal effects upon the logical domain), as distinct from all the things over which social groups can disagree, conflict or struggle, many of which contain no logical contradiction whatsoever.

Again, a few examples will flesh out the concept of competitive contradictions, which ironically, given their ubiquity, have rarely captivated the sociological imagination. Their ubiquitousness in academic, moral, political, theological or philosophical debate is undeniable and within our own specialisms or interests we tend to be highly aware of them, partly because they are conducted *as* debates and partly because they are about issues the logical nature of which makes fence-sitting excruciatingly uncomfortable. Thus, for example, in social theory most practitioners are acutely aware that they cannot view social structure both as an objective fact and as objectified facticity, or that they cannot endorse both methodological individualism and collectivism, because the premises of each pair are mutually inconsistent.

What is intriguing, however, is how the format, progress and outcome(s) of these debates have hardly ever been seen as interesting issues in their own right. Instead, the history of thought which preserves them is inordinately unilateral, typically portraying stages in the rise and demise of functionalist theory, for example, rather than depicting the historical thrust and counter-thrust, argument and riposte, retreat and rearmament, defeat and come-back, between Functionalists and their critics as a bilateral process of argumentative elaboration for both. Of course, the obvious reason for this one-sidedness, in what often passes for the history of thought, is simply that many of these accounts have taken sides – they are indeed part of the competition themselves and play their part by conducting hasty burials or premature celebrations of the ideas involved.

Nevertheless, the lack of theoretical interest displayed in this concept cannot be accounted for by partisanship alone, for this would not preclude the logical and sociological reconstruction of debates in areas where the investigator is disinterested (and many of us do not have an axe to grind about eighteenth-century scientific or theological controversies). Again, if I take some really significant exemplifications of the competitive contradiction – ideological conflict in society and programmatic conflict in science – then the interesting thing about commentators on them is their general failure to note *either* that these are competitive (that is, two-sided) *or* that they are (logically) contradictory, and sometimes both.

Thus in the philosophy of science, Kuhn is the supreme exemplar of this lack of interest.[1] His history of science contains no competition: in normal times there is only *one* group whose paradigm enjoys monopoly and after a period of crisis there is still no competition since the new paradigm is 'incommensurate' with the old one. Furthermore, no logical role is played by contradiction; for him anomalies always abound, they are admitted to accumulate but are only accorded a psychological effect ('can people stand them?' not 'how do they stand up to them?'). Popper, on the other hand, was preoccupied with the *contradictory* aspect but not with the *competitive* element in his logic of scientific discovery. To him scientists should be riveted by the urgency of anomalies, openly acceptant of falsification, and ever-ready to replace a refuted theory by a bold new conjecture. The competitive element however reduced to the survival of the fittest – the theory which had withstood the most stringent testing in an unpeopled historical *concours* between ideas (competition was philogenetic in nature, hence his adoption of an evolutionary approach to the growth of knowledge).[2] What is missing in Popper's work is basically an account of *current competition between groups and their theories.*

Yet not only does competition abound in science (which cannot be depicted as theories quietly queuing up for testing), but also competition is essential to scientific progress, since no experiment, observational statement or refuting hypothesis can *alone* lead to falsification (for auxiliary clauses can always be added to accommodate any of the foregoing anomalies). Thus, ultimately, there 'is no falsification before the emergence of a better theory'.[3] In this way Lakatos moves competition to the centre of the historical stage where science is concerned: '(s)ophisticated falsificationism thus shifts the problem of how to appraise *theories* to the problem of how to appraise *series of theories.* Not an isolated *theory*, but only a series of theories can be said to be scientific or unscientific: to apply the term "scientific" to one *single* theory is a category mistake.'[4]

In dealing with competition between 'research programmes', 'paradigms',[5] or conceptual frameworks, rather than the naked confrontation between an 'explanatory theory' and the 'observational' one (the substance of constraining contradictions), not only does the *competitive* element become crucial but in a manner which is highly consonant with our earlier definition. Research programmes are characterized by 'a remarkable *continuity*'[6] which connects their members (the fact that they share the conceptual framework and language of the programme) and since these paradigms have to be plural to fulfil the condition of competition, then this corresponds to our Socio-Cultural requirement of two social groups activating contradictory (CS) items in opposition to one another.[7] The programme members develop their paradigms semi-autonomously, with a weather eye to the opposition, but refusing to be drawn to work in terms of the other theory and thus maintaining the independence which is the hallmark of the competitive contradiction. As we will see, the battles which then ensue between them are very different in nature and in their end-product from the scenario of the constraining contradiction.

An almost identical lack of interest in ideologies as examples of competitive contradictions has characterized approaches to this type of collective belief. Kuhnian equivalents abound among the upwards and downwards conflationists already discussed. Fundamentally, for dominant ideology theorists there is no competition (because domination spells the incorporation of all into one view) and no contradiction (because domination equals the

elimination of other views). Universal socialization and internalization play just the same role in relation to the central value system
within upwards conflationism.[8]

Certainly, many have realized the significant 'peculiarity of
ideology as a belief system lies in its *connection with group interests in a
given social order*. This *sectional* nature of ideology *qua* belief system
may be deemed the central tenet of ideology theory proper . . . the
interest nexus is what provides ideologies with their *differentia specifica*
among the various kinds of collective beliefs.'[9] However, from our
point of view, this is often no more than an acknowledgement of
plural interests and associated ideologies. It concedes the existence
of oppositional groups at the Socio-Cultural level (indeed necessary
for the competitive contradiction) but it allows of no competition or
contradiction between the ideologies *themselves* at the CS level, since
the latter are mere epiphenomena or reflections of the former.

This is inadequate in two respects, both of which hinge on the
fact that ideologies are used against one another – they are quintessentially competitive. First, if they were no more than passive
duplications of interests then it is impossible that they could advance,
foster or defend those interests. Yet if they are performing such
tasks then they are necessarily doing so in *competition* with others
which perform the same job in relation to oppositional interests.
Second, the epiphenomenal view is fundamentally unable to
answer the 'riddle of ideological assent': '(i)f ideology is just a
"rationalization" of . . . interests, then how is it also believed by
those who do not share in the advantages it rationalizes.'[10] Since we
are bound to acknowledge the existence of this phenomenon and if
we also accept that plural interests are at work then we have to concede that there is a competition for assent amongst the ideologies
at play.

Finally, if we ask the theoretically interesting question about *competition* – namely, how do ideologies work against one another in
fostering particular interests or commanding assent from non-
beneficiaries? – then their most striking common denominator is a
claim to universal acceptability and a concealment of their intrinsic
sectional character. Each ideology seeks to legitimate itself by
reference to 'the imputed interests of the *totality* and the good of the
whole. It is on this claim that the moral authority and suasion of
ideology grounds itself. Ideological discourse is aimed continually
at denying the legitimacy of partisan interests; sometimes it even
denies the *reality* of partisanship. In the latter case, ideology may
seek to demonstrate that partisan interests are only *seemingly* such.'[11]

Since the protagonists of sectional interests *simultaneously* advance ideas which are said to be in the general good, then their *contradictory* nature has to be conceded too.

Ideologies are, then, genuine cases of competitive contradictions and in consequence have logical properties at the CS level which usually are either misrepresented (downwards conflation) or neglected (upwards conflation). Yet to answer questions about whether they protect interests or win assent it is vital to unpack and scrutinize their ideational contents (CS) independent of their social embodiment (S-C). For these are as embattled with one another as are the groups battling against each other, but the two fights are not identical; the outcome of the former can profoundly influence the latter. For as we have noted, the surest sign of ideational (CS) sucess is that it avoids the need for social conflict (S-C). (Socio-Cultural orderliness outstrips Systemic order.)

Contingent complementarities

Next it is necessary to examine how all the features which formally characterize these competitive contradictions may also be found in reverse – thus constituting the last of our four concepts, namely the contingent complementarity. The basic difference between the contingent and the concomitant complementarity is that here A and B are indeed consistent but they are also independent. There is no sense in which the invocation of A also entails the concomitant evocation of B. (As, for example, it was impossible even to describe the caste system without reference to reincarnation or to discuss political economy without recognizing that its laws were held to constitute a moral order; let alone explain the workings of either in the absence of their concomitants since, quite simply, without their complements they would not have worked – both would have foundered on manifest distributive injustice.) What this means is that concomitance, although man-made, becomes a Systemic given once it is made.

Its major components are indexed and permanently cross-referenced to one another. The extension, embellishment and articulation introduced through systematization essentially bulk out the catalogue and make its cross-referencing more elaborate. Complicated as the bibliographical labyrinth may become, there are always knowledgeable librarians on hand – those who helped form it, those born into it, those recruited and trained to it. For anyone showing an interest, the muniment room is thrown open and an archival guide provided.

Pursuing the simile, any large comprehensive library is a repository of the Cultural System where various groups and individuals, living or dead but usually unknown to one another, have deposited items which are independent but complementary. Because of their independence they are not cross-referenced, yet because of their complementarity they could be. However, since the two items are unrelated, then S-C action alone is responsible for whether they are brought into conjunction or not. Only through such action is attention drawn to particular complementarities (out of an unlimited number of equally congruent items which pass unnoticed), in order to make some point about this affinity which serves to advance social interests. In brief, to have any effect in society, this type of Systemic complementarity is contingent on its recognition and proclamation by human agency.

Like their counterparts, competitive contradictions, the *accentuation* of these complementarities is entirely dependent on action at the Socio-Cultural level. Usually, since A and B are unconnected, they will have independent origins being developed separately by different groups pursuing their particularistic interests – possibly generations or oceans apart. But the originators are not necessarily the key actors. Their part may end with lodging a given item in the Cultural System; its complement may be 'registered' far distant or much later. More time might pass (centuries, decades, years, months) before their congruence is noted – supposing it ever is. Because these items are independent and their originators can be long-dead, the derived sequence is important as it pin-pointed what increased the contingency of their interconnection, beyond the random effects of serendipity. (While not wishing to deny the latter, it is a completely fortuitous and generally individual phenomenon which will not manifest the social regularities which are our concern.)

The action chain began when the two components independently achieved high salience in society due to the separate activities of social groups (whatever their relationship or lack of it). Then the public visibility of both items increased *vis à vis* the pool of compatible but unaccentuated intelligibilia, and with it the chance of their harmony being recognized. For example, the cross-fertilization of ideas in academic life need not entail face-to-face contact or direct communication or any affinity of interests between their supporters: all that is required is that the compatible items are separately given a public airing, contact being established through the medium of the publications in which they appear – plus all the attendant paraphernalia of distribution and marketing. These provide the connective link between the items in question thus introducing A to B and leading both to become familiar to a wider 'audience'.

This is only the first step: the concept does not rest on some indeterminate probability of occurrence. Nevertheless, simple prominence is *one* reason why the most current theories and beliefs are compulsively handled for compatibility – yesterday afternoon's theory has the built-in Socio-Cultural advantage of guaranteed visibility.[12] Thus, just as social antagonism between two groups was necessary in order to keep a contradictory issue alive, so active partisanship is essential to keep the complementary components socially visible.

Thus, the complementarity of the items is a CS matter but the contingency of their conjunction is an S-C affair. The two interactional factors crucial for determining which of these items became joined up and then underwent elaboration are, first, social or sectional salience for the two items sustained by different social groups and, second, certain opportunists, possibly from a third group, who perceive some advantage to be derived from exploration of the complementarity. Of the two conditions, it is the second which is decisive, for even if some contact mechanism performs the introduction between A and B, unless the connection is exploited by someone, the two items slip back into the systemic repository to become indistinguishable from the pool of other undetected but potential complementarities.

In other words, S-C motivation is crucial, particularly since in the derived sequence it actively promotes the contact rather than just cashing in on it. The identification of those so motivated is as different from Kuhn's inspection of 'the state of mind' of established research communities (are they yet in anguish over the pile-up of anomalies?) as is the eventual form of ideational elaboration from his notion of a revolutionary re-definition of the field by its members. Although Kuhn has come to accept that 'scientific communities (i.e. networks) can and should be isolated without prior recourse to paradigms' he continues to maintain that 'the latter can then be discovered by scrutinizing the behaviour of a given community's members'.[13] His assumption is still that the Socio-Cultural element (the network) and the Systemic component (the paradigm) are superimposed. What we are dealing with here is prior to both and therefore we can start with neither a stable body of workers nor a consensual set of ideas. Instead, the problem is precisely the reverse, namely to account for how something even roughly akin to these two features in fact derives from their opposites – those who have quit the cosy confines of community to explore new combinations of ideas.

What is it then which furnishes the Socio-Cultural motivation to do this? The common denominator of 'having something to gain' from launching into a new uncharted area was clearly insufficient – partly because 'gain' is not assured and partly because for many it has to be weighed against potential losses. Like any form of exploration, risk is involved and it appeared helpful to reformulate our question in terms of 'who is willing to take cultural risks?' Mulkay's work on the social process of innovation was seminal here and gelled particularly well with the present approach since he is one of the rare thinkers who consistently utilizes analytical dualism, not conflating the Systemic with the Socio-Cultural, but gaining purchase on innovation through exploring their interplay.

His following formulation, although framed with reference to natural science alone, appears germane to the whole category of contingent compatibilities and who initiates their exploration:

There exists considerable but unsystematic evidence in support of the claim that significant innovations come disproportionately from young researchers at the foot of the scientific hierarchy and others at the margins of research networks . . . Let me just mention the foray of the inventor Edison into radio astronomy; the favourable response of the amateur astronomer Reber to Jansky's discovery; Wundt's redefinition of the problems and methods of speculative philosophy; and Pasteur's advocacy of the vitalist theory of fermentation and the germ theory of contagious diseases. These are all examples of major innovations being taken up by men on the margins of the research network centrally involved. The generalization that there is a connection between innovation and social marginality can be given a plausible interpretation in terms of risks and profits, along the line adopted . . . in relation to low-status researchers. Indeed, low-status within a research network is to be regarded as one form of marginality.[14]

This usefully identifies the Socio-Cultural mechanism (with both its push and its pull) which prepares a category of opportunists ready to seek the wherewithal for ideational innovation by venturing beyond their habitual boundary. Such marginal migrants are the agents who seize on complementarities – that is, those salient enough to be encountered – capitalizing upon new sources of variety compatible with their existing skills and goals by synthesizing the two.

Beyond this, however, it appears impossible to determine which *complementarity* a group will take up and exploit synthetically. This barrier is not due to sociological deficiency but derives from the logical properties of this type of Systemic complementarity. If they are genuinely contingent then the uncertainty of their occurrence (detection, actualization, exploitation) is definitional. It is of course part and parcel of the quintessential unpredictability of scientific development and, indeed, of ideational inventiveness in general.

Operative effects

Competitive contradictions

Competitive contradictions generate an entirely different situational logic for those confronting or brought to confront them. Basically, it is one which does not rub their noses in logical difficulties and keep them there. For to maintain A, whilst being fully knowledgeable about B, does not embroil actors in inescapable cognitive exigencies which inexorably drive them to personal or collective strategies of containment and correction – the only ways of avoiding relentless mental tension or the ultimate resignation of A. Dependency is responsible for this situation for it means that B can never be shrugged off, but this property does not feature in the competitive contradiction whose constituents are independent of each other.

Because of this, their operative effect is entirely different from the workings of the constraining contradiction. By contrast the situational logic created by the competitive contradiction is one which confronts people with *choice*. To be more precise, it is a logic which forces them to make choices, by accentuating differences, by insisting on their salience, by undermining indifference and by making the *question* of alignment inescapable.

This is not to argue that the situational logic enforces alignment with one side or the other but what it does inexorably extend is the awareness of choice in society. As many have pointed out, the traditionalist ceases to be one from the moment that he realizes he is one. What the logic does is to pull the rug from underneath unthinking traditionalism, habitualism and conventionalism by exposing their practitioners to the existence of alternatives. It presents the collectivity with the *possibility* of ideational diversity. The level of discursive awareness will vary enormously from the ideological protagonists and academic advocates immersed in the intricacies of the contest, through groups which having been bombarded by the crossfire have made their choice but do not penetrate the issue any further, to those who merely have the uneasy feeling that in sticking to the old ways they are somehow being old-fashioned. Even the latter are aware, however dimly, that alternatives exist, and indeed they do – this is the force of the situational logic.

But as far as the active opponents are concerned, those already aligned in ideational antagonism, the logical source of their opposition further conditions their course of action. In contradistinction to the constraining contradiction, here the situational logic dictates *elimination* not *correction*. In the former case, actors were driven to cope with ideas which contradicted their own (compromising, conciliating and usually conceding much *en route*) whereas those involved (and drawn into involvement) over a competitive contradiction have every incentive to *eliminate* the opposition.

Because partisans of A and of B are unconstrained by any dependence between these items, there is nothing which restrains their combativeness for they have everything to gain from inflicting maximum damage on one another's ideas in the course of competition. Victory consists in so damaging and discrediting oppositional views that they lose all social salience, leaving their antithesis in unchallenged supremacy. As in structural analysis there is, then, a different distribution of opportunity costs associated with different objective situations.[15] For protagonists of A, who find themselves confronting a constraining contradiction, penalties accrue if B is not somehow corrected; for partisans of another A who are faced with a competitive contradiction, bonuses are associated with unbridled injurious conflict. In the first case, the actors involved are conditioned to make the best of the situation, in the latter case to make the worst of it.

Since elimination of what is inconsistent with a given belief or theory is the goal dictated by the situational logic, and because two groups are involved in the activation of every competitive contradiction, what results is a battle-ground of ideas. The military simile is not far-fetched, for in both ideological and scientific conflict we are dealing with charge and counter-charge (counterfactuals and counter-arguments), with offensives and counter-offensives, with defensive re-groupings, loss of ground, retreat and, of course, the problem of deserters. Thus Lakatos paints us a typical combat scenario for science. 'When two research programmes compete, their first "ideal" models usually deal with different aspects of the domain' (in other words they avoid dependence and are activated as competitors, though war is not immediately declared between them).

As the rival research programmes expand, they gradually encroach on each other's territory and the n-th version of the first will be blatantly, dramatically inconsistent with the m-th version of the second. An experiment is repeatedly performed, and as a result, the first is defeated in *this battle*, while the second wins. But the *war* is not over: any research programme is allowed a few such defeats. All it needs for a comeback is to produce an n+1–th (or n+k–th) content-increasing version and a verification of some of its novel content.[16]

And hostilities go on, their outcomes being discussed in the next section.

The scenario for ideologies differs only in one non-crucial respect, namely that war may have been declared between oppositional groups (nakedly advancing or defending their interests) before their hostilities became embroiled in ideational conflict, let alone contradiction. Obviously, any group which is dominant in some part of society appeals to certain legitimatory ideas, consonant with its interests but not derived automatically from them, but initially these may be extremely vague – sometimes amounting to little more than a statement of traditional rights. The assertive group(s) which challenges it requires the dual functions of ideology from the start: not only must an ideology be developed to *legitimate* its claims and activities amongst its own members (and, ideally, a wider audience), but also the same principles must be extended to constitute a *negation* of the legitimatory basis of the dominant group. Because the claim to legitimate domination must be undermined before challenge is possible, assertive groups, in their earliest stages, concentrate almost exclusively on negation, on condemning and unmasking the interests concealed behind the proto-ideology of the dominant party. However, a group whose domination has been unopposed for a long period may only begin to elaborate this negative function in proportion to the attacks launched against it. Hence the typical response of a well-established dominant group is the immediate *reformulation* of its ideology[17] – extending it to negate the claims of its new rival, and thus finally crystallizing the competitive contradiction. (This corresponds to the point in science where n-th and the m-th verisons of two theories become blatantly inconsistent.)

However, these first rival interpretations of the problem situation do not remain frozen as static social alternatives. The further clarification of the original ideology, B, which actually crystallized the contradiction, simultaneously clarified the logical points at issue with A. Those asserting A then encroach further into enemy (CS) territory by concentrating their counter-arguments on the new (or newly clarified) claims of B. But however powerful these are, the defenders of B are never rendered speechless and, at best, can make a come-back by advancing a more sophisticated version of their ideology which both protects their initial position and answers the charges brought against it. As Lakatos argued, 'the idea of proliferation of theories can be generalized to any sort of rational discussion and thus serve as tools for a general theory of criticism'.[18] This naturally involves dismissing any view which holds the *differentia specifica* of ideology to be distortion but then no one, I believe, has ever made out an acceptable case for the existence of a separate sub-type of 'ideological ideas'. What is ideological is the uses to which they are put – in the context *of* interests but *in* argument. Both features are equally important in the competitive contradiction: it is undoubtedly the S-C interests which fuel the contest and keep it going but, also, as a (CS) argument, it can be examined like any other for features like 'progressive' or 'degenerating' problem-shifts, which will be taken up in the next section.

Contingent complementarities

The operative effects of *contingent complementarities* can best be elucidated by comparing them with the three concepts already discussed and the different kinds of situational logic associated with them – thus at the same time summarizing the main distinctions made in this connection. Although the situational logic generated by the contingent complementarity is indeed the loosest of the four (like a job description stressing initiative rather than itemizing duties), this does not prevent it from conditioning the Socio-Cultural level in a crucial fashion. For the existence of these (socially known) compatibilities represents a source of novelty which the Cultural System extends to human agency with few strings attached. These condition action precisely because they *objectively increase the opportunity for cultural free play* – for novel combinations and applications involving conceptual integration, theoretical reduction or doctrinal extension, all of which have ideational synthesis as their common denominator.

This, indeed, is the first contrast with the other three kinds of situational logic. When confronted by a constraining contradiction, the protagonists of A have no choice but to cope with B (or abandon ship); when faced with the concomitant complementarity their choice is between the wholesale adoption of B or flying in the face of its manifest benefits; when embroiled in a competitive contradiction, alternatives are indeed present but actors are presented with a forced choice between A and B. Only the contingent complementarity simultaneously holds out choices to the adherents of A but leaves them free to make what they will (if anything) of B. It is not merely that the objective availability of different courses of action is greater; so is the freedom to determine what to do with these opportunities.

Thus the second point of contrast is that unlike the other types of situational logic already discussed, there are no containment strategies or exposure policies associated with the contingent compatibility. While the constraining contradiction makes social containment tempting and logical correction mandatory (resulting either in restricted access to material or restrictions on intellectual enterprise), the concomitant compatibility operates in exactly the opposite direction, encouraging maximum exposure to congruent ideas but inducing maximum closure against innovation. With competitive contradictions, alternatives are objectively available but every pressure is brought to bear to decrease their subjective attractions, to discourage synthesis, and to foster stable alignment— again reducing the potential for ideational diversity. Only the contingent compatibility is free from Socio-Cultural manipulation, designed to induce avoidance or adoption or aversion. Certainly, distracting Socio-Cultural practices – habitual preoccupations, established routines, traditional preserves or conventional divisions of subjects – may well reduce subjective willingness to explore new and congruent possibilities, but these will usually coexist with various sticks and carrots which stimulate originality, innovation and experimentation (as in the derived sequence). The actors concerned have substantial freedom to survey or to ignore the broader horizon which has come into view and such is indeed the distinctive feature of this situational logic.

In sum, since the contingent complementarity presents a loose situational logic of opportunity, then this requires Socio-Cultural opportunists to take advantage of it. Their capacity to take advantage of contact with B and then to define what can advantageously be made of it, constitutes the final contrast with our other concepts.

For with the constraining contradiction, B can neither be neglected nor repudiated; with the concomitant compatibility, B cannot be neglected but must be incorporated; and with the competitive contradiction, B cannot be repudiated but must be attacked if not eliminated. Instead, the situational logic of the contingent compatibility provides no directional guidance about what is to be done with B (the consistency of which has recently become socially apparent).

Because the components making up the contingent complementarity are unconstrained by logical dependence and are not trapped in the either/or logic of competition, then there is nothing about their constitution which restrains what is made of their congruence. The components can be combined in any pattern and it is specialist interests which determine the actual patternings to take shape. Consequently, the net Systemic result is the generation of great cultural *variety*, which breaks down 'artificial' knowledge barriers, stimulates new departures and bold syntheses. At the CS level the contingent complementarity is the source of the wildest doctrines and the most daring theories (since its cognitive mode is untrammelled inductive generalization). At the S-C level the parallel effect of the contingent complementarity is diversification, specialization and, above all, recombination, as marginals disengage themselves to recoalesce in a group with a novel brief – for example, biochemistry, psychometrics, bio-technology, social statistics and, of course, cybernetics and systems analysis. Thus, in short, the net increase in the variety of the Cultural System is accompanied by a net decrease in uniformity at the Socio-Cultural level.

Hence, in conclusion, there is a major operative difference between the two kinds of contradictions and complementarities. The effects of the constraining contradiction and the concomitant complementarity are *imposed* by the CS level *inescapably* on the S-C level. In other words, these Systemic relationships (logical) impress themselves (causally) on S-C action. This is the element of truth in downwards conflation, but it is not the whole story. There are also the effects of the competitive contradictions and contingent complementarities and these are *activated* (causally) at the S-C level by the *selective accentuation* of certain CS level relationships (logical). In other words, social action determines which logical relations shall have cultural salience in society. And this is the element of truth in upwards conflation, which makes up the other part of the story. The truth is something of both, but it does not lie in the middle as central conflationists would have it.

For it has only been due to the use of analytical dualism that it has been possible to distinguish between these operative differences and to disengage the substantive elements to which the two versions of conflationism properly apply. In itself this constitutes some vindication of the dualistic approach, but its utility is far from exhausted. Having delineated the substantive and operative differences between the new types of contradiction and complementarities (simultaneously at work at T₁) we can now begin to theorize about their respective contributions to cultural stability and change ... if we maintain an analytically dualistic approach. The profitability of this becomes apparent when the final difference between the two kinds of emergent contradictions and complementarities is examined, namely their results. For these dissimilar products complete the nuts and bolts of a theory which can cope with cultural dynamics.

Divergent results

Competitive contradictions

The basic proposition advanced earlier was that the situational logic generated by competitive contradictions is one which prompts attempts at mutual *elimination*. The aim is to eradicate inconsistency by annihilating the incongruent viewpoint. However, since both competing groups have the same goal their confrontation generically results in an unintended consequence, totally at variance with the desires of the rivals, namely ideational Pluralism. The archetypical product of the competitive contradiction is thus a sustained differentiation of ideas from one another at the CS level which is associated with a polarization of the relevant population at the S-C level. This is exemplified equally by competing research programmes in natural science and by the dynamics of ideological debate.

The central argument that Pluralism is the generic consequence of competitive contradictions has four related components. Each of these will be presented in general terms and also shown to form common denominators of scientific and ideological competition.

The pin-pointing of differences – the dynamics of differentiation

Given that the name of the game is mutual elimination, these contradictions lead to *debate* (competitive by definition) in contrast with constraining contradictions which generate *dialogue* since there the ideal end-play is correction. In turn, the dynamics of debate entail a detailed inspection and dissection of opponents' views, geared to their destruction, and an equally detailed clarification and justification of the proponents' standpoint, geared to its vindication. Intrinsic, then, to debate is the identification of antitheses – the definition of differences being a necessary prelude to their demolition or refutation. Mutual clarification of one another's point of view is both a precondition of debating and an inescapable consequence of it. Thus, the committed Marxist knows his classical economics better than the average entrepreneur and needs to before he can satirize and criticize them. The concern, then, is to pin-point the differences at issue, not in order to sink them but with the goal of scuppering one of them.

Hence the primary feature of ideational competition is the differentiation of viewpoints from one another (through barbed interchange), and it stands in stark contrast to the efforts at effecting union between them (through mutual exchange), which are promoted by corrective contradictions. Equally, this close familiarization with opposing views differs greatly from protective closure against them which is typical of the concomitant complementarity. Finally, this spur towards ideational differentiation is entirely unlike the impetus towards the inclusive integration of ideas typifying the contingent compatibility. Indeed, this is only the start of their divergent consequences. Later we will also see that the *analytical* orientation which is part and parcel of debating also contrasts with the *synthetic* outlook fostered by the situational logic of opportunity and that the *exclusivity*, characteristic of rivalry, also places it in contradistinction to the *eclecticism* engendered by contingent complementarities.

Turning from differentiation as the consequence of debate for the Cultural System, it can also be seen to have a close parallel in Socio-Cultural polarization. Ironically, the very fact of debating, of confronting the logical issue rather than treating it as a social problem, is supremely counter-productive at the S-C level. For the result of mutual clarification (that is, an essentially public exercise) is to maintain the social salience of *both* points of view. Each increases in visibility and audibility, the two thus register an increase in objective social availability, more actors are then drawn into the debate and neutrality ceases to be a matter of ignorance. This ideational 'mobilization' again stands in contrast to the 'desertion' attending the corrective manoeuvres which stem from constraining contradictions.

The dynamics of differentiation are indeed the starting point of competition proper in both science and ideology. The analytical orientation is marked from the beginning in both forms of discourse. In science the source of a contradiction often originates from internal criticism of a particular theory – from the uneasy feeling that something is wrong and the germ of an alternative approach to the problem. Confrontation does not take place immediately because the new and undeveloped theory confronts a sea of anomalies at least as vast as that in which it was felt the old theory was busy drowning. Alternatively, two entirely different research programmes find that some development has placed them on a collision course but initially they may be far from certain about its implications and repercussions for each theory (which could be trivial or macroscopic). What follows in such cases is a sizing up of the opposition and a firming up of research strategy. Both involve what could be termed field-reconnaissance – the analysis of existing theories in relation to the 'hard core' of the fledgling theory, with the aim of discouraging lines of work which will probably prove antipathetic to it and encouraging those more likely to yield support. The orientation is analytical since it entails a bold self-definition which pin-points its own distinctive features and a wily awareness of what could prove damaging to them.[19] In other words, strategic differentiation precedes direct confrontation, attempts to anticipate it and, as we shall see, also accompanies it.

In the ideological domain the pin-pointing of differences is also the starting point for further differentiation. Generally, there is the same initial process of disentangling the embryonic ideology (which promotes a particular S-C interest) from the ideas advancing the position of its social opponents. This involves more than highlighting the interested nature of oppositional views: it entails detailing where they are 'wrong'. The modern phrase 'ideology critique' has been coined for this negative process which is as old as ideological discourse itself. Thus, for example, the first task of the early French socialists was to focus on their economic differences with the Physiocratic founders of classical economics: rejecting the theory of distribution as a bland account of the price of services, obedient to necessary laws and countering that the unequal relationships of people to property were historical artefacts the continuance of which generated further inequalities in distribution; denying that the spontaneous force of competition beneficently ensured the general interest; and counterposing the cruelty of this force which constituted the exploitation of man by man rather than serving the general good. The technical issues addressed in this process of distancing radical from established economics were complex and extensive.

The legitimation of the embryonic ideology to its target population also entailed a more positive form of differentiation, an alternative definition of who and what the productive forces of society were. Furthermore, since the third purpose of ideology is to specify a blueprint for the implementation of new policies, congruent with the social interests advanced but not directly derivable from interest alone, there was a further delineation of new economic policies in contradistinction to those advanced by political economy – for example, profit-sharing, land re-distribution, combination, state socialism, etc. The negative analysis of classical political economy went hand in hand with a positive self-definition of socialist economics, the two in combination representing the dynamics of differentiation of this new ideology.

The process of divergent elaboration

Second, the active involvement of two groups in debate means that each aims to clock up points which tell against the validity or credibility of the other side, by adducing counterfactual evidence or counter-arguments. Although the situational logic propels each rival to eliminate the other, because it does so to both simultaneously, elimination is rarely accomplished. Instead, what takes place is the refinement of both standpoints in the course of competition. In other words, a strong positive feed-back loop is generated through the process of debating thus amplifying the Pluralism which initiated the debate. Already we have seen the combat scenario that originates from Pluralism (from the ideational confrontation of two groups). As the two sides engage with one another each rival has a case to answer; then, as the protagonists respond to the reciprocal challenge by the refinement of both sets of ideas, the differences sharpen and the gap between them widens and deepens.

Competition is quintessentially a morphogenetic process, that is it amplifies deviations from the original starting point, namely the positions from which the rivals first crossed swords. For failure to elaborate in order to meet a challenge is to concede defeat and few will go down without an effort. Even if they are able to mount little more than a defensive rearguard action this still constitutes a refinement of their position. On the other hand, the successful elaboration of a viewpoint such that it overcomes a challenge is a morphogenetic development which has been stimulated by rivalry – and this is the case whether the rival proved a push-over or drove his opponent on to higher and higher elaborative feats.

This is amply demonstrated in the history of natural science. When inconsistent versions of 'strong' rival theories are advanced simultaneously, this prompts the search for a 'decisive experiment' to settle the issue in favour of one or the other. However, the course of competition shows a whole series of such experiments to have been anything but conclusive. For a revised (content-increasing) version of a theory can turn the first apparent defeat of a research programme into a resounding victory for it – successive 'refutations' being dealt with in like manner. The key point for the present argument is that each of the succeeding versions represented improvements on one another. Thus Lakatos presents the elaboration of Bohr's programme as one which required the development of sophistications in mathematics and refinements in auxiliary parts of physics in order to produce new versions of the theory capable of winning the next battles. But since we are dealing with competition, then a parallel elaboration must also have characterized the opposition for it to have remained a serious rival. Even if it has a set-back every theory *may* make a come-back, or several comebacks, including theories which appear to be entering a degenerating problem-shift, yet may still manage to get out of the degenerative trough.

If eventually, after an indefinite period of hindsight, something does indeed turn out to have been a crucial experiment,[20] establishing one programme as superseding its rival, this only serves to reflect 'the greatness of the two *programmes* involved'.[21] Both have undergone creative elaboration in the course of competition, under the force of competition. Ultimately, this elaboration turns out not merely to be the consequence of competitiveness but the criterion by which the outcome of the competition is determined – for only by meeting the 'requirement of continuous growth',[22] by which one theory registers a systematic increase in its theoretical and empirically confirmed contents does it out-distance its rival through its greater heuristic power.

Even if one opponent proves to have been unequal to the competition, nevertheless the consequence of the debate itself is morphogenetic. Thus, for example, in the controversy between the hereditarians and the environmentalists over the factors responsible for differences in mental ability, it is very easy to provide a perfectly correct but unilateral account of the geneticists' failure to answer charges through an effective theoretical elaboration of their position – depending instead on verbal reformulations and the production of controversial supporting data to stay in the ring. Hence the verdict of two very recent commentators: 'We consider that anybody approaching this field for the first time and expecting to find a gradually accumulating body of knowledge about the role of heredity in human intellectual variation would be sadly disappointed.'[23] What this account fails to note is the spur that the vociferous hereditarians gave to the debate itself.[24] With more perspicacity Medawar accentuates that lack of progress characterized only one of the competitors, 'the more disputative I. Q. psychologists give the impression of being incapable of learning anything from anybody'.[25] Environmentalists, on the other hand, have registered a progressive problem-shift – from criticizing cultural bias in testing, through itemizing psychogenic and sociogenic factors involved in intellectual performance, to theorizing about the interrelated (material, cultural, linguistic, etc.) constituents of social background which affect manifest ability. Although the environmentalist programme still has a long way to go, it would not have got so far without the pertinacity of the tenacious hereditarians (Galton, Spearman, Burt, Eysenk, Jensen), whose main merit lay in the opposition they stimulated.

Nevertheless, it is true that the tougher the competition the more it contributes to both morphogenesis and Pluralism, partly because it encourages both sides to elaborate boldly and partly because boldness itself has pluralistic consequences. If we consider any group locked in theoretical or ideological debate with another, then the deadlock can only be broken by one of them advancing some bold new conjecture or some radically new argument. The incentive to produce one impinges on the collectivity but given this stimulus a plurality of creative responses is typically forthcoming, each one claiming to be the best guide forward and the truest guardian of the group's key tenet. Fissiparousness ensues with different factions or sections pursuing a particular line of research or argumentation which to them is 'the' way out of deadlock. Internecine conflict intensifies, the tentative solutions crystallize into 'tendencies' and factionalism spurs each to extremism. If this happens to both contenders in the debate, then we have increasing Pluralism *on* both sides *and* a widening gap *between* their extremities.

If we take an ideological example this time, the long debate between political economy and socialist Marxist economics, it displays all the features of the divergent elaboration scenario plus the contribution of fissiparousness to the increase of Pluralism. Thus the sequential development of political economy under the pressure of constant, if minoritarian, criticism progressed through: (i) the Physiocratic system, which first enunciated the principle of *laissez-faire* but defended natural resources as the main foundation of wealth; through Adam Smith (ii), who refined the first principle but re-defined the second to assert that the wealth of nations was based upon the division of labour (although agriculture was still held to represent a special source of wealth); through Ricardo's elaboration (iii) of the theory of rent, which demystified the benefice of nature by providing an account of agricultural rents, where increases in farming prices were also shown to diminish the profits of capital – thus actually detracting from the main source of national wealth (and exacerbated by wage-earners whose increasing numbers drove up the demand for foodstuffs and hence agricultural prices, then enabling landowners to obtain further increments in rent).[26]

Although these principles came under fire from those like Hodgskin, whose *Labour Defended Against the Claims of Capital*[27] argued against there being a natural law of falling profits (merely a myth of growing rents perpetrated by capitalists to keep wages down), his economic attack did not go much further than asserting the oppression of workers by entrepreneurs (meaning the former were grossly under-paid compared with the excessive remuneration of the latter).[28] Since this was not yet underpinned by a theory of surplus value, the complaint could be dismissed as unjustified by reference to the beneficent effects of the classical laws for the generality. Thus the thirty years separating the appearance of Ricardo's *Principles of Political Economy* (1817) and J. S. Mill's book (iv), of the same title, were ones when the Classical Liberal School believed it had crushed its two main rivals, protectionism and socialism, and erected a complete science of economics composed of a series of universal laws – those of self-interest, of free competition, of supply and demand, of population, of rent and of wages.

Then for a time the liberal economists' response to renewed criticism became increasingly defensive: Mill conceded that wages, profits and rent were not determined by immutable laws (thus opening the door to social reform) and himself came to advocate a comprehensive policy to 'unite the greatest individual liberty of action, with a common ownership in the raw material of the globe, and an equal participation of all in the benefits of combined labour'.[29] Thus, while in 1852 Reybaud had written that 'to speak of socialism today is to deliver a funeral oration',[30] the end of Mill's work can be seen as a degenerative accommodation to it. The majority of the liberal school were unwilling to accommodate so quickly, but their successive works then had to contend with the publication of *Kapital* (1867) and displayed the typical defensive contraction of a theory on the run. Thus Cairnes (v),[31] for instance (*Some Leading Principles of Political Economy*, 1874) sought to rescue the classical position by the caveat that competition is not universal but operative between individuals in exactly similar circumstances; it thus works within small areas and is inoperative between one area and another. By making this allowance for non-competing groups, it was hoped to give a classically consistent account of the persistent inequality between wages and profits.

Meanwhile, socialist economics underwent their own divergent elaboration which constituted a progressive assault on the principles of political economy and the articulation of an alternative in competition with them. What is of particular interest here is that the two great 'discoveries' of Marx (according to Engels),[32] the materialist conception of history replacing immutable economic laws and the theory of surplus value replacing the classical theory of wage determination, stimulated the heirs of political economy to surmount their degenerative trough. Thus in the latter years of the nineteenth century the Hedonists (Jevons, Menger, Walras, Marshall) (vi) completely revamped the three major laws of demand and supply, of cost, of production and of distribution, by ditching the old cause and effect account in favour of feed-back relations. (For example, the old law stating that 'price varies directly with demand and inversely with supply' was jettisoned with the recognition that it was equally true that demand and supply are each in their turn determined by price. It was replaced by a reconceptualization of their interdependence, for example, demand is now shown to be related to price by a see-saw motion, demand falling as prices rise and rising when prices fall.)[33]

In this new version, price, demand and supply became three interrelated elements of a single mechanism, and the new problem for (neo-liberal) economics was to discover the law governing their interdependence. Since this new surge forward coincided with the time at which the question of when the Marxist crisis of excess production was ever going to manifest itself, the debate again reached stalemate.[34] The Marxists were far from speechless; they could point to the containing consequences of imperialism and war, amongst other reasons which postponed the crisis – a riposte eventually elaborated into the economic version of world-system theory.

In brief, both theories had undergone substantial elaboration in the course of their debate but so, by the twentieth century, had the economy. Since neither competitor had been victorious and the problem itself had altered substantially, what followed was fissiparousness on both sides – the plethora of theories the intricate 'tendencies' of which are still with us today in all their divergent extremism. Divergent elaboration thus lies at the heart of competitive contradictions and once again this pluralistic drive contrasts with the unificatory force of syncretism conditioned by the constraining contradiction.

Alive but not well – the maintenance of Pluralism

The argument that what results from competitive contradictions is elaboration rather than elimination might seem to imply that competitions cannot be won. This is certainly not the case, though victory at best constitutes a progressive problem-shift for a theory or belief in relation to its opponent and defeat, at worst, a degenerating one. What is true, however, is that it is impossible to 'kill' an idea whilst there are some committed enough and ingenious enough to defend it. And what happens in the competitive process is that the ingenuity committed to sustaining each idea is augmented through debate, rendering the idea even harder to 'kill' by removing the grosser inadequacies of the prototype or by retreating to a more circumscribed but more defensible position. The latter still represents a competitive strategy, even though the moves are purely defensive, but what is being competed for now is really survival rather than any realistic chance of overcoming the rival.

Survival on such degenerating terms is always possible: there are ever ways of maintaining the fidelity of the faithful. Provided there are sufficient Socio-Cultural reasons for some to want to keep the faith or to maintain a theory, then some ideational mish-mash can always be dished up to sustain them – even if it is totally indigestible to anybody else. Thus the fact that the 'vanquished' are still 'alive' at the end of the day and able to protect their distinctive (bizarre, arcane, fundamentalist) ideas from relegation to the history of thought is, of course, yet another argument for viewing Pluralism as the end-product of the competitive contradiction.

Indeed, some rational justification can be given for the dogmatic attitude of sticking to a theory as long as is possible: 'This dogmatism is to some extent necessary. It is demanded by a situation which can only be dealt with by forcing our conjectures upon the world. Moreover, this dogmatism allows us to approach a good theory in stages, by way of approximation: if we accept defeat too easily, we may prevent ourselves from finding that we were very nearly right.'[35] Often, however, dogmatism cannot appeal to this rationale but the fact remains that it is 'very difficult to defeat a research programme supported by talented, imaginative scientists. Alternatively, stubborn defenders of the defeated programme may offer *ad hoc* explanations of the experiments or a shrewd *ad hoc* "reduction" of the victorious programme to the defeated one.'[36] Yet again dogmatism may triumph over science: as the foundations of the genetic theory of intelligence crumbled, fraudulent findings were fabricated by Burt to prop up the tottering hereditarian edifice undermined by the 'environmentalists'.[37] Yet even after this had been exposed in 1974 by Kamin[38] and followed up by numerous studies the import of which was to withdraw scientific status from the 'theory' underlying IQ tests,[39] this spelt no diminution in the practice of testing. Socio-Culturally this may be explained, in part, by the vested interests of educational psychologists who uphold the instrumental utility of the tests as practical tools for placement and partly by the ideological function the tests still perform in legitimating selective placement! In either case the price of survival has been the loss of scientific status – downgrading to a rule-of-thumb or assumption of a metaphysical character. However, for the present argument, which is not about scientific progress *per se*, the key point is that Pluralism continues to live on – be it in a progressive, degenerating, or, as in the last example, degenerate form.

Precisely the same is true of beliefs themselves. Even the most stringent attacks on particular components of a belief system can always be met by some counter-argument, cobbled together for the purpose, provided only that the motivation to defend it exists. Thus, for example, in the debate between proponents of a very literal Christian theory of genesis and advocates of natural evolution, the latter consistently adduced the evidence of fossil remains of earlier life forms as a compelling counterfactual. One Christian defence consisted in denying it this status by countering it with the theory of 'spontaneous creation complete with fossil remains'. This example highlights the key feature of defensive degeneration, namely that it does nothing to convince the other side (S-C level) nor to eliminate the incompatibility of their views (CS level). This Christian defence becomes, if anything, even more unacceptable to the secular evolutionists, who having challenged divine intervention in the first place are logically not going to accept a double dose of it. It is purely a device for helping the faithful not to waver, whatever the 'faith' may be.

The Pluralism of the peacemakers

Obviously there is no logical reason which precludes the discovery of a syncretic formula uniting the views of the competitors through repair of the inconsistency characterizing them. It is simply that the situational logic of mutual elimination induces neither contender to search for one. However, this does not prevent unaligned groups from pursuing correction. Indeed, as it has been argued that the Socio-Cultural consequence of competition is the progressive involvement of more and more people in the debate, then the appearance of peacemakers is unsurprising. Quite literally, the enduring hostilities leave large numbers not knowing what to do or what to think: they are publicly confronted by alternatives but may find both arguments too compelling to be able to take sides. The typical response is to try to have the best of both worlds and to proceed along some *via media*, rough-hewn from slabs of both.

Since these 'middle ways' are usually forged from elements the premisses of which are mutually contradictory they are better seen as Socio-Cultural devices enabling people to live with contradictions rather than as resolutions of them. A genuine syncretic solution to a competitive contradiction generally comes from a line of thought or research far removed from the rivalry. Only rarely, and then after substantial creative work, does it emerge from the maelstrom of hostilities and here the least probable outcome is a discovery that the truth lies in the dead centre. 'Centrism'[40] is rather the birthmark of Socio-Cultural peace-making. It is ineluctably spawned by competition but is immediately spurned by both rivals. Each detests the centre more than one another for it not only concedes too much to the other side but also constitutes a travesty of their own views and a denial of any logical reason for opposition between the two groups. In other words, these arranged marriages of convenience enrage the families involved but do not prevent others from celebrating the union. Pluralism of the centre has emerged and, whatever its logical and sociological defects, it is generally here to stay while ever the outcome of the competition remains undecided.

In any realm then, the hallmark of a peace-making 'solution' is that it is no solution at all: it mutes but never transmutes the contradiction. In politics it is typically represented by the ideology of the Centre parties, like the old characterization of the French Radicals – 'with heart on the left and pocketbook on the right'. In natural science it usually takes the guise of 'instrumentalism', a supremely amoral criterion since it involves shackling together whatever concepts or propositions work best for certain practical problems, despite the fact that their premises (ontological and epistemological) may be at complete variance with one another. In social theory its standard feature is mindless eclecticism; we may have outgrown the crudities of 'conflict theory to account for dissensus and consensus theory to explain integration' but our growing up often appears to mean that we are playing the same game with more sophisticated perspectives.

These 'centrist' forms of Pluralism are essentially shelters from the storm, erected, as it were, in the eye of the hurricane but the moment competition moves on to different ground, produces a victor or is resolved by some genuine syncretic formula, they are promptly abandoned. If the debate moves onwards, new shelters will be erected and if the rivals complain that these clutter their battleground, then it is the dynamics of divergent elaboration which are to blame. For Socio-Culturally more and more have been dragged into the fray and Systemically they will indeed find something to be said for both sides as this is precisely the effect of competition between ideas.

In conclusion, then, competitive contradictions fuel Pluralism through the divergent elaboration of ideas in the process of debate and through their two corollaries – further internal differentiation of factionalist views on both sides and external attempts to delineate a *via media* between them. The basic thrust is thus the precise antithesis of ideational unification promoted by the constraining contradiction: it is the accentuation of ideational differences in the population. Since it is *differences alone* which are increasingly distributed throughout the population (actors are presented with choice and pressured to align themselves), then the Systemic impetus is towards *social cleavage*. This is reinforced by the fact that the rivals themselves manifest their mutual hatred of compromise formulae and direct their conjoint forces to undermining any credibility or legitimacy of 'centrist' views. In brief, the debate between them fosters *polarization* among the relevant population. Continued competition then augments choice within each polarized alternative through the proliferation of *factionalism*, which in turn multiplies cleavages. As Geertz puts it a '(c)ommonality of ideological perception may link men together, but it may also provide them, as the history of Marxian sectarianism demonstrates, with a vocabulary by means of which to explore more exquisitely *the differences among them.*'[41]

The spread of differences without compensatory similarities thus promotes cleavages and conflict as the conditional effect of competitive contradictions within the Cultural System. Nevertheless, we have to allow for the ways in which its Socio-Cultural reception can either reinforce or nullify such effects. It might be argued that since Socio-Cultural rivalry was a precondition of competition in the first place (opposing groups having won social salience for contradictory ideas) and because more by-standers are drawn into the fray, then the amplification of conflict in society (or the relevant part of it) is the most likely outcome. This I believe is indeed the likelihood given that an opposition of interests pre-dates the debate, which then accentuates them rather than muting them, but it is not the necessary outcome. Socio-Culturally, parts of the population may be predisposed to divisions over the issue in question but they may also feel that they have more imperative and more consensual concerns. Although they will not be able to evade growing awareness of the debate, nevertheless, if there are strong countervailing sources of Socio-Cultural integration then involvement with them may mean that many take refuge in one of the hastily constructed shelters until the hostilities are over. They cannot ignore the war but they can, as it were, preserve their civilian status. Furthermore, it is open to every actor to remain a conscientious objector, to consider that the cause is not worth a candle, that the way the dispute has been defined is unfruitful and to opt instead for the pursuit of an independent line of research, thought or argument. The fact that the Socio-Cultural effect of the on-going debate is to drag in more participants never means that it involves everyone and the independent activities of those who conscientiously refuse involvement can be the source of an ideational innovation which cuts across the battle-lines drawn by the competitive contradiction.

Indeed, this is precisely what we are about to discuss under the final rubric of the contingent complementarity: namely, how the opportunities presented by novel but congruent ideas can prove more attractive, particularly to marginal groups, than any amount of competitive bombardment – where alignment to either side appears tangential to their interests, while pursuit of their own line seems to offer a readier means of advancing them and also spells migration away from the site of the hostilities just discussed.

Contingent complementarities

The basic proposition advanced earlier was that the situational logic generated by the contingent complementarity, that of *opportunity*, which increases the objective availability of novel strands of thought, generically results in ideational *synthesis*, that is, the building up of *separate* elements – concepts, propositions, data – into a connected theory or system. This outcome is common to the exploration of any concomitant complementarity, whatever the way it was first encountered. The result at the CS level is the sustained generation of new variety, that is the continued addition of new items to the existing cultural stock, leading to a process of progressive Systemic diversification. Its direct counterpart at the S-C level is increasing specialization (of knowledge, skills, language, commitments and so forth) among the relevant population, which is reflected in social re-grouping along specialist lines.

Although the new Systemic additions are by definition compatible with one existing component (apart from a common language), they can assume any of the logical relations, previously discussed, with other items in stock. Whether what ensues is the overall Systemic integration of diversity or the instigation of a new set of contradictions is an empirical question not amenable to theoretical generalizations because of the quintessential unpredictability of innovations. Equally, although exploring the new item proves socially attractive to those opportunists grouping themselves around it, their ensuing specialization may dovetail smoothly with existing practices, conflict with entrenched preserves, or generate isolated and alienating enclaves.

Consequently, the central argument that synthesis is the generic consequence of contingent complementarities refers strictly to the work performed on two consistent elements (to what our opportunists do when they take up a compatible item) and the results of these endeavours which they then offer back to the Cultural System. How these are 'received', that is whether synthesis can itself be synthesized, is simultaneously a more macroscopic and a more substantive question. (So too is the whole issue surrounding the 'reception' of pairs of highly differentiated ideas resulting from competitive contradictions and whether they map onto existing

Systemic divides, thus reinforcing them, or prove marginal to most Systemic concerns.) Leaving aside the question of further repercussions, the production of synthesis from any *given* contingent complementarity is made up of three stages which culminate in the generation of cultural variety. These will be discussed sequentially, both in general terms but also with reference to the practical examples already introduced earlier in the chapter.

The transfer and fusion of ideas

The discussion of migration highlighted how some contingent complementarities are encountered because they are sought after and how our opportunistic seekers then engage in the synthetic transfer of ideas so as to further development in one domain or another. In other cases the encounter has nothing whatsoever to do with seeking it, though those who capitalize on it are also marginals and they too end up as migrants, but in any case the products of their activities share the same core features as the above. Synthesis itself takes the form of a combination of ideas transferred from one or more domains to another. In certain instances the transfer is more pronounced, in others the fusion is most prominent, but it would always be a mistake to neglect either element in the synthetic process. To begin with, let us take two straightforward examples, which roughly conform to an import-export analogy in the cultural field and where the transfer of ideas is thus particularly marked.

In terms of the traffic in ideas, the importing of technology is a matter of selecting an item which complements existing resources, can be accommodated and maintained by them and once in place will increase output, enhance environmental control or whatever the aim may be. The synthetic element may appear small, reducing to making the right selection plus a bit of fiddling about on the ground to make it fit. The appearance is deceptive. Make the wrong synthesis and you end up with an item which you cannot fuel, cannot repair and cannot work. In short, there is no such thing as the *straightforward* transfer of ideas from one domain to another which is not identical – some form of synthesis is always required.

Where exporting is concerned, and this may mean the movement of a whole group of thinkers into another area, the *leitmotif* is the same – a basic transfer of ideas which are then synthesized with their new environment. This is illustrated by the disenchanted physicists of the 1930s who deliberately initiated work on bacterial viruses (phages) with the avowed hope of making ideational innovations 'abroad'. 'In applying ideas and techniques developed within physics to biological problems, they gradually came to form the nucleus of a research network',[42] from which a new field, later to be called molecular biology, developed. Once again the transfer accomplished by migration was crucial but the accomplishment of transfer was a highly synthetic process. 'To some extent the cognitive and technical structure of the emerging speciality was brought in from other disciplines by the intellectual migrants. But many of the rules which came to govern the study of phages grew out of the attempt to impose order on an area of ignorance in which basic assumptions had yet to be defined.'[43]

In contrast to these two examples, the prolonged synthetic process eventually responsible for the official emergence of 'radio astronomy' as a novel area of study in the late 1950s (the formal actualization of this contingent complementarity) entailed the *fusion of ideas* between physics and astronomy; only as this combination progressed was there a *transfer of ideas* from both disciplines to constitute the new one. Thus, 'during the 1950s radio physics became increasingly dependent on astronomy, for example, for the measurement of stellar distance which is only possible optically. At the same time the physicists began to respond by supplying useful information to the astronomers, for example, information about very distant objects which are optically faint but which emit powerful radio waves. This convergence of research interests became so close that in 1959 the new area of study was officially named "Radio Astronomy" by the International Telecommunications Union.'[44] This example has been cited because it illustrates three key points about fortuitous contact between compatible items: how easily they could be ignored; how dependent their exploration is on the Socio-Cultural activity of opportunistic individuals and groups; and, more particularly in this connection, how their exploitation entails a lengthy synthetic fusion of ideas which brings two 'disciplines' together at some point beyond the ambit of both, thus transferring work to new ground outside the original pair of disciplinary boundaries.

The overall result of synthesis is an increase of variety since through it new items are added to the Cultural System. The process of synthesization is quintessentially morphogenetic: it amplifies deviations from their starting points and generates novelty. Thus the transfer of ideas is never the replication of those ideas in a new environment, for literal copying is possible only when the two domains are practically identical. Instead, the transferred ideas have to be synthesized with the properties of their new field of application and this itself is innovatory. The emergence of molecular biology from the application of physical methods to living matter provided a clear illustration of this. Equally, however, if we consider the large-scale transfer of industrial techniques, this has produced a diversity of paths to industrialization, none of which have duplicated the original English sequence and all of which constituted novel combinations which in their turn could be considered for transfer to yet new settings, where further synthesis would be required. Similarly, the fusion of ideas is never a facile matter of aggregating items, as the case of radio astronomy showed,[45] but a lengthy process in which novelty is elaborated and then becomes usable in its own right for a new range of purposes.

Finally, however, we should underline the fact that although synthesis increases systemic variety and is intimately linked with ideational innovation, nevertheless syntheses can either be productive or defective. The examples used so far have accentuated the former. The latter must also be signalled, partly to allay any impression of an 'open sesame' to intellectual progress and equally to alert us to the fact that a defective synthesis may still have significant consequences at the S-C level.

On the one hand, the facile combination of items with some superficial complementarity is a permanent temptation to over-zealous opportunists in all walks of life. In academe the desire to make quick progress often results in slapping a theory – carefully elaborated in some other field – onto an alien subject matter, without doing any synthetic homework. Then instead of regretfully concluding that the transfer is inappropriate, sloppy synthesis ensues blanketed by the apologetics of analogical reasoning. The successive adoption of the mechanical, organic and cybernetic models in social theory and their subsequent abandonment as the points of disanalogy have surfaced to deny the transfer are warnings against short-cuts in theory formation.[46] Perennially tempting, too, is an attempt to extend the appeal of a theory by instant fusion with another which is currently in vogue, again accentuating only superficial compatibilities and ignoring inconsistent premises or implications. Since the rise of psycho-analysis it is harder to think of any strand of sociological thought with which it has *not* been combined than to specify perspectives which have resolutely deemed fusion inappropriate. This temptation is shared by social movements, which succumb in the hope of buttressing their position and increasing their appeal – hence the facile compounds represented by 'feminist Marxism', 'liberation theology' or 'Rastafarianism'. These examples are all cases of what Etzioni terms 'ineffective' synthesis deriving from inadequate knowledge-processing.[47]

They differ from instances of 'excessive' synthesis where the synthesizing efforts are strenuous but the informational input is too inadequate for those involved to understand that the proposed combination is simply 'not on'. Cargo cults exemplify this process and Etzioni appears right in his general expectation that 'actors who use over-synthesized knowledge will suffer from poor reality-testing, not unlike that of actors who do not synthesize sufficiently'.[48] In other words, the exploration of contingent complementarities will be sources of some of the boldest and best ideational innovations but also of some of the wildest and occasionally the most pathetically ambitious intellectual excursions.

Synthesis, progressive specialization and institutionalization

The type of synthesis under discussion is not instantaneous; indeed, in most of the examples cited the process took several decades. The typical sequence is the publication of some new discovery, application or line of thought which serves to attract others with relevant skills or resources to work on it and particularly those who are marginal or subordinate in their own fields. Intense synthetic activity follows but as yet there is no formal network of co-workers, no estabished rules of procedure and no basic theoretical assumptions. These grow out of the process of exploration itself and they add up to a new form of intellectual specialization.

This is the scenario which Ben-David and Collins present for the origins of experimental psychology. They attach particular importance to the transfer of ideas from physiology to philosophy, effected by Wundt as he migrated from the former discipline to the latter. There he carried out 'a revolution in philosophy by replacing logical speculation with empirical research' and increased the social salience of this new endeavour by widely advertising 'the fact that he was in a different kind of enterprise than the traditional philosophers'.[49] In turn, the exploration of this novel departure drew many away from speculative philosophy itself. 'This new intellectual enterprise attracted the attention of a number of German philosophers, particularly Bretano, Stumpf, Müller and Ebbinghaus. Thus a new research network grew out of this attempt to apply scientific methods to some of the traditional problems of philosophy. Students from various disciplines and nations quickly attached themselves to the new network. The original problems were speedily redefined, the initial research techniques refined and the growth of modern psychology was set in motion'.[50]

Specialization intensifies as many new workers are drawn to the new field, especially younger ones who are as yet marginal to any discipline or enterprise and therefore have little to lose and much to gain. Influx can be stimulated by the founders of the new field: thus as far as molecular biology was concerned, 'steady recruitment was ensured when, in 1945, Delbruk initiated a regular summer school to train new entrants attracted by the group's increasingly obvious success'. In this way a new network crystallizes to explore the contingent complementarity; findings multiply as its activities grow; secondary synthesis re-orders these; and methodological procedures are consolidated by interchanges within the network. In brief this novel form of specialization represents the formation of a new specialism. The more successful the initial efforts, the more quickly this occurs, as the transformation of the phage network into the specialism now termed molecular biology again illustrates. 'Workers in related areas began to recognise the importance of the group's achievements, which often had implications for their own research. With the discovery of the Watson–Crick structure of DNA there was sudden increase in government funds, followed by a decade of explosive growth and the eventual award of five Nobel Prizes to members of the group.'[51]

Through such types of formal recognition, the institutionalization of the new specialism as a distinct field with a specialized body of knowledge and techniques takes place. At the S-C level this may indeed involve a struggle as Zloczower has documented for the dissociation of physiology from traditional anatomical studies as the basis of German medical training. What is significant in his account is the importance he attaches to the role of members of a new network in the pursuit of institutional differentiation. 'The struggle was spearheaded by young men, who as private lecturers had opened up new territory and were loath to dissipate their energies in other than their chosen fields. Characteristically, these men were striving not merely for personal recognition . . . what they wanted was the creation of new chairs for their respective disciplines.'[52] In other words, the sequence of exploration–specialization–institutionalization appears generic to the contingent complementarity as it stems from the successful synthetic endeavours of those first detecting it who then seek formal recognition for their achievements.

Generally speaking, institutionalization tends to have two main connotations – social recognition and practical routinization. Both are important here but they must be stripped of their morphostatic connotations for each of them has conservative overtones. Certainly the institutionalization of, say, a new academic discipline in universities plays something of both above roles: it becomes a respectable specialism to follow for which relevant training is available. Another way of looking at this is that it provides a guaranteed flow of new recruits and also serves to disseminate the newly synthesized items more widely in society thus making objective availability (CS) and social opportunity (S-C) more equal. In itself institutionalization is perfectly neutral with regard to morphostasis or morphogenesis. It lends its so-called force of inertia to the former when novel departures dry up and a network begins to ossify. On the other hand, it enhances morphogenetic developments in a field which is still forging ahead, by supplying personnel, a base and funding.

All then depends on the state of the new field itself and as far as the specialization which stems from synthesis is concerned it has a strong tendency to remain intellectually progressive, the rewards going to innovation rather than replication. The main reason for this is that as a *new* specialism, there is no body of orthodox elders with vested interests in reproducing their cultural capital and, as a *burgeoning* specialism, it shows no tendency to become the kind of stable solidary grouping in which they could develop. Thus, despite its spectacular successes, Mullins describes the movement into and out of the phage network as 'a rolling, boiling confusion of entries and exits',[53] where the average career length was just over three years and the founders remained in it for less than ten, some scanning new horizons as soon as an effective research framework began to be consolidated.

If the scenario of the contingent complementarity finished here it might be argued that the *progressive* nature of specialization ultimately rested on psychologistic foundations. Such an explanation would run along the following lines: some personality feature made for marginal misfits in the first place, their personal idiosyncrasies then accounted for their adventurism, but this rabid individualism, intellectual ambition, failure to form stable social relationships, or whatever, no more equipped them to settle down in the new field than it had in the old. To free the account from this (S-C) misinterpretation we have to proceed to the final step and demonstrate that the situational logic which produced additional variety in the Cultural System also stimulates the generation of further variety. If successful, we will also have shown how this situational logic engenders the precise opposite of that associated with the concomitant complementarity. Instead of the progressive systematization the tight internal articulation of which defied external disruption and thus fostered strong boundary maintenance, we find the exact antithesis. The contingent complementarity is born from external connections and continues to encourage them, thus leading to the continuous shifting and re-drawing of boundaries.

Variety stimulates more variety

As new specialisms emerge in any domain they represent not only an objective increase in variety but also, because of their novelty and the 'publicity' surrounding their institutionalization, they enjoy high social salience. Considered collectively, they therefore constitute settlements of intense and expansionist activity, each of which enriches the environment of the rest since it enlarges the pool of new but unmarked contingent complementarities. This is a purely logical property of the Cultural System and it is an emergent one. As several new items (pure and applied theories) are lodged in the System, the probability increases that the fund of undetected complementarities (either between novel items themselves or between the novelties and older items) also increases, though not in any fixed proportion. (Obviously, the same is true of their contradictory potential.) Although, as ever, the detection of any particular contingent complementarity remains indeterminate, a higher *rate* of discovery appears to be an empirical fact. In other words, there seems to be a tendency such that 'variety stimulates more variety, which feeds on existing variety to create still more variety'.[54] Empirical indicators of this include the increasing speed-up of technological innovations once Gellner's 'great hump' of industrialization has been passed[55] – from my point of view the 'hump' is also a 'heap'; a large stockpile of potentially exploitable complementarities. Another pertinent index is the increasing rate of academic specialization. In British universities the 'proliferation of subjects on which advanced students were engaged... rose from 123 in 1928–9 to 448 in 1964–5, including an increase from seven to twenty-six kinds of engineering and from one to five branches of economics'.[56] I want to argue that these empirical regularities constitute morphogenetic developments which stem directly from the situational logic of the contingent complementarity.

This logic, as has been maintained throughout, is a loose one of opportunity, so once again it is necessary to identify the factors (both CS and S-C) which either permit or encourage further opportunism. On the one hand, any group detecting further complementarities will meet with no organized S-C resistance: again no one is disturbed because there is nobody there with vested interests at stake. Equally, there is nothing in the situational logic restraining adventurism by dragging actors back to repair a pressing inconsistency, to answer a dangerous competitive attack or to devote their energies to unremitting protection. On the positive side, since rewards accrue to and reputations are made through innovation there is every incentive to keep moving before a seam has been worked bare (and only the less prestigious tidying up tasks remain). As Hagstrom[57] has pointed out, it is becoming fairly common practice for certain researchers to move into new areas, 'skim the milk' by making several important contributions and then move on before the significance of the remaining problems diminishes and the field shows signs of becoming defunct. Second, as Mulkay points out, the very absence of stable communities fosters both the transfer and the fusion of ideas thus encouraging new synthetic developments, 'even within those areas of research which persist for relatively long periods, there is a constant movement of personnel. This movement into and out of etablished networks produces a continuous cross-fertilization of ideas which is often responsible for intellectual change without the kind of redefinition of the field by a stable group envisaged by Kuhn.'[58]

Indeed, when Systemic features invite the exploration of novelty and contact mechanisms like the speed up in academic communication encourage it, then the more science emphasizes the production of variety and the less 'Kuhnian' is the research community in organization. Not only are numerous loose independent networks spawned but their characteristics are the reverse of those held to typify the stable, monopolistic, solidary community: 'They include (1) free flow of information and ideas; (2) temporary associations of individuals to bring together that variety which is essential to a particular kind of research; (3) status accorded to individually defined contributions with recogniton of unique additions to the pool . . . ; (4) clear identity of individual scientists with discoveries; and (5) the engagement of the total capacities of individual scientists, rather than their specific skills.'[59]

Thus both positive and negative factors join together to encourage the detection of further contingent complementarities out of the growing pool and to stimulate their exploitation, hence the continual addition of new items of variety to the Cultural System. The situational logic therefore furnishes untrammelled opportunities for morphogenesis while increased incentives for S-C opportunism ensure that many are taken up. For the two levels are intertwined in a positive feed-back loop. As past waves of CS specialization were successively institutionalized, through the creation of university departments, research institutes, development agencies, advisory bodies and consultative committees and the like, the S-C consequence was the attachment of groups of specialists to them whose institutional mandate was to innovate and whose personal interests were harnessed to doing so successfully. This assertion does not depend upon imputing some out of the ordinary drive, ambition or restless inventiveness to the people involved (though doubtless some self-selection on these lines determined which of the marginals actually got the new jobs), for, once in these positions, penalties accrued if ideational advances were not forthcoming (the most swingeing of which was to do oneself out of a job through the closure of an unproductive think-tank), while bonuses were associated with consistent innovation, thus encouraging every specialist to become an empire-builder. The best indicator of the influence exerted by opportunity and incentive, operating in tandem, is the steady expansion of areas of expertise in modern societies: we readily acknowledge new experts but we rarely withdraw this honorific title – at worst its pretentions are limited. Consequently, this interplay between the CS and the S-C levels means that the contingent complementarity is our only example of *unremitting* morphogenesis, from the four concepts examined.

In conclusion, then, the production of more and more variety is governed by positive feed-back. This is the exact obverse of the negative feed-back mechanism which regulates the protection and reproduction of the concomitant complementarity. Not only are the logics and the dynamics of the two kinds of complementarities the inverse of one another, but so are their results. Cultural variety is the opposite of cultural density. Variety feeds on what looks promising but is ill-defined; density deals with what feel like certainties yet are already over-defined. Variety pushes on to extend horizons haphazardly and unpredictably; density stays at home to embellish the local environment systematically.

These differences are equally marked in their Socio-Cultural effects – specialization prompts ideational diversification; systematization fosters cultural reproduction. Although the specialist groupings stemming from the contingent complementarity are not born to conflict (unlike the pluralist groups associated with competitive contradictions), nor are they endowed with internal stability or integrative relations to the rest of society. Their proliferation is fissiparous in effect, for as more and more sectional groupings are carved out they have less and less in common with one another and the rest of society. Specialist groups, unlike pluralist ones, are not defined by their opposition to others but by their differences from everyone. The detailed concerns which preoccupy them cannot be communicated satisfactorily or satisfyingly to those outside the group. Their members are condemned either to a separate 'social' and 'professional' life (having friends to whom they cannot talk about work and often finding that they do not have enough to talk about), or to becoming socially isolated (having colleagues with whom they can only talk shop and then being hard-put to keep it amicable). This is to look at the S-C effects within the specialist grouping where they are not particularly comfortable, its members being sustained by the temporary exhilaration of innovative surges but also terrified by the trough preceding the next intellectual high.

To view progressive specialization from the outside is to see the proportional exclusion of vast tracts of the population from larger and larger portions of specialist knowledge. The division of the population into laymen and experts is repeated over and over again as each new specialism emerges. This is a horizontal form of differentiation quite unlike the vertical stratification generated by the concomitant complementarity. The latter created strata with different degrees of mastery over the Cultural System: their mental maps were of the same universe but differed in terms of crudity or completeness. Where specialization becomes advanced, the differentiated cultural maps that sectional groupings carry in their heads may give more meaning to that dubious phrase about inhabiting 'different cultural worlds' than it has in its usual contexts. Here it would operate as an extreme type referring to two maps with no overlapping features, except language, which Socio-Culturally would mean no conversation.

There are, of course, other S-C factors militating against this, though they do not prevent my map from marking many entirely different features from those of my doctor's, car mechanic's, or farming neighbour's and vice versa. Consensual concerns over community, national and world affairs provide common reference points, though undoubtedly the superglue of our time comes from the ubiquitous flickering box. In short, the S-C level mediates the reception of the sectionalizing effects stemming from the contingent complementarity, as it does all forms of CS conditioning. Without its counteractive effects (themselves partly conditoned from the other Systemic sources) in supplying common meanings, concerns and commitments, specialization would provoke all the old Durkheimian anxieties about the absence of social cement. For unalloyed sectionalism would serve to invert General Pétain's quip, that culture is what remains when all else has been forgotten, by directing attention so closely to specialist knowledge that general knowledge is driven out of mind. In sum, then, the sectionalizing effect of the contingent complementarity is orthogonal to the reproduction of similarities generated by the concomitant complementarity and the widening of cleavages derived from the competitive contradiction. A simpler way of putting this is that specialization works against both conflict and consensus in Socio-Cultural life.

As is always the case, the state of affairs at the end of one morphogenetic cycle also constitutes the new conditional influences which are at work from the beginning of the next. Nevertheless our method of proceeding undoubtedly means that we will have failed to capture the full import of increased complexity at either the CS or S-C level. As has been stressed repeatedly, this enterprise was constrained to work in the barest and most basic terms, operating with logical relationships between pairs of propositions as our fundamental Systemic units in the absence of even the most rudimentary concepts of cultural components. It follows from this that the types of Cultural Elaboration it was possible to analyse were at the same basic level – additions to the CS of 'new' sets of logical relations between pairs of propositions the 'arrival' of which spelt increased systemic complexity and alterations in subsequent conditioning of cultural action. These were drawn out in the most general terms and at the expense of their historicity.

The 'original' elements (our constraining contradictions and concomitant complementarities) both generated situational logics which worked through negative feed-back and hence were predominantly culture-restoring. The associated influences upon S-C integration worked on the population to the same effect. The 'new' elaborated elements – the competitive contradictions and contingent complementarities – operate instead through positive feedback which amplifies deviations from the status quo to culminate in cultural change. Attendant S-C effects are the break-up of integration, induced by the intensification of polarized interests and sectional concerns, which in turn reinforce the push towards change. The immediate theoretical implication of this increase in complexity is the need to examine the interplay amongst these complex constituents of culture as well as their *combined* consequences for later action.

Imperative as this task is, it has not begun to be tackled in the present work. However, rather than conclude with an unbridged gap between what has been done and what still needs doing, it seems worth considering how the former links up with and would lead on to the latter – rough and ready as many of these suggestions will be.

Discussion will be aided by reference to Table 2 which provides a summary of the cultural features which have been distinguished, and (as far as the elaborated characteristics are concerned) derived through using analytical dualism. The Table is general in nature and could be applied to society as a whole or to some sector of it. Obviously this does not mean that the societal patterning of properties and relations will be replicated sectorally. The two may be very different, just as one institutional structure may differ greatly from another depending on the particular action sequence from which it arose. (Indeed when surveying the cultural field from a contemporary vantage point, we remain deplorably ignorant about which current doctrines developed according to one scenario or the other. Only sustained historical study of the emergence of theories and beliefs, conducted from the perspective of analytical dualism, would furnish this kind of map.)

The increased complexity of cultural relations by the last phase of morphogenetic cycle appears indisputable. The reason for this is that nothing whatsoever precludes both the right-hand side and the

Table 2. *Cultural Elaboration: summary*

Cultural System
Types of logical relations

| Which condition | Contradictions | | Complementarities | |
	Constraining	Competitive	Concomitant	Contingent
Situational Logic	Correction	Elimination	Protection	Opportunity
CS level	Syncretism	Pluralism	Systematization	Specialization
S-C level	Unification	Cleavage	Reproduction	Sectionalism

270

left-hand side of the Table from characterizing different cultural sectors simultaneously. Clearly it is not claimed that the array of doctrinal developments will display this four-fold patterning at all times and places. Nevertheless it seems useful to consider the co-existence of all the properties which appear in the Table, precisely because this raises the full range of tantalizing but wholly speculative issues about the importance of complexity for both the CS and S-C levels – in posterior cycles of cultural dynamics.

To take the Cultural System level first, let us think a little about relations in the middle horizontal band of the Table. Here we have already stressed the opposition between the original pair of logical relations and their respective derivatives. Thus emergent Pluralism opposes initial Syncretism, just as emergent Specialization opposes initial Systematization. However there are now four ideational features present and if we take these to be represented by four different doctrines, then things potentially become much more complex at the CS level for the emergent doctrines *may* be incompatible with *both* original doctrines. Formally it will be argued that this is the case.

The reason for this is that it is very hard to see how the development of Pluralism (considered *in toto*) could be anything other than opposed to Systematization. Since the various pluralistic strands are themselves embroiled in the situational logic of mutual elimination, then their joint incorporation into any systematized conspectus defies imagination. Similarly, if emergent forms of Specialization are also considered *in toto*, then their combined tendency to accentuate differences by exploiting the situational logic of opportunity runs directly counter to the generic aim of Syncretism which is the sinking of differences.

Because of the potential significance of this complex logical interplay in the elaborated Cultural System, the next step forward in theorizing would be to treat Syncretism, Pluralism, Systematization and Specialization as a parallelogram, and to conduct a pairwise inspection of their logical relations, moving around the cultural field as one's problem directs. However, until we have a body of 'doctrinal' or 'disciplinary' histories, compiled from the perspective of analytical dualism, we lack the empirical means to explore these speculations about and at a greater level of complexity.

Exactly the same is true of S-C life under the same assumptions about co-existence. Thus putting together the arguments advanced throughout Chapter 8, there would be an overall increase in the pushes and pulls to which social actors are subjected. It would in fact be perfectly possible for the population to be bombarded by four different pressures, each of which seeks to induce forms of S-C grouping which are at variance with one another. Indeed when all four conditional influences are at work on actors simultaneously, there are only two pairs which have any chance of pulling in the same direction, namely Unification/Reproduction and Cleavage/ Sectionalism – providing of course that they work to unite or to divide the population along similar lines. This cannot be taken for granted, for it is an empirical matter. All the other combinations of conditional influences seem necessarily to be pulling against one another.

Since all of these influences on actors would be co-terminous, the only certainty in this situation is that human agency would be and would feel increasingly badgered. In this context there is less and less possibility of just 'going on' because there is no life-world into which to retreat, since all of it becomes more and more subject to cultural raiding as morphogenesis proceeds. Any notion of a *Lebenswelt* as a sort of cultural redoubt for human agency betrays the same romantic nostalgia which prompts those who try to see *Gemeinschaft* surviving (or reborn) amidst *Gesellschaft*.

However, intriguing as considerations about cultural complexity may be and vital as they will become for theorizing about 'the next' morphogenetic cycle, we have to hold back for the time being until we know a good deal more about the origins, operations and eventual outcomes of the two sequences with which this study has dealt. At most perhaps one can venture the sketches in Figure 2, if only to show what one thinks one knows, what one suspects and what one would dearly like to discover when we have the wherewithal to tackle complexity.

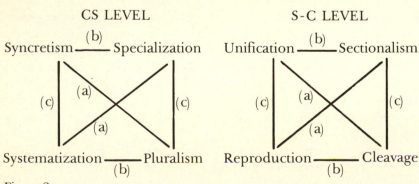

Figure 2

The bulk of the book has been concerned with establishing the (a) relationships of opposition alone. In the last few pages of speculation it has been suggested that the (b) relations are probably ones of opposition too, or at least predominantly so. However about the (c) relationships, which are empirical matters of content and congruence, we know nothing at all though are eminently capable of remedying this situation in the future.

CONCLUSION

Towards theoretical unification: structure, culture and morphogenesis

An introduction

Significantly when the morphogenetic perspective was elaborated within general systems theory, it was intended to apply to what Buckley termed 'socio-cultural systems'. Hence the direct implication that structure and culture could share the same theoretical umbrella – the framework of which is provided by the morphogenetic perspective, although the actual cultural fabric had still to be attached to it. This has been the task of the last four chapters. Perhaps however, we should pause to spell out just why it is so desirable to unify the ways in which we theorize about structure and culture. This has a rationale of its own which is quite separate from the idea of a more developed area giving a helping hand to a less advanced one.

The crucial point about theoretical unification is that it would foster a balanced view of the respective importance of structure and culture at any given time. Thus a unified theory would have an important deterrent effect by discouraging both the inflated importance assigned to culture, presented as society's bandmaster, or its relegation to a reflective role as society's looking-glass. Of course, both these distorted views of the place of culture in social life entail equal but opposite distortions of the part played by structure, for as the importance of culture is inflated or deflated it is really structure which diminishes or dominates at its expense. Effectively much of social theory has treated structure and culture as partners in a zero-sum relationship. The main alternative has been to represent their partnership as one of such tight mutual constitution that neither has any degree of autonomy from the other. Thus the ultimate

274

object of theorizing about structure and culture in the same kinds of terms is that it avoids any prejudgement of their relative importance at any time and makes it much easier to examine *their* interplay over time.

The promise of theoretical unification between structural and cultural analysis was implicit in the application of the morphogenetic perspective to the field of ideas. Fulfilment of this promise therefore depends upon this approach being successfully employed to deal with culture. Here its application entailed four basic propositions and its success depended upon each and every one of them commanding assent. These are the headings of the last four chapters, which were placed there to indicate the importance attached to them:

(i)   There are logical relationships between the components of the CS.

(ii)   There are causal influences exerted by the CS on the S-C level.

(iii)   There are causal relationships between groups and individuals at the S-C level.

(iv)   The S-C level elaborates on the composition of the CS by modifying current logical relationships and introducing new ones.

Why, however, am I arguing that this attempt to think and theorize about structure and culture in the same fundamental way depends upon the endorsement of all four propositions and founders if any one of them cannot be upheld? To begin with, proposition (i) is indispensable because it represents the charter of analytical dualism in the cultural domain. There may of course be serious dispute over the criterion I have used to delineate the Cultural System from the Socio-Cultural level, but unless some such analytical distinction is made between the two then all parallelism with social and System integration falls to the ground and this project for theoretical unification is still-born. The subsequent propositions, (ii), (iii) and (iv), correspond respectively to the three phases of the morphogenetic cycle. Once again there may be the deepest critical reservations about my treatment of them (in Chapters 6, 7 and 8), but the unificatory project would remain unimpaired if the propositions themselves carried conviction and only their discussion attracted criticism. However, since the three phases are essential parts of a single explanatory formula, then this whole theoretical approach collapses if assent is withheld from any of its three necessary components. The simplest way of expressing all of this is to say that propositions (ii), (iii) and (iv) make up the morphogenetic framework of explanation – for things cultural as for things structural – which is built on the foundations of proposition (i).

Obviously it is not difficult to identify theorists who subscribe enthusiastically to one of the last three propositions whilst rejecting the rest. Thus, although they would not use my notation because they reject the conceptualization underlying it (that is, based upon proposition (i)), nevertheless downwards conflationists would fully assent only to proposition (ii), which is where they see social actors being moulded by keys and codes. To them proposition (iii) would at most be theoretically redundant (just the sort of noise that people make in the System), while proposition (iv) is entirely repugnant to their approach since it postulates a two-way relationship, giving agency the power to modify culture. Exactly the opposite is true of upward conflationists who reserve their enthusiasm for proposition (iii), since causal relations between groups are what constitute culture. They would see proposition (iv) as superfluous, since the manipulation of culture in the interests of domination is what the causal relationships are all about. But they would totally repudiate proposition (ii), again because it postulates a two-way relationship – according culture the unacceptable power to mould even the most powerful groups. Central conflationists could only approve proposition (iv), which highlights the transformatory capacity of human agency, but would strenuously deny the propriety of advancing (ii) and (iii) as separate propositions – since to them any Systemic influence depends upon the instantiation of rules by agents and, equally, social relations between actors are reliant upon their drawing on shared signification systems.

Consequently in the various versions of conflationism we have either downright rejection of some particular proposition or outright condemnation of the propriety of stating these as distinct propositions. Both have the effect of damning the morphogenetic enterprise and any prospect of theoretical unification being introduced from that perspective. All of this is eminently understandable given that conflationists as such are intransigently opposed to the analytical dualism upon which the former is based. Correspondingly, however, each version of conflationary theorizing threw up the problem of culture and agency in different guises but ones which were immediately recognizable as counterparts of unsatisfactory solutions to the problem of linking structure and agency. Since the morphogenetic perspective can claim to have made a fair start on that problem, through the specification of the stringency of constraints and the degrees of interactional freedom, then it seemed at least to extend the same promise in the cultural field.

The last four chapters were a spare and preliminary exploration of this promise, with one chapter being devoted to each of the basic propositions in turn. The starting point was the introduction of analytical dualism in the cultural domain by distinguishing the Cultural System from the Socio-Cultural level. The distinction itself is crucial, for without it the mode of cultural analysis becomes a squabble between rival versions of conflationism – thus implicitly endorsing the validity and utility of conflation itself. But if the distinction between the levels is vital then it has to be convincingly drawn, anticipating the potential metaphysical and methodological objections reviewed in Chapter 5.

It was maintained that the most workable way of delineating the Cultural System was to restrict it to the register of propositions existing in any given social unit at a particular time. The propositional, though by no means exhaustive of the meaningful, constitutes the corpus of truths and falsehoods cherished in society at any given time. The self-evident importance of those things which are held to be true or false to the constitution and operation of culture is also considered to be sufficient justification for making the propositional register co-terminous with the Cultural System. Methodologically this enables the invariant rules of logic to be employed for the cross-cultural detection of contradictions and complementarities between items, despite their substantive differences.

This distinction and all that follows from it is grounded in analytical dualism, for the register we distinguish is not synonymous with or reducible to your or my Cultural System. If we are talking about the here and now, there will be overlap between the two but there will also be tracts of the register of which no one at present is aware. Equally, it will contain a series of emergent relational properties which confront current actors as obstructions or opportunities, yet ones for which contemporary agents are in no way responsible. Consequently we can never arrive at knowledge of a Cultural System through personal introspection or participant observation. A lifetime of fieldwork could only yield up partial knowledge – at best an inventory of those components and their relations which are within the cognizance of the collectivity. A simpler way of putting this is that Cultural Systems really pertain to libraries rather than to people.

Yet all libraries are vast and all catalogues are incomplete. Hence the basic problem of *how* to approach the Cultural System, of how to start to theorize about a phenomenon which we can never fully describe? This difficulty is not as bad as it looks; most of the natural sciences have forged ahead in an analogous situation. Indeed it is yet another misconception perpetrated by the conflation of the two levels that we can gain full entry to the cultural domain through the S-C door (all that conflationists differ on is whether this is a direct *entrée* as in the upwards version or an indirect one as in the other two kinds). Nevertheless, where to start remains problematic.

Lacking any existing cultural 'units' with which to work, exploration of proposition (i) was pared down to the bone. Without pre-existing groundwork on which to build, the discussion began at ground level by an examination of relations between two cultural components A and B. Obviously this involves considerable abstraction from reality since two propositions rarely relate to one another and to no others. Its advantage was the capacity to disentangle basic types of interconnections between unit items which could then be cast outwards and applied to practical examples which embodied them, despite enmeshment in a larger web of further relations with other items. Although the key A/B relations which were disengaged are abstracted from reality by stripping away additional connections, they remain none the less real as they entail none of the selection and one-sided accentuation which characterizes the ideal type. Through working in the barest and most basic terms, the aim was then to begin theorizing in the sparest yet boldest way.

These pairs of propositions thus constituted our fundamental Systemic units when moving on to examine the latter three propositions which together represent the key phases of the morphogenetic cycle. Clearly, in social life these pairs do not exist in isolation but are linked with other propositions to form theories and beliefs. The latter are then clustered and formalized into broader bodies of doctrine, schools of thought, rule systems and policy programmes – the resultant Cultural System at T_1 being made up of all these elements which display different contradictions and complementarities at the various levels. This approach to culture is entirely congruent with structural analysis, for there, too, structural contradictions maintain between *parts* of the social structure – it makes no sense whatsoever to assert that society as a whole is in contradiction. Thus the most macro unit of structural analysis is properly the 'institutional' for these are the parts between which contradictions develop – affecting the whole of society.

Indeed the units of structural analysis appear to have their direct cultural counterparts although the latter lack a well-established nomenclature. Thus the institutional level in the structural field, where operations in one sphere can obstruct those in another, setting up inescapable strains and contradictions as in Lockwood's prime examples, have their parallel in the cultural domain. At what could be called the doctrinal level, then, social policies can be inconsistent with economic planning, religious doctrine can contradict defence programmes and educational knowledge can stand in logical opposition to legal rules.

At the next floor 'down', structural analysis treats of intra-institutional strains and tensions which *may* involve entirely different properties from the inter-institutional contradictions just mentioned, and in any case are not homologous with the latter. Thus the particular structuring of an institution, such as an education system, generates distinctive strains *between* its component parts: a decentralized system suffers from semi-permanent anarchy amongst its highly autonomous components; a centralized system institutes a tension between the internal standardization of practices and the external diversity of educational demands. Similarly, each cultural 'doctrine' harbours or engenders incompatible elements or survives in a state of tension with its ideational environment.

Moving closer to the micro-level, just as any role within an organization can have contradictory requirements written into its formal constitution (which are analytically and empirically distinguishable from the incompatible expectations that people may entertain in relation to it), precisely the same is true of cultural rules. Similarly too this is not a matter of variations in Socio-Cultural interpretations (important as these may be) for a rule to which all *may* subscribe, such as 'human life should be preserved', can entail contradictory requirements as in the old 'mother or baby' dilemma. Certainly personal interpretation will determine what is done in such a situation but these do not abolish the contradiction; indeed the fact that each such interpretation is also a justification indicates a recognition of the contradiction and an attempt to live with it.

All the same it might well have been felt that the excessive abstraction involved in poring over the logical relations between two propositions was a very long way from a theory of cultural dynamics and, less charitably, was actually heading away from one. But inspection of the core A/B relationship did sterling service in erecting such a theoretical framework, when harnessed to the morphogenetic perspective. From consideration of pairs of propositions, it was possible to sketch one *generic* morphogenetic cycle for culture, using the same phases as employed in the analysis of social structure (Structural Conditioning → Social Interaction → Structural Elaboration), thus pointing the way to theoretical unification.

Doubtless this basic cycle of Cultural Elaboration has been played out innumerable times in different parts of the cultural realm (as the examples adduced in Chapter 8 serve to illustrate). Hence what I have talked about as 'newly' elaborated Systemic features are only 'new' in an abstract and analytical sense: the implication is not that they emerged yesterday, recently or even in modern times. It is a virtual certainty that the elaborated features discussed could be detected empirically at almost any point in recorded history.

Here, however, there is a major contrast with structural analysis: when theorists are dealing with concrete changes in social structures (for example, the emergence of capitalism from feudalism) or one part of them (for example, the emergence of state educational systems from a prior context of private ownership in education) they were able to put names and dates to changing social configurations or institutions. Their cycles, though analytic (and of course open to dispute on all sorts of grounds) had the advantage of being once and for all. Because of their concreteness they could utilize successive morphogenetic cycles to trace and account for actual developmental sequences over time within the social structure, in areas like production and education. But in the cultural field this is precisely where we are deplorably ignorant – largely because the Myth of Cultural Integration served to put the study of the sociological origins of cultural configurations out of business. Thus, until a corpus of work exists which, having forged its own concepts appropriate to cultural entities, events and changes, then provides equivalent substantive studies of cultural configurations, we are confined to generalities, to discussion of a generic sequence and to the elucidation of general similarities characterizing both Structural and Cultural Elaboration when suggesting the possibility of theoretical unification between them.

One thing that serves to encourage this enterprise is that it was by working the other way round, with reference to substantive work in the Marxist, Functionalist and Weberian traditions that Lockwood distilled his general points about system integration which were then linked to social integration and extended to the analysis of specific institutional orders. Equally, when Blau sought to show the derivation of complex structural features from simpler sociative processes, he too worked in terms of a generic sequence through which general properties like differentiation, power, opposition and legitimation were derived – argumentatively rather than empirically.

In other words it is possible to discuss morphogenetic and morphostatic mechanisms in both general and specific terms: the difference between structural and cultural analysis is that the two have already been done in relation to social structure, while in the cultural field we are still struggling to disengage the mechanism in its most basic form. Our present frustrating ignorance about the actual patterning of cultural configurations (with the exception of a few works like those of Elias and Needham) means that future advances in thinking and theorizing will have to confront culture in its full complexity – progressively but eventually. The A/B relations were a pair of strong bootstraps which served to lift analysis off the ground, by allowing the two morphogenetic scenarios to be disengaged. Useful as this was as a starting point, we cannot remain at the level of bootstrapped abstraction for good.

9   Uniting structural and cultural analysis

This book has been a flight from the Fallacy of Conflation and it is a flight which will continue to the very end. Throughout this work the two levels, the Cultural System and Socio-Cultural interaction, have been kept apart by means of analytical dualism in order to examine the relationship between them. Yet analysis of the S-C level involved ceaseless cross-references to the structural domain – to material interests, to power, to resources, to group alliances and antagonism. Because of the frequency with which such empirical connections have been mentioned, certain readers (especially the unrepentant upwards conflationists) may still be cherishing the idea of a 'hidden motor' throbbing away underneath the cultural floorboards. Their thinking would be basically as follows: S-C interaction has been admitted to be intimately involved with material power and interests; this interaction in turn makes or breaks cultural stability; therefore are not structural factors really at the bottom of cultural dynamics?

In what follows I want to take an axe to the 'hidden motor' without then falling back on the feeble assertion that there is an empirical connection but one contingent on a vast array of factors the frequency of occurrence of which is indeterminate. On the contrary, the conclusion advanced is that structural and cultural dynamics are indeed interrelated in determinate ways, without one of them ultimately determining the other. In other words, the relative autonomy of culture will be upheld, as will that of structure (and anyone thinking this needs no upholding should keep a weather eye on the current doings of the central conflationists), whilst saying some basic things about their relationship.

This becomes possible because their conceptual unification then paves the way for uniting structural and cultural analysis. Since the two domains are now conceptualized in the same morphogenetic terms there exists a common vocabulary in which to talk about them and a common framework from which to theorize about their relationship. This conceptual unification immediately allows two preparatory points to be made about the intersection of the two domains. In substance they are unoriginal, in presentation they gain in precision because we can point to where they intersect in the same framework and in consequence we can trace through the effects of their intersection for one domain on the other. These points, then, are a necessary preface to a propositional linking of structure and culture.

When both structure and culture are conceptualized from the morphogenetic perspective then *the two intersect in the middle element of the basic cycle*. In other words, the interactional phase, whether we are dealing with S-C interaction or that taking place between structured interest groups, always entails a great deal of interpenetration between the two – this entailment being a matter of *sociological* necessity.

Thus, when discussing S-C interaction in Chapter 7, constant reference did indeed have to be made to the power and material interests of groups, that is to structural factors defined somewhere other than in the cultural domain itself, which were therefore inexplicable in purely cultural terms but also indispensable to explaining Socio-Cultural interaction. This was simply because the degree of S-C orderliness or disorderliness, relative to the order or disorder prevailing in the Cultural System, often required recourse to statements about the power and interests of groups to explain it. From their incorporation some might have thought that the parts were being assembled from which the 'hidden motor' could then be constructed. For it was undoubtedly accepted that, to paraphrase Berger, those with the biggest stick did have the best chance of defending or disrupting a particular cultural status quo. Moreover, structural properties were incorporated into a general statement to which frequent appeal was made, namely that it was the divergence of material interests from the situational logic of ideas which frequently caused the CS to come unstuck. In short, it was concluded that a lack of gel between the two was a prime mechanism of cultural dynamics.

However, none of the above has as its corollary that the conflict of ideas is reducible to the ideational expression of the struggles between material interest groups. On the contrary, nothing stated above rules out a conflict of ideas which gets underway independently of material interests. Even more importantly, none of the foregoing serves to deny that ideational interaction can spawn its *own* vested interest groups – collectivities, as we have seen, who first acquire different ideal interests through which they later develop different material interests by receiving differential material rewards from their cultural capital. Nevertheless, most of the time it is empirically the case that we have to recognize that there is structural penetration of the cultural realm, and thus need to theorize about the intersection of the structural and cultural fields, for the simple sociological reason that actors themselves do have positions for both domains simultaneously.

Exactly the same is true of any discussion of group interaction in any part of the social structure. Again, logically and sometimes empirically there can be naked group antagonism, but to explain sociologically the outcome of conflict between material interest groups this is rarely sufficient on its own. Generally, it is necessary to introduce cultural factors, that is the battle between legitimatory and oppositional ideas which form part of most social struggles and transactions. In exact parallel to the previous argument, it needs be allowed that the discursive success of one set of ideas helps to account for the victory of the group advancing it, when structural factors alone (such as bargaining power, numbers, or organization) fail to provide explanatory purchase. Similarly, cultural factors often have to be deemed accountable for the failure of conflict to manifest itself although the structural conditions appear ripe. Again, then, discrepancies between the relative orderliness or disorderliness prevailing between groups compared with the orderliness or disorderliness prevailing between parts of the social structure have to be attributed to cultural influences. Thus, empirically and theoretically the cultural penetration of the structural field has to be recognized, for the same sociological reason as before – that social groups not only have interests, resources and power but they also have ideas (and if certain groups would like not to have some of these around, then their opponents certainly would).

These considerations lead directly to the most interesting questions of all. On the one hand, the inescapable intersection of the structural and cultural domains has just been underlined. On the other hand, this in no way denies that the two fields have their own morphostatic/morphogenetic dynamics (I have tried to demonstrate this generically for culture in the present book and attempted the same for the structuring of a social institution in its predecessor). If both these propositions are accepted, then we are immediately led to query the nature of the interplay between them. In other words, how does the fact that structure penetrates Socio-Cultural inter-action affect cultural dynamics? Equally, how does the intersection of culture with interaction between interest groups affect structural dynamics? The answers to these 'how' questions home in on the mechanisms through which (1) culture influences structure and (2) structure exerts its influence upon culture.

(1) The basic mechanism by which cultural factors find their way into the structural field through the intersection is extremely simple. Let any material interest group (call some groups 'domi-nant' by all means if their societal or sectional dominance can be demonstrated empirically) endorse any doctrine (theory, belief or ideology) for the advancement of those interests (that is their articulation, assertion, or legitimation), and that group is immedi-ately plunged into its situational logic. Structural benefits may indeed ensue from ideational back-up but they have their cultural price and not one which is paid in a single instalment.

By adopting a set of ideas the structural interest group enmeshes itself in a particular form of cultural discourse and its associated problems. Thus, whether it knew it or not in advance, the interest group has taken on a new job in a different kind of struggle. Depending on which situational logic it has voluntarily unleashed on itself, it now has to get busy correcting, protecting, competing or diversifying because these tasks are intrinsic to upholding ideas. Moreover, since interest groups embraced doctrines for the pur-pose of material advancement, they indeed set to work with a will, if not a great deal of cultural skill, for the options of irrational dogmatism or desertion, though objectively open to them once they have fully realized what they have let themselves in for, would be disastrous to their structural cause. (Irrational dogmatism is a dug-out for ideational groups on the run and can never be an asset to structural groups on the make: organized group desertion is not only expensive to marshall but is a collective admission of failure to sustain its source of legitimation.) Necessarily, then, material interest groups become subject to some form of situational logic in the cultural domain. They may not make the most ingenious con-tributions to correction or protection, they may not provide the most inventive competitive arguments or the most innovative

285

departures *but* they will have to keep abreast with them and attain sufficient mastery over syncretic formulae, the systematized conspectus or their ideational opposites, to engage in public discourse proficiently.

For the whole point of a material interest group adopting ideas is quintessentially public – to inform and unify supporters or to undercut opponents argumentatively, are all noisy exercises. And it is precisely because of this audible exposure of ideas that the full price of employing them is finally reckoned. The interest group had, as it were, surveyed the cultural field, selected congruent ideas from it and publicized them. In so doing, it alerts the entire relevant population (supporters, opponents, or quasi-oppositional groups) to a particular part of the Cultural System. If opposition or differentiation are already rife there, then structural opponents find ready-made cultural weapons in the CS which they have every interest in taking up and wielding against the material interest group which is attempting to generalize and naturalize those ideas it has adopted for its own advancement. Indeed, a quasi-oppositional group may be transformed into a 'group for itself' by taking sides in a more 'advanced' cultural struggle.

Sometimes the size of the final cultural bill will be considered too heavy by the interest group which first went out shopping for ideas but by that time it is too late to back out of paying it. The struggle has to go on, between ideas as well as between interests. At other times the doctrines adopted as yet incite little ideational opposition or deviation and, for the time being, those material interests which were first to ally with them reap structural support from them. Nevertheless, they have enmeshed themselves in a particular kind of situational logic, and as and when it unfurls they will find that they occupy an ideational stance which constrains them to engage in particular kinds of discursive tasks. These are the costs and benefits of elective affinities and no structural advantage which is gained from culture ever comes for free.

(2) Structural factors find their way into the cultural field by following the same path through the intersection, only here we have to look at what happens at the other end of it. Thus, let the advocacy of any doctrine (theory, belief or ideology) become associated with a particular material interest group and its fate becomes embroiled in the fortunes of that group *vis à vis* others. For all such attachments immediately enmesh cultural discourse in power play. There is no need to linger over this basic point for numerous examples have been given in the last three chapters,

illustrating its two main aspects. On the one hand, the effectiveness of morphostatic strategies can be greatly extended over time given the support of powerful social groups working for the authoritarian concealment of contradictions or blocking the accessibility of alternatives. On the other hand, since morphogenesis depends not only on the elaboration of new ideas, through counter-actualization or synthesis, but also upon their achieving social salience, then their sponsorship by powerful social groups can be crucial for them attaining and maintaining high visibility in society.

Again, however, there are costs attaching to involvement in power play. The first is a form of guilt-by-association which socially restricts the appeal of ideas. Thus, for example, a set of ideas the logical form of which is universalistic (like many religious ones) will find its Socio-Cultural reception far from universal, the more particularistic are the interests of its powerful sponsors. When the Anglican Church can become satirized as the Tory Party at prayer this is the end of a long action sequence in which the original connection between Church, king and country eventually fostered just that particularism which was intended to remain hidden. The quest by ideational groups for sponsors is a search to sign up the powerful, but the price of their support is that a second list of subscribers is simultaneously constituted – namely those willing to subscribe to practically any other ideas, providing these allow them to pursue their structural hostilities. Of course, this is only an immediate reaction and soon after these oppositional interest groups will be found busily engaged in ideational moulding and meddling to extract real cultural congruence out of a socially induced marriage of convenience.

At this point the second cost comes into play as discourse becomes caught in the cross-fire of the social struggle: ideational groups gloomily see shifting emphases, particular interpretations, and given lines of thought promoted or demoted by the shifting ploys of material interest groups, with scant attention to their own ideal commitments and interests. Here too, then, there are costs and benefits attaching to structural alliances but since the former appear after the latter the bill is often run up recklessly high, yet still has to be paid.

These general propositions about the mechanism by which structure and culture inter-penetrate one another are crucial but they are also ones from which few but the complete idealist or materialist would dissent. For basically they state that ideas are forces in social conflict and that the socially forceful are also culturally influential. So far we have only added a little precision to the 'how' issue. This by itself provides no escape from those banal statements that structure influences culture and that culture also influences structure, for although it tells what mechanisms are relevant, it does not specify which ones will be more important, when, where and under what conditions. Without such a specification we remain no better off than those arguing that structure and culture are 'dialectically related' or 'mutually constitutive' – which are different ways of saying that the two domains are connected but the nature of their mutual influence still eludes us. The present aim is to improve on this by answering the two underlying questions: 'when does structure exert more influence over culture than vice versa?' and 'when is culture more consequential for structure than vice versa?' By linking the above discussion of the 'how' mechanisms to a specification of the 'when' conditions it is hoped to produce a theory of mutual influence rather than a theoretical evasion.

It will be argued that it is possible to do better than this thanks to the theoretical unification of the two domains from the morphogenetic perspective. Now that we can theorize about sequences of structural and cultural dynamics in common terms, a new opportunity presents itself for examining the interplay *between* these sequences in the two different realms. Approaching the issue in this way has the advantage of skirting the futile idealist/materialist debate about 'which came first'. Instead of this pointless excursion, it can be taken for granted that all ideas are generated in a material setting and equally that all material interest groups emerge within a Cultural System – in order to get to the point of establishing when one is more influential than the other.

Thus the proposition will be advanced that it is when there are discontinuities between the morphostatic/morphogenetic sequences in the structural and cultural domains that one of these is found to be *more consequential* for the other, temporally and temporarily. Correspondingly, conjunction between the two cycles coincides with *reciprocal influences* between structure and culture. Finally, the argument will conclude by attempting to demonstrate that theorizing about the interplay of structure and culture in this way also gives some explanatory purchase on what actually results under various conditions of conjunction and discontinuity.

Logically, there are four basic combinations between morphostatic and morphogenetic cycles in the structural and the cultural domains. As exemplifications of each readily spring to mind, they are clearly more than theoretical extrapolations and are perhaps best considered as extreme types. In contrast to Ideal Types they are found in reality, so their discussion entails no one-sided theoretical accentuation; nevertheless, in relation to the bulk of empirical incidences they are extreme instances of perfect conjunction or total discontinuity. Probably this makes them rareties in reality, for the majority of cases are more likely to occupy slots between these two poles. The discussion will be conducted in relation to these four 'pure' combinations and theoretical statements will be disengaged in this context. It then remains a matter open to empirical testing whether these provide some explanatory grip on cases (societal or sectional) which are 'more like' one of the combinations discussed than any other.

Finally, it is essential to underline that what were referred to above as logical combinations, though they indeed have this property, are also real-life social configurations – a patterned interplay between structure and culture, revealing itself over time and never a static snapshot of their timeless combinatory pattern. Indeed, analysis of each configuration works in terms of the three phases of the morphostatic/morphogenetic cycles and, since these phases are temporal, then the Socio-Cultural affairs with which they deal cannot be timeless. By corollary, none of the theoretical propositions which are introduced can be atemporal either.

(i) The conjunction between structural morphostasis and cultural morphostasis

Let us begin from the point where we first set out with the community of shared meanings as the archetypical picture of the place of culture in society. From Figure 3 it can be seen that the reality in which this image was grounded is, in fact, that particular configuration which results when structural and cultural morphostasis coincide. Far from being universal, the supposed archetype is dependent upon this conjunction. In turn, the manifestation of this conjunction depends on specific states of affairs occurring simultaneously in the two domains.

On the one hand, cultural morphostasis signifies the hegemony of systematization or syncretism at the CS level (which are not (yet) subject to ideational opposition) accompanied by the S-C reproduction of ideas amongst a unified population, which is what makes this cycle morphostatic. On the other hand, structural morphostasis usually indicates a monolithic form of social organization with a superimposition of elites and heavy concen-

CULTURAL DOMAIN   STRUCTURAL DOMAIN

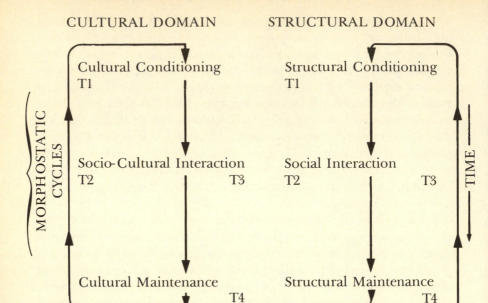

Figure 3

tration of resources which together prevent crystallization of opposition – this subordination of the population thus allowing the social (or sectional) structure to be perpetuated. When spelt out in this way it is obvious that this configuration is not universal; when examined more closely it is equally obvious that where it develops this conjunction will prove long-lasting. Perhaps such very durability was responsible for it acquiring the reputation of typicality among those seminal early anthropologists who confined themselves to the period of its duration.

Turning immediately to the mutual influences of the two domains upon one another, these display complete reciprocity. The force of hegemonic ideas imposes itself on stable social groups and the fortune of the dominant groups reinforces the stability of ideas, the two thus working together for maintenance of the status quo. The mechanisms responsible for these reciprocal influences at the intersection of the two domains are very similar.

First, the fund of cultural ideas which are *available* for adoption by social groups in structural interaction is extremely homogeneous. There are no visible alternatives (CS) with any social salience for those with inaudible grievances to latch onto and thus articulate the

290

sources of their smouldering discontent. Instead, by reproducing a stable corpus of ideas over time, cultural forces work to produce a unified population. Its members may indeed be the victims of pre-ceptual power rather than voluntary adherents to consensual precepts, but in any case they are incapable of articulating dissident views and of passing these over the intersection to stimulate structural disruption. On the contrary, the cultural forces generating S-C unification and reproduction work to depress incipient forms of structural opposition.

Second, and in direct parallel, the social structure contains no developed marginal groups or powerful malcontents with the motive or means to increase Socio-Cultural disorderliness. Subordination implies that there is no material interest group available to challenge CS conditioning. Since the emergence of both Pluralism and Specialization are utterly dependent on social groups pushing ideational diversification forwards, these are as yet lacking in the structural domain. Hence none traverse the inter-section to stir up S-C interaction by exploiting a Systemic fault-line or diversifying away from a systematized conspectus. On the con-trary, the subordination of potential oppositional interest groups works to delay the surfacing of cultural challengers.

Of equal importance in this configuration is the fact that elites find themselves in a similar position as far as alternatives are con-cerned. Thus, the structural elite is 'trapped' in the only kind of cultural discourse which is currently in social parlance; similarly the cultural elite is enmeshed by the monolithic power structure which is the present form of social organization. It might rightly be objected that these constraints are not determinants, for both kinds of elites have the means of resistance at their disposal. Thus, the concentration of resources in the hands of the structural elite means that in principle some could be diverted for the task of ran-sacking the CS for alternatives. On the other hand, the cultural elite enjoy a degree of social differentiation, as intellectuals, which could be directed towards the consolidation of an intelligentsia as an oppositional interest group in society – a group determined to equilibrate its material rewards with its intellectual expertise. However, although both kinds of elites have the means to resist mutual conditioning, both also lack the motive.

Given this conjunction, the two elites (whatever their origins) have no *immediate* alternative but to live together but what is much more important is that they have every interest in *continuing* to do so. Here, cultural morphostasis (through the stable reproduction of ideas amongst a unified population) generates an ideational environment which is highly conducive to structural maintenance. Structural morphostasis (through the control of marginality and subordination of the masses) in its turn produces an organizational environment which contributes greatly to cultural maintenance. Whatever private views the elites may entertain of one another (as out-and-out barbarians or high priests of mumbo-jumbo) the opportunity costs of turning on each other (to promote a different organization or different ideas) are much too high for this to become public practice.

Quite the opposite is the case. It is in these configurations that kings and emperors readily don the insignia of the high priest – given the chance they will pocket every personal reservation in order to palm the public pay-off. Here, too, the priests ratify the divine right of kings, the literati keep their books straight, the sooth-sayers arrange the entrails appropriately, and the intellectuals knuckle down to producing anything from conservative consti-tutions to confirmatory ceremonials. Those dominant in the struc-tural domain do not *have* to support the culturally dominant or vice versa but in this configuration both tend to do so with gratitude. Indeed, because of mutual recognition of benefits received, the two domains may become progressively intertwined, with interlocking roles and interchangeable personnel – thus approximating to the superimposition of structure and culture which Weber described for Ancient India and China.

Thus, where there is a conjunction between structural and cultural morphostasis, the consequences of each domain for the other are symmetrical and conducive to maintenance in both fields. When this state of affairs is detected it is probable that the cycle examined was preceded by anterior morphostatic cycles and suc-ceeded by posterior ones. Indeed, the fact that many 'old and cold' societies conformed to this pattern was what got the Myth of Cultural Integration off to such a good start. But since the Myth has now been shown to rest upon the existence of this particular con-figuration, it can at last be put in its proper place and perspective. It is not universal to 'primitive society' but conditional there on un-opposed cultural traditionalism and unchallenged structural domination – a combination not found everywhere. Nor where it is found will this configuration last for ever. As has been seen (Chap-ter 7), there are internal cultural dynamics which eventually engage to disrupt ideational traditionalism. These may be speeded up by structural disruption or slowed down by structural routinization.

Just because the wait may be long this does not make morphostasis eternal, universal or even typical, nor does it reduce one whit its reliance on the duration of the configuration under discussion. Because of this the question of what happens when there are disjunctions between morphostasis and morphogenesis in the two fields becomes of enormous interest.

(ii) The disjunction between cultural morphostasis and structural morphogenesis

Basically in this configuration culture retains the same formal features as those described above. Namely, its morphostatic character indicates that Syncretism is being made to stick or that Systematization is well protected. For the time being the population is subject to ideational control which prevents S-C interaction from working against maintenance of the cultural status quo. In the structural field, however, for any number of reasons, morphogenesis has got underway quite independently. Whatever the cause (the determinants of structural dynamics not being part of the present concern), the key result for the middle element of the cycle, where the two domains intersect, is a substantial growth in the differentiation of material interest groups. Depending on the types of structural development underway, these groups are preoccupied with self-definition, self-assertion and self-advancement through social interaction. But regardless of what kinds of structural change are being elaborated and whether some groups want to hold them back while others press them forward (and further groups act as arbitrators and yet others as opportunists), the fact remains that all this activity initially takes place in a stable cultural context. Culture provides no spur to the group differentiation which is the generic motor of structural change but acts as a drag upon it.

The differentiation of new collectivities (for example the rise of the European leisured aristocracy), or more particularly their development into self-conscious promotive interest groups, is itself restrained by cultural unification and reproduction. Indeed, cultural power will be deployed against them but, as has been seen, this is most efficacious against the weaker groups, lacking in both clout and confidence. But when change concerns those with the opposite attributes and simultaneously increases their ranks and augments their interests, the group which is already engaged in the 'brute' assertion of these interests soon recognizes that they do not gel with the prevailing form of cultural Syncretism or Systemization. Its members do so for two reasons – one at the CS level; the other operating at the S-C level.

Objectively, such a group derives no benefits from the cultural status quo. On the contrary, negative opportunity costs are associated with its support or passive acceptance. It might be argued that, all the same, in the absence of articulated cultural alternatives, this new group has no independent vantage point from which it can either know it or rebel against it. The notion that they must remain unaware that culture is costing them, holds no water at the S-C level. For there it receives independent indications that it is collecting cultural penalties whilst others reap cultural benefits. On the one hand, it makes comparisons with other social groups with which it interacts and can hardly fail to note that some of its competitors are beneficiaries of cultural support whereas their own promotive efforts attract cultural opprobrium. On the other hand, one of the very things which enforces awareness of this situation is the use of cultural force against the group. Members of competitive groups do not have to be endowed with the qualities of good sociologists to know that they are being sanctioned, censored and coerced when their opponents are not.

Nevertheless, they do indeed lack ideas to counterpose against those whose hegemony obstructs them. But they also have a structurally induced motive for acquiring them, in order to challenge the legitimacy claims of others and to establish their own. Consequently, just as their domain had been raided by the cultural controllers, so they now cross the intersection to ransack the CS for items conducive to their cause. Certainly, the nature of the CS will enmesh them in a particular form of discourse precisely because what they batten onto first are the most obvious *problems* presented by the hegemonic ideas.

Thus, where concealment or containment had cloaked a contradiction, the new interest group now rips this aside and precipitates the move towards Syncretism; if some syncretic formula was in place already this group refuses to let it stick and prompts a shift to more generous types of syncretic accommodation; when the schismatic tendencies associated with accommodative Syncretism have brought the contradiction out into the full light of day, the material interest group pounces on the contradictory items and brings about their counter-actualization. The fact that a single interest group can accomplish *all* of this is indicative of the stronger influence of structure on culture, given this conjuncture. All the same, the fact that what the material interest group unleashes is a competitive contradiction and that its members then become embroiled in the situational logic of elimination, shows that there is always a cultural influence on structure at the intersection – even when the latter sets the former in train.

Similarly, when Systematization has enjoyed unchallenged hegemony in the cultural domain, it is the material interest group most hindered by it who have the motivation to diagnose the problems it cannot solve and the issues with which it cannot deal. In so doing, they become nascent anti-traditionalists and traditionalism is on the skids the moment a group starts searching for its weak spots rather than viewing it as all-sufficient. Still it dominates social discourse and it is the only form of discourse the new interest group knows. Consequently, the latter is driven to interpretative adaptation and the accentuation of its more congruent elements (see Gouldner). In itself this neither rocks hegemony nor generates a distinctive source of self-legitimation. As a result the interest group not only remains on the alert for new compatible items which would increase its appeal without alienating potential supporters – it actually goes out looking for elements congruent to ideational diversification. What it develops is some form of contingent complementarity which buttresses its claim to a special status and special treatment, in terms which the rest of the population can still understand. To this extent its quest for a novel source of legitimation is culturally entrapped: complete novelty is not on. However, given its interests *in* sectionalism, which provide the impetus to pursue the logic of opportunity, the systematized conspectus is soon confronted with diversified ideas which complement it in one sense but are brought in from over a boundary which could no longer be maintained.

The development of these ideas by material interest groups eventually induces cultural elaboration. The structural groups that have just been discussed thus constitute those independent sources of cultural change which were introduced in Chapter 7, but remained unidentified in the text. In short, it is groups and interests which penetrate from the structural domain which account for cultural changes that are not derivative from internal cultural dynamics themselves. Hence, it is where there is a disjunction between cultural morphostasis and structural morphogenesis that the latter jolts the former into transformation, through what could be called the 'non-derived sequence'.

Cultural Elaboration is induced at the intersection of the two domains, through the influence of Social Interaction on S-C interaction. Once new material interest groups have unleashed novel ideas and providing that they continue to hold to them, then the old unification of the population has been undermined, by definition. Henceforth, the traditional reproduction of ideas has to contend with the new options on offer. Because the material interest groups seek to legitimate their advancement in the social structure, by appeal to the newly elaborated ideas, then they necessarily promote cleavage and sectionalism in the cultural domain. Those whose quietism had been the product of containment strategies and those whose conformity had been due to lack of alternatives may well now leap to competitive opposition or flock to the new opportunities, thus augmenting Socio-Cultural conflict way beyond its original structural impetus and issuing in dramatic Cultural Elaboration. But without the structural stimulus, rooted in the disjunction between the two domains this elaborative sequence would not have got off the ground. Here, then, Structural Elaboration exerts more of an influence upon Cultural Elaboration than vice versa.

(iii) The disjunction between cultural morphogenesis and structural morphostasis

In this configuration the fact that cultural morphogenesis is already underway, while structure remains morphostatic, points to the 'derived sequence' having worked its way through the cultural field. In other words, Pluralism or Specialization have developed from internal cultural dynamics and the groups attached to them refuse to let corrective repairs stick or stable reproduction last. However, the co-existing state of affairs in the structural domain is morphostatic and continues to work through negative feed-back, thus maintaining a particular form of social organization and eliminating deviations from this status quo. If such organization entails a significant degree of social differentiation, then the morphostatic process operates to reinforce the attendant social relations (based on a stable and hierarchical distribution of resources) and to prevent the crystallization of new material interest groups because of their disruptive potential.

Structural stability and the forces maintaining it will undoubtedly have acted as a brake at first on cultural change, by sanctioning the capacity of social actors for mobilization or regrouping; for, quintessentially, social control is directed against re-differentiation in society. Yet ideational diversification is totally dependent on differentiated groups who have enough freedom to introduce and then sustain pluralistic or specialized ideas. Structural restraints will delay their emergence. Indeed, it is highly likely that it was the effect of morphostatic structural processes which accounted for the existence of greater S-C orderliness than could be attributed to the state of the CS or to the deployment of cultural power. When this state of affairs was noted in the text, it was attributed to the pursuit of more compelling interests: these, of course, are likely to be material interests, rooted in the structural status quo. However, given the relative autonomy of the two domains, structural influences can restrain the emergence of new material interest groups but they can do no more than retard the development of new ideal interest groups.

Whatever the delays and vicissitudes involved in cultural change, the eventual elaboration of either Pluralism or Specialization has immediate effects at the S-C level. The two developments respectively entail competitive conflict between ideas and progressive diversification of ideas. As they amplify, they promote deeper cleavages or further Sectionalism in a population previously subject to ideational unification or the stable reproduction of ideas. Earlier in the text we concentrated purely on the Socio-Cultural consequences of the erosion of these morphostatic influences, namely more actors are drawn into cultural competition and more agents are drawn to cultural specialization. But, of course, these changes have repercussions on the other side of the intersection.

The most obvious of these is the withdrawal of that very cultural unity on which structural stability had partly rested. Certainly, notions about a common cultural framework which distributes similarities amongst the population and develops a community of shared meanings tend to be exaggerated as features of cultural morphostasis, but at least successful Syncretism or Systematization saved the social structure from pronounced ideational division and diversity. This is no longer the case. Cultural morphogenesis not only means that ideational uniformity ceases to be produced, but that what takes its place is a new fund of divisive ideas (presenting competitive advantages or new opportunities to material interest groups) which now intrudes in the structural domain. When the story is told from the structural side of the intersection this intrusion is pictured as some inexplicable 'rise of ideas', or what could be called the 'great-wave theory', in which the upsurge of the Renaissance, Enlightenment, or scientific revolution, washes over and around social institutions, reducing them to crumbling sand-castles.

The 'great wave' is, of course, no 'theory' at all, but one can respect its imagery while deploring its lack of grounding in human interaction. Yet the mechanism is there and its influence is ineluctable – though it works on people and only indirectly through them on social institutions. For what cultural morphogenesis does is to change people (or at any rate some people), from unthinking traditionalists into evaluators of alternatives and from passive conformists into potential competitors. And although this occurs in the cultural domain, its effects do not stop there because cultural actors are also structural agents. Thus, cultural change leads to the reconstitution of structural subjects. Here the 'great wave' image is pretty accurate, for the sandbags of social control cannot stem the flow of ideas.

Furthermore, it must not be assumed that the socially or institutionally dominant are necessarily resistant to either form of cultural change. Particularly where specialization is concerned, its incursion need not incite repressive social control nor does its warm reception indicate the previous suppression of structural grievances. As was seen in Chapter 7, groups who are in no sense discontented with their social positions or current activities themselves undergo change as they become intrigued by ideational novelty and, by following it up, they precipitate further change – without encountering any initial resistance. Structural changes ensue (like new types of formalization, institutionalization or organization) but all are fundamentally based upon sectional re-grouping among the relevant part of the population. Sectional interests have by then indeed developed and will subsequently be promoted by some and condemned by others but their emergence itself was largely unintended and unopposed. Moreover, there is no reason to assume that the social groups most responsive to the new ideas with which they come into contact, thanks to cultural morphogenesis, are always the structurally subordinate ones. This is where structure exerts its influence on culture at the intersection of the two – by determining *who* opts to pursue a novel contingent complementarity.

Precisely the same is the case for the socially or institutionally dominant when confronted by the emergence of competitive contradictions. For the first time they are presented with cultural alternatives and the ineluctable force of Pluralism is that they must now choose to come down on one side or the other. The cultural context has shifted beneath their feet and this means that there is no longer anything 'automatic' about the ideas they endorse and work with. Certainly, they may be compromised by their past ideational commitments but on the other hand the opportunity costs for continued support of the old syncretic or systematized formula have risen and the benefits derived from them have fallen as they no longer provide a steady source of social unity. What is important here is that whichever side the socially dominant come down on, social conflict is augmented in the new context of pluralistic competition. The reason for this is that the population themselves have become pluralists, given their constant bombardment by ideal interest groups seeking support. Cleavage has been introduced across the intersection and provides a powerful impetus to the proper consolidation of what were previously latent interest groups.

Clearly, the two sides of a competitive contradiction between ideas will not be equally or sufficiently congruent with all latent material interests to prompt complete social mobilization, but it is not necessary to presume that cultural cleavages have the effect of neatly partitioning the population in two for them to initiate a conflict which eventually introduces structural elaboration. All that is being asserted is that in some institutional areas the dominant groups will stick to the old ideas as their source of legitimation, while certain quasi-groups find the new opposing notions consonant with their nascent ambitions – the former not merely articulating but also shaping the latter. Alternatively, the socially dominant group can throw in its lot with the competitive formula, in which case it faces rearguard conflict from 'old believers' defending the traditional institutional practices around which they are *already* organized, as for example in most State/Church educational struggles.

Thus the generic effect of cultural morphogenesis on structural morphostasis is that ideational change stimulates social regrouping. It can quietly prompt the sectional differentiation of new interest groups or can intensify conflict by bringing about the polarization of existing latent interests. In either case subsequent social interaction changes because of the introduction of diversity or intensification of divisions between material interest groups. When this social destabilization issues in structural elaboration, it can be seen as the long-term consequence of cultural change which has exerted this influence on the social structure by precipitating group differentiation, or re-differentiation.

(iv) The conjunction between cultural morphogenesis and structural morphogenesis

The final pure case deals with instances where morphogenesis is concurrent in the two domains. It is indeed an extreme type because it is unlikely that the two cycles would manifest precise simultaneity (as represented in Figure 4). Obviously, it is more probable that change gets underway in one field somewhat before the other, that interaction may be more protracted in one than the other and that they do not complete the final phase at exactly the same time. Temporal discontinuities between the phases are important and it is unfortunate that their closer examination has had to be sacrificed as the price for bringing out the coarser-grained contrasts in this section in order to maintain comparability with the three preceding ones. Indeed, future work will have to devote more attention to their analysis than any other matter, for the effect of temporal precedence on *positions prises* probably explains many of the elements left open as uncertainties and possibilities here.

This last state of affairs can be seen as one possible future for cases (ii) and (iii), where the elaborated features foster further changes in *both* fields (their alternative futures being a return to (i), if the elaborated properties each then conditions maintenance; or a repetition of disjuncture if this is only true of one domain). However, the intention is not to switch analytic procedures at this stage and to start treating this case as part of a historical sequence by investigating how it is intertwined with the three configurations already discussed. It will again be examined in abstraction because, as before, the influences disengaged are intended to be sufficiently general to apply to instances where 'structure' and 'culture' do not share a common history of development, as in conquest or colonialism for example.

The basic feature of this configuration is a mêlée of competing and diverging groups in both structural and cultural realms, in neither of which is domination unopposed or diversification unfamiliar. Given this high level of interaction between differentiated interest groups, seeking structural and cultural advancement respectively, the question is how material and ideal interests now intersect. Although the empirical alliances formed in reality are matters of historical contingency, this does not blur the generic reciprocity of their mutual influence across the intersection.

Let us abstract completely from history and simply picture an array of material interest groups surveying a variety of ideas, with the single thought of which will serve their structural designs best. Confronting them is a series of ideal interest groups which assesses the former purely in terms of their value as potential sponsors. Of course, real life is not like this if only because we are usually, though not necessarily (indigenous culture/foreign rulers), talking about (some of) the same people. The key point remains that it really does not matter who makes the first move or in which direction the first move is made. Whether some alliance is initiated from the cultural side (in quest of sponsorship) or from the structural side (seeking a legitimatory source), eventually all ideational options are taken up in social interaction as all interest groups become involved in Socio-Cultural interaction. The only difference in real life is that the first move has probably already been taken or at least is practically predetermined.

To see how this intense and reciprocal set of influences works at the interface, let us consider the two sides separately. Supposing quite baldly that one set of cultural ideas gains the sponsorship of a powerful material interest group, perhaps indeed because the protagonists of these ideas sought this support in order to break out of deadlock with their cultural opponents. Then the latter too are irresistibly drawn towards the structural domain, for if one group alone makes headway in winning support there, all others will suffer from the augmented power and resources now brought to bear against them. Consequently, they must woo *other* material interest groups to acquire their support in order to ensure the survival or the salience of their own ideas. Thus, the patterning of cultural diversification aligns itself to the pattern of structural differentiation. This alignment has further repercussions, both of which are themselves morphogenetic, namely structural mobilization and cultural accommodation.

The first material sponsor into the cultural arena probably had close social relations with the ideational group in question (overlapping membership or shared class, status, or party affiliations) which accounted for its readiness to be the first in. Simultaneously, their entry costs the cultural group very little in terms of ideational accommodation, the knowledge of which presumably made them quite so ready to issue the invitation. The same is not true of the other alliances forged between ideal and material interest groups.

Indeed, subsequent sponsorship can best be pictured as a gradient, involving more and more strenuous efforts to mobilize support from social groups who basically have less and less immediate reason for giving it. Since its acquisition is crucial because cultural survival and salience are at stake, then ironically the price of obtaining it is ideational adjustment. Ideas must be adapted, often substantially, to appeal to material interests and thus mobilize the groups associated with them. The price is rarely considered too high to pay because the alternative is that the cultural group goes under – assaulted and battered by their ideational opponents and the latter's social allies.

The consequence is, first, an intensive mobilization of material interest groups, vastly exceeding the most generous definition of their initial 'elective affinities' and eventually including some improbable forms of sponsorship. The latter have been activated through the most radical forms of cultural accommodation, for now opportunity costs attach to the *lack* of structural support. Finally, if the ideational stalemate which first prompted the quest for material supporters is not quickly broken by a substantial imbalance in the sponsorship acquired, then a variety of ideational adaptations, extensions and extrusions attempt to involve every section of the population in Socio-Cultural interaction.

Alternatively, the intersection can be examined from the other side, although of course this is purely a matter of analytical convenience since the mutual interpenetration of cultural and structural affairs is simultaneous. In the context of unfinished morphogenesis, the outcome of social interaction is unresolved at this stage. However, the fact that it is underway means that differentiated interest groups have developed divergent material interests which they now attempt to advance in the face of one another, including the opposition of any antecedent dominant group. Because interaction is intense but its outcome uncertain to participants, each attempts various ploys to gain an edge over its opponents. The one which is of concern here is the endorsement of ideas for the advancement of their cause.

Again, it matters little who makes the first move; this certainly is not the prerogative of dominant groups since frequently domination develops no well-articulated form of justification until it comes under severe challenge or pressure. The group which is the first to go in for ideational endorsement does two things: it introduces a Socio-Cultural dimension to social interaction and, in so doing, it unleashes the effects of situational logic upon itself and the rest of society. What follows is the direct counterpart of the argument about embattled ideal interest groups; let one acquire a sponsor and the others have to seek sponsorship. So here, let one material interest group present its claims as legitimate and those opposing them have to take up ideas which undermine this legitimatory source and buttress their own counter-claims.

This is where the situational logic of the cultural domain comes into play because it conditions both the fund of oppositional ideas available to be taken up and the form of the ensuing ideational battle. Structural opponents can hardly endorse the same ideas as one another if these are to play a role in legitimation and counter-legitimation. Hence, those not first in are constrained to adopt the opposing set of ideas, if necessary adapting their cause to them in the process. Thus, what is culturally on offer can make for strange bed-fellows but the opportunity costs of having no source of legitimation are usually too heavy for a group to refuse the accommodative effort (by diluting and re-defining its precise material demands). Consequently, all ideational options are taken up and the more differentiated is social interaction, so the more the minor and extremist strands of cultural division and diversification become activated.

In sum, social interaction and S-C interaction reinforce one another; this, in turn, fosters morphogenesis in both domains. Structural sponsorship means that oppositional and sectional ideas are assured of retaining salience in social life, which is a necessary though not sufficient condition for their victory. However, the very fact that Pluralism and Specialization enjoy continuing social support *is* sufficient *to prevent* the re-establishment of old-style cultural morphostasis. Re-unification around the original syncretic formula or resumed reproduction of the traditional systematized conspectus are simply not on in the face of divided or sectionalized S-C groups. Similarly, though it is not our concern here, the interaction of a variety of material interest groups, each of which has become articulate in its own defence and capable of detecting self-interest in the claims of others, is enough to preclude any drift back to unquestioned structural morphostasis. The groups have mobilized, ideas have helped them to do it, and assertion will not fade away because the material interests it seeks to advance do not evaporate.

Hence, social interaction and S-C interaction reinforce one another, leading to morphogenesis after intense competition, diversification, conflict and reorganization in the two domains. The process is not endless; the very fact that Structural and Cultural Elaboration takes place signals that some alliance has won out to a sufficient degree to entrench something of the change it sought – and thus to re-start a new cycle of interaction embodying this change as part and parcel of its conditional influences. Fundamentally, the outcome at the end of these two co-terminous cycles is highly dependent on the fortunes of the social groups involved in interaction; what results from it is equally dependent upon the ideas endorsed by the successful alliance. For, in turn, these will introduce their own situational logic – be it new efforts directed towards correction, elimination, protection or opportunity, depending on the nature of the victorious ideas. These will then exert their influence on subsequent interaction in the next cycle, whatever the new balance of material power turns out to be. Thus, in configurations where there is a conjunction between cultural and structural morphogenesis, the two processes are intimately intertwined but they retain their relative autonomy, not only during this cycle but also in the next and thereafter.

This final leg of the journey has only been completed by holding hard to first principles. Through consistently adhering to analytical dualism and persistently withstanding the seduction of conflationism it has been possible to lay the foundations of a comprehensive account of cultural dynamics from the morphogenetic perspective. Throughout this has depended on maintaining analytical distinctions which other approaches would readily com-

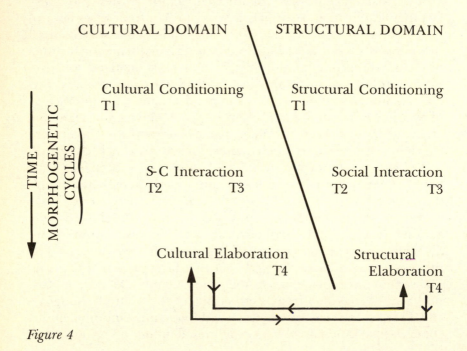

Figure 4

pact together. This, of course, was our starting point – a tenacious defence of the distinction between the Cultural System and Socio-Cultural interaction in opposition to every version of the Myth of Cultural Integration. It is also the finishing point, for the siren-call of conflationary thought persists to the end, bidding us finally to fuse structure and culture into one compacted entity which once again would proscribe examination of interplay between the two, by denying their relative autonomy.

This last chapter has taken as its key premiss that the structural domain and the cultural realm are analytically separable. Its object was then to utilize the fact that the two could be conceptualized in the same terms in order to examine the relationship between morphostatic and morphogenetic cycles in the two domains. The whole point of this exercise was to define the conditions under which structure and culture were reciprocally influential and those which resulted in one having a greater influence on the other. This point can never be reached from the predicate that the two domains exist in a state of complete fusion.

Certainly, in substantive analysis, as in everyday life, the two are indeed fused together in one sense – we often meet them and treat them as an amalgam. Thus, on entering a school, for example, one does not separately and self-consciously encounter a social organization and its cultural contents, or on taking an examination one does not engage in distinct acts of cultural communication and participation in structural allocation. Yet there is nothing in these daily experiences of fusion which warrants their extension into a methodological injunction to study their two components in this way, any more than the daily drinking of water enjoins us not to examine it as one combination of the two elements, hydrogen and oxygen.

On the contrary, social organization and cultural organization are analytically separable. Once this is done it becomes possible to assert that discursive struggles are socially organized and that social struggles are culturally conditioned. Even more importantly, it becomes possible to specify which is more influential for the other, when, where and under what conditions. Any formula which serves to compact structure and culture – like Foucault's 'power–knowledge' complex, Habermas's 'knowledge constitutive interests' or Bauman's 'culture as praxis' – merely defies and defeats analysis of different configurations. What is more, these latter are just as important experientially as they are theoretically. What we confront in daily life are, in fact, *particular* configurations and what we meet and treat as amalgams are, in fact, *specific forms of amalgamation*. To maintain otherwise is, ironically, a denial of the reality of experience the contextual richness of which is a direct reflection of configurational nuances.

Actors, of course, will not necessarily analyse their experiences in such terms but neither do their practices dictate the terms necessary to a theory about agents, situations and contexts.

In this work, theorizing about cultural dynamics entailed a long journey, paved with the intention of discovering whether analytical dualism would yield the same explanatory pay-off in the cultural field as it had in the structural domain. This appeared, indeed, to be the case and it was possible to identify changes in discourse which were generated by processes proper to the cultural field – that is, elaborated through the interplay of properties pertaining to the Cultural System with those belonging to Socio-Cultural interaction. Although the disengagement of sequences of Cultural Elaboration that the utilization of analytical dualism made possible was the purpose of the journey, this was not its terminus.

Once cultural properties and processes had been reconceptualized from the morphogenetic perspective, it became clear that we had not reached the end of the line. Cultural change was indeed susceptible to conceptualization in the same terms as structural change, but when this conceptual unification had been accomplished it opened up new theoretical possibilities and a further unanticipated stage was added to the journey. What had at first seemed a towering ambition – namely, to gain the same kind of explanatory purchase upon slippery cultural entities as on their sturdier looking counterparts – now appeared a partial accomplishment if the two forms of analysis were merely parked alongside within the same framework and left there.

Now that structural and cultural analysis were both formulated from the morphogenetic perspective, curiosity obviously demanded whether extra explanatory mileage could be gained from (the new possibility of) running them in tandem. Although much more detailed examination is still needed, it seems indubitable that as morphostatic/genetic cycles work their way through the structural and cultural domains, then their mutual intersection, conjunction and disjunction hold the key to much that had remained obscure in both fields and opened the door to a more comprehensive theory of change *per se* – a theory which accorded relative autonomy to both domains but could also venture to define the conditions of their relative influence on one another.

Thus, in social theory to date the morphogenetic perspective has already made signal contributions to structural analysis, it has here made possible some advance in cultural analysis, but it now seems likely that its most seminal accomplishment will be to weld a general theory of change from the two – once more overcoming dualism by making consistent use of analytical dualism.

Notes

Preface

1 Percy Cohen, *Modern Social Theory*, London, Heinemann, 1968, p. 93.
2 M. Markovic, *From Affluence to Praxis*, Michigan, Michigan University Press, pp. 10–11.

1. The Myth of Cultural Integration

*A similar version of this chapter first appeared in *The British Journal of Sociology*, vol. 36, no. 3, 1985.

1 Amitai Etzioni, *The Active Society*, London, Free Press, 1968, p. 146.
2 'Culture' in the German Romanticist tradition stemming from Herder, referred to a unique collective pattern of life, an integrated whole, pertaining to particular peoples. It was viewed as a 'meaningful' historical product, transmitted within the collectivity but not transferable beyond it. Herder's concept of culture as an integrated whole is closely akin to the notion of *Gestalt*.
3 B. Malinowski, *A Scientific Theory of Culture*, Chapel Hill, University of North Carolina Press, 1944, p. 38.
4 Ruth Benedict, *Patterns of Culture*, London, Routledge & Kegan Paul, 1961. In fact she used the terms 'pattern' and 'style' interchangeably in this work. Coherence of a given culture is indicated by her usage of the 'broken cup' metaphor for cases when any mixing of cultures occurs.
5 Cf. 'Style', in Sol Tax (ed.), *Anthropology Today*, Chicago, University of Chicago Press, 1962, p. 278.
6 A. L. Kroeber, *Anthropology; Culture, Patterns, & Processes*, New York, Harcourt Brace, 1963. See sections 122 (integration) and 125 (ethos/eidos and values).

7 Mary Douglas, *Purity and Danger*, London, Routledge & Kegan Paul, 1966, p. 69.

8 J. G. Merquior, *The Veil and the Mask*, London, Routledge & Kegan Paul, 1979, p. 48.

9 Ernest Gellner, 'Concepts and society', in Bryan R. Wilson (ed.), *Rationality*, Oxford, Blackwell, 1979, pp. 36f.

10 Perry Anderson, *Considerations on Western Marxism*, London, Verso, 1979, pp. 75–8.

11 David Lockwood, 'Social integration and system integration' in G. K. Zollschan and W. Hirsch (eds.), *Explorations in Social Change*, Boston, Houghton Mifflin, 1964.

12 'Cultures are individual psychology thrown large upon the screen, given gigantic proportions and a long time span', Ruth Benedict, 'Configurations of culture in North America', *American Anthropologist*, vol. 34, 1932, p. 24.

13 E. E. Evans-Pritchard, *Witchcraft, Oracles and Magic Among the Azande*, Oxford, Oxford University Press, 1937, p. 195.

14 Edward Sapir, *Culture, Language and Personality*, California, University of California Press, 1949, p. 90. Sapir's views were not typical but they were highly congruent with Functionalism and its universalistic pretentions. Later on they retained salience as they meshed equally well with cultural projects based on linguistic relativism.

15 As Lockwood rightly argued, Max Weber was equally aware of the potential for strains and conflicts developing between interdependent parts as is illustrated by the example of patrimonialism. See Lockwood, 'Social integration and system integration', pp. 253–5.

16 E. E. Evans-Pritchard, *The Position of Women in Primitive Society and Other Essays in Social Anthropology*, London, 1965, p. 110.

17 Ernest Gellner, *Legitimation of Belief*, Cambridge, Cambridge University Press, 1974, pp. 143–4.

18 Evans-Pritchard, *Witchcraft, Oracles and Magic Among the Azande*, p. 195.

19 Ibid., p. 13.

20 Edmund Leach, *Political Systems of Highland Burma*, London, Bell & Sons, 1954.

21 Gellner, *Legitimation of Belief*, p. 156.

22 Gellner, 'Concepts and Society', p. 36.

23 Anthony Giddens, *Central Problems in Social Theory*, London, Macmillan, 1979, p. 219.

24 Merquior, *The Veil and the Mask*, p. 51.

25 Zygmunt Bauman, *Culture as Praxis*, London, Routledge & Kegan Paul, 1973, p. 5.

26 Ernest Gellner, *Thought and Change*, London, Weidenfeld & Nicolson, 1964, p. 154.

27 Ibid.

28 Gellner 'Concepts and society', pp. 42–3.

29 Robin Horton, 'African traditional thought and western science', *Africa*, vol. 37, no. 2, 1967, p. 154.

30 Claude E. Shannon and Warren Weaver, *The Mathematical Theory of Communication*, Urbana, University of Illinois Press, 1963.

31 Roger C. Owen, 'The patrilocal band: a linguistically and culturally hybrid social unit', *American Anthropologist*, vol. 67, 1965.

32 From an earlier unpublished version of this paper cited by Walter Buckley, *Sociology and Modern Systems Theory*, Englewood Cliffs, New Jersey, Prentice Hall, 1967, p. 91.

33 Merquior, *The Veil and the Mask*, p. 53.

34 Henry Teune and Zdravko Mlinar, *The Developmental Logic of Social Systems*, London and Beverly Hills, Sage, 1978, pp. 94–5, 107, 127.

35 Gellner, 'Concepts and society', p. 47.

36 See Giddens, *Central Problems in Social Theory*.

37 Margaret S. Archer, 'Morphogenesis versus structuration', *British Journal of Sociology*, vol. 33, no. 4, 1982.

2. 'Downwards conflation': on keys, codes and cohesion

1 P. Sorokin, *Social and Cultural Dynamics*, London, Peter Owen, 1957, p. 621.

2 Ibid., p. 7.

3 Ibid., p. 8.

4 Ibid.

5 Ibid.

6 Ibid., p. 606.

7 Ibid., p. 609.

8 Ibid., p. 14.

9 Ibid., p. 23.

10 Ibid., p. 24.

11 Ibid. Sorokin's distinction between the two types is the following: 'The Sensate mentality views reality as only that which is presented to the sense organs. It does not seek or believe in any supersensory reality . . . The Sensate reality is thought of as a Becoming, Process, Change, Flux, Evolution, Progress, Transformation. Its needs and aims are mainly physical and maximum satisfaction is sought of these needs. The method of realizing them is not that of a modification within the human individuals composing the culture, but of a modification or exploitation of the external world. In brief, the Sensate culture is the opposite of the Ideational in its major premises'. Those of Ideational culture are, '(1) Reality is perceived as nonsensate and nonmaterial, everlasting Being (Sein); (2) the needs and ends are mainly spiritual; (3) the extent of their satisfaction is the largest, and the level, highest; (4) the method of their fulfillment or realization is self-imposed minimization or elimination of most of the physical needs, and to the greatest possible extent.' Ibid., pp. 27–8.

12 Ibid., p. 52.

13 Ibid., p. 24.

14 Ibid., p. 49.

15 Ibid., p. 639.

16 This point is rammed home when Sorokin does deal with 'fractures' in what he terms 'intermediate systems', i.e. those which are *neither* perfectly integrated nor completely incoherent. Even here external intervention rather than internal dynamics are accorded the prime role in introducing change, as the following quotation illustrates: 'In such systems there always is found what Max Weber, M. Scheler and E. Barthel style *Spannung*, a kind of tension or latent antagonism; a hidden split or crack, which flares into an open split of the system *as soon as the respective adverse interference of the external conditions takes place.*' Ibid., p. 643 (my emphasis).

17 Ibid., p. 608.

18 Ibid., p. 609.

19 Ibid., p. 621.

20 Ibid., p. 615.

21 Ibid., p. 187.

22 Ibid., pp. 615–17.

23 Talcott Parsons, *The Social System*, London, Routledge & Kegan Paul, 1951, p. 350.

24 David Lockwood, 'Social integration and system integration', in G. K. Zollschan and W. Hirsch, *Explorations in Social Change*, London, Routledge & Kegan Paul, 1964.

25 'On norms and values', in R. A. Manners and D. Kaplan (eds.), *Theory in Anthropology*, Chicago, Aldine, 1968, pp. 465–72.

26 Parsons, *The Social System*, p. 350.

27 Ibid., p. 379.

28 Ibid., p. 351.

29 Ibid., p. 327. Using the same terms as employed here, Alexander has effectively criticized Parsons for having explicitly conflated the analytical problem of the relation between social system level and Cultural System level with the empirical problem of Socio-Cultural consensus and the values held by human agents which are treated as 'specifications' of a common value system. Jeffrey C. Alexander, *Theoretical Logic in Sociology*, vol. 4, Berkeley, University of California Press, 1983.

30 Talcott Parsons, 'The social system: a general theory of action', in R. Grinker (ed.), *Toward a Unified Theory of Human Behaviour*, New York, Basic Books, 1956, pp. 190, 194.

31 Helmut R. Wagner, 'Displacement of scope: a problem of the relationship between small-scale and large-scale sociological theories', *American Journal of Sociology*, vol. 59, no. 6, 1964.

32 J. G. Merquior, *The Veil and the Mask*, London, Routledge & Kegan Paul, 1979. 'If, on the one hand, the integration of common values with the deeply internalized need – dispositions of the socii is for

Parsons the "core phenomenon" of social dynamics, and, on the other hand, the very springs of action are reduced by his outright anti-instinctivism to *learned* dispositions shaped by the cultural system, then the motivational issue by which Parsons appears to be so beset – "the Hobbesian problem of order", described by him as the fons et origo of the sociological quest – actually is no problem at all; it is rather a foregone conclusion.' p. 55.

33 Parsons, *The Social System*, p. 327. Jeffrey Alexander takes this stance to task for in it there 'is no long-term basis for division or conflict. Such a model need not examine the detailed structure of subcultural traditions, for each more detailed tradition is principally derived from the roots and structures of a single more generalized cultural theme'. 'Three models of culture and society relations', *Sociological Theory*, vol. 2, 1984, p. 293.

34 Merquior, *The Veil and the Mask*, p. 55.

35 Cf. David Lockwood, 'Some remarks on "The Social System" ', in N. J. Demerath and R. A. Peterson, *System, Change and Conflict*, New York, Free Press, Collier-Macmillan, 1967.

36 A. Gouldner, *The Coming Crisis of Western Sociology*, London, Heinemann, 1971, p. 242.

37 Claude Lévi-Strauss, *Structural Anthropology*, London, Allen Lane, 1968, p. 62.

38 Anthony Giddens, *Central Problems in Social Theory*, London, Macmillan, 1979, p. 22.

39 Ruth Benedict, 'Configurations of culture in North America', *American Anthropologist*, vol. 34, 1932, p. 24.

40 Lévi-Strauss, *Structural Anthropology*, p. 280.

41 Robin Horton, 'African traditional thought and western science', *Africa*, 36, 1967.

42 John Skorupski, *Symbol and Theory*, Cambridge, Cambridge University Press, 1979.

43 Claude Lévi-Strauss, *L'homme nu*, Paris, Plon, 1971, p. 560.

44 Giddens, *Central Problems in Social Theory*, p. 24.

45 Dan Sperber, *Rethinking Symbolism*, Cambridge, Cambridge University Press, 1975.

46 'Although the possibility cannot be excluded that the speakers who create and transmit myths may become aware of their structure and mode of operation, this cannot occur as a normal thing, but only partially and intermittently. It is the same with myths as with language: the individual who conscientiously applied phonological and grammatical laws in his speech, supposing he possessed the knowledge and virtuosity to do so, would nevertheless lose the thread of his ideas almost immediately.' Claude Lévi-Strauss, *The Raw and the Cooked*, New York, Harper Row, 1969, p. 11.

47 Merquior, *The Veil and the Mask*, p. 96.

3. 'Upwards conflation': the manipulated consensus

1 In primitive society a 'sheep-like or tribal consciousness receives its further development and extension through increased productivity, the increase of needs, and what is fundamental to both of these, the increase of population, with these develops the division of labour . . . Division of labour becomes truly such from the moment when a division of material and mental labour appears (The first form of ideologists, the priests, is concurrent).' Karl Marx, *The German Ideology*, in David McLellan, *Karl Marx: Selected Writings*, Oxford, Oxford University Press, 1978, pp. 167–8.

2 See A. Aulard, *Christianity and the French Revolution*, Boston, 1927. Michalina Vaughan and Margaret S. Archer, *Social Conflict and Educational Change in England and France; 1789–1848*, Cambridge University Press, 1971, Chapter 9.

3 C. Morse, 'The functional imperatives', in M. Black (ed.), *The Social Theories of Talcott Parsons*, Englewood Cliffs, New Jersey, Prentice-Hall, 1961, p. 148. A. Giddens, ' "Power" in the recent writings of Talcott Parsons', *Sociology*, vol. 2, no. 3, 1968, p. 269.

4 Nicholas Abercrombie, Stephen Hill and Bryan S. Turner, *The Dominant Ideology Thesis*, London, Allen & Unwin, 1980, pp. 1–2.

5 Perry Anderson, *Considerations on Western Marxism*, London, Verso, 1979, pp. 75f.

6 Marx, *The German Ideology*, in McLellan, *Karl Marx: Selected Writings*, p. 176.

7 In fairness to the later contributors with whom we are concerned, Marx was not unambiguous about the constitution of the Cultural System and it would be perfectly possible for them to adduce the following type of quotation in support of their view. Starting from the social intercourse associated with material production, it is possible 'to explain all the different theoretical products and forms of consciousness, religion, philosophy, ethics, etc., etc., and trace their origins and growth from that basis; by which means, of course, the whole thing can be depicted in its totality' (ibid., p. 172). As usual it is the question of where the weight of argument is to be assigned in Marx, but the broader context of his work does not reinforce this polemical portrayal of the cultural realm in its totality. Indeed even this trenchant quotation, stating that there is a material basis from which the cultural realm can be 'depicted in its totality' which *seems* a simple statement of the epiphenomenalism of ideas, immediately casts doubts on this view since it reads on, 'and therefore, too, the reciprocal action of these various sides on one another' (ibid.). 'Reciprocal action' denies epiphenomenalism – culture is not *simply* a dependent variable.

8 T. B. Bottomore and M. Rubel, *Karl Marx: Selected Writings in Sociology and Social Philosophy*, London, Watts, 1956, p. 79.

9 Karl Marx, *The Poverty of Philosophy*, in McLellan, *Selected Writings*, p. 209.

10 F. Engels, *The Condition of the Working Class in England in 1844*, Oxford, Blackwell, 1892, p. 114.

11 Nicholas Abercrombie *et al.*, *The Dominant Ideology Thesis*, p. 8.

12 Marx, *The German Ideology*, in McLellan, *Selected Writings*, p. 173.

13 Ibid., p. 167.

14 Ibid., p. 181. Moreover, as Raymond Williams comments 'the historical process . . . includes both *residual* and *emergent* forms of thought and belief, which can in practice enter into very complex relations with the more specifically and locally dominant. In any developed social order, we can expect to find not only interaction but also actual conflict between residual, dominant and emergent forms of thought, in general as well as in special areas. Moreover there is often conflict, related to this complexity, between different versions of the dominant, which is by no means always a ready translation of a singular material class interest.' 'Culture', in David McLellan (ed.), *Marx: The first hundred years*, Fontana, 1983, p. 51.

15 E.g. 'As philosophy finds in the proletariat its material weapons, so the proletariat finds in philosophy its intellectual weapons, and as soon as the lightening of thought has struck deep into the virgin soil of the people, the emancipation of the Germans into men will be completed . . . Philosophy cannot realize itself without transcending the proletariat, the proletariat cannot transcend itself without realizing philosophy.' Karl Marx, *Towards a Critique of Hegel's Philosophy of Right: Introduction*, in McLellan, *Selected Writings*, p. 73.

16 Marx, *The German Ideology*, in McLellan, *Selected Writings*, p. 168.

17 'If these material elements of a complete revolution are not present . . . then, as far as practical development is concerned, it is absolutely immaterial whether the idea of this revolution has been expressed a hundred times already, as the history of communism proves', ibid., p. 173.

18 Bottomore and Rubel, *Karl Marx*, p. 80.

19 Marx, *The German Ideology*, in McLellan, *Selected Writings*, p. 181.

20 Engels, *The Condition of the Working Class*, p. 114.

21 Abercrombie *et al.*, *The Dominant Ideology Thesis*, pp. 24f.

22 Perry Anderson, 'The antinomies of Antonio Gramsci', *New Left Review*, no. 100, 1976–7, p. 26.

23 Antonio Gramsci, *Selections from Prison Notebooks*, London, Lawrence & Wishart, 1971, pp. 3–23.

24 R. Miliband, *The State in Capitalist Society*, London, Allen & Unwin, 1969, p. 266.

25 Herbert Marcuse, *One-Dimensional Man*, London, Routledge & Kegan Paul, 1964, p. 14.

26 J. H. Westergaard and H. Resler, *Class in a Capitalist Society*, London, Heinemann, 1975.

27 Abercrombie, *et al.*, *The Dominant Ideology Thesis*, p. 4.

28 'Above all, within the realm of culture itself, it was *Art* that engaged the

major intellectual energies and gifts of Western Marxism. The pattern in this respect is arresting. Lukács devoted the largest part of his life to work on literature, producing a serried file of critical studies on the German and European novel – from Goethe and Scott to Mann and Solzhenitsyn, culminating in a massive general *Aesthetics* – his longest and most ambitious published work. Adorno wrote a dozen books on music, including both global analyses of the musical transformations of the twentieth century and interpretations of individual composers such as Wagner or Mahler, besides three volumes of essays on literature; he too completed his oeuvre with an overall *Aesthetic Theory*. Benjamin's most significant theoretical legacy within Marxism was an essay on *Art in the Age of its Mechanical Reproduction*, and his major critical achievement in the thirties was a study of Baudelaire. His accompanying concern was the work of Brecht. Goldmann's principal work was an analysis of Racine and Jansenism – *The Hidden God*, which at the same time set out a general canon of literary criticism for historical materialism; his other writings explored the modern theatre and novel (Malraux). Lefebvre in turn wrote a *Contribution to Aesthetics*. Della Volpe, for his part, produced another full-scale aesthetic theory, *Critique of Taste*, besides essays on films and poetry. Anderson, *Considerations on Western Marxism*, pp. 76–7 f. (Further illustrations of this theme are found in the work of Marcuse, Sartre and Gramsci himself.)

29 Gramsci states as the first fundamental principle of political science 'that no social formation disappears as long as the productive forces which have developed within it still find room for further forward movement'. Gramsci, *Selections from Prison Notebooks*, p. 106.

30 Common sense, the 'philosophy of non-philosophers' is uncritically absorbed and heterogeneous – a kind of philosophical 'folklore': 'Its most fundamental characteristic is that it is a conception which, even in the brain of one individual, is fragmentary, incoherent and inconsequential, in conformity with the social and cultural position of those masses whose philosophy it is. At those times in history when a homogeneous social group is brought into being, there comes into being also, in opposition to common sense, a homogeneous – *in other words coherent and systematic* – philosophy.' Ibid., p. 419. Note the italicized properties of the revolutionary values and how these form part of the general credo of upwards conflation.

31 Abercrombie *et al.*, *The Dominant Ideology Thesis*, p. 55.

32 See Pierre Bourdieu and Jean-Claude Passeron, *La Reproduction*, Paris, Minuit, 1970. The analysis of education begins from Proposition 1 which states: 'All *pedagogic action* is, objectively, symbolic violence insofar as it is the imposition of a cultural arbitrary by an arbitrary power' (p. 19).

33 The above is predicated on an even more basic proposition, stressing the two-fold nature of arbitrariness: 'Every power to exert symbolic violence, i.e. every power which manages to impose meanings and to impose them as legitimate by concealing the

power relations which are the basis of its force, adds its own specifically symbolic force to those power relations.' What is significant is the importance attached by the authors to the gloss which follows this axiom. 'To refuse this axiom, which states simultaneously the *relative autonomy and relative dependence of symbolic relations* with respect to power relations, would *amount to denying the possibility of a science of sociology.*' Ibid. (my emphasis), p. 18.

34 See Samuel Bowles and Herbert Gintis, *Schooling in Capitalist America: Educational Reform and the Contradictions of Economic Life*, New York, Basic Books, 1976.

35 For a discussion of the deficiencies of treating education as fully permeable see Margaret S. Archer, 'Process without system', *Archives Européennes de Sociologie, vol. 24, 1983, pp. 196–221.*

36 Samuel Bowles, 'Unequal education and the reproduction of the social division of labor', in Jerome Karabel and A. H. Halsey, *Power and Ideology in Education*, New York, Oxford University Press, 1977, p. 147.

37 Margaret S. Archer, 'The sociology of educational systems', in Tom Bottomore, Stefan Nowak and Magdalena Sokottowska (eds.), *Sociology: The State of the Art*, London and Beverly Hills, Sage, 1982, pp. 242–6.

38 Critical theory is a sustained critique of Marx's sociology of knowledge, which Habermas holds defective on two counts – that it is too restrictively tied to relations of production and is destructively linked to the natural sciences in its methodology. Jürgen Habermas, *Knowledge and Human Interests*, London, Heinemann, 1978, pp. 54–63.

39 See Jürgen Habermas, *Toward a Rational Society*, Heinemann, London, 1971, especially pp. 100–14.

40 Ibid., p. 99.

41 Ibid., p. 104.

42 Marcuse, *One-Dimensional Man*, pp. 158–9.

43 Habermas, *Towards a Rational Society*, p. 109.

44 Ibid., p. 111.

45 The deficiencies of this position can be illustrated by the simple example that new applications of science can be stumbled on or actually propose themselves through spin-off, quite independently of or in contradiction to any corpus of rules about application. Whether something *is* applied certainly is a social question; whether it *can* be is not, this is an independent logical issue.

46 Habermas, *Towards a Rational Society*, p. 111.

47 Habermas, *Knowledge and Human Interests*, p. 4.

48 Ibid., p. 314.

49 Ibid., p. 310.

50 As an example of cultural constraints unsusceptible of change, one can cite the unalterability of a religious cultural tradition: this remains *as such* (a permanent point of back-reference and

ideational Pluralism) even if its influences on social institutions and beliefs are subject to a contemporary policy of secularization. For a discussion of cultural properties which are not susceptible of immediate change, see my example of literacy rates, 'Structuration versus morphogenesis', in S. N. Eisenstadt and H. J. Helle (eds.) *Macro-Sociological Theory: Perspectives on Sociological Theory*, vol. 1, London and Beverly Hills, Sage, 1985, p. 72–5.

51 Habermas, *Knowledge and Human Interests*, p. 314.
52 Habermas, *Toward a Rational Society*, p. 122.
53 Habermas, *Legitimation Crisis*, London, Heinemann, 1979, p. 75f.
54 Habermas, 'What does a crisis mean today? Legitimation problems in late capitalism', *Social Research*, vol. 40, no. 4, 1973, p. 660.

4. 'Central conflation': the duality of culture

1 Anthony Giddens, *New Rules of Sociological Method*, Hutchinson, London, 1976, p. 121.
2 Zygmunt Bauman, *Culture as Praxis*, Routledge & Kegan Paul, London, 1973, p. 86–7.
3 '(I)n short, we speak of communication whenever there are some limits imposed on what is possible or what can happen and what the probability of its occurrence is. We speak of communication whenever a set of events is ordered, which means to some extent predictable' (ibid., p. 94). Now this definition which equates 'communication' with 'influence' is in itself I believe entirely unacceptable (Weber's colliding cyclists certainly influence one another but he rightly wanted to reserve this as a case of non-social, let alone communicative action).
4 Ibid., p. 94–5.
5 Ibid.
6 Giddens, *New Rules of Sociological Method*, p. 127.
7 Ibid., p. 122.
8 Anthony Giddens, *Central Problems in Social Theory*, Macmillan, London, 1979, p. 5.
9 To Bauman the 'orderliness of the world they live in is so vitally important to human beings that it seems entirely justified to ascribe to it an autotelic value. It is hardly necessary, if not redundant, to seek a further explanation to the above need by pointing to a purpose which "making the world meaningful" allegedly serves.' In satisfying this need, culture reduces uncertainty, introduces predictability, eliminates ambiguity and minimizes insecurity; it orders and it orientates and in so doing it integrates. Bauman, *Culture as Praxis*, p. 98.
10 Ibid., p. 51.
11 Giddens, *Central Problems in Social Theory*, p. 5.
12 Bauman, *Culture as Praxis*, p. 52.
13 Ibid., p. 117.

14 Ibid., pp. 119, 88.
15 Giddens, *Central Problems in Social Theory*, p. 53.
16 Ibid., p. 83.
17 Ibid., p. 67.
18 Ibid., p. 65.
19 Ibid., pp. 4–5.
20 Bauman, *Culture as Praxis*, p. 81.
21 Ibid., p. 116.
22 Ibid., p. 5.
23 Ibid., p. 56.
24 Cited ibid., p. 52.
25 The 'iota of creativity, of active assimilation of the universe, of imposing on the chaotic world the ordering structure of the human intelligent action – the idea built irremovably into the notion of praxis – is indeed comprehensible only if viewed as an attribute of community' (ibid., p. 118).
26 Ibid., p. 143.
27 Ibid., p. 80.
28 Giddens, *Central Problems in Social Theory*, p. 81.
29 Quoted in ibid., p. 98.
30 Ibid., p. 64.
31 Ibid., p. 104.
32 Ibid., p. 99.
33 Margaret S. Archer, 'Morphogenesis versus structuration: on combining structure and action', *British Journal of Sociology*, vol. 33, no. 4, 1982, pp. 472–7.
34 Giddens, *Central Problems in Social Theory*, p. 210.
35 Ibid., p. 71.
36 Ibid., p. 77–8.
37 Bauman, *Culture as Praxis*, p. 146.
38 Giddens, *Central Problems in Social Theory*, p. 63.
39 Ibid., p. 114.
40 Jürgen Habermas, *Knowledge and Human Interests*, Heinemann, London, 1978.
41 Archer, 'Morphogenesis versus structuration', pp. 466–71.
42 Giddens, *Central Problems in Social Theory*, p. 93.
43 This argument about explaining *cultural* change is precisely the same as that developed by David Lockwood in relation to those theories of social change which are based on the examination of social conflict alone, i.e. unrelated to structural contradictions at the Systemic level. See his 'Social integration and system integration', in G. K. Zollschan and W. Hirsch (eds.), *Explorations in Social Change*. Houghton Mifflin, Boston, 1964.
44 Giddens, *Central Problems in Social Theory*, p. 88. Also, 'power must be treated in the context of the duality of structure: if the resources which the existence of domination implies and the exercise of power draws upon, are seen to be at the same time structural components of social systems. The exercise of power is not a type of

act; rather power is instantiated in action, as a regular and routine phenomenon.' Ibid., p. 91.

45 Steven Lukes, *Essays in Social Theory*, London, Macmillan, 1977, p. 18.
46 Giddens, *Central Problems in Social Theory*, p. 91.
47 Steven Lukes, *Power: A Radical View*, London, Macmillan, 1974, p. 54.
48 Lukes, *Power: A Radical View*, p. 35n.
49 Giddens, *Central Problems in Social Theory*, p. 215.
50 Bauman, *Culture as Praxis*, p. 150–1.
51 Ibid., p. 146.
52 Giddens, *Central Problems in Social Theory*, p. 7.
53 Ibid., p. 229.

5. Addressing the Cultural System

1 Mary Hesse holds that this is a 'positivist point in the sense that it presupposes that there can be no language unless we (now, or perhaps at some future time) understand it as a language' in which beliefs are expressed (*Revolutions and Reconstructions in the Philosophy of Science*, Harvester, Brighton, 1980, p. 37). On the contrary I would argue that the untranslatable *could* constitute a different Cultural System but since it was nothing more than the emission of sounds (marks or smells etc.) it *could* equally be a literary spoof or a deliberate randomization of sounds. Even given her gesticulating Martians and strong circumstantial evidence for their using language, if we failed to establish consistent signs for 'yes' and 'no' then we could never *know* that they had either language or beliefs – but the relativist would be in exactly the same position.

2 Cultural Systems are open ones and in principle actors can penetrate any part of them, though in practice there may be both physical, social and intellectual barriers preventing some or all of them from doing so. At times, for example, attempts are made at the Socio-Cultural level to make the Cultural System operate as a closed one. Ironically there is no better evidence of the openness of the System to its social environment than efforts to manipulate it in this way: ultimately the failure of all such attempts from Edicts of Seclusion, stringent censorship, to Top Security measures show that, because of their intrinsic ease of transfer, ideas are generically incapable of closure. Equally, at times physical obstacles like uncrossable mountains or unnavigable oceans have appeared to shut one part of the cultural universe off from another. But even under these circumstances, since we cannot predict future discoveries, then at any given T_1 penetration is not simply a principle for it may be accomplished at any moment. Historically (and that also means to the best of our historical ability) it could well be maintained that at least two different 'societies' S1 and S2 (tribes or islanders for example) possessed cultures which had emerged

autonomously and operated in isolation with no knowledge of the other *prior* to T_1. (The possibility of the discovery of S1 by S2 or vice versa at T² remains open of course.) If such isolation can be established there appears to be no objection to someone asserting the plurality of Cultural Systems as a temporary empirical fact, provided that this state of affairs is accepted to be time-bounded and is not assumed to have been universal for or almost synonymous with primitive societies (many of which had extensive contacts).

3 The use of T_1, T_2 etc. does not imply linear cultural development through time. Certainly a strong case can be made for this in relation to scientific knowledge over the last four centuries, but allowance must also be made for periods of cultural stagnation (i.e. T_1 lasts for centuries) and of cultural regression (i.e. the CS at T_2 is impoverished compared with T_1).

4 Karl R. Popper, *Objective Knowledge*, Oxford, Clarendon, 1972, pp. 298–9.

5 It might immediately be objected that all that is intelligible is not propositional – the usual contenders being either desires, questions or commands. There, however, intelligibility rests upon assumptions, which involve propositions, that certain states of affairs do obtain. Other contenders are concrete objects, artefacts or events. Here the relevant proposition is the relation asserted to hold between them or their parts, since sense experience alone never yields knowledge without a reflective analysis, entailing language, of what we are experiencing. For knowledge is knowledge of propositions and can only be known by discriminating between abstract features which are aspects of the concrete situation or object.

6 'The student of the history of ideas will find that ideas have a kind of life (this is a metaphor, of course); that they can be misunderstood, rejected, and forgotten; that they can reassert themselves, and come to life again. Without metaphor, however, we can say that they are not identical with any man's thought, or belief; that they can exist even if universally misunderstood, and rejected.' Popper, *Objective Knowledge*, p. 300.

7 Peter Winch, *The Idea of a Social Science*, Routledge & Kegan Paul, London, 1958, p. 126.

8 Peter Winch, 'Understanding a primitive society', in Bryan R. Wilson (ed.), *Rationality*, Oxford, Blackwell, 1979, p. 82.

9 Steven Lukes, 'Some problems about rationality', in Wilson (ed.), *Rationality*, p. 204.

10 'One might sum up all this by saying that nothing is more false than the claim that, for a given assertion, *its use is its meaning*. On the contrary, its use may depend on its lack of meaning, its ambiguity, its possession of wholly different and incompatible meanings in different contexts, *and* on the fact that, at the same

time, it as it were emits the impression of possessing a consistent meaning throughout – on retaining, for instance, the aura of a justification valid only in one context when used in quite another.' Ernest Gellner, 'Concepts and society', ibid., p. 45.

11 Amitai Etzioni, *The Active Society*, New York, Free Press, 1968, pp. 26–7.

12 Winch, *The Idea of a Social Science*, p. 102.

13 Ibid., pp. 100–1.

14 Lukes, 'Some problems about rationality', p. 209–10.

15 'What, then, is special about Identity, Contradiction and Inference? The answer is, I believe, that these notions set the conditions for the existence not only of a particular kind of logical reasoning but also of any kind whatever . . . They express, rather requirements for something's being a system of logical reasoning at all. To look for alternatives is like looking for a novel means of transport which is novel not only in that it has no engine but also that it does not convey bodies from one place to another.' Martin Hollis, 'Reason and ritual', in Wilson (ed.), *Rationality*, pp. 231–2.

16 Winch, 'Understanding a primitive society', p. 100. Immediately, however, he resists the implication of having accepted general logical criteria by adding that 'these formal requirements tell us nothing about what in particular is to *count* as consistency'. This seems to be an innocuous statement that it is the contents of propositions rather than their logical relations which are socially variable.

17 The main works to which reference is made are: David Bloor, *Knowledge and Social Imagery*, London, Routledge & Kegan Paul, 1976; Barry Barnes, *Interests and the Growth of Knowledge*, London, Routledge & Kegan Paul, 1977; David Bloor, 'Polyhedra and the abominations of Leviticus', *The British Journal for the History of Science*, vol. 11, no. 39, 1978; 'The strengths of the strong programme', *Phil. Soc. Sci.*, 11, 1981; Barry Barnes, 'On the "hows" and "whys" of cultural change', *Social Studies of Science*, vol. 11, 1981. Barry Barnes and David Bloor, 'Relativism, rationalism and the sociology of knowledge', in Martin Hollis and Steven Lukes (eds.), *Rationality and Relativism*, Oxford, Blackwell, 1982; David Bloor, *Wittgenstein: A Social Theory of Knowledge*, Macmillan, London, 1983.

18 H. M. Collins, 'What is TRASP?: the radical programme as a methodological imperative', *Phil. Soc. Sci.*, 11, 1981. Instead of TRASP, 'the tenet of symmetry implies that we must treat the natural world as though it in no way constrains what is believed to be' (p. 218). That the strong programme is incompatible with a realist ontology is a conclusion hard to avoid – at least on most interpretations of it.

19 Bloor, *Knowledge and Social Imagery*, p. 5. This principle opposes 'conventional' philosophical approaches for their supposedly 'teleological' character, i.e. for the assumption that the truth or reasonableness of a belief was itself sufficient to explain its adop-

tion. Simultaneously this wrongly absolved the philosopher of any need to advance causes for such beliefs and equally wrongly condemned the sociologist to reserve his causal explanations for cases of error.

20 For a general criticism of this position see Larry Laudan, 'The pseudo-science of science', *Phil. Soc. Sci.*, 11, 1981. Bloor's reply 'The strengths of the strong programme' is in the same issue.

21 Barnes and Bloor, 'Relativism, rationalism and the sociology of knowledge', p. 27.

22 Bloor writes of Mannheim: 'Despite his determination to set up causal and symmetrical canons of explanation, his nerve failed him when it came to such apparently autonomous subjects as mathematics and natural science', *Knowledge and Social Imagery*, p. 8.

23 Erik Millstone, 'A framework for the sociology of knowledge', *Social Studies of Science*, vol. 8, 1978, p. 117.

24 Bloor, *Knowledge and Social Imagery*, p. 141.

25 Ibid., pp. 88 f.

26 Thus by driving the social element through the gap between physical reality and the mathematical principles imposed on it, 'Bloor has opened the way to the idea – indispensible for his entire project – of socially determined "variations in mathematical thinking". Each such variant, then, constitutes – in parallel to the Kuhnian "paradigm" in natural science – an "alternative mathematics", and the relation of these variants to one another is analogous to that which (in Kuhn's account) exists between different paradigms.' Gad Freudenthal, 'How strong is Dr Bloor's "strong programme"?', *Studies in History and Philosophy of Science*, vol. 10, 1979, p. 72.

27 Bloor, *Knowledge and Social Imagery*, pp. 95–6.

28 Freudenthal, 'How strong is Dr Bloor's "strong programme"?' pp. 73 f. He concludes that Bloor's theoretical affirmations about an alternative mathematics and 'above all his claim that logical necessity is a social phenomenon – are not tenable and, moreover, that the allegedly confirming case-studies do not, in fact, bear upon them' (p. 82).

29 Bloor purports to 'offer illustrations of 4 types of variation in mathematical thought each of which can be traced back to social causes'. However, his delineation of the examples to come represents a departure from his original specification of an alternative, i.e. alien consensus on something we deem erroneous and which entails violation of our notions of logical propriety. The four instances are '(i) variation in the broad cognitive style of mathematics; (ii) variation in the framework of associations, relationships, uses, analogies, and the metaphysical implications attributed to mathematics; (iii) variations in the meanings attached to computations and symbolic manipulations; (iv) variation in rigour and the type of reasoning which is held to prove a conclusion'. *Knowledge and Social Imagery*, p. 97.

30 Ibid., p. 98.

31 Exactly the same argument can be used against Bloor's most
    extended example, the polyhedron as a negotiated mathematical
    concept. Indeed since much of his argument deals with the fact
    that for a given set of definitions of what constitutes polyhedra a
    theorem may be shown not to hold, then the notion of
    mathematical validity is shared by the negotiators rather than
    being the subject of negotiation. See Bloor, 'Polyhedra and the
    abominations of Leviticus'.

32 Bloor, *Knowledge and Social Imagery*, p. 103.

33 Freudenthal, 'How strong is Dr Bloor's "strong programme"?',
    p. 77.

34 Barnes and Bloor, 'Relativism, rationalism and the sociology of
    knowledge, p. 41 n.

35 Ibid., pp. 41–2n.

36 Ibid., p. 43.

37 The following are typical avowals of upwards conflationism: 'When
    Durkheim and Mauss said that the classification of things rep-
    roduces the classification of men, they were nearer to the truth
    than their critics have allowed', Bloor, 'The strengths of the strong
    programme', p. 212; 'People, it is agreed, are not under the con-
    trol of their discourse or their own verbal artefacts: the relationship
    is the other way round', Barnes, 'On the "hows" and "whys" of
    cultural change', p. 481.

38 'At whatever point it is found necessary, the explanation of
    credibility may swing from social to biological causes', Barnes and
    Bloor, 'Relativism, rationalism and the sociology of knowledge',
    p. 44.

39 Ibid.

40 Mary Hesse, *Revolutions and Reconstructions in the Philosophy of Science*,
    Brighton, Harvester, 1980, p. 38.

41 Ibid., pp. 37–8.

42 Obviously I am not arguing that only the propositional is intellig-
    ible and even where *beliefs* or *theories* are concerned, I fully accept
    Sperber's argument for the incidence of 'pre-propositional' ideas
    in many societies and areas of discourse. The point is however that
    if and when such pre-propositional terms are completed, then
    their completion is in conformity with, and not in abrogation of,
    the principle of contradiction whose invariance is defended here.
    See Dan Sperber, 'Apparently irrational beliefs', in Hollis and
    Lukes (eds.), *Rationality and Relativism*.

43 J. C. Crocker, 'My brother the parrot', in J. D. Sapir and J. C.
    Crocker (eds.), *The Social Use of Metaphor: Essays on the Anthropology of
    Rhetoric*, Philadelphia, University of Pennsylvania Press, 1977.

44 As Sperber comments: 'So, the enigmatic subject-matter of so
    many learned discussions turns out to be but an indirect form of
    expression well within the bounds of commonsense rationality. No

doubt, many other puzzling cases around the world could be handled in similar fashion'. Dan Sperber, 'Apparently irrational beliefs', in Hollis and Lukes (eds.), *Rationality and Relativism*, p. 153. Doubtless too we can 'invent' puzzles by treating doctrines like Trinitarianism as if we had just come across an isolated hymn containing the strange assertion: 'Firmly I believe and truely God is three and God is one.'

45 Hesse, *Revolutions and Reconstructions in the Philosophy of Science*, p. 38.
46 '(C)laims to have identified the metaphorical uses of words and gestures must be rationally justified. This involves cashing the metaphors and therefore the notion of "metaphorical use" never has any explanatory force.' Martin Hollis, 'Reason and ritual', in Wilson (ed.), *Rationality*, p. 238.
47 Henry Bettenson (ed.), *Documents of the Christian Church*, Oxford University Press, 1967. See section IV, 'The person and work of Christ'.
48 Sperber, 'Apparently irrational beliefs', p. 175.
49 The key statement about Apostolic succession, advanced by St Iranaeus and used by the Catholic Church against its doctrinal rebels ever since, is that 'with this church, because of its position of leadership and authority, must needs agree every church, that is, the faithful everywhere' p. 69. This basing of belief on authority is remarkably clear in the original Creed of Nicea (AD 325), where after the profession of articles of faith are specially listed seven propositions which 'the Catholic and Apostolic Church anathematizes', Bettenson (ed.), *Documents of the Christian Church*, p. 25.
50 Hesse, *Revolutions and Reconstructions in the Philosophy of Science*, p. 38.
51 Ibid., p. 39.
52 Barnes and Bloor, 'Relativism, rationalism and the sociology of knowledge', p. 39.
53 W. Newton-Smith, 'Relativism and the possibility of interpretation', in Hollis and Lukes (eds.), *Rationality and Relativism*, p. 114.
54 Hollis, 'Reason and ritual', p. 238.
55 Barnes and Bloor, 'Relativism, rationalism and the sociology of knowledge', p. 38.
56 'What is here true of two languages applies equally to one.' Hollis, 'Reason and ritual', p. 230.
57 This is the implication of their conceptual relativism. 'One clear implication arises from the character of concepts as arrays of judgements of sameness. Every such array, being the product of a unique sequence of judgements, is itself unique. No array in one culture can be unproblematically set into an identity with an array from another culture', Barnes and Bloor 'Relativism, rationalism and the sociology of knowledge', p. 39. But what is a culture to them? Clearly not 'all English language speakers', nor anything so big as a nation – a region then? a community? a locality? a family? or a small group of like-minded thinkers?

58 Ibid., p. 36.

59 Ibid., p. 38.

60 Note the relativists' ambivalence *vis à vis* the notion of a 'simple perceptual situation'. On the one hand they wish to deny them to any rationalist translator in the field, but on the other hand they are quintessential to Barnes' and Bloor's account of language learning, either by the young native or by the mature anthropologist (see pp. 122–6). Their account of learning concepts through processes of ostension and correction, leading the similarities and differences between 'birds' and 'aeroplanes' to be arranged and judged in a particular way is in fact perfectly compatible with Hollis's procedure *for* establishing the bridgehead. Indeed if the latter is not on, neither is language learning on this account.

61 R. Bulmer, 'Why is the cassowary not a bird?', *Man*, n.s., 2, 1967.

62 Barnes and Bloor, 'Relativism, rationalism and the sociology of knowledge', pp. 39–40.

63 Mary Hesse, *The Structure of Scientific Inference*, London, Macmillan, 1974, pp. 16f.

64 Thus Lukes appears to be completely correct that 'the considerations advanced by Barnes and Bloor – that classifications are "socially sustained" and patterns of knowledge "institutionalised", that language learning involves the acquisition from the culture of specific conventions, that concepts seen as arrays of judgements of sameness may not coincide across cultures, and that the "facts" are "theory-laden" and have different imports to different scientists depending on their theoretical frameworks – all of this argues at best for conceptual and perhaps perceptual relativism.' Lukes, 'Relativism in its place', in Hollis and Lukes (eds.), *Rationality and Relativism*, p. 266. Evidential support can be adduced against perceptual relativism (e.g. colour discrimination appears to be universal rather than linguistically determined. See B. Berlin and P. Kay, *Basic Color Terms*, Berkeley, University of California Press, 1969) and against conceptual relativism (since variations can be given a non-relativistic explanation). And, once let down by linguistic determinism in areas like basic colour terminology or geometric forms (where the human perceptual system appears to determine linguistic categories rather than the reverse), then their argument amounts to an assertion that the fact that something is round and red plays the same role in leading us to believe that it is and that it isn't. The absurdity of this conclusion undermines the equivalence postulate of the 'strong programme'. See also Eleanor Rosch, 'Human Categorization', in N. Warren (ed.), *Studies in Cross-Cultural Psychology*, vol. 1, 1977.

65 With one exception the whole bridgehead procedure is empirically grounded. The only *a priori* assumption made is that the very possibility of meaningful disagreement is entirely dependent on *some* foundation in agreement, which no state of affairs can falsify.

'But *what* that foundation is, what must be presupposed for the interpretation of beliefs and belief systems to proceed is in a sense an empirical matter, or at least revisable in the light of experience', Lukes, 'Relativism in its place', p. 272.

66 Hesse, *Revolutions and Reconstructions in the Philosophy of Science*, p. 56.
67 Lukes, 'Relativism in its place', pp. 264–74.
68 Moreover, inspection of references shows the use of translations to be common practice amongst members of the school. It might seem uncharitable to note that the bibliography of *Knowledge and Social Imagery* contains no item which is not in English, were it not for the fact that I find translation both unobjectionable and necessary. It is Bloor who has objected to it, yet for example he states that his illustrations of Diophantus's thought are 'taken from Heath's (1910) translation and commentary', *Knowledge and Social Imagery*, p. 99.
69 Martin Hollis, 'The limits of irrationality', in Wilson (ed.), *Rationality*, p. 214.
70 Barnes and Bloor, 'Relativism, rationalism and the sociology of knowledge', p. 37.
71 Ernest Gellner, *Thought and Change*, London, Weidenfeld & Nicolson, 1964, pp. 105–13.
72 Newton-Smith, 'Relativism and the possibility of interpretation', p. 114.
73 Ibid., p. 115.
74 Gellner, 'Concepts and society', p. 48.
75 Ibid., p. 43.
76 Cf. Hollis, 'Reason and rituals', p. 226.
77 Gellner, 'Concepts and society', p. 22.
78 Ibid., p. 19.
79 Ibid., p. 43.
80 Ibid., p. 44.
81 Ibid., p. 45.
82 Ibid., pp. 38–9.
83 Ibid., p. 48.
84 Ernest Gellner, 'The savage and the modern mind', in Robin Horton and Ruth Finnegan (eds.), *Modes of Thought*, London, Faber, 1973, p. 169.
85 This Gellner continues to demonstrate, in ibid. However, in the lead-up to the statement cited about the need for a Dividing Line, he accepts that 'There are two principal methods normally employed for identifying, isolating a "belief system": one uses the observer's own sense of coherence, and the other invokes written sources and documents. The possibility of bias or arbitrariness inherent in the first method is obvious. But the danger is clearly not absent from the second method either.' Ibid., p. 168. However, while in 'Concepts and society' Gellner had really plumped for the first method, this article represents a cautious shift to the second, which is what I am exploring here.

86 Eleanor Rosch, 'Universals and cultural specifics in human categorization', in R. Brislin, S. Bochner and W. Lonner (eds.), *Cross-Cultural Perspectives on Learning*, New York, Halstead Press, 1975. E. Rosch and C. B. Mervis, 'Family resemblances: studies in the internal structure of categories', *Cognitive Psychology*, vol. 7, 1975.

87 Eleanor Rosch, 'Linguistic relativity', in A. Silverstein (ed.), *Human Communication: Theoretical Perspectives*, New York, Halstead Press, 1974.

88 Eleanor Rosch, 'Principles of categorization', in E. Rosch and B. Lloyd (eds.), *Cognition and categorization*, Hillsdale, New Jersey, Erlbaum, 1978, p. 29.

89 Consequently for *this* purpose not only is the S-C context irrelevant, but so too are tracts of the CS itself because some of its constituents, like musical scores or paintings are not propositional and thus whatever their importance, these components cannot figure in contradictions.

90 Incidentally this rule solves the problem (at the CS level) of the context itself being socially specific and therefore precluding any cross-contextual generalizations. For if what is being dealt with is exclusively the presence or absence of logical connections, the specificity of their contents is immaterial. Moreover, since it is none of our business to pass judgements on contents we must therefore be prepared to declare that an alien belief system based on some metaphysical entity (let us call it 'Alpha'), the existence of which is not open to falsification, may be of a much higher logical consistency (i.e. a coherent 'Alpha theology') than that of a modern science-based Cultural System.

This is what Hollis has termed taking the stance of the 'unbelieving theologian'. Any religion may begin in revelation (unintelligible or perhaps incredible to the investigator) but its communication demands theology and it is no accident that every world religion has laboured for centuries on the consistency of the latter. Without this, how else could unbelievers find the logic of many theologians impeccable but still reject their premises? Only because it is the contents of propositions which may take 'many and varied forms', but not the logical relations between them. Thus I trust that we have disposed of both the supposed difficulty of contextual specificity and the potential criticism that ethnocentricism lurks within the use of logical criteria to identify contradictions. On the contrary, logic, being universal, is also neutral. It is an empirical matter whether any particular modern Cultural System turns out to manifest fewer contradictions than medieval or primitive ones. Using logical criteria does not stack the cards in favour of either modernity or the primitive world.

91 Cf. E. Leach, 'Ritual' in *International Encyclopaedia of the Social Sciences*, vol. 13, New York, Macmillan, 1968; M. E. Spiro, 'Religion: problems of definition and explanation', in M. Banton (ed.), *Anthropol-*

ogical Approaches to the Study of Religion, London, Tavistock, 1966;
S. Turner, *Sociological Explanation as Translation,* Cambridge,
Cambridge University Press, 1980; Robin Horton, 'Tradition and
modernity revisited', in Hollis and Lukes (eds.), *Rationality and
Relativism;* D. Sperber, *Rethinking Symbolism,* Cambridge, Cambridge
University Press, 1975.
92 Sperber, 'Apparently irrational beliefs', in Hollis and Lukes (eds.),
   Rationality and Relativism, p. 165.
93 Lukes, 'Relativism in its place', p. 292.
94 Evans-Pritchard, *Witchcraft, Oracles and Magic Among the Azande,*
   Oxford, Oxford University Press, pp. 475–9.

6. Contradictions and complementarities in the Cultural System

1 'A thorough-going relativism that removes any objective realm of
   reality accessible to all systems also apparently removes the
   possibility of understanding and comparing them', Roger Trigg,
   'The sociology of knowledge', *Philosophy of the Social Sciences,* vol. 8,
   1978, p. 295. This article provides a pointed critique of Bloor as
   an upwards conflationist.
2 Gad Freudenthal, 'How strong is Dr Bloor's "strong programme"?',
   Studies in History and Philosophy of Science, vol. 10, 1979, p. 82.
3 Karl Popper, *Objective Knowledge,* Oxford, Clarendon Press, 1972,
   p. 299.
4 To examine a Cultural System in terms of the contradiction or
   consistency between its items implies that there are additional relations obtaining between some components beyond the shared
   language which makes them members of the system. If this was all
   that related them we would be dealing with a system characterized
   by complete summativity where variation in the whole was simply
   the sum of independent variations in the parts. However, by their
   very nature, cultural components (ideas, theories, beliefs etc.) have
   further logical relationships amongst one another. Every such relation removes the Cultural System from complete summativity and
   is a move to the other extreme – Systemic wholeness. This state of
   affairs exists when 'every part of a system is related to all other
   parts such that a change in one causes a change in all others and
   the system as a whole – it is said to behave as a *whole* or *coherently*',
   A. D. Hall and R. E. Hagen, 'Definition of a system', in Joseph A.
   Litterer, *Organizations, Systems, Control and Adaptation,* vol. 2, New
   York, Wiley, 1969, pp. 34–6.
      Now it is not my expectation that we will discover complete
   wholeness – it is upholders of 'the Myth' who tend to assume this
   – but to set out with the intention of examining the consistency or
   contradictory nature of items *is* to presume that at *least some* of
   them are logically related in these ways. This appears a warranted
   a priori assumption since it is a virtual impossibility that the corpus

of 'ideas' constituting any Cultural System should have *no* logical implications, no interconnections, no problematic conjunctions with some of the others. If in doubt, try the thought experiment of designing an artificial System, none of the components of which have any logical relations at all.

5 Even if sociologists do not make extensive use of the notion of a plurality of Cultural Systems, they will justifiably employ the concept of subsystems. Indeed, the less they make reference to the former the more they will conceptualize in terms of the latter. A subsystem exists wherever a boundary has developed (for whatever reason) across which the exchange of items/information is less than that on either side. Technically the delineation of boundaries boils down to deciding what magnitude of difference in the rate of exchange one accepts as indicative of a boundary and this is largely determined by the problem in hand – although empirically the scope for delineation increases with cultural differentiation over time.

6 'It has been almost completely ignored by writers on Durkheim and on the history and sociology of education, though it is unquestionably a major work', Steven Lukes, *Emile Durkheim: His Life and Work*, London, Penguin, 1973, p. 357.

7 Emile Durkheim, *The Evolution of Educational Thought*, London, Routledge & Kegan Paul, 1977. All subsequent citations are taken from this edition.

8 Maurice Halbwachs' 'Introduction' to Durkheim, *The Evolution of Educational Thought*, p. xiii and p. 278.

9 Jeffrey Alexander attributes much of this neglect and misconstruction to Parsons' dismissal of *The Elementary Forms of Religious Life* as epistemological idealism, which in turn was due to Parsons' own lack of awareness that between it and the 'middle works' lay numerous unpublished lectures of which *The Evolution of Educational Thought* contained some of the most important. 'Rethinking Durkheim's Intellectual Development: Working Out a Religious Sociology', *International Sociology*, vol. 1, 1986.

10 Durkheim, *The Evolution of Educational Thought*, p. 21.

11 Ibid., p. 22.

12 Ibid., p. 210.

13 Ibid., p. 255.

14 Ibid., p. 209.

15 Ibid., p. 23.

16 Ibid., p. 25.

17 R. B. Braithwaite, *Scientific Explanation*, London, Cambridge University Press, 1953, p. 368.

18 Imre Lakatos, 'Falsification and the methodology of scientific research programmes', in I. Lakatos and A. Musgrave (eds.) *Criticism and the Growth of Knowledge*, London, Cambridge University Press, 1970, p. 96.

19 See Ernest Gellner, *Thought and Change*, London, Weidenfeld & Nicolson, 1964, pp. 73–81.
20 Lakatos, 'Falsification', p. 99.
21 Ibid., p. 130.
22 Thomas S. Kuhn, *The Structure of Scientific Revolutions*, Chicago, Chicago University Press, 1962.
23 For a more detailed discussion of these ideas in the structural domain see my *Social Origins of Educational Systems*, London and Beverly Hills, Sage, 1979, chap. 1.
24 Lakatos, 'Falsification' in Lakatos and Musgrave (eds.), *Criticism and the Growth of Knowledge*, p. 129.
25 Ibid., p. 130.
26 Ibid., pp. 130–1n.
27 Ibid., p. 131.
28 Ibid., pp. 138–40.
29 Durkheim is particularly scathing about attempts to portray syncretic manoeuvres as nothing but S-C censorship. He specifically condemns the 'lost knowledge regained' view of the Renaissance by documenting continuous historical familiarity with classical literary sources. Rather it was the fact that each new reinterpretation was punctured by a re-emergence of the basic contradiction which led to 'an uninterrupted series of renaissances', *The Evolution of Educational Thought*, p. 34.
30 Ibid., p. 280.
31 Ibid., pp. 58–60.
32 Ibid., pp. 71–2.
33 Ibid., p. 96.
34 Ibid., p. 73.
35 Ibid., p. 250.
36 Ibid., p. 252.
37 Lakatos, 'Falsification', p. 139.
38 See A. Leroy-Beaulieu, *Les Catholiques libéraux, l'Eglise et la libéralisme de 1830 à nos jours*, Paris, 1885. 'The Liberalism against which he fought was not Liberalism in the political sense, but Liberalism as Newman understood it – the setting up in the sphere of religion of free thought and free discussion in the place of revealed truth' (p. 80).
39 J. H. Newman, *Idea of a University*, London, 1893.
40 Ibid., p. 42.
41 Ibid., p. 120.
42 Ibid., pp. 432–3.
43 Ibid., p. 434.
44 Ibid., p. 454.
45 Ibid., p. 431.
46 A. D. Hall and R. E. Hagen, 'Definition of a system', in Litterer, *Organizations, Systems, Control and Adaptation*, vol. 2, p. 36.
47 H. H. Gerth and C. Wright Mills, *From Max Weber*, London, Routledge & Kegan Paul, 1967, p. 291.

48 Ibid., p. 293.

49 See Max Weber, *Economy and Society*, New York, Bedminster Press, 1968, pp. 524–5.

50 See E. Daire (ed.), *Les Physiocrates*, Paris, 1946.

51 Adam Smith, *An Inquiry into the Nature and Causes of the Wealth of Nations* (ed. Cannan), London, 1904, vol. 2, bk. 4, chap. 9, p. 176.

52 Ibid., vol. I, bk. 2, chap. 3, p. 323.

53 F. A. Cavenagh, *James and John Stuart Mill on Education*, Cambridge, 1931.

54 Hall and Hagen, 'Definition of a system', pp. 35–6.

55 'Since its beginnings, religion has been an inexhaustible fountain of opportunities for artistic creation, on the one hand, and of stylizing through traditionalization, on the other', Gerth and Wright Mills, *From Max Weber*, p. 341.

56 See Margaret Masterman, 'The nature of a paradigm', in Lakatos and Musgrave, *Criticism and the Growth of Knowledge*, p. 84.

57 Zygmunt Bauman, *Culture as Praxis*, London, Routledge & Kegan Paul, 1973, p. 140.

58 Kuhn, *The Structure of Scientific Revolutions*, p. 5.

59 Gerth and Wright Mills, *From Max Weber*, p. 413.

60 Kuhn, *The Structure of Scientific Revolutions*, pp. 47, 11.

61 Bauman, *Culture as Praxis*, p. 122.

62 Ibid., p. 119.

63 Ibid., p. 123.

64 Mary Douglas, *Purity and Danger: An Analysis of Concepts of Pollution and Taboo*, London, Routledge & Kegan Paul, 1966, pp. 139f.

65 If the semiotician attempts a defence that he is giving a truly genetic account way back to the 'first meaning' where in his view a cow must have been opposed to something to give it the very identity of a cow, he would (a) be starting a different debate in the area of philosophical anthropology, where I would contend that prior to the 'emergence' of logical universals it is impossible for us to know what was going on mentally at all, and (b) speculative as accounts of their emergence *must* remain, alternative, simpler, and certainly ontologically less dubious reconstructions exist, such as trial-and-error learning.

66 Bauman, *Culture as Praxis*, p. 124.

67 Lakatos, 'Falsification', p. 137.

68 Julien Freund, *The sociology of Max Weber*, London, Penguin, 1968, p. 189.

7. Socio-Cultural interaction

1 See Walter Buckley, *Sociology and Modern Systems Theory*, Englewood Cliffs, New Jersey, Prentice-Hall, 1967. Morphostasis '(R)efers to those processes in complex system–environment exchanges that tend to preserve or maintain a system's given form, organization or state. Morphogenesis will refer to those processes which tend to

elaborate or change a system's given form, structure or state',
pp. 58–9. Sustained use of morphogenetic cycles in the explanation of structural change is found in Margaret S. Archer, *Social
Origins of Educational Systems*, London and Beverly Hills, Sage, 1979.

2 In the previous chapters discussion was pared to the bone by formulating it simply in terms of the logical relationships between
two cultural items A and B. The propositions advanced were of
sufficient generality to apply equally to:

(i)   Logical relations within a system.
(ii) Logical relations between two empirically or temporally separate
      systems.
(iii) Logical relations between two subsystems.
(iv) Logical relations between a system or a subsystem and its environment.

Consequently the term 'system' was used throughout chapters 5
and 6 to refer to all of the above. Since propositions of the same
order of generality will be advanced about social interaction in the
present chapter, here the term 'society' refers equally to causal
relations between groups at either societal or sectional levels. In
neither case is there any truck with the fallacy of displaced scope:
the propositions advanced are highly abstract ones the practical
application to particular cases of which would entail the introduction of those emergent properties pertaining to the scope of the
phenomena in question.

3 Steven Lukes, *Power: A Radical View*, London, McMillan, 1974. For
example see J. G. Merquior, *The Veil and the Mask*, Routledge &
Kegan Paul, London, 1979, pp. 15–23. Obviously using this
approach means that power is viewed as a relational property and
not as some kind of 'generalized capacity'. However, it is beyond
the present brief to explain which past S-C transactions produced
the particular distribution of power between groups at T_1.

4 Emile Durkheim, *The Evolution of Educational Thought*, London,
Routledge & Kegan Paul, 1977, p. 22.

5 Ibid., p. 35.

6 John Watkins, 'Against "Normal Science" ', in Imre Lakatos and
Alan Musgrave (eds.), *Criticism and the Growth of Knowledge*, London,
Cambridge University Press, 1970, p. 33.

7 Thomas S. Kuhn, *The Structure of Scientific Revolutions*, Chicago,
Chicago University Press, 1962, p. 5.

8 The notion of groups having 'a high tolerance of contradiction'
appears to be of no analytical utility since the designation of such
must either be *post hoc* or entail unwarranted ethnocentrism, i.e.
they are different from us in this respect because of their primitive
mentality etc.

9 See Ernest Gellner, *Thought and Change*, London, Weidenfeld &
Nicolson, 1964, chs. 7 and 8.

10 Obviously analysis has to be restricted to contemporary or foresee-
able impingement: while we can all be wildly wrong in the matters

we dismiss, no one can be considered to be constrained by the unforeseen. Thus Prout's chemical problem did not concern the enormous majority of the nineteenth-century population, while their twentieth-century counterparts all live in the shadow of an atomic physics indebted to Prout.

11 Imre Lakatos, 'Falsification and the Methodology of Scientific Research Programmes', in Lakatos and Musgrave (eds.), *Criticism and the Growth of Knowledge*, pp. 14 ff.

12 Ignatius de Loyola, *Rules for Thinking with the Church*. The text appears in Rule 13.

13 A. Gramsci, *Prison Notebooks*, (ed. Nowell Smith, Hoare), London, Lawrence & Wishart, 1971, p. 340.

14 A. W. Gouldner, 'Reciprocity and autonomy in functional theory', in N. J. Demerath and R. A. Peterson, *System, Change and Conflict*, New York, Free Press, Collier Macmillan, 1967.

15 Durkheim, *The Evolution of Educational Thought*, pp. 17 f.

16 Pierre Bourdieu and Jean-Claude Passeron, *La Reproduction*, Paris, Minuit, 1970.

17 See E. E. Schattscheider, *The Semi-Sovereign People: A Realist's View of Democracy in America*, New York, Rinehart & Winston, 1960. Also Steven Lukes, *Power: A Radical View*, chaps. 3 and 4.

18 M. J. Mulkay, *The Social Process of Innovation*, London, Macmillan, 1972, p. 15.

19 James Mill, 'On education', in F. A. Cavenagh, *James and John Stuart Mill on Education*, Cambridge, 1931, p. 365.

20 Adam Smith, *An Inquiry into the Nature and Causes of the Wealth of Nations*, (ed. Cannan), London, 1904, vol. 2, bk. 5, chap. 1, p. 273.

21 Thomas S. Kuhn, 'Logic of scientific discovery or psychology of research', in Lakatos and Musgrave (eds.), *Criticism and the Growth of Knowledge*, p. 5.

22 Bourdieu and Passeron, *La Reproduction*.

23 J. G. Merquior, *The Veil and the Mask*, London, Routledge & Kegan Paul, 1979, chap. 1.

24 For a discussion of this difference see Margaret S. Archer, 'Process without system', *Archives européennes de sociologie*, 24, 1983.

25 Gouldner, 'Reciprocity and autonomy in functional theory'.

26 Ernest Gellner, 'concepts and society', in B. R. Wilson (ed.), *Rationality*, Oxford, Blackwell, 1979, p. 43.

27 '(A)t any moment we are prisoners caught in the framework of our theories; our expectations our past experiences; our language. But we are prisoners in a Pickwickian sense: if we try, we can break out of our framework at any time. Admittedly, we shall find ourselves again in a framework, but it will be a better and roomier one; and we can at any moment break out of it again', Karl Popper, 'Normal science and its dangers', in Lakatos and Musgrave (eds.), *Criticism and the Growth of Knowledge*, p. 56. However, where there is strong protection of the concomitant complementarity, strenuous

attempts are made to eliminate the objective or social availability of alternative frameworks, or both – which is why physical escape (migration) is the only means of breakout.

28 Amitai Etzioni, *The Active Society*, London, Collier Macmillan, 1968, pp. 177f.

29 Margaret T. Hogden, *Early Anthropology in the Sixteenth and Seventeenth Centuries*, Philadelphia, University of Pennsylvania Press, 1946, p. 86.

30 Mulkay, *The Social Process of Innovation*, p. 38.

31 See Harold R. Isaacs, *India's Ex-Untouchables*, New York, John Day, 1964, ch. 12.

32 Mulkay, *The Social Process of Innovation*, p. 44, secs. 43–4.

33 Ibid.

8 Elaboration of the Cultural System

1 Thomas S. Kuhn, *The Structure of Scientific Revolutions*, Chicago, Chicago University Press, 1962.

2 Karl Popper, *Objective Knowledge: An Evolutionary Approach*, Oxford, Clarendon Press, chap. 7.

3 Imre Lakatos, 'Falsification and the methodology of scientific research programmes', in I. Lakatos and A. Musgrave (eds.), *Criticism and the Growth of Knowledge*, London, Cambridge University Press, 1970.

4 Ibid.

5 Lakatos writes that his 'concept of a "research programme" may be construed as an objective, "third world" reconstruction of Kuhn's socio-psychological concept of paradigm', 'Falsification', p. 179n. The same usage is employed in this text.

6 Ibid., p. 132.

7 Still the naive falsificationist, who might have been brought to accept the existence and importance of competition between sets of theories, might now jib and contend that even so does not the competitive process reduce to attempts at mutual falsification thus dragging it into the domain of *constraining contradictions*, by forcing the competitors to speak the same language, work in the same terms and become riveted on rebutting their refuters? Lakatos scrupulously disposes of this objection, the implication of which in the present context would be to rob us of a separate category of *competitive contradictions* (between theoretical paradigms rather than between isolated theoretical propositions and their testing). He argues that those working on a paradigm are not constantly forced to bury their noses in the anomalous and that to maintain otherwise leaves one incapable of explaining the relative autonomy of theoretical research (ibid., p. 137). Often the paradigmatic scientist refuses to be drawn into observation. Instead he will 'lie down on his couch, shut his eyes and forget about the data' (ibid., p. 135). It is not that they are unaware of empirical difficulties but they

rely on the competitive conviction that further development of the research programme will later be able to deal with these recalcitrant or residual instances.

8 Talcott Parsons, for example, assimilated ideology to the 'cognitive legitimation of patterns of value orientation', in *The Social System*, London, Routledge & Kegan Paul, 1951, p. 351.

9 J. G. Merquior, *The Veil and the Mask*, London, Routledge & Kegan Paul, 1979, pp. 3–4.

10 Ibid., p. 9.

11 Alvin W. Gouldner, *The Dialectic of Ideology and Technology*, London, Macmillan, 1976, p. 278.

12 It accounts for the curious 'rule' in social theory: 'refer to every theory prominent in the last decade; ignore the rest of the century unless a theory has retained exceptional salience; but hallow any rediscovery from the more distant past.'

13 Thomas S. Kuhn, *The Structure of Scientific Revolutions*, Chicago, Chicago University Press, 1970, p. 176.

14 M. J. Mulkay, *The Social Process of Innovation*, London, Macmillan, 1972, pp. 51–2.

15 See Margaret S. Archer, *Social Origins of Educational Systems*, London and Beverly Hills, Sage, 1979, p. 26–30.

16 Lakatos, 'Falsification', p. 158.

17 Michalina Vaughan and Margaret S. Archer, *Social Conflict and Educational Change in England and France: 1789–1848*, London, Cambridge University Press, 1971, pp. 31–2.

18 Lakatos, 'Falsification', p. 180n.

19 Even more importantly, from our point of view, Lakatos details strategies employed by the groups involved to keep the competition going – especially their initial and deliberate avoidance of constraining contradictions which would stop the programme in its tracks (at least *pro tem*). This is the joint role of the paradigm's 'negative heuristic' and its 'positive heuristic'. Thus, for example, the Cartesian programme, the mechanistic theory of the universe, according to which the universe is a huge clockwork mechanism (and system of vortices) with push and pull as the only cause of motion, initially 'discouraged work on scientific theories like (the "essentialist" version of) Newton's theory of action at a distance – which were inconsistent with it (*negative heuristic*). On the other hand, it encouraged work on auxiliary hypotheses which might have saved it from apparent counter-evidence – like Keplerian ellipses (*positive heuristic*)', Lakatos, 'Falsification', p. 133.

20 Thus, there *are no such things as crucial experiments*, at least not if these are meant to be experiments which can *instantly* overthrow a research programme. In fact, when one research programme suffers defeat and is superseded by another one, we may – *with long hindsight* – call an experiment crucial if it turns out to have provided a spectacular corroborating instance for the victorious programme and a failure for the defeated one (in the sense that it was

never 'explained progressively' – or briefly, 'explained' – within the defeated programme). But scientists, of course, do not always judge heuristic situations correctly. A rash scientist may *claim* that his experiment defeated a programme, and parts of the scientific community may even, rashly, accept his claim. But if a scientist in the 'defeated' camp puts forward a few years later a scientific explanation of the allegedly 'crucial experiment' within (or consistent with) the allegedly defeated programme, the *honorific title may be withdrawn and the 'crucial experiment' may turn from a defeat into a new victory for the programme* (Ibid., p. 173).

21 Ibid., p. 163.
22 Ibid., p. 175.
23 B. Evans and B. Waites, *I.Q. and Mental Testing: An Unnatural Science and its Social History*, London, Macmillan, 1981, p. 177.
24 Ibid., p. 180.
25 Cited in ibid.
26 D. Ricardo, *The Principles of Political Economy*, (ed. Gonner), London, 1891, pp. 179f. Fissiparousness is increased at the S-C level too since Ricardo thus emerges as 'the representative, the theoretician and the spokesman of an occupationally optimistic class: the great English industrialists who dream of the economic conquest of the world', E. Halévy, *Le Radicalisme Philosophique*, Paris, 1904, p. 54.
27 T. Hodgskin, *Labour Defended Against the Claims of Capital or the Unproductiveness of Capital with Reference to the Present Combinations amongst Journeymen*, (ed. Cole), London, 1922.
28 'The manual labourers, oppressed by the capitalist, have never been paid highly enough, and even now are more disposed to estimate their own deserts rather by what they have hitherto received than by what they produce', ibid., p. 89. By contrast, 'the incomes of those who live on profit and interest, and who have no just claim but custom to any share of the national produce' are disproportionately high, ibid., p. 92.
29 J. S. Mill, *Autobiography and Literary Essays* (ed. Robson and Stillinger), Toronto, University of Toronto Press, 1981, p. 239. The following reflections on his *Principles of Political Economy* reveal Mill's own views on argumentative elaboration: 'In the first edition the difficulties of socialism were stated so strongly, that the tone was on the whole that of opposition to it. In the year or two which followed, much time was given to the study of the best socialistic writers on the Continent, and to meditation and discussion on the whole range of topics involved in the controversy: and the *result was that most of what had been written on the subject in the first edition was cancelled, and replaced by arguments and reflexions which represent a more advanced opinion*', p. 241. In Mill's view then a progressive problem-shift had taken place in his own work when faced by opposition.
30 M. Reybaud, in the *Dictionnaire d'economie politique*, Paris, 1852.
31 J. E. Cairnes, *Some Leading Principles of Political Economy*, London, Macmillan, 1874.

32 F. Engels, *Anti-Dühring*, Moscow, Foreign Languages Publishing House, 1962.

33 E. von Böhm-Bawerk, summarized the relationship between the liberal and neo-liberal economics as follows: 'The errors of the Classical School are, so to speak, the ordinary diseases of the childhood of every science', in 'The Austrian Economists', *Annals of the American Academy of Political and Social Science*, January 1981.

34 The Pessimistic neo-Marxist reaction is summed up by the Italian syndicalist Arthur Labriola, 'while we Marxians are trying to repatch the master's cloak political economy is making some headway every day', *Revue socialiste*, vol. 1, 1899, p. 674.

35 Karl Popper, *Conjectures and Refutations*, London, Routledge & Kegan Paul, 1963, p. 49.

36 Lakatos, 'Falsification', p. 158.

37 Evans and Waites, *I.Q. and Mental Testing: An Unnatural Science*, p. 100. The authors also indicate that, '(I)t was suggested . . . that the onset Burt's career in fraud can be most plausibly interpreted as a response to an intellectual environment which had become hostile to his views', p. 107.

38 Leon J. Kamin, *The Science and Politics of I.Q.*, Hillsdale, New Jersey, Erlbaum, 1974. The actual allegation of fraud was made by a journalist, Oliver Gillie, *The Sunday Times*, 24 October 1976; and *New Statesman*, 24 November 1978.

39 See H. J. Eysenck versus Leon Kamin, *Intelligence: The Battle for the Mind*, London and Basingstoke, Pan and Macmillan, 1981, pp. 182–7.

40 A term used by Maurice Duverger to characterize the situation where a multiplicity of political parties condition government from the centre. See his 'The central morass: French Centrism', in M. Dogan and M. Rose (eds.), *European Politics: A Reader*, London, 1971.

41 Clifford Geertz, 'Ideology as a cultural system', in David E. Apter and Charles F. Ardrain (eds.), *Contemporary Analytical Theory*, Englewood Cliffs, New Jersey, Prentice-Hall, 1972, p. 56.

42 Mulkay, *The Social Process of Innovation*, p. 38.

43 Ibid.

44 Ibid., pp. 44–5.

45 See F. Graham Smith, *Radio Astronomy*, Harmondsworth, Penguin, 1960.

46 See Walter Buckley, *Sociology and Modern Systems Theory*, Englewood Cliffs, New Jersey, Prentice-Hall, 1967, ch. 2, 'Social system models', and pp. 172–6.

47 Amitai Etzioni, *The Active Society*, London, Collier Macmillan, 1968, pp. 143–51.

48 Ibid., p. 146.

49 Joseph Ben-David and R. Collins, 'Social factors in the origins of a new science: the case of psychology', *American Sociological Review*, 31, 1966, p. 463.

50 Mulkay, *The Social Process of Innovation*, p. 43.
51 Ibid., p. 39.
52 A. Zloczower, *Career Opportunities and the Growth of Scientific Discovery in 19th Century Germany, with Special Reference to Physiology*, Jerusalem, Hebrew University of Jerusalem, 1966, p. 42.
53 N. Mullins, 'The prelude to scientific specialities: cluster development within patterns of association among scientists', cited by Mulkay, *The Social Process of Innovation*, p. 39.
54 See Henry Teune and Zdravko Mlinar, *The Developmental Logic of Social Systems*, London and Beverley Hills, Sage, 1978, pp. 76f.
55 Ernest Gellner, *Thought and Change*, London, Weidenfeld & Nicolson, 1964, see pp. 68–73.
56 Harold Perkin, *Key Profession: The History of the Association of University Teachers*, London, Routledge & Kegan Paul, 1969, p. 235.
57 See W. O. Hagstrom, *The Scientific Community*, New York, Basic Books, 1965.
58 Mulkay, *The Social Process of Innovation*, p. 36.
59 Teune and Mlinar, *The Developmental Logic of Social Systems*, p. 123.

Index

Abercrombie, N., 47–9, 51, 58, 313n, 314n, 315n
Alexander, Jeffrey, 329n
Althusser, Louis, 47
analytical dualism, xiv–xvii, xxii, xxiii, 4–6, 14, 18, 21; in Marx, 55–6; 77; denial of, in central conflation, 77–93; and analysis of Cultural Systems, 104–13; 130–42, 143, 145, 183–4, 206, 228, 245, 270, 275–80, 282, 304–7
Anderson, Perry, 309n, 314n–15n
Archer, Margaret S., 310n, 316n, 318n, 330n, 332n, 335n
Augustine, St, 151
Aulard, A., 313n

Barnes, Barry, 112, 115, 116, 117, 121, 122, 125, 321n, 322n, 323n, 324n, 325n, 326n
Barthes, R., 179–80
Bauman, Zygmunt, 12; and central conflation, 72–95; 177, 179, 181, 305, 309n, 317n, 318n, 319n, 331n
beliefs, 4, 9, 18, 34, 76, 104, 107, 110, 112, 113; and logic, 118–20; and translation, 124–7; 129, 131, 139, 141, 144, 145, 146, 148, Christian, 149–51, 157, 162–5, 166–7, 169–70; Hindu, 172–3, 177, 182; 186, 194, 200–1, 215, 229, 230, 270, 285, 286, 327n
Ben-David, Joseph, 262, 337n
Benedict, Ruth, 3, 41, 308n, 309n, 312n
Berger, Peter, 283
Berlin, B., 325n
Bettenson, Henry, 324n
Blau, Peter, 281
Bloor, David, 112, 113, 114, 115, 116,

117, 121, 122, 125, 321n, 322n, 323n, 324n, 325n, 326n
Böhm-Bawerk, E. von, 337n
Bottomore, T.B., 313n, 314n
Bourdieu, Pierre, 60–1, 214, 215, 315n, 316n, 333n
Bowles, Samuel, 61, 316n
Braithwaite, R.B., 152, 329n
Buckley, Walter, 274, 310n, 331n, 337n
Bulmer, R., 123, 325n

Cairnes, J.E., 252, 336n
caste, xxi, 235
Cavenagh, F.A., 331n
Chomsky N., 39
Christianity, 118, 119–20, 149–51, 155, 162–5, 166–7, 169–70, 171, 191–2, 200–1, 202, 204, 209, 230, 231, 254–5, 287
classical economics, 154, 172, 173–4, 178, 214, 235, 246, 247–8, 250–3
classicism, 150–1, 157, 162–5, 167–8, 171, 194, 200, 231
Cohen, Percy, xix, 308n
Collins, H.M., 112, 321n
Comte, A., 47
competitive contradictions, concept of, 203–5, 206–9; 221, 226, 228, definition of, 229–35; effects of, 239–42; results of, 245–58, 269, 270; 295, 298–9
concomitant complementarities, concept of, 153–4; effects of, 157–8; results of, 171–84; and change, 211–19; 220, 221, 226, 243, 246, 267, 268, 269, 270
Condorcet, M.J.A. de, 46
conflation, fallacy of, xiii–xiv, xviii, xxv; 7, 13, 20–1; downwards version, 25–45;